Reimagining North African immigration

Manchester University Press

REIMAG*I*NING NORTH AFRICAN IMMIGRATION

Identities in flux in French literature, television, and film

Edited by
Véronique Machelidon and Patrick Saveau

Manchester University Press

Copyright © Manchester University Press 2018

While copyright in the volume as a whole is vested in Manchester University Press, copyright in individual chapters belongs to their respective authors, and no chapter may be reproduced wholly or in part without the express permission in writing of both author and publisher.

Published by Manchester University Press
Altrincham Street, Manchester M1 7JA
www.manchesteruniversitypress.co.uk

British Library Cataloguing-in-Publication Data is available

ISBN 978 0 7190 9948 9 hardback
ISBN 978 1 5261 4353 2 paperback

First published by Manchester University Press in hardback 2018

This edition first published 2020

The publisher has no responsibility for the persistence or accuracy of URLs for any external or third-party internet websites referred to in this book, and does not guarantee that any content on such websites is, or will remain, accurate or appropriate.

Typeset by Servis Filmsetting Ltd, Stockport, Cheshire

Contents

Notes on contributors		*page* vii
Acknowledgments		xi
	Introduction Véronique Machelidon and Patrick Saveau	1
1	'Qui fait la France?' New configurations of Frenchness in contemporary urban fiction Steve Puig	17
2	Breaking the chains of ethnic identity: Faïza Guène, Saphia Azzeddine, and Nadia Bouzid, or the birth of a new Maghrebi-French women's literature Patrick Saveau	31
3	From daughter to mother, from sister to brother: building identities in Faïza Guène's novels Florina Matu	49
4	The immigrant in Abdellatif Kechiche's cinematic work: transcending the question of origins Emna Mrabet	63
5	Seeking paths to existence in Rachid Djaïdani's *Rengaine* Mona El Khoury	77
6	*Beur* and *banlieue* television comedies: new perspectives on immigration Caroline Fache	97
7	They had a dream: out-marching exclusion and hatred Jimia Boutouba	116
8	Narrativizing foreclosed history in 'postmemorial' fiction of the Algerian War in France: October 17, 1961, a case in point Michel Laronde	134
9	Unearthing the father's secret: postmemory and identity in *harki* and pied noir narratives Véronique Machelidon	153

10 Representations of the *harkis* in contemporary French-language films 178
Susan Ireland

11 'L'oued revient toujours dans son lit': Franco-Maghrebi identity in Hassan Legzouli's film *Ten'ja* 196
Ramona Mielusel

12 Rewriting the memory of immigration: Samuel Zaoui's *Saint Denis bout du monde* 212
Mireille Le Breton

13 *Harragas* in Mediterranean *illiterature* and cinema 232
Hakim Abderrezak

Index 253

Notes on contributors

Hakim Abderrezak is Associate Professor at the University of Minnesota. He teaches in the Department of French and Italian. His research focuses on Mediterranean, Maghrebi, and Francophone Studies. He is the author of *Ex-Centric Migrations: Europe and the Maghreb in Mediterranean Cinema, Literature, and Music*. A major part of his work examines representations of clandestine sea crossings in literary and artistic works that have appeared in French, Arabic, Spanish, and Italian. He has contributed to *Francophone Studies*, *Expressions maghrébines*, and the *Journal of North African Studies*, and co-edited a special issue of *Expressions maghrébines*.

Jimia Boutouba is Associate Professor of French and Francophone Studies at Santa Clara University, specializing in twentieth/twenty-first-century French and francophone literature and cinema, and nineteenth-century colonial discourse. Her research focuses on women writers and filmmakers from the Maghreb and contemporary France. She has published articles on issues pertaining to the representation of women in Maghrebi cinema, on the memory of the Algerian War of Independence, as well as on issues of immigration and national identity in contemporary France. Her teaching interests include postcolonial francophone literature and cinema from North Africa, French cultural studies as they relate to the questions of colonialism, immigration, nationalism, and the representation of gender and race in contemporary French films as well as French colonial literature.

Mona El Khoury is Assistant Professor at Tufts University. Her dissertation titled 'Remnants of the Franco-Algerian fracture: the struggle with postcolonial minority identity in contemporary francophone literature,' focuses on French-Algerian minority identities. In 2014 she published '*Pagli* d'Ananda Devi. La recherche d'un sol hybride insulaire' in *Fert-îles 2. L'occupation littéraire des sols insulaires* (CNRS, Bastia). She is also the author of 'To Be or Not To Be "Métis": Nina Bouraoui's Embodied Memory of the Colonial Fracture' (*Journal of the Theoretical Humanities*, 2017).

Caroline Fache is Associate Professor of French and Francophone Studies and Africana Studies at Davidson College, North Carolina. Originally from Lille, France, she first studied movie translation before working for a subtitling company in Paris. Fache then completed a Ph.D. in francophone literature and film in 2007 at Indiana University Bloomington. Her research interests include métissage (mixed race studies), West African film, immigration, and transnationalism. Her co-translation of Boris Diop's *Africa Beyond the Mirror* was published in 2012. She has also published on métissage and gender identity, immigration, and memory, and most recently on francophone film production. Her current book project looks at immigration comedy as a subgenre in French film, and more specifically at the evolution of the representation of immigrants from tragic figures to comedy agents.

Susan Ireland is Orville and Mary Patterson Routt Professor of Literature at Grinnell College. Her research interests include contemporary French fiction, Quebec women writers, the Algerian novel, and the literature of immigration in France and Quebec. She is an editor of *The Feminist Encyclopedia of French Literature* (1999) and, with Patrice Proulx, of *Immigrant Narratives in Contemporary France* (2001), and *Textualizing the Immigrant Experience in Contemporary Quebec* (2004). She has also published articles in journals such as *L'Esprit Créateur*, *Québec Studies*, *World Literature Today*, and *Nottingham French Studies*.

Michel Laronde is Professor of French and Francophone Studies at the University of Iowa. He is the author of four books on the postcolonial literatures and cultures of immigration in contemporary France, an area of global transit and cross-cultural encounters. *Rethinking Reading, Writing, and a Moral Code in Contemporary France: Postcolonializing High Culture in the Schools of the Republic* (2014) is the translation by the author of *Postcolonialiser la Haute Culture à l'Ecole de la République* (2008) and 'Autour du roman beur: Immigration et identité' (1993) is an article on the 1980s "*beur*" generation of writers of North African origins. He has edited two volumes: *L'Ecriture décentrée, La langue de l'Autre dans le roman contemporain* (1996), and *Leïla Sebbar* (2003). His next book observes how a foreclosed event from the traumatic colonial history between France and Algeria, the massacre of Algerians on October 17, 1961 in Paris, resurfaces in post-colonial history through its inscription in postmemorial French fiction.

Mireille Le Breton is Associate Professor of French and Francophone Studies in the Department of Modern Foreign Languages at Nazareth College, in Rochester, New York. Her research interests include the interrelation between poetics and politics, francophone postcolonial studies, women and gender studies, and theories of narrative. Her publications explore themes related to identity, cultural memory, religions, and human rights in contemporary narratives.

Véronique Machelidon is Associate Professor and Department Chair in the Foreign Languages and Literatures Department at Meredith College (Raleigh, North Carolina). She holds a degree in Germanic philology from Liège University (Belgium) and a Ph.D. in comparative literature from the University of North Carolina at Chapel Hill. Her research deals with nineteenth-century fiction by George Sand and Charlotte Brontë. While publishing articles on George Sand and book reviews for *French Review*, *Rocky Mountain Review*, and *Nineteenth-Century French Studies*, she prepared an English translation of Rachid Boudjedra's play *Mines de rien* (titled 'Underground, Unknown, Unseen' in 2009) and co-wrote a translation of Wahiba Khiari's *Nos silences* (forthcoming). Her research interests include gender, feminism (post)colonial studies, translation, and immigration.

Florina Matu is Assistant Professor of Francophone Studies at St. Edward's University in Austin, Texas. Her main research interests include representations of shame and guilt in North African literature written by women. She is also interested in the socio-critical analysis of francophone crime fiction and pedagogical approaches to the French presence in the Americas.

Ramona Mielusel is Assistant Professor in the Department of Modern Languages at the University of Louisiana, Lafayette. Her research deals with migrating francophone literature and cinema – more specifically second-generation writers and directors – as well as French-North African artists in the francophone world. She is interested in the immigration process that is analyzed from post-colonial and transnational points of view. She also shows a specific interest in nomadism and frontier theories in regard to marginal characters in literature and cinema. At the moment, she is working on a book titled *Artists Build Their (Own) France: The Evolution of 'Beur' Artists in the Light of Transnationalism*.

Emna Mrabet is affiliated with the Ecole Doctorale Esthétique, Sciences et Technologie des Arts, University Paris 8, where she has been teaching since 2010. Her research interests lie in Maghrebi-French cinema. She has written several articles on the works of film directors of Maghrebi origins, in particular, 'Contestation et défense des droits humains chez les cinéastes Abdellatif Kechiche et Rabah Ameur-Zaïmeche' (*Studies in French Cinema*), 'La question identitaire chez les cinéastes issus de l'immigration maghrébine,' in *L'identité nationale à l'épreuve des identités culturelles en Allemagne, en France et au Royaume-Uni* (2013), and 'De la citation à la performance: processus en œuvre(s) dans le cinéma d'Abdellatif Kechiche,' in *Les œuvres d'art dans le cinéma de fiction* (2014).

Steve Puig is Assistant Professor of French at St. John's University in New York, where he is doing research on French Caribbean literature and urban culture in metropolitan France. He holds a Ph.D. in French from the City University of New York, where he worked with Edouard Glissant. His latest publications include articles on Maryse Condé, on Haitian literature for the *Journal of Haitian Studies*, on urban literature for *Présence Francophone*, an article titled 'Littérature-monde et littérature urbaine: deux manifestes, même combat?' for *Nouvelles Francographies*, as well as articles on Rachid Djaïdani, Abd Al Malik, and Disiz. He is also interested in representations of New York in contemporary French literature.

Patrick Saveau is Professor of French and Cultural Studies at Franklin University Switzerland. He holds a degree in French literature from New York University. In 2011, he published *Serge Doubrovsky ou l'écriture d'une survie* (Editions Universitaires de Dijon). While he continues to write about autofiction, his research interests focus on Maghrebi-French literature and cinema. He has published '*Confidences à Allah de Saphia Azzedine ou le rejet d'un Islam patriarcal*,' in *Les Écrivains maghrébins francophones et l'Islam. Constance dans la diversité* (2013), 'Topographie d'une identité désirante dans *Confidences à Allah* de Saphia Azzeddine,' in *Les Espaces intimes féminins dans la littérature maghrébine d'expression française* (2014), and '*Quand Beretta est morte* de Nadia Bouzid ou le refus d'une appellation d'origine contrôlée,' in *Les Franco-Maghrébines: autres voix / écritures autres* (2014).

Acknowledgments

We would first like to thank all our contributors, whose original chapters, reflections, and questions for further analysis have given shape to this collaborative endeavor. Their work contributes to enriching the field of postcolonial literature and film. Our gratitude also goes to the anonymous reviewers, whose thoughtful reports enabled our volume to be more incisive, focused, and coherent throughout the various stages of its development.

Our thanks go to our respective institutions for their unwavering support and generosity: Sara Steinert-Borella, Dean of Franklin University Switzerland, Garry Walton and Sarah Roth, Deans of the School of Arts and Humanities, and Matthew Poslusny, Provost, of Meredith College in Raleigh, North Carolina, as well as the Faculty Development and Instruction Technology program at Meredith, which awarded a sabbatical to work on this project. We received invaluable assistance from student worker Alyssa Wilson, who provided editing help in the initial stage of the preparation of the typescript, and from from Nigel Butterwick and Jake Vaccaro, librarians at Franklin University Switzerland and Meredith College respectively, whohelped locate and obtain research materials. Both Franklin University Switzerland and Meredith College provided continuing financial support for participation in conferences where the two co-editors met and decided to collaborate on a project born out of joint research interests. These conferences further gave us the chance to meet many of the contributors featured in this volume, who have since become more than colleagues.

We would like to thank Dr. Alice Kuzniar, University of Waterloo, Canada, who provided the professional expertise and unwavering emotional support, which cannot be taken for granted and can never be repaid.

Finally, this volume would not have materialized without the expert help and encouragement of the staff at Manchester University Press. Martin Barr, especially, has been the most meticulous copy-editor and attentive reader we could possibly have hoped for.

Introduction

Véronique Machelidon and Patrick Saveau

In a stunning televised speech in the French National Assembly in 2013, then minister of justice Christiane Taubira surprised her (primarily white male) fellow politicians by reciting by heart the poem 'Nous les gueux,' from *Black Label*, a 1956 collection of poetry by colonial subject and Négritude writer Léon Gontran Damas. The event was immediately recorded in the national press and online on newspaper websites, blogs, YouTube, and Daily Motion. Taubira's spirited invocation of colonial poetry denouncing the French politics of assimilation in Guyana was openly intended to promote respect for difference, defend the equality of gay and heterosexual rights, and give a voice to silent social and cultural minorities. Taubira herself, in spite of her French nationality, can be described as a (post)colonial subject[1] as well as a Franco-French immigrant, due to her Guyanese roots. Of interest to us here is the potential for (post)colonial subjects and minorities who stand squarely in the middle of the French Republic (as Taubira stood in the center of the *hemicycle*) to interpellate the dominant group and inflect the discussion of a contemporary event (the issue of the marriage for all) through the citation of a foreclosed political or historical narrative (colonization, colonial resistance, and decolonization), embedded in literature. At the same time, Taubira was enlisting the power of literature[2] to redress present and past injustices, refresh repressed memories, denounce the hierarchy between the postcolonial margin and the hegemonic metropolis, and undermine the hegemonic narrative of French politics and history. Taubira's faith in the transformative power of literature and of cultural production more generally, was unshakeable. Her unmatched passion for poetry and social justice, applied to the current political arena, made her an instant star in the media and on the Internet.

Contributors to this volume discuss similar issues related to the mimetic and transformative powers of literature and film. They examine literary works and films that help deflate stereotypes regarding France's post-immigration population, promote a new respect for cultural and ethnic minorities, and give a new dignity to the subjects supposedly located on the margin of the Republic. The writers and filmmakers examined in this collection have found new ways to conceptualize the French heritage of immigration from North Africa and to portray the current state of multiculturalism in France, within, and in spite of, a continuing republican framework. More generally, this volume seeks to take the pulse of French postcoloniality by studying the evolving representations of trans-Mediterranean immigration to France in recent literature and films produced by a range of authors, most of whom with roots in North Africa and using French as their language of choice.

Literature and cinema by authors of North African descent discussed in this volume have been frequently labeled as "*beur*" or "post-*beur*," terms with a long and controversial history, which it is useful to recall here briefly. In his 2012 attempt to evaluate the status of *beur* writing, Najib Redouane revealed the common malaise generated by the label and showed how some ten years after its inception, this body of literature 'se distingu[ait] ... par un renouvellement des modes d'expression et des choix de création' (2012b: 20) (stood out ... through a renewal of creative modes of expression). Since 2000, with the advent of a new generation of writers who have chosen different literary practices to assert their place and their voices, the shift away from time-worn clichés has taken a new dimension. As a matter of fact, post-*beur* authors' new practices in both literature and film strive to break the chains of ideological, literary, memorial, spatial, gender, sexual, and ethnic constraints. They stage identities in flux, undermining the ideological division of (cultural) space and society along binary lines (dominant/dominated; French literature/*beur* literature; center/periphery; French/Maghrebi; mainstream/minority), crisscross national and trans-Mediterranean spaces, engage in postmemorial work, and collapse clichés and stereotypes.

In more than one way, the post-*beur* writers and filmmakers discussed in this volume can be regarded as heirs to the early pioneers of *beur* literature and cinema. The limitations and post-colonial coloring of the term *beur* have been frequently pointed out by critics before. When considering *beur* literature and cinema, scholars are quickly confronted with an abundance of books and articles which point out the difficulty of defining what *beur* literature and cinema are. For instance, when examining *beur* literature, Alec G. Hargreaves and Anne-Marie Gans-Guinoune note that 'il n'existe en effet aucun consensus quant à la façon dont il convient de désigner le corpus littéraire produit par les auteurs issus de l'immigration maghrébine' (2008: 2) (there is no consensus as to how we should define the literary corpus written by authors with roots in Maghrebi immigration). Some years later, the very same Hargreaves turned to the exploration of full-length feature films by second-generation Maghrebi directors, stating that 'there has been a vigorous and ongoing debate about how best to categorize and label them' (2011: 25). Critics feel repeatedly compelled to explain how problematic the term *beur* is when attached to literature and cinema (Durmelat, 1998: 191–207; Tarr, 2005: 3–4; Durmelat and Swamy, 2011: 12–14; Redouane,

2012a: 18–21; Higbee, 2013: 9–14). A first reason for critical discomfort is that from the very beginning, the label was rejected by some of the authors it was supposed to designate. Second, it confined *beur* authors to a literary and cinematic ghetto: *beur* writers and filmmakers were said to produce sociological testimonies devoid of aesthetic qualities. In an interview with Frédérique Chevillot, Tassadit Imache summarizes the situation *beur* authors were confined to: 'Très vite, il a été déclaré que nous ne saurions pas créer, sortir de notre histoire, comme si nous étions assignés à résidence, interdits de fiction, incapables d'invention' (Chevillot, 1998: 639) (It was quickly pronounced that we would not know how to create, go beyond our own story, as if we had been put under house arrest, forbidden to write fiction, incapable of creativity). Yet, *beur* literature and cinema did not remain static. One goal of this volume is to highlight the overall renewal of literary and cultural production initiated by post-*beur* and post-colonial authors with roots in North Africa. As our contributors convincingly argue, descendants of the *beur* pioneers in film and cinema continually transcend the assigned boundaries, renew creative modes of expression, develop novel aesthetics, and explore uncharted territories. For these reasons and while recognizing the ideological weight and critical legacy of the term post-*beur*, the editors of this volume have chosen to stay away from the term in the volume's title, as the authors examined here regard themselves not as marginal, ethnic commentators on French society, but rather claim their place as full-fledged members and renovators of French literature and cinema at large (see Chapters 1 and 2). Additionally, we find that the continued use of the word "*beur*," even when qualified by the prefix "post-," is too restrictive and implies that post-*beur* cinema and fiction are not entirely free to develop their own themes, narrative strategies, and fictional spaces.

Mobility, space appropriation, transgression, fluidity, and hybridity are key concepts showcased in films of the 2000s, as filmmakers express their desire to break down social, geographical, and ethnic barriers, in other words, to go beyond the formulaic *beur* or *banlieue* cinema of the 1980s and 1990s respectively. To achieve this goal, they tackle a 'greater range of narrative themes and genres than before,' a characteristic of post-*beur* cinema according to Higbee (2013: 25). Indeed, post-*beur* cinema has come a long way from the essentialist approach of *beur* and *banlieue* film and the guarded conclusion that Tarr formulated at the end of her seminal book on Beur and banlieue filmmaking in France (2005: 185).[3] Post-*beur* cinema's self-appointed major mission is to 'combat the oppression or exclusion effected by hegemonic discourse' (Higbee, 2013: 13) through a creative, flexible, self-reflective, and inquisitive practice that refuses to limit itself to standardized narratives and genres. Furthermore, films by directors of Maghrebi descent examined in this volume steer away from the leitmotifs of integration (Durmelat and Swamy, 2011) and split identity, which characterized the production of the 1980s and 1990s, to emphasize a sociological and cultural reality which is less easily appropriated by hegemonic discourse and goes largely unrecognized by the dominant media. Thus, their film work transcends the geography of the local, represented by the substandard lifestyles of the *cité* (housing project) and the culturally impoverished *banlieue*, to embrace richly diverse spaces, stories and cultures that pertain to the national and transnational.

Cinematic production nowadays is tightly linked in different ways to the television industry. As television channels regularly contribute to the funding of full-length feature films and therefore facilitate the shooting of works by relatively unknown or inexperienced film directors, post-*beur* authors seek broader audiences for their ideas by writing scripts for television films (Dalila Kerchouche) or by favoring the small or big screen over the written page. *Téléfilms* and television series are ideal media to address broader audiences, they 'have the potential to be viewed by a greater number of spectators than most short films, documentaries, or even certain feature films, whose screenings are often – but not always – limited to film festivals, small venues or non-peak viewing hours on television' (Kealhofer-Kemp, 2015: 7). Due to the overall 'privileged position cinema occupies in contemporary French culture and the column space and airtime dedicated to it in media coverage and analysis' (Johnston, quoted in Kealhofer-Kemp, 2015: 3), authors with roots in North African immigration like Azouz Begag and Rachid Djaïdani have successfully used both literature and film as media to convey their messages. Novelist Azouz Begag foregrounds his easy crossover from novel to film, and back to novel, affirming in a yet unpublished interview: 'I now write for readers who could also be viewers in movie theaters. I write novels the same way I write movie scripts. Each time, I am trying to turn the book into a movie.'[4]

As literature and cinema have a long and productive history of cross-pollination and partnership, 'critics and scholars have often worked with a mixed corpus, to foreground the rich interweaving of different strands of creative arts, novels and films that have contributed to the construction of the contemporary French cultural moment' (Swamy, 2011: xxviii–xxix). Our contributors explore the intertextual relation between literature and film in the cinema of Abdellatif Kechiche and discuss television's sociocultural role in increasing the representativeness and visibility of immigrant minorities through the popular comic genre. While the aim of this book is not to focus on generic and medium specificities (literature versus film or telefilm), but rather on the joint construction of a cultural corpus dealing in new ways with the issues of immigration to France and of post-colonial heritage, some of the chapters invite the reader to bridge the gap between literature and film. Placed at the center of this volume, Michel Laronde's chapter outlines a postmemorial methodology intended to correct the foreclosures of French memory through the reading of multiple fictional representations of a significant event of Algerian decolonization. Laronde's methodology opens promising avenues for film studies also and finds its counterpart in Jimia Boutouba's chapter on the film *La Marche*, where she demonstrates cinema's potential to rewrite, complement, and fill in the epistemological gaps of the official historical discourse. In turn, both contributions share Christiane Taubira's faith in the corrective and inclusive hermeneutic powers of (post) memorial literature and film.

While most of the contributions address the heritage of French (de)colonization in North Africa and are therefore informed by the North–South axis of the trans-Mediterranean diaspora, the volume ends with a chapter pointing to a new, international type of immigration from the global South caused by a broader form of neo-imperialism, which is no longer the product of French (de)colonization, but rather the effect of a more insidious, worldwide ideological and economic hegemony of the North and West. Thus, this last chapter calls for a shift in the field of critical inquiry from the North Africa–France axis to a different, ex-centric pattern of trans-Mediterranean migrations, where refugee-migrants from the global South (including former French colonies), victims of war, ethnic cleansing, political strife, and environmental disasters, set their hopes on 'burning' the intercontinental divide for various European destinations, and not exclusively, or preferentially, France.

Mediterranean Sea crossings have received a lot of media attention, but the contributors to this volume also focus on characters who journey across metropolitan France, from the periphery to the center and vice versa, and from the province to the capital or the other way round, thereby undermining a preconceived map of immigration and State-sanctioned allocations of space and power. This spatial mobility suggests that the so-called "issue" of immigration and the post-colonial heritage of France can no longer be contained within, or relegated to the margins of, a dominant republican discourse. Accordingly, the contributors explore existing and new modalities of Frenchness as represented in Maghrebi-French literature and cinema and seek to dislodge the prevailing stereotypes of "immigrant" populations still propagated by the French media and by French nationalist political discourse in the light of recent terrorist scares. In so doing, our contributors build upon, add, or contest previous critical works.

Invoking *Identities in flux* in the title of our volume is a reference to Stuart Hall's distinction between identity and identification, where identity is considered a static entity and identification is viewed as a dynamic process. The refusal of fixed positions is the unifying thread that runs through this volume. In 2011, Fiona Barclay argued that contemporary France 'is haunted in various forms by the legacy of its history in North Africa' which remains 'largely unacknowledged' (2011: xiv), while historian Benjamin Stora warned against an overload of competing and divisive memories (2006: 66). Many of our contributors (El Khoury, Fache, Matu, Mrabet, Puig, Saveau) demonstrate that French people whose parents crossed the Mediterranean Sea to settle down in France refuse to 'function as embodied ghosts haunting the Hexagon' (2011: xxxiv), but instead want to assert their being-in-the-world within French society. As characters in the works discussed in this volume negotiate various identifications, with different cultural, ethnic, racial, religious, sexual, national, international, or global accents, they break out of the prison of predetermined identities imposed by the dominant social agents and testify to the complexity of French multiculturalism.

The authors' self-conscious avoidance of the clichés of *beur* literature (integration, racism, identity, *banlieue*, marginalization, discrimination, etc.) and their protagonists' refusal of assigned fixed identities does not mean, however, that connections with North African heritage have been severed. Quite on the contrary, they remain 'in the form of memories, structures of thought and ideologies which often serve to call into question conceptions of classical, Hexagonal-based Frenchness,' while at the same time preventing single narratives, 'totalizing discourses such as republicanism' (Barclay, 2011: xxi–xxiii).

Building on these various critical insights, the editors of the present volume have resisted the temptation of dividing the chapters along a generic line, neatly separating literature from the moving image. This generic division does not correspond to the profile of some of the authors discussed here, like Rachid Djaidani, Faïza Guène, and Dalila Kerchouche, who are comfortable using either medium. In the case of Abdellatif Kechiche, the inclusion of canonical French literary intertexts in his films serves not only to promote a generic fluidity mirroring his own professional *parcours*, but also to break down the symbolic divide between *banlieue* and a fantasized French cultural essence, in order to articulate 'ideals of liberty, justice, and social protest' (p. 70). Read side by side, Chapters 2 and 4 of our volume, devoted to literature and film respectively, further suggest that common strategies of identification can be found in literature and cinema by authors with North African heritage. Patrick Saveau's analysis of the novels by post-*beur* women writers and Emna Mrabet's study of Kechiche's films both highlight a common refusal of the 'binary logic of us/them, self/other' (p. 32) and an effort to 'stay away from clichés and stereotypes … to avoid the trap of communitarianism and to transcend the issue of origins' (p. 64). Contributors like Susan Ireland and Hakim Abderrazak have further chosen to examine the recent representations of *harkis* and *harragas* respectively through a dialogue between literature and cinema.

In a similar move, the editors have resisted the need to separate theory and hermeneutics, politics and aesthetics, history, and literature. As Steve Puig argues, the representation of North African immigration is in itself political, and the (urban) authors who explore the life, experiences, and journeys of French citizens with trans-Mediterranean heritage, are, for the most part, *auteurs engagés*. Political engagement can take lighter or more radical tones, ranging from the issue of the representativeness of ethnic minorities on French television series to ensure their visibility on the Paysage Audiovisuel Français (Fache) to the more complex effort to use film that 'weaves a new relationship between present and past' and give subaltern subjects, the right and power of dissensus (Boutouba). Finally, as Michel Laronde argues about literature's relation to history – an argument that is relevant to cinema also – fiction has the power to fill in the silences of State-enforced amnesia on (post-)colonial events and to initiate necessary revisions of the State-sanctioned historiography through the recovery and restoration of foreclosed memories.

The volume opens with Steve Puig's helpful recapitulation of the development of *beur*, *banlieue*, and urban literatures, closely related and partly overlapping taxonomies describing the cultural production of second-generation, postcolonial immigrants to France. Noting that the term "*beur*" has become politically incorrect and obsolete in the 1990s and opting for the concept of "urban literature," Puig argues that the innovation of urban culture is to overcome the dichotomy of France versus North Africa through a global, transnational dimension which points to new modes of Frenchness beyond post-colonial relations. While post-*beur* literature is no longer connected to a particular place (the *banlieue*), urban culture designates a global movement inflecting French culture with Afro-American influences and Antillean accents and embodied in a new generation of writers who are more informed than the *beur* generation about French colonialism and 'consider themselves fully French culturally speaking' (p. 20).

Similarly, Patrick Saveau studies female authors who claim their legitimate place as full-fledged writers in their own right, rather than second-generation immigrants tied to time-worn representations of the economically deprived *banlieue*. His chapter, 'Breaking the chains of ethnic identity: Faïza Guène, Saphia Azzeddine, and Nadia Bouzid, or the birth of a new Maghrebi-French women's literature,' considers authors who 'do not necessarily examine the world along an ethnic binary logic' (p. 32) but in Higbee's terms offer 'a more diverse spectrum of socio-economic space and geographic locations,' (2013: 25) while claiming to belong to French literature at large. Guène's narrative technique in *Les gens du Balto* allows characters to escape the chains of rigid identity; Azzeddine's protagonists adopt fluid cultural and identity positions according to circumstances; Bouzid does not anchor her work in the *banlieue*, nor does she dwell on themes of disenfranchisement, her characters being defined by their sexual orientation and their way to 'be in, act in, and see the world' (p. 43). Saveau concludes that 'the three writers claim their right to fiction, imagination, and poetic license, something denied to their predecessors' (p. 43) who were tied to mimetic representations of marginality.

Faïza Guène is also the object of Florina Matu's chapter titled 'From daughter to mother, from sister to brother: building identities in Faïza Guène's novels.' Her chapter examines how the fictional portrayal of women in Guène's novels differs from the representation of female characters in traditional *beur* literature. More often than not, families depicted in *beur* novels followed the social paradigm described by Camille Lacoste-Dujardin, with the father as the dominant figure, the eldest son prevailing over the mother because of his gender, 'the hierarchy of gender [having] priority over the hierarchy of generation,' and the daughter being therefore relegated to the lowest social rank, 'doubly dominated because of her gender and her generation' (2000: 64). Matu shows female identities in flux, questioning these traditional hierarchies. She demonstrates that Guène's female characters epitomize 'a new approach to identity configuration along with its translation into more articulated destinies' (p. 49).

Emna Mrabet's chapter, 'The immigrant in Abdellatif Kechiche's cinematic work: transcending the question of origins,' explores the development of Abdellatif Kechiche's cinema and argues that the filmmaker consciously 'chooses to create characters that stay away from clichés and stereotypes, while simultaneously managing to avoid the trap of communitarianism and to transcend the issue of origins' (p. 64). By using Arab literature and canonical French literature as intertexts, by giving characters access to a rich, hybrid, trans-Mediterranean cultural heritage, Kechiche allows protagonists to 'cross boundaries' and occupy a space 'where young men of Maghrebi origins are traditionally absent, confined as they are to the margins' (p. 67). Characters are not described as victims or rebels in a miserable environment, but, instead, are portrayed as 'proactive youth … in harmony with the older generation' (p. 73) and 'in love with France and its poetry' (p. 68). French literary intertexts further help Kechiche to articulate ideals of liberty, justice, and social protest, while the refusal of a hierarchy between *banlieue* culture and "high" culture represented by classical theater allows him to 'shift his emphasis from the center to the periphery' (p. 72), giving the *banlieue* a new cultural dignity' and offering a fresh image of Maghrebi-French youths and immigrants. Thus, for the film director, the periphery offers the promise of renewing and enriching the culture of the center, a position departing from the traditional representation of the *banlieue* as a locus of unemployment, violence, drugs, racism, and generational conflict.

The non-traditional representation of minorities in France is also the object of Mona El Khoury's chapter, 'Seeking paths to existence in Rachid Djaïdani's *Rengaine*.' She argues that in both film and fiction, Djaïdani tirelessly holds on to a view of identity as being in constant negotiation, a view also illustrated in his own changing professions and experiences. El Khoury finds that Djaïdani's work combines a universal scope and an autobiographical accent, thus oscillating between the universal and the particular. In *Rengaine*, characters serve to denounce the fantasy of a pure cultural identity and an all-determining origin. The film director pioneers a reflection on urban culture, ethnicity, religion, and sexual orientation, pleading for mutual respect between different immigrant minorities and for a view of Muslim identity as 'ever-changing and multifaceted. His film thus complicates and transcends the binary tension between majority and minority by emphasizing the plurality of evolving identifications within the so-called minority and the intersection of ethnicity with other dimensions of identity (sex, gender, religion, and culture). El Khoury concludes by showing how the film performs the author's own hybridity and virtual childbirth in a celebration of cultural and racial diversity.

In *Reframing Difference*, Tarr noted that television channels in recent years 'have fostered both the work of directors of Maghrebi descent and television films addressing questions of ethnic difference' (2005: 11). In '*Beur* and *banlieue* television comedies: new perspectives on immigration,' Caroline Fache examines television's role in increasing the visibility of minorities on the Paysage Audiovisuel Français (French audiovisual scene) and raises the question of whether comedy is the most appropriate genre to serve the cause of immigrants. Studying two television series, *Aïcha* and *Fortunes*, she shows how the portrayal of strong-willed, entrepreneurial, resourceful, and ambitious male and female characters breaks away from the pessimism usually associated with the image of immigration and frees the protagonists from the 'sticky *beur*, *banlieue*, and second-generation immigrant identity' (p. 103). Through the characters' dreams and through intertextual allusions to American movies in *Fortunes* (in particular, Quentin Tarantino's works) and to American civil rights activism in *Aïcha*, the two series directors promote a wide audience identification with the characters. As they conjure up the idea of transnationalism and globalization, they triangulate the binary opposition *banlieue* versus center, minority versus French mainstream. *Aïcha*, in particular, promotes the idea of intergenerational feminine solidarity, the global fight for women's rights, and the transmission of civil values and women's rights within a universal context.

Placed in the middle of our volume, Jimia Boutouba's chapter refers to one particular historical event that signaled a change in the French perception of Maghrebi-French youth through the demonstration of its plural identities. *La Marche pour l'égalité et contre le racisme* (the March for equality and against racism) took place in 1983 and soon became 'le symbole de la reconnaissance sociale de la "seconde génération" [qui] consacr[a] l'accès à la citoyenneté de ces enfants d'immigrés' (Beaud and Masclet, 2006: 809) (the symbol of the second generation's social recognition [which] consecrated access to French citizenship for immigrants' offspring). Boutouba examines the cinematic representation of this historical event in her chapter 'They had a dream: out-marching exclusion and hatred.' The narrative of mobility developed by Moroccan-Belgian filmmaker Ben Yadir's 2013 film *La Marche* transforms the story of the long journey through France's hinterland into a metaphor of 'solidarity and connectedness across gender, class, race and sex divides' and a paradigm for political intervention (p. 118). Undermining the stereotypical association *banlieue*–immigration–lawlessness and the French State's systemic discrimination against immigrants from former colonies based on national amnesia, *La Marche* is a 'heterogeneous text that weaves a new relationship between present and past' and transforms France's national historiography (p. 123). Using Jacques Rancière's theory of police ordering and dissensus, Boutouba argues that the filmic text 'disrupts and puts into crisis the political language attached to the modern French nation.' It offers 'a model of a micro-political challenge to State police, whereby marginalized characters become political subjects by disrupting the litigious distribution of places and roles' (p. 131). The open road as political activity points to a 'cartography of mobility that challenges and overturns the physical and ideological containment of minorities' and replaces the concept of fixed "roots" with that of fluid routes (p. 127). Transitional spaces and contact zones create encounters and dialogue, new public sites of political exchange and creativity. As interpreted by Boutouba, Ben Nadir's film participates in the postmemorial effort to dispel collective amnesia.

Boutouba's chapter serves as an appropriate thematic transition to the second half of this volume, which is explicitly or implicitly articulated around the concept of postmemory pioneered by Marianne Hirsch as 'a *structure* of inter- and transgenerational return of traumatic knowledge and embodied experience. It is a *consequence* of traumatic recall but … at a generational remove' (2012: 6). Characteristics of postmemory, such as 'the continuities and discontinuities between generations, the gaps in knowledge, the fears and terrors that ensue in the aftermath of trauma' (2012: 6), have found a fertile ground in French post-colonial literature and film. Postmemory has the potential to uncover the buried traumas inherited from French decolonization and perhaps to heal the silences of the first generation of North African immigrants to France, while simultaneously repairing the gaps in State-sanctioned national myths on both sides of the Mediterranean. If, as Fiona Barclay suggests, post-colonial French society has been haunted by the specter of its past imperialism, and Maghrebi immigrants and their offspring function in the collective psyche like the return of the repressed (Freud's uncanny), can the voice of the ghost/s, once restored by the post-generation, serve to mend State-sanctioned amnesia and facilitate collective anamnesis at the national level? Can the work of postmemory, as articulated by individual writers and filmmakers, promote reconciliation between various generations of immigrants and different constituencies of the Algerian War and of decolonization more generally? Can the process of postmemory, unlike that of 'monumentalization,' bridge the divide between 'competing narratives of the past' and 'facilitate the fusion of memories'? (Barclay, 2011: xxx). The following contributions seek to address these questions and more.

In 'Narrativizing foreclosed history in "postmemorial" fiction of the Algerian War in France: October 17, 1961, a case in point,' Michel Laronde outlines an ingenious methodology for studying across different writer generations the repeated literary inscriptions of a traumatic historical event, namely the massacre of Algerian demonstrators in Paris on October 17, 1961. Using works written both by authors of North African origins and by mainstream French novelists, he suggests that postmemorial immigration fiction has the potential to 'decipher and rehabilitate pieces of history that have been repressed, ignored, manipulated, or silenced by the State' (p. 135). He further hypothesizes that the inscription of the event in fiction may entail new forms of narration, replacing the chronological mode of the classical historical novel. Conversely, differences in fictional re-presentations over a thirty-year period will likely reveal an evolution in 'postcolonial mentality.' Laronde argues that postmemorial literature initiates a 'slow process of mending' trauma at the individual, collective, and intergenerational levels.

The second-generation's healing of national amnesia regarding the Algerian War and of the fathers' self-repression is at the core of Véronique Machelidon's contribution titled 'Unearthing the father's secret: postmemory and identity in *harki* and pied noir narratives.' Machelidon explores the literary representations of the physical or metaphorical trans-Mediterranean journey through time and/or space initiated by a *harki* daughter, Dalila Kerchouche, and a pied noir son, Thierry Galdeano, in search of their fathers' lost dignity. Through similar narrative techniques, the narrators of *Mon père ce harki* and *Harkis, Pieds-noirs, nos cœurs orphelins* succeed in constructing complex and integrated identities that reconcile diverse memories (Galdeano) or multiple cultural heritages (Kerchouche). Bearing in mind Benjamin Stora's imperative to 'decloister' memories and deflate the competition between different communities for the status of the most deserving war victim (Stora, 2006: 66), Machelidon concludes that the reconciliation of *harki* and pied noir memories takes place only in Galdeano's novel, 'at the levels of plot and narrative technique, in its title and postface,' whereas Kerchouche is 'unable to envisage a peaceful dialogue between *harki* and pied noir memories and prefers to point to the urgent need for a reconciliation between *harkis* and other Algerians' (p. 171). The critic warns that the exchange established by Galdeano between *harki* and pied noir plots and memories may, however, be a belated expression of pied noir idealization of colonial society.

Susan Ireland continues the exploration of postmemorial literature and cinema in her 'Representations of the *harkis* in contemporary French language films.' Drawing a diachronic panorama of *harki* literature and cinema since the 1960s through the twenty-first century, she notes that the end of official amnesia in the 2000s initiated 'a phase of memorialization and memory work' which finds its reflection in autobiographical and fictional literary works as well as cinema. As authors 'participate in the creation of collective memories, strive to heal the wounds of the past, and contest the reductive national scripts' (p. 180), literature and film about *harki* experience and identity offer 'counter-narratives' which, like Higbee's concept of 'counter-heritage' cinema, 'propose an alternative version to the dominant narrative of French colonial history' (p. 178). *Harki* films and literature thus constitute the sort of re-historicization of the Algerian War that Laronde explores in his analysis of the fictionalization of the October 17, 1961 massacre. Ireland does not restrict her study to the works of *harki* descendants, but instead she includes side by side films and documentaries by *harki* children and mainstream French directors. After a detailed examination of films produced in the 2000s, she agrees that 'the Harki remains a marginalized figure on the fringe of all cultural production' (Howell, 2014: 190) and adds that *harki* characters 'occupy only a very small place' in fiction films. They continue to be primarily represented in the historical context of the war or the camps, in liminal spaces at the margin of mainstream French society, 'a kind of transnational no-man's land that is neither fully French nor Algerian' (p. 188). While the Tasma/Kerchouche documentary *Harkis* emphasizes the 'need to go beyond oppositional discourses' in order to promote healing, the negotiation of a 'new identity at the confluence of two cultures' remains challenging (p. 191).

The next two contributions deal with cinema and literature respectively. They both explore the theme of the transformative journey across space and time, where a young protagonist retraces the biological or metaphorical father's footsteps, back to the family's roots in North Africa (Mielusel) or across France, revisiting the various *lieux de mémoire* of Algerian immigration in metropolitan France (Le Breton). In '"L'Oued revient toujours dans son lit." Franco-Maghrebi Identity in Hassan Legzouli's film *Ten'ja*,' Ramona Mielusel studies the director's revision of the road movie genre and shows how Nordine's trip to Morocco to bury his father becomes a cultural journey of personal initiation for the main character, who learns to reconcile his multiple identities. Exploring Hamid Naficy's concept of 'accented cinema,' Mielusel argues that the 'psychological and cultural exploration of identity' initiated by the geographical displacement allows the central protagonist to bridge the gap between parents and children, native and adopted cultures. As Nordine turns into a 'keeper of the parental memory,' he is able to give his life an 'added value: being the same (French) and the Other (Moroccan) at once,' a vivid paradigm for contemporary French identity, which is itself 'in transformation' (p. 206). In her reading of the film, Mielusel suggests that through the acceptance of the fathers' cultural heritage, immigrant descendants can play a vital role in French society, as agents of reconciliation bringing 'the [different] communities closer, instead of pulling them apart' (p. 206). Legzouli's film also initiates a trans-Mediterranean dialogue between Moroccan and Maghrebi-French youths across gender.

The symbolic significance of the postmemorial journey is further explored in Mireille Le Breton's chapter 'Rewriting the memory of immigration: Samuel Zaoui's *Saint Denis bout du monde*.' In Zaoui's novel, a young woman and second-generation immigrant, Souhad, joins and interacts with three elderly *chibanis*, single men who came to France in the first wave of labor immigration. Zaoui's central female protagonist bridges the gap between the two generations and gives a voice to the invisible generation of *chibanis* who were, for the most part, illiterate. As in Legzouli's film, the younger generation gives 'new meaning to the trope of the "myth of returning"' to the homeland often found in migrant literature (p. 214). The novel follows Souhad during her travels with the three *chibanis* from Saint Denis to Marseille, hence departing from the 'traditional tropes found in migrant literature' (p. 216). While they retrace their past along the paradigms of space (the different places they lived in) and time (their arrival in France), the young woman learns about her own father, who never shared his past experiences with her. Le Breton shows how the purposeful meandering trip across France becomes a 'metaphor of memory itself, the collective memory that is being written as the sum of their individual memories' (p. 222). As Souhad becomes 'the repository of migratory history,' she stands as the heir to a 'forgotten generation,' who can repair individual and collective amnesia (p. 226). This contribution intersects with Laronde's and Machelidon's chapters in the way it highlights a path for (re)-covering 'memories of immigration in France,' which have been silenced by official historiography, due to the 'colonial fracture' (Bancel and Blanchard, 2006).

Hakim Abderrezak situates the issue of trans-Mediterranean immigration within the larger, international context of the recent upheavals that have caused thousands of people to cross the Mediterranean Sea in search of safety and peace. His chapter, '*Harragas* in Mediterranean *illiterature* and cinema,' announces the recent shift from a South/North, Maghreb/France, and colonial/post-colonial axis to a wider, more global, and more diffuse pattern of migrations. With the concept of *illiterature* – a neologism he has coined to define 'literary works that tackle the phenomenon of clandestine migration' – Abderrezak outlines the codes of a new genre, which writers and filmmakers born and living in countries of the west Mediterranean use to give a voice to the silent victims of transcontinental abuse (p. 233). As he discusses works by Tahar Ben Jelloun and Mohamed Teriah along with films by Merzak Allouache and Mohsen Melliti, he uncovers the common themes, leitmotifs, tropes, and codes running through cinema and literature alike. Abderrezak's chapter unpacks western rhetoric (which conflates terrorism, clandestinity, and drug trafficking) with regard to a 'war on terror' that thinly disguises, under the pretext of international security, the implementation of murderous borders to safeguard Fortress Europe. At a time when European political parties from England to Poland defensively retreat into nationalist agendas and platforms (as shown by the recent Brexit in the United Kingdom and the prominence of the Front National on France's political scene), this chapter reminds us of the pressing need for critical vigilance toward the dominant discourse and points to a time in the future when *harragas* (clandestine immigrants) will, it is hoped, find their own voice.

At the beginning of the new millennium, the themes explored by writers and film directors are far removed from those of the previous *beur* generation. The binary logic (center/periphery; mainstream/minority; Franco-French/Maghrebi-French) that confined *beur* authors in the 1980s and 1990s has been undermined in many different ways suggested by our contributors. While this logic began to be questioned with the advent of *banlieue* literature and cinema in the mid 1990s, it is by the end of the century that writers and filmmakers clearly moved away from the *banlieue* to offer readers and viewers representations of (post-)immigrants involving more complex, hybrid, and fluid identifications and to celebrate racial and cultural diversity (see El Khoury). Instead of portraying the *immobilisme* (lack of mobility) of characters living in the *banlieue* as a predetermined, 'emblematic space of marginality' (Higbee, 2013: 17), authors and directors of the late 1990s began to show protagonists evolving in more open spaces and engaging in richer encounters and explorations of the self. Among the overarching paradigms found in this volume, mobility plays a crucial role, in particular in the literary and cinematic works studied by Abderrazak, Boutouba, Fache, Le Breton, and Mielusel. The emphasis on mobility as a key to identity formation enables writers and filmmakers to move away from the autobiographical and sociological narratives that tended to dominate *beur* literature and film, while deconstructing fixed identities and exposing the stereotypes associated with them. Furthermore, as shown in El Khoury's, Mrabet's, and Saveau's respective contributions, authors with immigrant roots who decline ethnic (*beur*) and spatial (*banlieue*) labels offer innovative narratives and encourage critics to focus on the aesthetic dimension of their works.

Christiane Taubira's strategic mobilization of poetry in her postcolonial and postmemorial move revealed that literature and cinema have the critical potential to mend the gaps of State discourse, correct the official historiography, promote political activism and the respect for all, and involve all political constituents across the post-colonial divide in the creation of an inclusive and rich multicultural democracy. As demonstrated by Boutouba, Ireland, Laronde, and Machelidon, novels and films contribute to fill out the epistemological void left by mainstream republican discourses. They help build postmemorial narratives that produce plural, decentered memories and deconstruct national myths. Bridging the silence between generations (Le Breton, Machelidon) and the memorial divide between (ex)colonizer and (ex)colonized denounced by Benjamin Stora, film and literature can further promote "democratic politics" that resists the established police order (Boutouba). In an age of nationalist anxiety fed by the fear of Islamic fundamentalism, promoted by demagogues in the wake of terrorist attacks in France since the years 2010s, and fed by mono-vocal readings of past and present history, *Reimagining North African Immigration: Identities in Flux in French Literature, Television, and Film* can deflate the temptation of the dominant group's retreat into simplified narratives of identity and challenge the dominant perceptions and stereotypes affixed to minorities. The transformative potential of trans-Mediterranean literature and film offers a much-needed antidote and a reason for hope in cultural, post-colonial, and ethnic reconciliations in France.

Notes

1 In this introduction the editors have used the helpful distinction introduced by Michel Laronde in Chapter 8. 'Postcolonial' refers to the concept, while 'post-colonial' indicates historical time. 'Post(-)colonial' designates both the concept and the time frame. In the following chapters of this book, contributors have been free to adopt this distinction or not. In this introduction, terms like 'postmemory' and 'postmemorial' as well as 'postgeneration' have been

spelled following the terminology coined by Marianne Hirsch, who pioneered the theory and the concepts. Christiane Taubira can be described as both a colonial subject, since Guyana never went through a process of decolonization, and a postcolonial subject because she is consciously referring to, and working within, a postcolonial context.
2 Some of the shock created in the *hemicycle* can be attributed to the pugnacious immediacy of the language used by Damas and his attack on the European canon of poetry through colonial prosaism: 'pisser un coup, tout à l'envi, contre la vie stupide et bête qui nous est faite' (take a piss, piss at will, piss at the stupid living conditions which are imposed on us).
3 Contrary to Tarr's guarded evaluation of the progress achieved by *beur* filmmakers in the new millennium, post-*beur* filmmakers have shown since the 2000s that they are able 'to imagine young men from the banlieue either successfully investing the spaces they inhabit or negotiating alternative spaces' (2005: 185).
4 Interview with the authors, Lyon, October 23, 2015.

References

Bancel, N. and Blanchard, P. (2006). 'Les Origines républicaines de la fracture coloniale,' in P. Blanchard, N. Bancel, and S. Lemaire (eds), *La Fracture coloniale: La société française au prisme de l'héritage colonial*, Paris: La Découverte, 35–45.

Barclay, F. (2011). *Writing Postcolonial France: Haunting, Literature and the Maghreb*, Lanham, MD: Lexington Books.

Beaud, S. and Masclet, O. (2006). 'Des "marcheurs" de 1983 aux "émeutiers" de 2005: Deux générations sociales d'enfants d'immigrés,' *Annales. Histoire, Sciences sociales*, 4, 809–43.

Chevillot, F. (1998). 'Beurette suis et beurette ne veux pas toujours être: Entretien d'été avec Tassadit Imache,' *French Review*, 71(4), 632–44.

Damas, L. G. (2011). *Black Label* et autres poèmes. Paris: Gallimard.

Durmelat, S. (1998). 'Petite histoire du mot beur: Ou comment prendre la parole quand on vous la prête,' *French Cultural Studies*, 9, 191–207.

Durmelat, S. and Swamy, V. (eds) (2011). *Screening Integration: Recasting Maghrebi Immigration in Contemporary France*, Lincoln, NE: University of Nebraska.

Hall, S. (1996). 'Who Needs Identity?,' in S. Hall and P. du Gay (eds), *Questions of Cultural Identity*, London: Sage, 1–17.

Hargreaves, Alec G. and Gans-Guinoune, A. M. (2008). 'Introduction,' *Expressions maghrébines*, 7(1), 1–9.

Higbee, W. (2013). *Post-Beur Cinema: North African Emigré and Maghrebi-French Filmmaking in France Since 2000*, Edinburgh: Edinburgh University Press.

Hirsch, M. (2012). *The Generation of Postmemory: Writing and Visual Culture after the Holocaust*, New York: Columbia University Press.

Howell, J. (2014). 'Reconstructing Harki Sites of Memory in the Graphic Novel,' in K. Moser (ed.), *A Practical Guide to Harki Literature*, Lanham, MD: Lexington Books, 187–207.

Johnston, C. (2010). *French Minority Cinema*. Amsterdam: Rodopi.

Kealhofer-Kemp, L. (2015). *Muslim Women in French Cinema: Voices of Maghrebi Migrants in France*. Liverpool: Liverpool University Press.

Lacoste-Dujardin, C. (2000). 'Maghrebi Families in France,' in J. Freedman and C. Tarr (eds), *Women, Immigration and Identities in France*, Oxford: Berg, 57–68.

Redouane, N. (2012a). 'Pourquoi les filles des émigrés maghrébins en France prennent-elles la plume?,' in N. Redouane and Y. Bénayoun-Szmidt (eds), *Qu'en est-il de la littérature "beur" au féminin?*, Paris: L'Harmattan, 13–47.

Redouane, N. (2012b). 'Qu'en est-il des écrits des enfants d'immigrés maghrébins en France?,' in N. Redouane (ed.), *Où en est la littérature "beur"?*, Paris: L'Harmattan, 13–53.

Stora, B. (2006). 'Quand une mémoire (de guerre) peut en cacher une autre (coloniale),' in P. Blanchard, N. Bancel, and S. Lemaire (eds), *La Fracture coloniale: La France au prisme de l'héritage colonial*, Paris: La Découverte, 59–67.

Swamy, V. (2011). *Interpreting the Republic: Marginalization and Belonging in Contemporary French Novels and Films*, Lanham, MD: Lexington Books.

Tarr, C. (2005). *Reframing Difference: Beur and Banlieue Filmmaking in France*, Manchester: Manchester University Press.

1

'Qui fait la France?' New configurations of Frenchness in contemporary urban fiction

Steve Puig

The riots of October and November 2005 will be remembered in French history as a time of conflict between the government, who passed a law aiming to promote 'the "positive aspects" of French colonialism' in February of that year, and the youth living on the outskirts of Paris (the *banlieue*), the majority of whom are descendants of formerly colonized people now living in France. Since the 1980s, the term "integration" has been used by French politicians to describe the process through which immigrants are being assimilated into French culture. In the 1980s, the concept of *beur*[1] culture emerged to express the feeling of belonging to two cultures: one that originated in the Maghreb (Algeria, Morocco, or Tunisia) and a French one, which has been increasingly challenged by the arrival of new immigrants from former French colonies.

In the 1990s, *beur* literature as well as the word *beur* itself started to become obsolete, as this new generation felt more and more assimilated or "integrated" into French society. In 2007, a collective of writers named 'Qui fait la France?' (What is Frenchness?) published a collection of short stories named *Chroniques d'une société annoncée* (Chronicle of a society foretold), in which writers such as Faïza Guène and Rachid Djaïdani, whom some critics regard as *beur* writers, shared their opinion on French society. Along with newcomers like Mabrouck Rachedi, Jean-Eric Boulin, and Thomté Ryam, they gave new representations of the *banlieue* and its inhabitants. Not only did they change the way urban youth was perceived as a whole, they also exposed France's colonial past, which is still taboo in many aspects of French society – whether it be history books or just public debate – in order to shed new light on contemporary social issues like unemployment or racism. At the same time, postcolonial studies began to blossom in France, notably because historians started to establish a continuum between the colonial era and the present post(-)colonial situation, in which the *banlieue* itself can be seen as an internal colony. In this chapter, I wish to establish a parallel between the development of postcolonial studies in France and the emergence of urban literature, as both contribute to our understanding of "postcolonial France." My aim is to show that urban literature can be seen as a kind of postcolonial literature as it contains references to, and a critique of, France's colonial past that are informed by a new generation of historians.

The 2005 riots were not exactly a new phenomenon. Since the 1980s, France has been beset by various forms of protest, mostly coming from the children of immigrants living on the outskirts of major cities and even within major cities. One example is the city of Vaulx-en-Velin near Lyon, a name that was ubiquitous in the media at the time when young adults of North African descent rebelled against discrimination and racism, making the news around the world, including the *New York Times* (October 19, 1990). Protests of this sort were part of France's history throughout the 1990s. As Alec Hargreaves pointed out, the 2005 riots were only a little more widespread than previous ones: 'While unprecedented in scale, the events of 2005 were not in any significant respect new. At a lower level of intensity, there had been similar disorders in the banlieues since the late 1970s' (2007: 136).

Although I agree with Hargreaves' statement, I would like to argue that they were different in the sense that much of the French-Maghrebi youth is now aware of France's colonial past, and especially the French presence in Algeria, which gave these riots a new meaning. In that sense, they were not only protesting discrimination and racism on the outskirts of Paris but also expressing their anger toward a country that colonized their parents' homeland and marginalized them once they moved to France. Paradoxically perhaps, they were also demanding to finally be treated as French citizens, which they have been for decades, and to exist in the way sociologist Abdelmalek Sayad defines the word "existence," meaning to exist politically, to have some kind of political representation in politics and in society more generally, and in the cultural spheres as well (Sayad, 2006: 13–21).

Although the field of postcolonial studies has been vibrant for more than two decades in the anglophone world, it only started to blossom in France at the beginning of the new millennium. In the last decade, several historians have published on France's colonial past and a few intellectuals have shown that there is a continuum between the colonial era (and the way immigrants were treated in the 1960s) and the post-colonial era (with the riots in 2005). For instance, Sadri Khiari (2009) clearly states that not much has changed between the colonial period and 2005 in terms of how the French see minorities, still perceiving them as foreigners and refusing to consider them as fully French or *citoyens à part entière*.

Since 2005, a plethora of books have been published on France's colonial past in Algeria, in the Caribbean, in Africa and elsewhere, but it is mostly due to the civil unrest on the outskirts of Paris that the presence of immigrants and their descendants has become the subject of public debate. Marie-Claude Smouts (2007) claims that France cannot ignore the repercussions of the French colonial presence in the world upon today's society. Along with a group of historians called ACHAC (Association Connaissance de l'Histoire de l'Afrique Contemporaine), she suggests that France is now entering a post-colonial era, one where the (lack of) space granted to minorities in political and cultural spheres must be negotiated. Just as Sartre wrote that existentialism is a kind of humanism, Smouts seems to suggest that the postcolonial lens is also a way to re-evaluate the past and its repercussions on contemporary French society. It represents an attempt to understand current events, giving the postcolonial field a humanist perspective. For instance, the curfew planned by Dominique de Villepin in November 2005 was very reminiscent of the curfew imposed by Maurice Papon in 1961 during the massacre of Algerians and French citizens of North African descent in Paris, something that Tom Heneghan from the *Washington Post* noted on November 8, 2005: 'The renewed violence followed a warning by Prime Minister Dominique de Villepin that he would take a firm line against lawbreakers, including reinforcements for police and curfews not seen here since the Algerian war of 1954–1962.' Other publications, mostly led by the collective ACHAC, have informed a new generation of writers who are now much more aware of the relationship between France and its former colonies, and therefore of the reasons for their presence on the French territory. The emergence of postcolonial studies in France coincides with the realization by a new generation of French citizens that the practices of French imperialism still have a major impact on contemporary French society.

Since 2005, several novels and essays have been published about the riots and, more generally speaking, about life in the *banlieue*. Many of these novels include the word *banlieue* or *cités* in their title: *Banlieue noire* by Thomté Ryam, *Cités à comparaître* by Karim Amellal, *Banlieue Voltaire* by Didier Mandin or *La guerre des banlieues n'aura pas lieu* by Abd Al Malik, just to name a few. Some of these writers have united their voices to form the aforementioned collective Qui fait la France?, whose name interrogates what it means to be French or how Frenchness can (and should) be redefined in the new millennium. Most of these novels deal with daily life in the *banlieue*, but they also have a political aim. Some openly criticize French society today, others denounce the lack of interest for the urban (i.e. mostly non-white) youth of France by the Sarkozy government, which did very little to improve the conditions in the *banlieue* despite the 2008 *Plan Espoir Banlieues* (a kind of Marshall Plan for the projects outside Paris), which never fully came to fruition (*Le Monde*, February 7, 2008).[2] Several names have been used to describe this new trend: among them, *littérature urbaine* and (post-)*beur* literature.

In an article called 'Authors on the Outskirts: Writing Projects and (Sub) urban Space in Contemporary French Literature,' Harry Veivo defines urban literature as a literature of the city and analyzes novels by four writers: François Maspéro, Jean Rolin, Georges Perec, and Jacques Jouet. His definition includes mostly established writers, whose topics are linked with daily life in the city but does not include any of the writers previously mentioned in this chapter. Christina Horvath defines urban literature as a kind of literature that describes daily life in the city (2007: 16). Both scholars define urban literature in a French context as a literature based on urban topics and daily life in Paris. Since their publications came out just a couple of years after the riots, it is likely that they have not been able to include most of the new wave of urban fiction that came out in 2006 and 2007 (although Horvath dedicates a few pages to Djaïdani and Guène in her book). Andrew Gallix's definition seems to take into account this new generation of writers:

> So what is this 'littérature urbaine' lark really about, then? Above all, it reflects the advent of a new generation; a changing of the guard: Faïza Guène was only 13 when Georgia de Chamberet edited her anthology of fresh French fiction back in 1999. Giving voice to the vernacular of the banlieues – with its backslang ('verlan') and borrowings from Arabic – may not seem a big deal in post-Trainspotting Britain, but it is truly novel, and perhaps even revolutionary, given the conservative nature of the French literary establishment. (*The Guardian*, September 12, 2008)

Gallix's definition suggests that urban literature not only gives a voice to the marginalized youth, but also creates a space in the literary establishment for a new kind of literature which includes the vocabulary and the collective imagination of urban youth.

Various scholars have suggested that these urban writers write from a different perspective than the *beur* writers torn between their origins and their "Frenchness" (like Azouz Begag's character in *Le Gone du Chaâba*). In 'New Writing for New Times: Faïza Guène, *banlieue* Writing, and the Post-*beur* Generation,' Dominic Thomas states that banlieue writing recognizes 'the pluridimensionality of ethnic struggles in France today (whereas Beur literature [was] predominantly constituted by a Maghrebi-centric corpus), and is accordingly working towards articulating a trajectory in which social exclusion and injustice are denounced, in order to work productively and responsibly in seeking solutions' (Thomas, 2008: 35). Ilaria Vitali shows how themes have evolved from *beur* literature to urban literature and that *beur* writers are not the only ones who try to redefine Frenchness, as they are joined by a new generation of French urban writers with roots in French-speaking sub-Saharan African countries (2009: 181–2). I have shown elsewhere the transition between *beur* literature and urban literature and the shift in the vocabulary linked to both genres (Puig, 2011: 21–46). Indeed, whereas *beur* writers struggled with the concept of integration, the new wave of writers consider themselves fully French culturally speaking and therefore demand to be treated as such. In an interview, Mohamed Razane, one of the leaders of Qui fait la France?, denounced the constant marginalization of minorities in the political and cultural spheres and insisted on the need to hear new voices in French literature. For Razane, writing is also a way to rebel against the domination of the literary establishment, 'L'écriture comme un écho ou plutôt comme un porte-voix de cette plèbe dominée, comme une possibilité de se disputer avec ceux-là même qui vous méprisent' (Puig, 2008: 86) (Writing as an echo or rather as a voice for the oppressed people, a way to argue with those who despise you).

The *beur* movement came into existence thanks to the combination of a political movement aiming to improve the conditions of second-generation immigrants and a cultural production (literature, music, dance, and theater) that echoed the 1983 *Marche pour l'égalité et contre le racisme* (March for equality and against racism).[3] I would argue that the same is true of urban culture, which is not just a cultural movement but also a political one, moving from the kind of autofiction that has characterized much Parisian literary production since the *nouveau roman*, to a more politically inclined kind of literature. One of the main differences between *beur* literature and urban literature is that the latter is less ethnically marked than the former. *Beur* literature was written by writers with Tunisian, Moroccan, and Algerian origins, whereas urban writers come from various backgrounds: Jean-Eric Boulin is from Marseille, Faïza Guène was born in France to Algerian parents, and Thomté Ryam was born in Chad before moving to France as a child. Born in Marrakech, Mohamed Razane came to France at the age of 9, while Didier Mandin's parents are from Martinique, and so on. The concept of urban literature, then, is connected to a place (the *banlieue*) rather than a specific ethnicity.

The term "urban literature" has emerged in various articles after 2005, mostly from scholars who try to go beyond *beur* literature, like Alec Hargreaves, or seek to analyze a new trend like Najib Redouane, but the reasons for using the word 'urban' are not completely clear. In a strict sense, the word refers to the city (*urbanus* meaning 'from the city' in Latin) and yet, urban writers come mostly from the periphery of Paris, hence a paradox between the actual meaning of the word and its use to describe cultural production that has emerged from the outskirts of the city (urban sports, urban music, etc.). The word is used in Rachid Djaidani's 2012 movie *Rengaine*, where a young man doing a survey asks a few ethnic youths about 'les minorités urbaines dans l'espace public' (urban minorities in public space).[4] This example reveals the use of *urbain* as a euphemism, replacing another often-used word: *ethnique*. In the realm of music, the French award ceremony Victoires de la musique gives prizes to the best-selling artists each year and includes a category called *musique urbaine*, which was created to reward the best hip-hop, raï, or R&B albums, all mostly by Afro-French or Maghrebi-French youths. Some websites and magazines like *Respect Mag'* are also dedicated to urban culture in France.[5]

If the French word *urbain* does not refer to the city, then one can assume that the term works the same way as in the United States, where it refers to minorities, with the difference that in the United States, minorities often live in the inner city. In a cultural context, the word is mostly being used as a euphemism to describe African-American and Latino cultural productions and to refer to cultures that have emerged from hip-hop. Though "urban literature" was used in the 1970s to describe writers like Iceberg Slim, nowadays the term evokes a kind of fiction that describes life in the streets (mostly of New York and other major cities), a life filled with violence, sex, drugs, and hip-hop. The genre has even gone 'from the streets to the libraries,' to quote the title of an article in the *New York Times* (October 23, 2008). In fact, American urban culture is probably responsible for inspiring urban cultures internationally, including in France, which now has the second biggest hip-hop market in the world.

Some critics have noticed the new corpus of novels that have emerged since 2005. Najib Redouane suggested that these writers have been distancing themselves from the *beur* condition since the 1990s and that in recent production, writers have been less concerned with traditional themes like that of belonging (or not) to French society: 'Après les années quatre-vingt-dix, la continuité de l'écriture des beurs prend une nouvelle direction ... Cette nouvelle vague tente de se forger une nouvelle identité en dépit du poids familial et des orientations sociétales' (Redouane, 2012: 20) (After the 1990s, *beur* writing takes on a different direction ... This new wave tries to forge a new identity in spite of the weight of family and society's new trends).

The hesitations and tensions between North African culture and French culture which were part of *beur* literature have shifted to other preoccupations. One of the main features of urban literature is its political side, which shows the influence of postcolonial studies and the awareness of France's colonial past. Urban literature has democratized and in some way also broadened the reach of literature, as it has made fiction accessible to a new generation of readers who might not identify with bourgeois fiction. The multiple references to pop culture – whether French or American – also represent an attempt to get away from the way literature is generally perceived in France, where the difference between high and popular culture is much more marked than in the United States. In the United States, urban fiction has become part of contemporary American culture. In the 1960s and 1970s, urban literature served as a way to express African-American pride and to denounce racism, which was a source of inspiration for urban French writers.

The question of naming the new post-*beur* movement is also an issue with cinema, as Sylvie Durmelat and Vinay Swamy have noted: 'Although labels such as *beur* and *banlieue* cinema overlap, and may well be temporary, they have highlighted the contributions of films that have renewed the images of immigrants and their descendants by providing a perspective from within the North African immigrant experience' (2011: 4). Many critics have used the term *beur* within quotation marks or with italics. They wish to show their reluctance to use a word that very much belongs to the generation who grew up in the 1970s and 1980s and that has been criticized by the very people it refers to. One of the main advantages of the word *urbain* is that it is more inclusive than the word *beur*, allowing writers to come together, regardless of their origins, in order to address problems that are not specific to one group but are relevant to France as a whole, especially at a time when the definition of Frenchness is changing.

As I suggested earlier, France, like other European countries, now has to deal with a growing population of immigrants and redefine what it means to be French, something President Sarkozy's government attempted rather awkwardly with the 2007 creation of the Ministère de l'Immigration, de l'Intégration, de l'Identité nationale et du Développement solidaire (Ministry of Immigration, Integration, National Identity and Codevelopment of France).[6] Part of the problem is that French society is reluctant to give space to minorities, whether in the political or cultural sphere, and one of the issues is the silence around France's colonial past, a past that explains, in part, the presence of some minorities on its soil. Interestingly enough, some urban writers go as far as accusing France of silencing its colonial past on purpose, whether by censoring books (like the essays and novels that came out after October 17, 1961, the day when Algerian demonstrators were massacred by the Parisian police)[7] or by ignoring the topic in history classes. In his book *Celui qui écrit une lettre au président*, Adel Fernane writes: 'Si l'Éducation Nationale ne nous apprend pas l'histoire complète et réelle de notre pays, et que nos parents sont trop perturbés et traumatisés pour nous en parler sans neutralité, pourquoi s'étonner alors que des centaines de jeunes sifflent la Marseillaise lors d'un match France-Algérie?' (2007: 16) (Since we aren't told our real history in schools and since our parents are so disturbed and traumatized to talk about it without feeling embarrassed, then we shouldn't be surprised when hundreds of ethnic youths boo the Marseillaise during a soccer game between France and Algeria).[8]

Fernane describes a point of view which is typical of a new generation of writers and activists who have read, or at least heard, about France's colonial past and decided to address it in their work, or to create awareness about the historical implications of France's presence in its former colonies. In his *Open Letter to the President*, he points to one of the main obstacles that plague the *vivre-ensemble*, which remains the goal of many French people: the lack of recognition of France's colonial past in North Africa. This critique, which one can describe as postcolonial, is omnipresent in urban novels published after the 2005 riots.

In his 2006 *Supplément au roman national*, a book whose title echoes Diderot's 1772 *Supplément au voyage de Bougainville*, Jean-Eric Boulin, a member of Qui fait la France?, writes that the silence around France's presence in Algeria has been lingering for too long and that it is time for France to face its past in order to move on and build a future together with its minorities. As the title suggests, French history can be read as a novel that needs to be denationalized, by incorporating the experiences of the colonized or ex-colonized and of their descendants on French soil. In that regard, the Musée de l'immigration, which opened in 2007, was an important move toward decolonizing France's history. Unfortunately, the museum has failed to attract a lot of visitors, maybe another symptom of French people's disinterest in the history of immigration in France.

Many urban writers tend to include France's colonial (or post-colonial) history in their works in order to create awareness among a new (post-*beur*) generation of readers. For instance, in her most popular novel *Kiffe kiffe demain*, Faïza Guène aims to evoke France's troubled history with Algeria as she tells the story of Doria, a teenage girl of Moroccan descent, who researches the October 1961 massacre of Algerians in Paris and comments on Paris mayor, Bertrand Delanoë's commemoration of the tragic events:

> Elle (Maman) est amoureuse du maire de Paris. Elle kiffe Bertrand Delanoë depuis qu'elle l'a vu à la télé poser la plaque de commémoration à Saint-Michel. C'était en souvenir des Algériens balancés dans la Seine pendant la manifestation du 17 octobre 1961. J'ai emprunté des bouquins sur ça à la bibliothèque de Livry-Gargan. Maman a trouvé Bertrand très bien de faire ça pour la mémoire du peuple algérien. (2004: 164)

> Turns out she likes the mayor of Paris. Yeah, she's been in love with Bertrand Delanoë ever since she saw him on telly laying the memorial plaque at Saint-Michel. It was in honour of the Algerians who were thrown into the Seine during the demonstration on 17 October 1961. I borrowed books about it from Livry-Gargan library. Mom thought it was big of Bertrand to do something in memory of the Algerian people. (2006: 153–4)

In this quote, Guène approves of Delanoë's gesture through the point of view of Doria's mother. Although the novel's main theme is the story of Doria growing up in the *banlieue*, there are a few references to France's colonial presence in North Africa which contribute to the reader's awareness of the tragic events of October 1961. The filmed interviews Faïza Guène and Bernard Richard put together with historian Jean-Luc Einaudi's help in 2002 (*Mémoires*) and the publication of *Kiffe kiffe demain* in 2004 have allowed the long-repressed date of October 17, 1961 to resurface in French collective memory, inviting other artists, writers, or musicians, to talk about the massacre. The collaboration between historians and urban writers or musicians later materialized in the book *Don't Panik*, co-written by historian Pascal Boniface and rapper Médine, who is also famous for the song '17 octobre' describing the October 1961 tragedy.

In his 2006 novel *Banlieue Voltaire*, Didier Mandin describes the daily life of young adults of Caribbean descent and explores the cultural gap between the experiences of the parents, who grew up in Martinique or Guadeloupe, and those of their offspring, who grew up as products of the Parisian *banlieue*. The title clearly indicates that life in the *banlieue* is the main topic of the novel but it also mentions Voltaire, which is both the main protagonist's nickname and the name of the famous eighteenth-century philosopher, whose ideas on slavery in the French Caribbean were ambiguous. Part of the young adults' unease is due to their lack of awareness of their parents' history and the obscure relation between the mainland and the two islands, a colonial history that has been taught neither in school nor by their parents. This two-fold silence, on the parents' part and in official discourse, is often denounced in urban literature (as in the Adel Fernane quote above) and remains a major obstacle in the making of a new and more inclusive French identity:

> A ma grande surprise, Ludo m'a répondu que l'Education Nationale fait son job: elle s'adresse à des êtres indifférenciés, des particules de République partageant légalement une histoire commune ... Mais surtout elle devra veiller à ce que cette histoire ne soit pas enseignée à travers des prismes de lecture multi-centenaires, ceux-là même qui font passer des lois vantant les mérites de la colonisation dans les manuels scolaires. (2006: 93)

> Much to my surprise, Ludo answered that the curriculum designed by the National Education Ministry does its job: it is designed for undifferentiated members of the Republic, atoms of this whole, who by law all share a common history ... But most importantly, the Ministry must make clear that this history should not be taught through the lens of age-old approaches, like those inscribed in laws praising the positive effects of colonization in school textbooks.

In Mandin's book, the narrator makes a clear case for decolonizing history as it is traditionally taught in French textbooks, something that has been the topic of many books by Pascal Blanchard, Nicolas Bancel, and Sandrine Lemaire, particularly in their collective work *La Fracture coloniale*, which includes a study on high school students' lack of knowledge of colonial history (2005: 273–304).

Chroniques d'une société annoncée, includes a short story by Thomté Ryam who creates a dialogue between a character whose parents came to France from Sub-Saharan Africa, and a former history teacher of his. When the ex-student meets the teacher many years later, he tells her: 'C'est toujours en retard un prof d'histoire. Ça te parle des conflits d'il y a cinquante ans et jamais de ceux du moment ... En fait, je me suis renseigné sur Napoléon, Colomb, l'esclavage, de Gaulle, et ses mensonges. Vous mériteriez des heures de colle, madame pour vos trous de mémoire' (2007: 257–8) (History teachers are always one step behind. They speak of conflicts that took place fifty years ago and never of current ones ... Actually, I did some research on Napoleon, Columbus, slavery, de Gaulle and his lies. You deserve some detention time for your memory gaps, Ma'am). The *'trous de mémoire'* the character is talking about refer to certain topics that are not taught in French schools, such as colonialism, de Gaulle's failure in Algeria, Napoleon's restoration of slavery and Columbus' massacres in the New World. Even when these historical figures are mentioned, they are often portrayed as heroes within the context of a glorified past.

In most urban novels, the reader finds references to France's presence in Algeria, Tunisia, Morocco, the Antilles, Haiti, Indochina, and other places, which explain the existence of many minorities in France today, whose parents – some of them former colonized subjects – moved to France after their country of origin gained independence. Urban writers are more informed about French colonialism than the *beur* generation, not only because French colonialism is less of a taboo more than fifty years after the Algerian War, but also because they have read works by, or have been in contact with, the new generation of historians like Pascal Blanchard, Benjamin Stora, or Pascal Boniface, who are more present in the media than most historians.

In *Writerly Identities in Beur Fiction and Beyond*, Laura Reeck argued that the aim of the collective Qui fait la France? is not merely to criticize the French literary establishment for its lack of inclusiveness, but simply to exist through the act of writing (2011: 128), and in so doing, offer new representations of French identity in literature. In today's globalized and increasingly digitized world, the visibility of minorities in the media and in politics is crucial in order to ensure a minimum of social cohesiveness, a goal which many urban writers seem to be striving for, not only in their novels but also through various forms of activism, thus redefining the concept of *littérature engagée*. For instance, Mohamed Razane is a social worker, Mabrouck Rachedi has participated in many writing workshops, and Karim Amellal has appeared on television multiple times to defend the possibility of developing the French equivalent of affirmative action, which was unfortunately named *discrimination positive*. The manifesto that opens *Chroniques d'une société annoncée* clearly states that the writers are fighting to create an awareness of the living conditions of minorities in the periphery of Paris.

Marc Cheb Sun's publication, titled *D'ailleurs et d'ici: L'affirmation d'une France plurielle* is a sign that multiculturalism in France is here to stay. In his introduction, Marc Cheb Sun alludes to France's current postcolonial situation: 'Ce monde colonial, dont nous sommes les héritiers ... sévit encore dans la relation française à d'autres terres, outremer, ou sur d'autres continents. Sans parler du rapport crispé, apeuré, que, trop souvent, ce pays entretient avec son identité' (2014: 2) (This colonial world we have inherited ... still affects the relation between France and other territories, overseas or on different continents. Additionally, there's France's tense and frightened rapport to its own identity).

For the last decade, the light shed on francophone writers and the interest for so-called *francophonie* and *littérature-monde* in French has been growing, culminating in a manifesto titled 'Pour une "littérature-monde" en français' and signed by Edouard Glissant, Abdourahman A. Waberi, Maryse Condé, Dany Lafferière, Anna Moï, Wajdi Mouawad, and many more in favor of a world literature in French. Let us hope that urban writers can find their place in today's literary world as some of the 'francophone' writers have. For many activists and intellectuals, the French tradition of color-blind republicanism, supposedly based on equality, actually perpetuates discrimination and racism. France's colonial past, so long repressed, is the topic of a great many books, whether in the field of history or sociology. Francophone writers like Aimé Césaire and Assia Djebar have more or less explicitly offered a critique of French colonialism in their works for many years, while urban writers have analyzed colonialism's consequences on today's urban youth, but have yet to find a space in the French academic world.

The primary focus of *beur* culture was for Maghrebi youth to negotiate cultural affiliations with both French cultural society and their culture of origin. *Beur* activists helped develop *beur* literature, while writers voiced their concerns in the media. In a way, the political component of *beur* culture and its literary aspect reinforced each other. As a global movement, urban culture added a third component which makes it possible to go beyond the dichotomy of French versus North African cultures: indeed, as French youth has become more and more Americanized, they have found new ways of expressing their sense of revolt. Several urban writers have found inspiration in Spike Lee (like Mohamed Razane), Mohammed Ali (like Rachid Djaïdani) or Martin Luther King (like Axiom in *J'ai un rêve*).

The debates following the traumatic events of January 2015 and the terrorist attacks at the *Charlie Hebdo* offices proved that France still has to work on accepting cultural and religious differences, especially as the country is undergoing political turmoil. Even though one might fear that the Paris attacks against *Charlie Hebdo* and the kosher supermarket will create a kind of racial apartheid, one can also hope that they will provide opportunities for dialogue and for fulfilling the promises of the republican ideals, or maybe for adapting them to the new make-up of France, as new waves of immigration bring in refugees from countries that are not former French colonies. In that sense, the new generation of urban writers can help relay the point of view of an increasingly important urban youth, whose voice has yet to be heard, especially in the literary world. As urban literature deals with France's colonial past, it also helps explain the reasons for the presence of ex-colonial subjects on French soil and explore the sometimes conflicting relationships between the idea of Frenchness, as it is generally conceived, and what it is becoming. Urban literature can therefore be categorized as a kind of postcolonial literature that seeks to re-evaluate the weight of the past on contemporary socio-economic realities and to fulfill the goals of postcolonial studies, including a better understanding of the power dynamics behind racism and exclusion in France today.

Notes

1 I am using italics here to signal a critical distance regarding the use of the word.
2 The *Plan Espoir Banlieues* was considered simply as a way to gain votes during Sarkozy's presidential campaign (*Le Monde*, 2008).

3 See Chapter 7 in this volume.
4 See Chapter 5 in this volume.
5 The website 'Urban-Culture' tackles all topics of urban life, from art to sports to politics.
6 From the start, the Ministry of Immigration, Integration, National Identity, and Solidarity was controversial among intellectuals and other personalities. The same month it was created, in May 2007, eight university scholars – including Patrick Weil and Gérard Noiriel, specialists in the history of immigration – resigned from the Cité nationale de l'histoire de l'immigration to express their dismay, stating that the association of 'immigration' with 'national identity' was unacceptable. In the following months, various petitions and colloquiums denounced the risk of institutionalized xenophobia resulting from the existence and operation of this Ministry. It was eliminated in November 2010.
7 See Chapter 8 in this volume.
8 All translations are mine, unless otherwise specified.

References

Abd Al, M. (2009). *La guerre des banlieues n'aura pas lieu*, Paris: Cherche midi.
Amellal, K. (2006). *Cités à comparaître*, Paris: Stock.
Axiom (2012). *J'ai un rêve*, Paris: Denoël.
Barnard, A. (2008). 'From the Streets to the Libraries,' *New York Times*, October 22. Web. June 4, 2016.
Begag, A. (1986). *Le Gone du Chaâba*, Paris: Seuil.
Bernard, P. (2005). 'Banlieues: la provocation coloniale,' *Le Monde*, November 29.
Blanchard, P., Bancel, N., and Lemaire, S. (2005). *La Fracture coloniale: La société française au prisme de l'héritage colonial*, Paris: La Découverte.
Boniface, P. and Médine (2012). *Don't Panik*, Paris: Desclée de Brouwer.
Boulin, J.-E. (2006). *Supplément au roman national*, Paris: Stock.
Cheb, Sun M. (2014). *D'ailleurs et d'ici! L'affirmation d'une France plurielle*, Paris: Philippe Rey.
Dendoune, N. (2007). *Lettre ouverte à un fils d'immigré*, Paris: Danger public.
Djaïdani, R. (2000). *Boumkoeur*, Paris: Seuil.
Djaïdani, R. (2004). *Mon Nerf*, Paris: Seuil.
Djaïdani, R. (2007). *Viscéral*, Paris: Seuil.
Djouder, A. (2006). *Désintégration*, Paris: Stock.
Durmelat, S. and Swamy, V. (2011). 'Introduction,' in S. Durmelat and V. Swamy (eds), *Screening Integration: Recasting Maghrebi Immigration in Contemporary France*, Lincoln, NE/London: University of Nebraska Press, 1–23.
Fernane, A. (2007). *Celui qui écrit une lettre au président*, Paris: Publibook.
Forsdick, C. and Murphy, D. (2003). *Francophone Postcolonial Studies: A Critical Introduction*, London: Arnold.

Gallix, A. (2008). 'The New Wave of French Urban Fiction,' *The Guardian*, September 12. Web. June 4, 2016.
Greenhouse, S. (1990). 'Vaulx-en-Velin Journal; Arab Youths of France: Their Anger Boils Over,' *New York Times*, October 19. Web. June 4, 2016.
Guène, F. (2004). *Kiffe kiffe demain*, Paris: Hachette.
Guène, F. (2006). *Just Like Tomorrow*, trans. S. Adams, London: Random House.
Hargreaves, A. (2007). *Multi-Ethnic France: Immigration, Politics, Culture and Society*, 2nd edn, New York: Routledge.
Heneghan, T. (2005). 'French Youths Riot Again Despite Curfew Threats,' *Washington Post*, November 8.
Henley, J. (2005). 'French Angry at Law to Teach Glory of Colonialism,' *The Guardian*, April 15. Web. June 4, 2016.
Horvath, C. (2007). *Le roman urbain contemporain en France*, Paris: Presses Sorbonne nouvelle.
Khiari, S. (2009). *La contre-révolution coloniale en France: De de Gaulle à Sarkozy*, Paris: La fabrique éditions.
Laronde, M. (1988). 'La "Mouvance beure": Emergence médiatique,' *French Review*, 61, 684–92.
'Le Plan "Espoir banlieue" de Nicolas Sarkozy devrait être moins ambitieux que prévu,' *Le Monde*, February 8, 2008. Web. June 4, 2016.
Mahany, H. (2008). *Kiffer sa race: roman*, Paris: J.-C. Lattès.
Mandin, D. (2006). *Banlieue Voltaire*, Fort-de-France: Desnel.
Puig, S. (2008). 'Interview avec Mohamed Razane,' in A.-M. Gans-Guinoune and A. Hargreaves (eds), *Au-delà de la littérature "beur"?* Barcelona: Centre dona i literatura, Universitat de Barcelona, 85–92.
Puig, S. (2011). 'Du roman beur au roman urbain: de *L'intégration* d'Azouz Begag à *Désintégration* d'Ahmed Djouder,' in I. Vitali (ed.), *Intrangers (II): Littérature beur, de l'écriture à la traduction*, Paris: L'Harmattan, 21–46.
Qui fait la France? (2007). *Chroniques d'une société annoncée*, Paris: Stock.
Ratner, A. (2009). *Street Lit: Teaching and Reading Fiction in Urban Schools*, Columbus, OH: McGraw-Hill.
Razane, M. (2006). *Dit violent*, Paris: Gallimard.
Redouane, N. (2012). 'Qu'en est-il des écrits des enfants d'immigrés maghrébins en France?,' in N. Redouane (ed.), *Où en est la littérature "beur"?* Paris: L'Harmattan, 13–53.
Redouane, N. and Szmid, Y. (eds) (2012). *Qu'en est-il de la littérature "beur" au féminin?* Paris: L'Harmattan.
Reeck, L. (2011). *Writerly Identities in Beur Fiction and Beyond*, Lanham, MD: Lexington Books.
Ryam, T. (2006). *Banlieue Noire*, Paris: Présence Africaine.
Sané, I. (2006). *Sarcelles-Dakar*, Paris: Éditions Sarbacane.
Sartre, J.-P. (1970). *L'existentialisme est un humanisme*, Paris: Nagel.
Sayad, A. (2006). *L'immigration ou les paradoxes de l'altérité: 2*, Paris: Raisons d'agir.
Smouts, M.-C. (2007). *La Situation postcoloniale: Les postcolonial studies dans le débat français*, Paris: Fondation nationale des sciences politiques.

Thomas, D. (2008). 'New Writing for New Times: Faïza Guène, *banlieue* writing, and the post-Beur Generation,' *Expressions maghrébines*, 7(1), 33–51.
Veivo, H. (2008). 'Authors on the Outskirts: Writing Projects and (Sub)urban Space in Contemporary French Literature,' *Knowledge, Technology & Policy*, 21(3), 131–41.
Vitali, I. (2009). 'De la littérature beure à la littérature urbaine: le regard des Intrangers,' *Nouvelles Etudes Francophones*, 24(1), 172–83.

Filmography

Djaïdani, R. (2012). *Rengaine*. Haut et court. Arte Editions.
Gauthier-Pavlov, S. (2002). *Mémoires du 17 octobre 1961*, L'Autre Film.

2

Breaking the chains of ethnic identity: Faïza Guène, Saphia Azzeddine, and Nadia Bouzid, or the birth of a new Maghrebi-French women's literature

Patrick Saveau

Some labels are hard to get rid of. They provide a helpful taxonomy to classify, sort out, or separate. They enable us to distinguish what can be included or excluded from the epistemological field we are exploring, and ultimately they give us a sense of order and clarity in a world that is becoming ever more complicated to understand, let alone to explain. This is particularly true in the humanities, when talking about a particular literary, cinematic, or artistic genre. For instance, knowing where a literary text belongs, what other texts or movements can be related to it, makes us feel safe as teachers and enables us to offer courses that will fit in particular slots: African literature, Caribbean literature, or even more encompassing, francophone literature, even if we are perfectly aware that in the postmodern age characterized by fluidity, hybridity, bricolage, métissage, we would be hard pressed to try to define these literary categories because there are always some exceptions. This is the case of *beur* literature which appeared in the first half of the 1980s. Some thirty years later,[1] this literary category was still in use when in 2012 two large volumes titled *Où en est la littérature "beur"?* and *Qu'en est-il de la littérature "beur" au féminin?* came out.[2] The titles had in common tell-tale quotation marks framing the adjective '*beur*,' and question marks, suggesting that the appellation was problematic and questioning the very existence of this literature.

As Alec G. Hargreaves and Anne-Marie Gans-Guinoune remind us in *Au-delà de la littérature 'beur'? Nouveaux écrits, nouvelles approches critiques*, the word '*beur*' was problematic right from its inception. Some authors labeled as '*beur* writers' felt hesitant to endorse this designation or were frankly hostile to it since, in their eyes, it was tantamount to a form of ghettoization or exclusion from French literature per se (Hargreaves and Gans-Guinoune, 2008: 2). Curiously, their reluctance was disregarded not only by the media but more problematically by literary critics, who used and abused this label for their own benefit. In an all-out attack on these critics, Jimia Boutouba rightly points out that this categorization served to confine so-called *beur* writers and their literary productions to a binary system where French people of old stock are opposed to immigrants and their descendants, and sameness, secularity, modernity, and center are contrasted with otherness, religion, tradition, and periphery. She adds that critics 'créent un système référentiel et un modèle interprétatif figé qui s'appliqueraient ainsi à tout texte, dès lors que ce dernier est identifié comme étant "beur." Le romancier n'existe pas en tant que tel. C'est sa singularité d'enfant d'immigré, de produit des banlieues qui le distingue' (Boutouba, 2007: 152–3) (create a fixed referential system as well as a static interpretative model which could be applied to any text, as long as it is identified as "beur." The novelist as such does not exist. What distinguishes a *beur* writer is his or her status as an immigrant's child and product of the *banlieue*).[3]

If labeling may have advantages by providing a sense of direction to critics researching this particular literature or professors teaching it, it simultaneously denies writers any pretense to creativity, muffles voices that may not want to identify with this so called *beur* literature as it is defined and theorized, and serves to keep them in a subaltern position. Accordingly, their work is treated as documents that are preformatted to fit a particular category with predetermined themes, style, narrative strategies, and language; in other words, these writerly productions lack literariness as delineated by the French literary establishment. The fact that some writers of Maghrebi origins produce novels that have nothing to do with the usual definition of *beur* literature, where their status of 'child of immigrant' is irrelevant, and whose narrative content is dissociated from any idea of periphery or margin, points to the most recent generation of young Maghrebi-French writers' desire to break the chains of a confining naming game and reject the discursive myth that they all speak with a single voice and tell one identical story.

In the following pages, I will examine how Faïza Guène, Saphia Azzeddine and Nadia Bouzid not only blur the lines of the literary movements with which media and scholars would like to associate them, but also exceed the literary confines of appellations such as minority literature, decentered literature, literature of the margins, exile literature, and *banlieue* literature. This postulate has several consequences: since these novelists' works do not stand in a systematic opposition to the French canon, critics have been at pains to determine whether or not their work should be kept in the margins. Furthermore, in terms of narrative content, the writers do not necessarily examine the world along an ethnic binary logic of "us/them," "self/other," but instead open the door to new and different ways to narrate the world we all live in, while offering 'a more diverse spectrum of socio-economic space and geographical locations' (Higbee, 2013: 25).[4] In other words, I would like to demonstrate how these novels seek 'to be grounded and not simply "deterritorialized" or "deterritorializing" for that matter' (Mehrez, 1993: 33),[5] in a literary landscape that does not pertain to a minority literature, but to literature at large.

In her hugely popular novel *Kiffe kiffe demain* (2004), Faiza Guène offered 'an insider's perspective into the daily struggles of the Maghrebi working class as it negotiates gender, racial, and social marginality within confining urban spaces and debilitating economic conditions' (Mehta, 2010: 176). Since then, she has continued to situate her novels in the *banlieues*, broadening her palette to include disenfranchised characters, who do not exclusively belong to the 'Maghrebi working class,' but to what she calls 'la France d'en-bas' (Guène, 2008) (disenfranchised France). This class of people is intrinsically more encompassing and inclusive of different ethnic groups and in line with France's sociological reality: 'In France, areas containing relatively large concentrations of residents of foreign origin are almost always multi-ethnic, i.e. it is common to find people of many different national origins within the same neighborhood; while a few groups often dominate, it is extremely rare for a single group to make up virtually the whole of the minority population' (Hargreaves, 2007: 67).

In *Les gens du Balto* (2008), Guène gives voice to a multi-ethnic France, avoiding traditional stereotypes and misrepresentations, whose iteration tends to produce essentialist views of the *banlieues* and their inhabitants, typical of Maghrebi-French literature from the 1980s and 1990s. The choral novel, a literary genre that readers of *beur* literature are not accustomed to, enables her to develop each character as the narrative progresses. In order to show how much Guène deconstructs the buzz-words which are systematically applied to *beur* literature, I will introduce the different characters who, beside sharing social disenfranchisement, turn out to be much more complex than anticipated. Joel Morvier, whose death is announced right at the beginning of the book, is the detestable French owner of the Balto bar, the only social place where residents of Joigny-les-Deux-Bouts can meet. Tanièl, aka Quetur, or Turk in *verlan*, is actually Armenian;[6] he does not live in the housing projects, but walks over there to meet with friends, which shows that the exchanges between the housing project and the center are multidirectional and not exclusively one-way from the periphery to the center. His mother, a working woman dissatisfied with her life, cannot stand her husband and has a foul mouth, while his father, who used to be a heavy gambler, is unemployed and spends time watching game shows on television. Tanièl's younger brother, Yezig, is mentally handicapped. Magalie Fournier, Tanièl's girlfriend, has a racist father and peppers her narrative with English words, a way to assert her discontent with living in a 'hole' and her wish to live in America. Finally, Nadia and Ali, the only Maghrebi-French characters in the novel, are unhappy living in a house in the countryside where their mother cultivates her own garden. Guène's choice of characters who are not of one single ethnic origin and whose characteristics do not fit within traditional *beur* narratives, breaks down the stereotypes of the *banlieue* and its inhabitants provided by a deterritorialized literature. In other words, her determination to resist used and abused clichés allows her narrative to literally regain territory in its abstract and concrete meaning, namely to reterritorialize a literature which was kept in the margins for the longest time.

While the characters introduce themselves to the reader, Guène adds another twist to her choral novel. From chapter 1, the reader knows that the owner of the Balto bar has just died, something the character himself announces: 'Je baigne dans mon sang, à poil' (Guène, 2008: 10) (I am lying stark naked, bleeding). Instead of focusing on the investigation of Joël Morvier's death as a traditional detective fiction would, this choral novel is more interested in examining the socio-familial and ethnic background of the different characters, allowing the readers to learn more about the disenfranchised community each time the characters are summoned to explain themselves, each new testimony adding complexity to their identity. From a narrative perspective, Guène demonstrates that any event, tragic or not, cannot be narrated in an identical manner. Indeed, within the little town, the sociocultural parameters that frame each character's life preclude one single way of telling a story.[7] The polyphony illustrated by *Les gens du Balto* is an undisguised criticism on Guène's part of the way media tends to have only one story line when talking about a dramatic event in the French *banlieues*. Indeed, the discovery of the dead body allows for only one stereotypical news report by the regional radio channel France Bleu Île-de-France, part of the Radio France group. At no other point in the novel, will the media tell a different version of the event. The codes and conventions of journalistic speech are all reproduced here: people's incomprehension in the face of a brutal act of violence, the tribute to the bar tender who was appreciated by the whole community, although the reader knows him to be a racist bastard, a mention that this crime could have been committed by a serial killer, and finally the mayor's call for the community to stay united in order to overcome the tragedy.

Since the publication of *Kiffe kiffe demain*, Guène's depiction of the 'France d'en-bas' (disenfranchised France) has drastically changed. *Kiffe kiffe demain* portrayed the adventures, moods and thoughts of one character, Doria, within a more monolithic ethnic environment which stood in opposition to the dominant society represented by the social workers. By choosing the choral novel form in *Les gens du Balto*, Guène can gradually unveil her characters' identities, while preventing a priori judgments and stereotyping. Indeed, there is a stark contrast between their initial self-presentation and their successive testimonies, which add new information about their respective identities, family situations, and socio-economic environment. This technique enables Guène to portray *banlieue* characters who are neither static nor confined to the typology of traditional characters in *beur* literature. The choral nature of the novel makes it difficult for the reader to pin them down: their identities remain elusive, slippery, in a permanent state of flux, as they are summoned by the police to explain and go over their relationships with each other, and in particular with the bar owner before he died.

Even Joël Morvier, whose personality throughout the novel is strongly condemned by the other characters, turns out to be someone who cannot be reduced to a sexist, misogynist, and racist man. In the last chapter, after every character has tried to shed some light on the bartender's death, the reader learns more about this particular character who was so disliked by the regulars of the bar. Further, the chapter brings the story full circle, with Joël Morvier opening and closing the novel, and brings to the readers unexpected information that renders his character more likeable. Among the 'zones d'ombre' (Guène, 2008: 149) (grey areas) that no other character was able to elucidate, we learn that he truly missed having a family, a social structure that all the other characters benefit from. His father was a tyrant, so much so that Joël considers himself a softie in comparison, and his mother a slut, *dixit* his father. After Joel's mother left, the father took him to the woods; Joel was excited because he thought they were going to spend time together rabbit hunting, as the father had promised. After a long walk in the woods, the father stopped, started to sing the national anthem at the top of his lungs, and asked his son to kill him: 'TIRE MOI DESSUS JE TE DIS!' (Guène, 2008: 152) (shoot me, for God's sake), enjoining him to tell the authorities it was just an accident. Joël Morvier told this gruesome story to no one but his uncle Louis, who thought he was just plain crazy. Instead of being a victim of a serial killer as the media suggested, Morvier was just a man tired of pretending that everything in his life was fine and who begged one of the characters, mentally handicapped Yezig to kill him. Unfortunately, after stabbing Morvier once, Yezig got scared and ran away, leaving the bar tender no other option than stabbing himself six more times. This gruesome scene shows that identities are not to be reduced to the used and overused soundbites the media associate with *banlieue* inhabitants and plainly demonstrates that each character's identity is indeed more complex and plural than meets the eye.

Through her choral novel Guène reworks the traditional 'antagonistic workings of differentiation (we/they, self/other)' to eschew the confining binary system we, as readers, have been so used to (Emery, 2004: 1152). Moreover, she shows that traditional workings of differentiation tend to occult the idea that defining people's identities by the place they live, their ethnic group and social milieu is difficult, even impossible. Indeed, in the socially disenfranchised small town whose name Joigny-les-Deux-Bouts appropriately reflects the challenges of daily life ('joindre les deux bouts' means making ends meet), characters should not be viewed in relation to their spatially defined territory, or differentiated along ethnic lines. For instance, within the same Maghrebi-French family, Ali and Nadia do not think of Tanièl the same way. Ali, the young boy, defends him, saying Tanièl could not have done such a horrendous act, while Nadia, on the contrary, states that he is, no doubt, the murderer. Instead of focusing on difference, *Les gens du Balto* follows the destinies of several characters who are seen as sharing the ups and downs of the human condition. As a matter of fact, *Les gens du Balto* breaks away from the 1980s and 1990s reductive representation of the *beur* community and shows that Faïza Guène's literature cannot be confined to formulaic definitions of *beur* literature. What matters in her novel is that the reader is led to follow the transformation of characters who, once confronted with an unexpected situation, escape the identity straight-jacket that predefined them. Finally, by having a dying character tell his own story, Guène emphasizes the novel's literariness and reminds the reader that Joel Morvier's narrative situation has some famous antecedents from Agamemnon in Book XI of Homer's *The Odyssey* to William Faulkner's Addie in *As I Lay Dying*.

Contrary to Guène, who was raised in the *Courtillières* housing project of Pantin, a Paris suburb, Saphia Azzeddine never lived in a *banlieue*. Born in Agadir (Morocco), she moved to Ferney-Voltaire (France) as a child. The daughter of tailors working in Geneva, she had the opportunity to attend fittings for the wealthy, like the royal Saudi family. It is hardly possible then to associate Azzeddine with Maghrebi-French writers born and raised in the *banlieue*. Yet, among the books she has published so far, *La Mecque-Phuket* (2010) takes place in a *banlieue* and at first sight seems to include some of the traditional components of *beur* literature, in particular the divide between the parents' and the children's cultures. For instance, the main character's mother is perceived as the guardian 'of tradition incapable of developing new and original forms of knowledge and agency' (Freedman and Tarr, 2000: 5). The narrator is unable to remember her mother outside the kitchen, a domestic space usually associated with *beur* mothers. The mother also thinks that the main goal of a woman's life is to find a husband, whereas the daughter is more concerned with her studies. Fairouz, the main character, cannot relate to her parents' modesty when they are invited to a family reunion where they prefer to be the objects of pity rather than envy. As to the male characters, the father changes television channels each time there is a sex scene, and Najib, the narrator's brother, is the king at home but a nobody outside, only involved in monkey business. Although these examples show characters who are similar to what readers of *beur* literature have come to expect, they cannot conceal the different ways in which Saphia Azzeddine renews *beur* literature, by focusing on her main character's hybrid identity and the fluid positions of a subject who adapts to the different and multiple situations she is exposed to.

Beur literature's 'inevitable paradigm of depicting young women … torn between two cultural worlds' (Geesey, 2008: 57) seems to belong to a buried past in this novel. Indeed, the narrator has enough insight to understand the pros and cons of each culture, to navigate between them, and to state clearly what she wants to preserve or reject. Right from the title page, the reader wonders how Fairouz is going to reconcile Mecca, the holy site of Muslim faith, and Phuket, a popular vacation site for well-to-do westerners in search of exoticism. On the one hand, she can please her parents who want to go to Mecca to fulfill one of the five pillars of Islam. In order to do so, she and her sister Kalsoum save money and make regular down payments to the travel agency that specializes in organizing the *hajj*, or pilgrimage to Mecca. On the other, she can think of herself, stop being the dutiful daughter that she is expected to be in her parents' culture, and decide to go to Phuket without feeling guilty. When Kalsoum asks her how she can feel so relaxed lying in the sun on a beautiful beach while she imagines her parents crying, Fairouz replies that one choice does not exclude the other, Phuket and Mecca being both present in her head: 'ce n'est pas l'un ou l'autre mais dans ma tête c'est l'un *et* l'autre. Il y a un temps pour tout et là, il était temps pour nous d'aller à Phuket' (Azzeddine, 2010: 154) (it is not one or the other, in my head it is both. There is a time for everything, and well, it was time for us to go to Phuket).

Her adopting an identity that is not fixed in time and space is even more relevant when examined in the light of her feelings toward religion and Allah, a theme that is repeated throughout the novel.[8] According to the narrator, a believer can fear God, ask for forgiveness, and claim responsibility for nothing s/he does because everything can only be achieved *Inch'Allah* (God willing), or conversely, be a doer knowing that God will appreciate the efforts s/he will put in each venture or task. As a doer, Fairouz can only be thankful for all the marvels she has the possibility to enjoy.

Far from the traditional ethnicization of identity that was the focus of novels in the 1980s and 1990s, Azzeddine has been concerned with the way Islam has been interpreted to enforce a lifestyle contrasting with today's lifestyle in the western world, and implemented to uphold men's domination over women. The narrator claims to be a secular Muslim, thus invalidating the opinion commonly propagated by the media that Muslims in France are fervent believers, an opinion which does not take into consideration that 'religious belief and observance are far weaker among the descendants of immigrants than among first-generation Muslims in France' (Hargreaves, 2007: 103). Asserting that she believes in secularism,[9] Fairouz finds herself in a position to denounce the inconsistencies of religious practices in a postmodern society. Every practice which lacks fluidity, which is rigorist and uncompromising, is met with the narrator's wrath because it reinforces the inequality between men and women. For instance, offering to pay for her parents' *hajj* is not really a material issue for Fairouz and her sister, but rather an ideological one, for Fairouz is ready to explode at the idea that a woman cannot enter Saudi Arabia without being accompanied by a man. Her anger also manifests itself when she sees young women wearing the burqa in her neighborhood. As far as she is concerned, the burqa is not a symbol of religious piety but a sign of submission not only to the male gaze but also to the male libido: 'Qu'on se voile ou qu'on se dévoile, finalement c'est encore le regard de l'homme qui détermine notre surface à abriter. Minijupe et burqa même combat, quand l'une aguiche, l'autre s'éclipse et c'est toujours Mustapha et Jean-François qui se tend' (Azzeddine, 2010: 62–3) (Whether we are veiled or unveiled, in the end, it is still the male gaze that determines what we should cover. Miniskirt and burqa, same fight! When one teases, the other hides away and in each case Mustapha and Jean-François get a hard-on).

Azzeddine's criticism of Islam as enforced by male religious authorities goes further when her character criticizes the role of amulets in religion, discrediting the Eye of Horus[10] as an agent of protection and adopting a Cartesian approach to religion to question anything that is not based on pragmatism and rational thinking. For instance, she questions one of the five pillars of Islam, namely the five daily prayers recommended by the Sunna, wondering why Allah would rejoice over workers taking time off to go and pray, calculating the number of wasted working hours due to praying on the workplace, and stressing the notion of individual achievement instead.[11] Finally, she condemns Christians who convert to Islam, adopt a rigorist attitude, and convey an archaic view of this religion which is not shared by the majority of Muslims. She wonders why religion cannot be a source of joy, and she regrets that believers need to put on a stern face to pray. Her discourse on religion stands in opposition with the monolithic media discourse that tends to focus on the excesses of Islam.

Included in her embracing of a fluid identity is a strong condemnation of social movements that distract from what is really important, i.e. education. Among these movements, we find *Ni putes ni soumises* (Neither sluts nor slaves) which, as the narrator claims, essentializes the life of young women in the *banlieue*. When Shéhérazade, her younger sister, asks if she can attend one of their meetings, Fairouz, who acts as her mentor, tells her that she has no reason to do so since the male family members respect her, are not violent with her, and do not force her to wear the veil. She then concludes her speech by ordering her to go back to her studies. In opposition with the *Ni putes ni soumises* movement's essential view of women living in the *banlieues*, the narrator forcefully rejects the idea that women are condemned to be weak and subservient members of the community. The patrilinear model described by Camille Lacoste-Dujardin in 'Maghrebi Families in France' does not have a leg to stand on in the face of what the narrator thinks of the male–female relationships inside and outside *banlieue* families. According to the sociologist, in the traditional Maghrebi family structure, daughters are at the bottom of the hierarchical order, being 'doubly dominated because of [their] gender and [their] generation' (Lacoste-Dujardin, 2000: 64), while fathers are at the top, immediately followed by the sons. In Azzeddine's work, this structure is turned upside down. Since the collective ego which used to crush the individual is a thing of the past, individualism now prevails over the collective. So, the narrator ends up choosing her personal well-being and spends her vacation in Phuket instead of funding her parents' pilgrimage. When it comes to her relations with men, it is eye for eye, tooth for tooth: 'D'une manière générale, quand une femme reçoit des coups, j'étais pour les rendre en plus fort et en double ... Répondre à la barbarie par de la barbarie ne me semblait pas barbare, simplement juste' (Azzeddine, 2010: 27) (As a rule, when a woman would get beaten up, I was in favor of returning the blows, just stronger ... Responding to cruelty with cruelty did not seem to me barbarous, only fair).

Adopting such a strong attitude toward male dominance enables Azzeddine to assert her disdain for anything close to a rhetoric of victimization. The idea that *banlieues* are inhabited by subordinate people who should remain the passive victims of the post-colonial system does not agree with Azzeddine. Her brother Nabil is involved in petty crimes, but she sees so much potential in him that she decides to help him find a job in the company belonging to the family for whom she babysits . When she mentions a job opportunity to her brother, his initial reaction is to rehearse the stereotype of the discriminated Maghrebi-French youth and assert he does not have a chance: 'Paris? Déjà ici ils aiment pas ma gueule, neuf postes ils m'ont refusés, alors à Paris, ils vont m'accueillir comment tu crois?' (Azzeddine, 2010: 127) (Paris? In our housing project, they don't like my face and turned me down nine times, so imagine in Paris, how do you think they are going to welcome me?). This does not mean that Azzeddine is blind to forms of discrimination in French society but she refuses all stereotyping or essentializing of French and Maghrebi-French relationships, where the dominant group uses categories of alterity like ethnicity, social class, and gender to suppress Maghrebi-French people.

This de-essentialization also manifests itself in the way she considers her brother. At no time is he represented as a bully who controls his sisters. The stereotype of the Maghrebi-French family order is revisited to offer readers a totally different view of who Maghrebi-French people are nowadays. Nabil is not portrayed as a dominant and controlling brother who enforces the patriarchal model. On the contrary, he only intervenes when Fairouz calls for his help after she is insulted by some men whose origins are not mentioned. In fact, Nabil is not in control, his sister is, when she advises Nabil on how to behave himself and watch his language. In *La Mecque-Phuket*, language and its mastery are essential tools to succeed. The main protagonist urges her brother to leaf through a dictionary so that he can expand his vocabulary range.

In fact, the problematic around language takes a new turn here. French is not perceived as 'a language of external domination' (Hargreaves, 2007: 90), but as a tool to exercise socio-economic power and accomplish personal goals. Azzeddine's novel is replete with slang and Arabic, but using *verlan* (backslang) and Arabic is not necessarily a way to assert one's origins and ethnicity, but rather a medium used to circulate freely between different languages and sociolects, or use them in relation to specific social contexts the characters find themselves in. Indeed, *verlan* and Arabic have entered common French language usage more and more. Even if the narrator systematically gives translations of Arabic words and expressions in her narrative, she insists on communicating to her siblings how essential it is to master different language registers according to the different people they are talking to. She reprimands her sister Kalsoum on her very limited vocabulary and advises her to learn to express herself with distinction because, as a make-up artist, she will rub shoulders with people from higher social strata: 'Ne parle pas comme ils attendent que tu t'exprimes, parle en français, un point c'est tout' (Azzeddine, 2010: 98) (Don't speak as they expect you to, speak in French, that's all). According to Fairouz, peppering standard French with slang and Arabic confirms the stereotype of the Arab girl whose language is colorful but the object of mockery. The techniques of resistance suggested by the narrator are not those that traditional *beur* literature used to develop. For the narrator, it is not a question of feeling alienated when using only standard French, it is rather a call to embrace context-dependent linguistic diversity. There is no desire of *départenance*,[12] but a wish to crisscross linguistic borders according to the specific social context. However, this crisscrossing does not preclude the belief that French should remain the dominant language. As a matter of fact, *La Mecque-Phuket* epitomizes what Hargreaves calls the 'policy of cooption,' namely a policy that 'tolerates differences but seeks to ensure that minorities limit their distinctive patterns of behavior in ways that are compatible with the dominant cultural norms' (2007: 199). As a matter of fact, Fairouz wants her siblings to adopt these dominant cultural norms and make them theirs when necessary. It is only by doing so that they will succeed.

In the same vein, opposing what used to predominate in traditional *beur* literature, *La Mecque-Phuket* does not portray ethnic and gender relationships in terms of conflict (us against them). The stereotypes usually linked with *banlieue* living such as violence, social misery, ethnic discrimination, gender inequalities, and marginalization are absent. Azzeddine replaces exclusionary and confrontational identity politics with fluid cultural and identity positions which are adopted or relinquished according to the circumstances but in any case are not pitted against one another. At no time does the main character feel torn between her dual cultures. Instead she shows her knowledge of the ins and outs of each culture, adopting what is or is not acceptable for a young woman of her age in order to assert herself and find a place in society. She is shown 'in a dynamic process' (Freedman and Tarr, 2000: 5), not as the object of a homeostasis which traditionally confined such characters to the margin, immobility, and disenfranchisement. Consequently, she challenges 'la vision ancrée dans l'imaginaire national' (Le Breton, 2011: 113) (the vision that is anchored in the national imagination) and breaks down the barriers which are traditionally associated with literature by Maghrebi-French authors.

Decompartmentalizing a literary field so that it can be embraced and judged as non-marginal literature Maghrebi-French writers can be fully part of, is the task some female writers have undertaken. Among them, novelist Nadia Bouzid who has no interest whatsoever in documenting a socio-ethnic space she does not identify with. When I first wrote to her, awkwardly focusing on her patronym, I asked her why there was no reference to the *banlieue* and to Maghrebi-French characters in her work. She immediately replied: 'Je suis d'origine arabe sans avoir grandi dans une banlieue, sans nourrir le mythe du retour au bled, sans être dans une logique communautariste, et je ne parle même pas de religion' (I am of Arabic origin but did not grow up in a *banlieue*; the myth of the return to my parents' village was not part of my growing up; I was never raised in the logic of communitarianism and I don't even want to talk about religion).[13] Being from what she calls a 'demi-deuxième génération' (half-second generation) since her father is of Algerian origins and her mother is from Alsace, she grew up in a little village in Alsace and attended a very good school in Strasbourg. She claims Germanic and French republican cultures as her cultural roots instead of a Maghrebi-French heritage.

Not sharing 'la marginalisation ethnique et sociale qui touche une large partie [des Maghrébins de France]' (Hargreaves, 2008: 199) (the socio-ethnic marginalization that concerns a large part of [Maghrebi people living in France]), Nadia Bouzid would de facto be excluded from the narrative corpus Hargreaves tried to elaborate in 2008, the very same year her novel *Quand Beretta est morte* was published. Refusing to anchor her work in the *banlieue* and to focus on issues that plague people living in these disenfranchised areas is a way for Nadia Bouzid to reterritorialize her work in literature at large, without the qualifiers that are usually associated with Maghrebi-French literature. Therefore, there is no 'institutional tension' (Laronde, 2005: 179) when it comes to determining where her books belong and nothing that could allow the French literary establishment to pigeonhole her books outside mainstream literature.[14] It is interesting in this regard to note the way Grasset, her publisher, introduces the author on their site: 'Nadia Bouzid est née en 1970 à Strasbourg. Elle a été successivement professeur de philosophie, modèle aux Beaux-Arts, factrice, gardienne de musée au Louvre, régisseuse cinéma. Elle travaille actuellement aux Archives Nationales' (Nadia Bouzid was born in Strasbourg in 1970. She successively worked as a philosophy professor, a model at the Fine Arts school, a postwoman, an attendant at the Louvre museum, and a movie assistant-director. She currently works at the National Archives). In this succinct biography, there is no mention of the usual identity markers attached to Maghrebi-French authors; as a matter of fact, Beaux-Arts and Archives Nationales pertain to a cultural capital associated with the dominant class. As she indicated to me, Bouzid does not feel legitimate to document life in a *banlieue* where she has never lived, or talking about her Algerian origins when the focus of her cultural heritage is Germanic and French. Her novel *Quand Beretta est morte* spans 'spaces that are far more diverse than those suggested by the ethnic marker "Beur"' (Hargreaves, 2011: 31), a qualifier she rejects when talking about her work. Yet this does not mean that the question of identity is not a topic of concern in this novel, but it is not expressed along ethnic lines.

The novel's main characters, Isabelle and Beretta, are first of all adolescent girls. Isabelle lives with her father in an apartment, while Beretta comes from a very affluent social milieu. The disenfranchised *banlieue* as a geographical and ethnically defined referent is absent from the novel. Even more so than the two writers studied above, Bouzid deconstructs what publishers and media have so long denied to Maghrebi-French writers, namely the power to create a story that is not confined to a stereotypical socio-ethnic context. With *Quand Beretta est morte*, Bouzid is definitely demonstrating how preposterous it is to consign Maghrebi-French writers to the writing of autobiographies and testimonies on *banlieue* experience, something Tassadit Imache was already protesting more than fifteen years ago: 'Très vite, il a été déclaré que nous ne saurions pas créer, sortir de notre histoire, comme si nous étions assignés à résidence, interdits de fiction, incapables d'invention' (Chevillot, 1998: 639) (Right away, the claim was that we would not know how to create, get out of our own histories, as if we had been placed under house arrest, prohibited from writing fiction, incapable of being inventive). Far from adhering to a preconceived literary mold, Bouzid imagines two lesbian characters whose thirst for the absolute manifests itself in their admiration for Filippo Tommaso Marinetti's *Futurist Manifesto* which glorified risk-taking, recklessness, and violence and called for a literature exalting aggressiveness, audacity and revolt.[15] This manifest is then used *à la lettre* by the two lovers, when they decide to eliminate those who lack distinction as Bourdieu defined it in his eponymous book.[16] Distinction is the combination of qualities that characterize someone's class: 'port, prestance, maintien, diction et prononciation, manières et usages, goût dans le choix des biens, culturels et matériels, et façon de consommer ces biens' (Détrez: 2006, 44) (deportment, poise, bearing, elocution and pronunciation, manners and customs, taste for cultural and material goods, ways to consume them). In the narrator's view, Beretta exudes distinction: she is 'la plus belle fille de la classe' (Bouzid: 2008, 11) (the most beautiful girl in the class), she comes from the upper class; when Isabelle first goes to Beretta's home, she feels like she is "dans un catalogue, tellement tout était bien rangé et respirait l'harmonie' (Bouzid: 2006, 164–5) (in a catalog, where everything was in its place, exuding harmony); further, Beretta has read the complete works of seventeenth-century playwright Racine and only reads the French classics in the *Pléiade* edition.[17] However, the two characters resist the social identities they were born into in different ways. Isabelle overcomes the fear that her working-class status will bar her from befriending and falling in love with Beretta; Beretta achieves what her conservative bourgeois milieu frowns upon through her strict adherence to the *Futurist Manifesto*.

Contrary to what Alec Hargreaves could state in the middle of the 90s, there is no desire on Bouzid's part to 's'affranchir de la culture dominante' (Hargreaves, 1995: 28) (free herself from the dominant culture) since this is not even an issue, her book being grounded in dominant French literature. Refusing to be pigeonholed, calling upon French, Italian, and Russian classic literary intertexts, Nadia Bouzid's book cannot be part of a *beur*, testimonial, or *banlieue* literature, as these labels just do not fit. In other words, she breaks away from a literature where writers are confined to their ethnic origins. Not only does she distance herself from Michel Laronde's decentered literature, which characterizes texts 'produits à l'intérieur d'une Culture par des écrivains partiellement exogènes à celle-ci' (Laronde, 1995: 29) (texts produced within a Culture by writers who are partly exogenous to it), but she asserts her endogenous position among writers who, according to critic Mustapha Arzoune, 'se situent ... en dehors d'une logique de groupe ou communautaire [et] entendent inscrire leur travail dans l'universel, en dehors de tout déterminisme ... Ce n'est point comme "produit" de la migration qu'ils entendent voir aborder leurs livres mais selon les critères communs au commun des écrivains' (Arzoune, 2001: 19) (situate themselves outside a group or community logic, and seek to inscribe their work within the universal, away from any determinism ... They do not intend for their books to be read as a "product" of migration but according to criteria common to all writers). Finally, I would like to argue that through *Quand Beretta est morte* and the answers the author gave me during our correspondence, Nadia Bouzid subscribes to the idea that 'l'identité ne se compartimente pas, elle ne se répartit ni par moitiés, ni par tiers, ni par plages cloisonnées' (Maalouf, 1998: 8) (identity cannot be compartmentalized, or divided in halves, thirds, or self-contained segments). Therefore, she breaks down the barriers of a decentered literature where her name and her Algerian origins could have confined her. In the end, what prevails through her novel is its literariness, since *Quand Beretta est morte* calls upon multiple intertexts to assert its belonging to a transnational literature.

Although I have referred to the three above writers as Maghrebi-French, their quest for *départenance*, namely for a space and an identity that are neither French nor Maghrebi, seems moot, even irrelevant. If Guène's characters in *Les gens du Balto* come from a disenfranchised space, the main focus is not on the difficulty to integrate themselves in French society or their daily struggles in the housing projects, but on the testimonies of the different characters, which reveal their fluid identities. Through Fairouz, the narrator of *La Mecque-Phuket*, Saphia Azzeddine embraces the best of both Maghrebi and French cultures, which contribute to shape a hybrid identity whereby she picks and chooses what allows her never to stagnate, but instead, be in a state of permanent mobility. As to Nadia Bouzid, her characters are not defined by their ethnicity, but by their sexual orientation, and most of all by their way to be in, act in, and see the world. The three writers claim their right to fiction, imagination, and poetic license, something that was denied to their predecessors, who were only deemed capable of producing testimonies, decentered narratives, and the like. Guène, Azzeddine, and Bouzid further demonstrate that through fiction, they can disengage themselves from social, ethnic, spatial defining criteria which could impede not only their writing but also their being in the world.

In choosing these three writers to examine the relevance of labeling, I could well be accused of naivety. These appellations such as *beur* literature, minority literature, decentered literature, literature of the margins, exile literature, and *banlieue* literature are, as we have seen, numerous and various and work along an inclusion/exclusion dialectics. According to Hargreaves, they have the disadvantage of separating post-colonial writers from French writers and writers per se (2008: 3), something the three novelists examined above have no control over and disagree with.[18] Guène, Azzeddine, and Bouzid are collapsing the various appellations critics have thrived upon, bringing readers and scholars to focus on their *travail d'écriture*. This does not mean this new Maghrebi-French women's literature will silence critics who have repeatedly said that writers with high media visibility are not representative of Maghrebi-French writers at large.[19] As a matter of fact, we should not be duped when Saphia Azzeddine is invited to Laurent Ruquier's television show on France 2, *On n'est pas couché*, each time she publishes a new book. She is the tree that hides the forest within an ideological system which relishes the success of a happy few to demonstrate that everything is fine in France as far as literature is concerned. Should we then only focus on 'les images à contre-emploi qui contredisent cette volonté bien pensante' (images used against type which contradict this self-righteousness) at the risk of ignoring those who are often 'mis en scène dans les médias pour faire la démonstration vivante d'une intégration rassurante' (Guénif-Souilamas, 2000: 11) (cast by the media to give the reassuring image of a successful integration)? The answer belongs to the future readers of this chapter, but the idea that these successful writers could be seen as sell-outs by critics is as narrow-minded as rejecting them as insignificant because they dare to write narratives which cannot be easily labeled, except that they belong to Literature with a capital L.

Notes

1 In *Où en est la littérature "beur"?*, Najib Redouane writes that Hocine Touabti's *L'Amour quand même* published in 1981 is the first novel representative of this new literature of immigrant origin, but points out that it is with Mehdi Charef's *Le Thé au harem d'Archimède* that this literature, which came to be known as *beur* literature, started to emerge (16).
2 These two volumes were preceded by a special issue of *Expressions maghrébines* published in 2008, titled *Au-delà de la littérature 'beur'? Nouveaux écrits, nouvelles approches critiques*.
3 All translations in this chapter are mine.
4 In Higbee's argument, this remark applies to Maghrebi-French filmmaking since 2000. I am arguing here that it is equally relevant for Maghrebi-French literature.
5 Deterritorialized and deterritorializing refers to deterritorialization, a term theorized by Gilles Deleuze and Felix Guattari (1972) and (1980). If, etymologically speaking, deterritorialization refers to a deprivation of territory, for the two philosophers, this concept allows them to question structures of power and domination.
6 Tanièl's opening line is 'Je ne suis pas Turc' (Guène, 2008: 11) (I am not

Turkish), thereby introducing a character who rejects an identity that is forced upon him by others who refuse to see the difference between Turks and Armenians. Tanièl's words are all the more significant, since Armenians have been the victims of a genocide Turkey has yet to officially recognize. Through this line, Guène points out the dangers of lumping ethnic groups together when defining someone's identity.

7 If this sounds like as a truism, it is worth repeating in view of the narratives that were used to explain the events that took place in France in 2015. Regional and national newspapers, magazines, television and radio programs, left-wing and right-wing scholars among others, each told and interpreted the terrorist attacks of January 7 and November 13, 2015 differently.

8 Right from her first novel *Confidences à Allah*, Saphia Azzeddine has been questioning the way Muslims should live their religion. In *Confidences à Allah*, the main character Jbara shows how, when left in the Ulamas' hands, religion is used as a tool of domination to victimize women. In her recent novel, *Bilqis* (2015), Azzeddine follows the trial of the eponymous character who has been sentenced to death by stoning because one morning she took the role of the muezzin and went on top of the minaret to call for prayer, a task forbidden to women. Additionally, and most importantly, Bilqis took some liberties with the dogma and decided to absolve the baker, the gardener, and the history professor for not attending prayer early morning as they were busy serving their community. Questioning a strict adherence to the dogma, she replaces it with a concrete and pragmatic commitment to Islamic faith.

9 Under secularism or *laïcité* in French, I am referring not just to the separation of State and church, but to freedom of conscience.

10 Symbol of Egyptian origin which is now used to ward off evil.

11 In *La Mecque-Phuket* Saphia Azzeddine continues the critical examination of prayer observance in Islam that she started in *Confidences à Allah*. In this novel, the main character, Jbara, after her mother tells her to drop everything to go and pray, explains that she cannot envisage Allah telling the believers they are sinning if they do not pray on time: 'Tu n'as rien demandé de tout ça, j'en suis sûre' (2008: 31) (You did not ask for any of this, that I am sure). Her criticism is tied as well to the notion that believers are first and foremost members of a society where labor and achievements are of paramount importance: 'Tu n'as demandé qu'une chose, c'est qu'on se bouge le cul nous tous!' (2008: 31) (The only thing you asked for is that we get our asses in gear!).

12 In 'The "Beur Nation": Toward a Theory of "Departenance,"' Rosello explains that this neologism '"belongs to the family" of words like "départ" (leave), "appartenance" (belonging), and its questionable antonym "désappartenance" (un-belonging)' (1993: 23). Several years later, she writes in *Declining the Stereotype* that '"Departenance" is both the state and the always incomplete process of departure from one's group of origin, one's supposedly natural community' (1998: 182). There is no desire on the part of *La Mecque-Phuket*'s narrator to initiate a 'process of departure,' whether

incomplete or not, but rather a willingness to straddle both cultures and linguistic systems, take the best of what they have to offer, and remain in a state of permanent fluidity.

13 Email to the author, October 12, 2012.
14 In his effort to classify works written by offspring of Maghrebi immigrants, Laronde suggests that this particular literature is 'in a cultural and linguistic position of being an insider with regard to French literature' while intersecting with 'the new national literatures of the Maghreb' (2005: 182). This overlap between these two literatures could not be further from Nadia Bouzid's own work and the way she would like it to be perceived.
15 The *Futurist Manifesto* was first published on February 20, 1909 in the French newspaper, *Le Figaro*. It called for a different type of aesthetic beauty, a new literature, a new way of dealing with reality.
16 In *Distinction* (1979), Bourdieu studies the lifestyles of social classes and the power relations they engender.
17 La Pléiade is a prestigious book collection published by Gallimard editions. For a writer, to be published in this collection is the ultimate accolade.
18 In 'Dialogues avec Faïza Guène' on September 17, 2008 (www.youtube.com/watch?v=dnJwOL28ZnA), Guène comments on a review of *Les gens du Balto*, where the journalist took a vulgar expression out of its context to point out that it was the way Guène wrote. Talking about her writing, she tells the audience: 'cela a l'air simple comme ça, on dit "elle [Guène] écrit comme elle parle, c'est du langage parlé," mais il y a un travail d'écriture, il y a une construction des personnages, et ce que je fais, ce n'est pas juste d'écouter des gens parler et d'écrire, ce serait tellement simple' (It looks simple, people say 'she writes the way she speaks, it is spoken language,' but there is a writing process, characters are constructed, and what I do cannot be reduced to listening to people talk and then writing it down, that would be too simple). The journalist's remark reinforces a discourse of exclusion that Guène must counteract by justifying what she does.
19 High-media visibility applies primarily to Saphia Azzeddine and to a lesser extent to Faïza Guène, who have been invited on popular television shows like Laurent Ruquier's *On n'est pas couché* or Thierry Ardisson's *Tout le monde en parle*.

References

Arzoune, M. (2001). 'Littérature: Les chausse-trapes de l'immigration,' *Hommes & Migrations*, 1231, 15–28.
Azzeddine, S. (2008). *Confidences à Allah*, Paris Editions Leo Scheer.
Azzeddine, S. (2010). *La Mecque-Phuket*, Paris: Editions Leo Scheer.
Boutouba, J. (2007). 'La République des Lettres: Ses écrivains, ses critiques, ses limites ou comment décoloniser la critique,' *Synergies Monde arabe*, 4, 149–58.
Bouzid, N. (2008). *Quand Beretta est morte*, Paris: Grasset.

Chevillot, F. (1998). 'Beurette suis et beurette ne veux pas toujours être: Entretien d'été avec Tassadit Imache,' *French Review*, 71(4), 632–44.

Détrez, C. (2006). 'Distinction,' in J.-P. Cazier (ed.), *Abécédaire de Pierre Bourdieu*, Mons: Editions Sils Maria, 44–5.

Emery, M. (2004), 'Azouz Begag's "Le Gone du Chaâba": Discovering the Beur Subject in the Margins,' *French Review*, 77(6), 1151–64.

Freedman, J. and Tarr, C. (2000). 'Introduction,' in J. Freedman and C. Tarr (eds), *Women, Immigration and Identities in France*, Oxford/New York: Berg, 1–10.

Geesey, P. (2008). 'Global Pop Culture in Faïza Guène's *Kiffe kiffe demain*,' *Expressions magrébines*, 7(1), 53–66.

Guène, F. (2008). 'Dialogues avec Faïza Guène,' YouTube, Web. June 9, 2016.

Guène, F. (2010). *Les gens du Balto*, Paris: Fayard.

Guénif-Souilamas, N. (2000). *Des 'Beurettes' aux descendantes d'immigrants nord-africains*, Paris: Grasset.

Hargreaves, A. G. (1991). *Immigration and Identity in Beur Fiction*, Oxford/New York: Berg.

Hargreaves, A. G. (1995). 'La littérature issue de l'immigration maghrébine en France: Une littérature mineure?,' in C. Bonn (ed.), *Littératures des immigrations: Un espace littéraire émergent*, Paris: L'Harmattan, 17–28.

Hargreaves, A. G. (2007). *Multi-Ethnic France: Immigration, Politics, Culture and Society*, 2nd edn, New York: Routledge.

Hargreaves, A. G. (2008). 'La littérature issue de l'immigration maghrébine en France: Recensement et évolution du corpus narratif,' *Expressions magrébines*, 7(1), 193–213.

Hargreaves, A. G. (2011). 'From "Ghettoes" to Globalization: Situating Maghrebi-French Filmmakers,' in S. Durmelat and V. Swamy (eds), *Screening Integration: Recasting Maghrebi Immigration in Contemporary France*, Lincoln, NE/London: University of Nebraska Press, 25–40.

Hargreaves, A. G. and Gans-Guinoune, A.-M. (2008). 'Introduction,' *Expressions magrébines*, 7(1), 1–9.

Higbee, W. (2013). *Post Beur Cinema: North African Emigré and Maghrebi French Filmmaking in France Since 2000*, Edinburgh: Edinburgh University Press.

Lacoste-Dujardin, C. (2000). 'Maghrebi Families in France,' in J. Freedman and C. Tarr (eds), *Women, Immigration and Identities in France*, Oxford/New York: Berg, 57–68.

Laronde, M. (1995). 'Stratégies rhétoriques du discours décentré,' in C. Bonn (ed.), *Littératures des immigrations: Un espace littéraire émergent*, Paris: L'Harmattan, 29–39.

Laronde, M. (2005). 'Displaced Discourses: Post(-)Coloniality, Francophone Spaces, and the Literatures of Immigration in France,' in A. Donadey and H. A. Murdoch (eds), *Postcolonial Theory and Francophone Literary Studies*, Gainesville, FL: University Press of Florida, 175–92.

Le Breton, M. (2011). '"Re-penser" l'identité et la citoyenneté françaises dans les romans *Dit violent* de Mohamed Razane et *Kiffe kiffe demain* de Faïza

Guène,' in I. Vitali (ed.), *Intrangers (I): Post-migration et nouvelles frontières de la littérature beur*, Louvain-la-Neuve: Editions Academia, 93–117.

Maalouf, A. (1998). *Les Identités meurtrières*, Paris: Grasset.

Mehrez, S. (1993). 'Azouz Begag: un di zafas di Bidoufile or the Beur Writer: A Question of Territory,' *Yale French Studies*, 1, 25–42.

Mehta, B. J. (2010). 'Negotiating Arab-Muslim Identity, Contested Citizenship, and Gender Ideologies in the Parisian Housing Projects: Faïza Guène's *Kiffe kiffe demain*,' *Research in African Literatures*, 41(2), 173–202.

Redouane, R. (2012). 'Qu'en est-il des écrits des enfants d'immigrés maghrébins en France?,' in N. Redouane (ed.), *Où en est la littérature "beur"?*, Paris: L'Harmattan, 13–53.

Rosello, M. (1993). 'The "Beur Nation": Toward a Theory of "Departenance,"' trans. R. Bjornson, *Research in African Literatures*, 24(3), 13–24.

Rosello, M. (1998). *Declining the Stereotype: Ethnicity and Representation in French Cultures*, Hanover, NH/London: University Press of New England.

3

From daughter to mother, from sister to brother: building identities in Faïza Guène's novels

Florina Matu

A new generation of women writers

Integration, social rejection, and educational struggles, as well as challenging gender dynamics are favorite topics in the works of second-generation Maghrebi-French women writers. Determined to present an accurate image of their generation, these ambitious writers do not hesitate to depict painful episodes inspired by their own personal and societal battles. While many of these literary productions tend to have a rather somber tone, especially in the 1980s and the 1990s, more recent works reveal a significant change that reflects not only contemporary societal shifts, but also a different balance of power in the domestic sphere, where traditions, solidarity and respect become reinvented family values. While still impregnated by a critical and realistic representation of social and gender inequalities, freedom from patriarchal constraints and a more optimistic vision of a promising future characterize the works of Maghrebi-French women writers in the 2000s. Their characters are the product of a new, more articulate generation of women who claim their legitimate belonging to the French society, to the country where they were born, the only one they know. Strong, tenacious, and resourceful, these female protagonists possess significant amounts of energy, ready to be converted into personal and professional accomplishments. Just like a powerful engine, they propel not only themselves but also their families on the path of emancipation and social inclusion.

Such is the case of Faïza Guène, whose novels showcase a new approach to identity configuration along with its translation into more articulated destinies. The French writer and film director portrays young female characters, their struggle with their parents and siblings, and their own quest for a harmonious dual identity in the Parisian housing projects or *cités*. The author depicts the tortuous, but impressive, tension between valiant female protagonists' journeys of rejection and integration with sarcasm and humor, in a touching and hopeful tone. Highly entertaining and authentic, the characters' street language, a mix of French, Arabic, and slang, contributes to Guène's unmistakable style and complements her vision of contemporary French society. In an interview with Elaine Sciolino about her first novel, *Kiffe kiffe demain*, Guène affirms her desire to give a different portrayal of the Parisian suburbs populated by Arab immigrants: 'I was sick and tired of hearing only somber stories about the suburbs, so I wrote about the trivial, daily things that happen there. It's important to show that the suburbs are not only about cars that are set on fire, or girls who get gang-raped in basements' (Sciolino, 2004). In addition to acknowledging the literary and linguistic qualities of Guène's novels, Dominic Thomas highlights several other factors that contribute to the readers' interest in her innovative work: 'a concerted effort to avoid the kind of *misérabilisme* that has defined so much Beur and banlieue writing; a commitment to accessibility and to the democratization of reading … and an alternative perspective on the cultural and social circumstances of the banlieue' (2008: 42).

This chapter will analyze Guène's novels from a socio-critical perspective, as it looks at the texts as representations of societal dynamics. Many literary works of Maghrebi-French women writers reflect their involvement in contemporary societal issues and convey a powerful optimistic view of an entire generation whose voices, unlike those of their parents, project their aspirations more articulately. Najib Redouane, the editor of a volume dedicated to post-*beur* women writers, validates their work and its liberating impact on a personal and community level. Their novels constitute an audacious commitment to articulate their identity as women, 'le symbole d'une liberté acquise et l'expression d'un courage certain dans un monde contraignant' (Redouane, 2012: 47) (the symbol of an acquired freedom and the expression of an undoubted courage in a constraining world).[1] This emancipatory process within the constraints of a society still defined by patriarchal norms is the subject of Guène's work and is reflected in her portrayal of female characters. The characters serve as fictional representations of a new generation of Maghrebi descendants who seem to gradually perceive themselves as more integrated, more self-assured, and prone to fulfill their own potential.

This chapter aims to analyze the evolution of young women characters, bearers of responsibilities that are normally delegated to adults, particularly men. It will emphasize Guène's determination to reject stereotypes associated with the Maghrebi-French youth and it will highlight her development as a writer in the past ten years, as well as her shift in thematic interest. The readers will notice a visible progression in the construction of her protagonists, whose behaviors are symbolic of transformations in French society. Undecided, but capable of discerning some of their identifying features in *Kiffe kiffe demain* (2004) and *Du rêve pour les oufs* (2006a), her characters evolve into balanced individuals, aware of their place in French society and determined to enforce their values upon their families and representatives of social institutions in *Les gens du Balto* (2008) and *Un homme, ça ne pleure pas* (2014).

In *Kiffe kiffe demain*, the main character, teenage Doria assumes the role of head of household, struggling not only with her own indecision about education and love, but also fighting against her mother's depression and hopelessness after her husband abandoned her for a younger, more fertile wife. In *Du rêve pour les oufs*, Guène assigns a similar protective role to another young female character, Ahlème, who is bravely taking care not only of her mentally disabled father, but also of her teenage brother Foued. Just like Doria in *Kiffe kiffe demain* and like Nadia, one of the strong female characters in *Les gens du Balto*, Ahlème does not represent a stereotypical submissive woman, but rather one who emasculates male characters incapable or unwilling to take over their traditionally assigned authority role. While Doria and Ahlème display a profound attachment to their family members, Dounia, the female protagonist in *Un homme, ça ne pleure pas*, takes the liberating initiative of denying all family ties and completely rejecting all Maghrebi traditions. Her incredible social climbing and her attempts to build a new and radically different identity could, without a doubt, constitute the foundation of a convincing success story, skillfully told in this engaging fictional work. Such an inspirational character could not possibly be the sole product of Guène's imagination, a writer who, ever since she published her first bestseller in 2004, has consolidated her reputation by shaping plausible, yet complex protagonists, whose ups and downs reflect societal transformations.

From daughter to mother

As Soumaya Naamane-Guessous states in her sociological study *Au-delà de toute pudeur. La sexualité féminine au Maroc*, 'la femme n'a souvent que la maternité pour combler le vide de sa vie conjugale; avoir un enfant est d'ailleurs partie intégrale de son devoir d'épouse, et l'on sait que ce devoir est, dans notre société, fondateur du lien marital. La position de l'épouse se renforce lors de la grossesse, de l'accouchement, et surtout lorsque l'enfant né est de sexe mâle' (1991: 105) (a woman often only has motherhood to fill the void of her married life; having a child is also an integral part of her wifely duty, and we know that this duty is, in our society, the foundation of the marital bond. The wife's position within the family strengthens during pregnancy and childbirth, especially when the newborn is a male). The mother's situation in *Kiffe kiffe demain* partly corroborates the Moroccan sociologist's assertion. She filled out the void in her life when she became the mother of Doria. Unfortunately, instead of strengthening the marital bond, this birth has led to the father's abandoning them in order to have a male child with another woman. Unable to comply with the ideal of the fertile woman, Doria's mother feels humiliated and unworthy. Her marital status has been shaken by her inability to procreate, while her husband's abrupt desertion leaves her shameful, her emotions blocked, and wondering about herself.

Doria's world, too, is profoundly destabilized by her father's departure. Despite her sarcasm and apparent bravery, the narrator and protagonist defines her birth as a failure, a stigma, whose justification lies in traditional Arab culture. The young protagonist insists that, whether steeped in tradition or not, these outdated values fail to justify her father's act: 'Papa, il voulait un fils. Pour sa fierté, son nom, l'honneur de la famille et je suppose encore plein d'autres raisons stupides' (Guène, 2004: 10) ('Dad wanted a son. For his pride, his reputation, the family honour and probably tons of other stupid reasons') (Guène, 2006b: 2). Similar to undervalued merchandise, women do not have any rights nor do they deserve to be respected. Doria and her mother are banned from any activity related to physical and intellectual mobility that would allow them to shape their identities. Forbidden activities include: attending neighborhood fairs, taking the subway to Paris, working outside the home, getting educated, and displaying posters with favorite artists on their bedroom walls. Despite her sarcasm, bitterness, and camouflaged sensitivity, the teenaged narrator refuses to accept her mother's resignation and interpretation of the patriarch's desertion as an inevitable consequence of fate: 'Ma mère, elle dit que si mon père nous a abandonnées, c'est parce que c'était écrit. Chez nous, on appelle ça le mektoub' (Guène, 2004: 19) ('Mum says my dad walked out on us because it was written that way. Back home, we call it *mektoub*') (Guène, 2006b: 11). As for Doria, the explanation is much simpler: if only she were a boy! The guilt of being born a girl runs in a somewhat fantastic scenario that unveils idyllic images: 'Ouais, tout se serait mieux passé si j'avais été un mec. J'aurais eu plein de photos de moi étant gosse, comme la petite Sarah. Mon père m'aurait appris à chiquer du tabac. Il m'aurait raconté pas mal d'histoires salaces qu'il aurait entendues sur les chantiers' (Guène, 2004: 170) ('Yeah, it'd all of gone better if I'd been a boy. I'd have loads of photos of me as a little kid, like Sarah does. My father would of [*sic*] taught me to chew tobacco, told me a pile of smutty stories he'd picked up on building sites') (Guène, 2006b: 160).

As painful as initially depicted, the father's departure, the very event that generated a powerful identity crisis, gradually transforms into an event with positive connotations. Doria, an observant teenager who struggles to understand her own place in French society, realizes that, in fact, the once distressing event represents her mother's chance to build a new identity. Motivated by their love for each other and newly acquired solidarity, the two former "prisoners" learn the taste of freedom and discover a world of opportunities: for the mother, the chance to integrate into French society through her efforts to become literate and to obtain decent employment, and for the daughter, a broader understanding of her native France and of her own skills and ambitions, and the promise of a more meaningful future. United by their desire to succeed and fulfill their dreams, the two female characters develop a relationship that transcends the benefits of emancipation. According to

Brinda Mehta, Doria's and her mother's diegetic roles are not limited to embracing challenging experiences on a personal level: 'stereotypical representations of the housing projects as sites of deviance and violence' are humanized in the novel 'through a tender mother–daughter relationship and communal affiliations found in female solidarity bonds, popular music, and the sharing of food' (Mehta, 2010: 174).

From sister to brother

'J'ai vingt-quatre ans et le sentiment d'en avoir quarante' (Guène, 2006a: 38) ('I'm twenty-four, going on forty') (Guène, 2008: 31), says Ahlème, the narrator of Faïza Guène's second novel, *Du rêve pour les oufs*. With its realistic assessment of the protagonist's tortuous life, this statement is a clear indicator of a complex and crushing experience. It also represents a sample of the author's skillful use of a complex and ingenious language characterized, as Stéphanie Boulard notes, by 'cet humour franc et ce rire tonique, qui donnent à son œuvre une vivacité qui est celle de la vie même' (Boulard, 2012: 243) (this candid humor and tonic laughter which give her work a vivacity which is that of life itself).

The first pages of the novel reveal that the protagonist's identity is not clearly articulated. Unlike Doria in *Kiffe kiffe demain*, Ahlème struggles not only with poverty and a difficult family situation, but also with a precarious legal status. The readers get acquainted with the character as they watch her on her way to the temporary employment agency, mingling with a crowd of busy working people who are paralyzed by the winter cold. A twenty-minute slot is all the time she has to submit yet another application, struggling to fill in the dreaded field titled 'projet de vie' (Guène, 2006a: 9) ('life plans') (Guène, 2008: 3), a concrete symbol of her temporary, fragile position in her adoptive country, and a representation of her indecisiveness.

Grey, unpromising, and fluctuating, life for 24-year-old Ahlème is a continuous challenge. Her refuge is the warm and love-filled home of an older Senegal-born friend. In Auntie Mariatou, a strict but incredibly affectionate woman, Ahlème finds an absolute role model as a woman, wife, and mother. Four delightful children and a loving and hard-working husband complete this idyllic family portrait. Auntie Mariatou personifies a happy and so necessary mother figure, successfully filling in for all the care, affection, and support that Ahlème's long-deceased mother would have given her, if she were still alive: 'Elle m'a toujours consolée quand j'avais des peines de cœur, encouragée à prendre confiance en moi et poussée à devenir plus féminine, ce qui n'était pas une mince affaire car j'étais un vrai petit mec' (Guène, 2006a: 42) ('She's comforted me in times of heartache, she's encouraged me to be more confident in myself and she's even nudged me towards being more feminine, which was no small undertaking as I used to be a real tomboy') (Guène, 2008: 36).

Being a tomboy was not quite what destiny seemed to have in mind for little Ahlème. Clinging to her mother's skirt in her native village in Algeria, the protagonist lived the first eleven years of her life in an all-female environment to later immerse herself without the slightest transition in the all-male atmosphere of her father's entourage in France. The brutal metamorphosis from a polite and enthusiastic little girl into a fierce companion of merciless soccer players in the housing projects of Ivry, still represents a traumatic episode in the narrator's life. On her cousin Djamila's wedding day, the protagonist's mother traveled to a neighboring Algerian village to attend the ceremony. The young woman was the sole designer of the bride's seven luxurious traditional outfits, true works of art, craftsmanship, and incredible beauty. That day, little Ahlème, whose name signifies "dream" in Arabic, was left home, thus being saved from a brutal massacre in her cousin's village. On that fateful day, her mother's dream to see her daughter adorned in the bride's seven outfits was shattered, as were the dreams of the two little orphans, transplanted from their tranquil *bled* to the grey sky of Ivry. Building a new identity in a completely different, and often hostile, environment constitutes an arduous task for the protagonist, who realizes that she is responsible not only for her own destiny, but also for those of her younger brother and father. This provides a triple challenge for the protagonist, who shares her worries in a simple, touching confession: 'Parfois, j'ai l'impression d'être née pour m'occuper des autres' (Guène, 2006a: 33) ('Sometimes I get the feeling that I was born to look after other people') (Guène, 2008: 26).

Ahlème's father also called 'le Patron' (the Boss), is the bearer of an ironic nickname, given that he cannot think straight ever since an almost fatal accident changed his family life. Three years before, the narrator recalls, the Boss had a horrible accident, while working on a French construction site. After lending his hard hat to a co-worker, he fell from a girder and smashed his head. Mentally unstable, the former pillar of the Galbi household became another burden for the young protagonist, who is already acting as a mother substitute to her 15-year-old brother. Foued is a passionate soccer player and a rebellious teenager who constantly questions his sister's values, among which are a solid commitment to education and respect for hard work. While Ahlème appears quite undecided as far as her own professional path, she invests a great amount of energy and dedication into her brother's future. Just like a devoted, ambitious mother, she understands that Foued's destiny could radically differ from her father's. He belongs to a generation that could either rehearse the parents' battle with poverty and humiliation, or overturn all the stereotypes that French society associates with young Arab immigrants. 'Il est à l'âge où l'on commence à bâtir – pas sur les chantiers, comme a fait le Patron toute sa vie pour gagner deux francs six sous et rentrer à la maison sale et épuisé, les mains ruinées et le dos brisé par l'effort' (Guène, 2006a: 33) ('He's at that age where he's got to start building stuff–and I don't mean on building sites, like the Boss did his whole life, earning zilch to come home dirty and worn out, his hands destroyed, and his back broken by the strain') (Guène, 2008: 26).

Despite his sister's aspirations for him, Foued is rather determined to prove how content he is with his predictable path. After he once again disrespects his sister's curfew, she comes down to summon him back inside, taking a moment to contemplate their somber, disappointing environment:

> Je suis entourée par tous ces immeubles aux aspects loufoques qui renferment nos bruits et nos odeurs, notre vie d'ici. Je me tiens là, seule, au milieu de leur architecture excentrique, de leurs couleurs criardes, de leurs formes inconscientes qui ont si longtemps bercé nos illusions. Il est révolu le temps où l'eau courante et l'électricité suffisaient à camoufler les injustices, ils sont loin maintenant les bidonvilles. (Guène, 2006a: 29–30)

> (I'm surrounded by all these screwball housing blocks that hem in our lives here, our noises and smells. I'm standing alone, in the middle of their wacky architecture, their garish colours, their mad shapes that have cradled our illusions for so long. The days are over when running water and electricity were enough to camouflage the injustices, and the shantytowns are far away). (Guène, 2008: 22–3)

Fuming after being humiliated in front of his buddies, Foued understands nonetheless that he does not have any other choice than to follow his sister's orders because she brought him up, and he owes her obedience. As in a western movie, the two characters challenge each other in a comical scene of surrender: 'On est à environ vingt mètres l'un de l'autre, on se tient droit tous les deux, et là, commence une grande baston de regards' (Guène, 2006a: 32) ('We're about twenty meters apart, both standing tall, and it's a battle of stares') (Guène, 2008: 25).

Despite their daily struggles and countless challenges, what makes Guène's female characters stand out is their incredible optimism and capacity to enjoy fortuitous moments of happiness. Ahlème, for instance, is simply grateful to celebrate her father's birthday: a few treasured hours full of laughter, the joy of being together and enjoying the sight of a small cake, some festive candles, and the 61-year-old wearing his best suit. Life is good every now and then, as the protagonist suggests, while prolonging this privileged moment in the privacy of her room. In front of the mirror, with the deodorant for a microphone, she sings at the top of her lungs, carried away by the music and dreaming of a spectacular appearance on stage, alongside her favorite rap singer, Diam's. The 24-year-old protagonist cherishes these rare and meteoric moments, slowly tasting every bit of them, and noting with an uncharacteristic openness to the reader, the witness of her joy and sorrow: 'Si on me voyait! Il ne m'en faut pas beaucoup pour être contente. Me sentant heureuse, je me dis que ça ne dure jamais longtemps mais que c'est bien bon quand ça arrive' (Guène, 2006a: 51) ('If you could see me now! Doesn't take much to cheer me up. I'm happy – it never lasts of course but it feels nice when it happens') (Guène, 2008: 85). These simple, touching words describing a tiny slice of joy, are abruptly interrupted by the phone ringing, a symbol of the imperious need to return to earth. Back in her protective, motherly role, Ahlème mercilessly rejects the insistent female voice on the other end who is trying to get hold of Foued. Not a chance! He is already in more trouble than he should be. Just the other day, the narrator recalls, she was summoned to her brother's school to hear how all his teachers agree on the imminent expulsion of this rude, disrespectful, and violent student.

While Ahlème creates the impression of replicating her father's respect for authority, her younger brother's deviations escalate to the point where one day, his involvement in a petty DVD theft lands him in police custody. Furious and deeply saddened at the sight of the *beur* teenager who has prematurely engaged in a glorious criminal career, Ahlème comes once again to his rescue, confirming Guène's preference for reversed gender stereotypes. Just as in a movie, the young man is portrayed timidly sitting on a bench, confined in a small office at the police station, fearful, comparable to a caricature, his former insolence just a distant memory. The narrator describes the two siblings' contradictory feelings in a touching scene, a mix of shame, heartache, and solidarity: 'En me voyant entrer dans la pièce, il n'ose pas affronter mon regard et préfère baisser les yeux. Il a honte et il fait bien. Mon frère est menotté au radiateur contre le mur et ça me fait un mal que ces types en bleu n'imaginent même pas' (Guène, 2006a: 69) ('He doesn't dare look me in the eye when he sees me come into the room, he lowers his gaze instead. He's ashamed, and so he should be. My brother is handcuffed to the radiator on the wall, and it hurts me in a way the boys in blue can't begin to imagine') (Guène, 2008: 66). He is repentant but only for a short while, as Ahlème soon discovers. After a random incursion in her brother's room, a true Ali Baba's cave, she stumbles upon a stash of fake merchandise, which offers an irrefutable proof that the teenager is perfecting his illegal maneuvers. A violent quarrel, reinforced with a hard slap to the rebellious teenager's face, might not be sufficient this time. Foued is clearly on a dangerous trajectory, and it is just a matter of time before he joins the ranks of hopeless delinquents. Such urgent menace requires prompt action from the only authority figure in the family, Foued's valiant sister.

The protagonist is thus forced to go after the leaders of the neighborhood gang who trapped the vulnerable teenager into a perilous life of illusions. Her adventurous visit to the much-dreaded Block 30 becomes more than a social visit when Ahlème confronts the unscrupulous Magnum, Leper, and Escobar. It is only by a stroke of luck that she manages to elude the undesirable outcomes of her trespassing when she realizes that the prominent gang leader, whose nickname, Cafard (Cockroach), sends chills down her spine, is in fact her old classmate, Didier. Happy ending, no doubt, to what could have turned into a violent, stereotypical scene from the vicious housing projects. Not only does Ahlème remain unharmed, but she also manages to gloriously escape from the lion's den, carrying with her the formal promise that Foued will from now on be banned from any of the gang's meetings.

The teenager's forced separation from the suspicious, organized group is quickly followed by another exclusion. Just like his sister, who dropped out of high school, Foued is permanently expelled from school for having dared to insist on pursuing his dream (which is also that of many other Maghrebi young men) of becoming a soccer player. What the future holds for the troubled teenager is highly uncertain; he will, most likely, not become the accomplished young man of Ahlème's dreams. Meanwhile, a two-week trip to their native Algeria appears to be a necessary experience for the entire family, even if it generates a mixture of anticipation and worry. It is, unquestionably, a journey that will either clarify or deepen the narrator's profound identity crisis: 'J'avais tellement peur de ne plus rien avoir à partager avec les miens, je craignais que la France m'ait tamponnée au point de me sentir encore plus étrangère là-bas' (Guène, 2006a: 142) ('I was so scared of not having anything in common with my relatives any more, I was afraid of France having left its mark on me so I'd feel even more of a foreigner over there') (Guène, 2008: 145). After a joyous welcome party and an emotional visit to her mother's tomb, the young protagonist carefully digests her pertinent observations about her people and their struggle. She immerses herself in this sweet, therapeutic return to her roots but nonetheless understands that, indeed, France has left its mark on her. With its immigration office, France is where she finds herself once again, standing in line at 6 a.m., along with other tired and worried faces, building her new identity and a path to a better life where dreams do come true. It is the last image of the protagonist that the reader gets to contemplate, an image of a hopeful, bright young woman who loves life with all its endless battles and above all its little ephemeral moments of happiness.

Building (illusory) identities

In *Les gens du Balto* (*Bar Balto*), the female voice narrating each of Guène's two previous novels is replaced by a plurality of narrators, beginning with Joël Morvier, the victim in this thriller, and continuing with some residents of the small community of Joigny-les-Deux-Bouts (Making-Ends-Meet). These narrators, as Anouck Alquier notes in an article discussing 'le pot-pourri langagier' (the novel's polyphony), give the language a complex, creative dimension, and transform communication into 'l'affirmation de leur identité' (Alquier, 2011: 457) (an assertion of their identity). The narrative focal point is neither the murder itself nor the progress of the investigation, but rather a parade of picturesque characters described in Guène's humorous language. As in *Kiffe kiffe demain* and *Du rêve pour les oufs*, the author delegates a great amount of power to her female characters, among which Yéva. The middle-aged, hard-working wife and mother of two is easily recognizable, and most of the time she is blamed for her questionable taste, vulgarity, and ostentatiousness. She is the pillar of the household, constantly crushing her unemployed, obese husband under her tremendous dominance, seriously diminishing his self-worth: 'Ça fait bien longtemps que je me sens plus un homme. Seulement quelque chose d'inutile posé sur le canapé' (Guène, 2010: 81) ('Haven't felt like a man in a long time now. Just something pointless dumped on the couch') (Guène, 2011: 81).

In another household in the same community, the readers witness a similar domineering tendency, this time within a Maghrebi family. Among the five children, Nadia and Ali Chacal appear to be more particular. Despite the prejudice they face in their small town, they are proud of being French and, unlike their parents, dispute any doubt regarding their identity: 'Toujours en train de dire qu'il faut rester discrets, se comporter comme des invités, pas faire d'histoires, parce que c'est pas notre pays. Elle, d'accord. Mais nous, c'est notre pays! Comment! On est nés ici' (Guène, 2010: 41) ('Mom's always saying we've got to keep a low profile, behave like guests, not kick up a fuss, because it's not our country. Well, that's OK for her. But this *is* our country! We were born here!') (Guène, 2011: 39). The characters' determination to assert their legitimate place in society reflects a new tendency in the corpus of the post-*beur* literature. As Mireille Le Breton remarks, 'ces jeunes écrivains repensent la culture urbaine du quotidien et la culture politique, ainsi que le social et le monde. Ils "pansent" aussi l'identité en revendiquant leur "citoyenneté" de droit au sein de la société française' (2012: 115) (These young writers are rethinking the daily urban culture, the political culture, as well as the social and the world. They are 'healing' their identity by claiming their rightful citizenship within French society).

Just like Ahlème and Foued in *Du rêve pour les oufs*, the two siblings in *Bar Balto* have a relationship that is characterized by their different personalities. Ali tends to be more rebellious and easily gets in trouble. For instance, the night before the murder he came home with a hideous bleeding nose, the result of a fight with Yéva's son, Tanièl. While the parents' reaction is a mix of panic and anger, Nadia remains calm and promptly cleans up the wound, taking care of her brother who, as she sarcastically insists, cannot possibly have inherited the same genes.

A similar contrast in characters represents one of the focal points in Guène's fourth and latest novel, *Un homme, ça ne pleure pas* (*Men don't cry*), published in 2014. Her most elaborate work of fiction so far, it reflects the writer's experience and depicts more maturely some sensitive aspects of France's society and its modern, hybrid family dynamics. Literary chronicles, among which François Busnel's in *L'Express*, praise the writer's metamorphosis, as well as her coherent style and pertinent depiction of contemporary society: 'Elle signe une chronique sensible et cocasse, le portrait subtil d'une époque où tous les repères volent en éclats' (She signs a sensitive and funny chronicle, a subtle portrait of a time when all points of reference are shattered).

In this novel, two strong characters, Mourad and his sister, Dounia, vie for the title of main protagonist. For the first time in Guène's works, an important narrative voice belongs to a male character. It is through his lens that the readers get acquainted with his family's transformation, a true reflection of how tradition and modernity can clash when parents of Maghrebi descent and one of their daughters choose different paths. Dounia is typical of a new generation who, according to Camille Lacoste-Dujardin, perceives integration into French society as an individual experience: 'The young, and especially the girls, do not appreciate their ambitions being limited by the priority given to a rigorous and to them outdated conception of the patrilinear family' (2000: 61).

The narrator, Dounia's younger brother Mourad, is astonished to witness his sister's metamorphosis. In his opinion, not so long ago, she was no more than a plain, almost dull teenager with braces and austere glasses. Attractive and confident, Dounia is now determined to succeed and to take initiatives that go against her family's traditions. Mourad is fascinated to find out that his sister is smoking and occasionally drinking wine, not to mention that she is earning money behind her parents' back while working as a waitress, a job that the father considers as degrading as a prostitute's. Professional success and emancipation characterize rebel Dounia, who prefers to turn her back to her family rather than to follow in their footsteps. In a review published in the online magazine *Hommes et migrations*, Mustapha Harzoune insists on the fact that this character had to renounce a part of her identity and pay a heavy price for her emancipation: 'Dounia incarne la figure de l'intégration labellisée, un parcours d'émancipation synonyme de reniement, de négation d'une partie de soi-même et des siens' (2014: 118) (Dounia embodies the figure of sanctified integration, a path to emancipation synonymous with the denial of her own self and her family). The separation from her traditional family environment is brutal and complete, especially when she gets closer and closer to achieving her biggest dream of becoming a lawyer. Her admission to the Bar in Nice does not generate the approval that any gifted young woman would have expected from her parents. On the contrary, Dounia's own mother minimizes her accomplishment with an appalling lack of enthusiasm: 'Y a pas de quoi sauter au plafond, à ton âge, tu n'es toujours pas mariée!' (Guène, 2014: 26) (No reason to make such a big fuss about it, after all, you're still unmarried at your age). The mother does not seem to realize that with this forbidding statement, she manages to alienate her daughter even more. Mourad's recollection of his sister's radical break with her family is still vivid, as he portrays the young woman in tears, struggling to carry an overweight suitcase, without ever looking back at her parents' home.

The readers are, without any doubt, tempted to interpret Dounia's dramatic gesture as the first act in a spectacular play whose heroine will climb mountains of success and become an almost implausible character. That is without counting on Faïza Guène's capacity to deride any character and situation that risk becoming too serious or cliché. Dounia does put some distance between her aspirations and her family's suffocating environment. Yet, it is rather a symbolic gesture since she moves only 8 kilometers from her parents' house! Ironically, while escaping undesirable parental control, she is willing to place her image and career in the hands of a small-town mayor, whose political agenda includes exploiting the diversity associated by voters with young women of Maghrebi heritage. Her involvement with a feminist association, ironically named Fières mais pas connes (Proud but not stupid, most likely a parody of Ni putes ni soumises), is another indicator that the author is committed to creating plausible characters that reflect societal dynamics, while emphasizing young people's vulnerability and blindness on their way to professional and political success.

Dounia's rise to power is nonetheless quite spectacular, though her actions are often met with severe criticism from the traditional North African community depicted in the novel. She is a valuable political capital. According to her cynical brother, her popularity is not as much the result of true merit but rather a consequence of her becoming a puppet in the hands of powerful fellow politicians: 'Dounia plaît parce qu'elle symbolise ce que la République fabrique de mieux: la réussite accidentelle' (Guène, 2014: 82) (Dounia is liked because she symbolizes what the Republic manufactures best: fortuitous success). Mourad's merciless political insight reveals the true dimensions of his sister's achievements. His view seems to mirror what Hassina Mechaï (2010) calls 'la beurette méritante' (the deserving beurette). In an article about Rachida Dati and Fadela Amara, the journalist defines them as 'des créatures incertaines pour lesquelles on a substitué un paternalisme culturel ou religieux à un autre paternalisme, républicain celui-là' (Mechaï, 2010) (ambiguous creatures trapped between cultural or religious patriarchy and Republican paternalism).

Unlike Dounia, whose increasing influence on the political scene makes her less and less accessible, Mourad appears to be a sharp observer of this convoluted environment and he does not waste any opportunity to express his true feelings regarding his sister's corrupt entourage. On one occasion, Mourad penetrates Dounia's upscale world when he is invited to join her at a party in the elitist seventh *arrondissement* of Paris. Borrowed from a resourceful cousin, his own expensive attire is symbolic of a fabricated identity in what looks like a masquerade ball. Mourad's social uneasiness amplifies as he realizes that he is indeed an outsider in a luxurious room, populated by fifteen high-ranking politicians with broad electoral smiles and mechanic, firm handshakes. At this point in the narration, the readers might be tempted to believe that the young, possibly impressionable Mourad will either embrace the values of this glamorous world or, at least, remain a humble product of his lower-middle-class condition. A pompous and defying speech by one of the illustrious guests, Secretary of State Bernard Tartois, triggers the young teacher's indignant reaction. None of the guests are really paying attention to the politician's delirious racist analysis of 'les difficultés d'acculturation' (Guène, 2014: 282) (the difficulties of acculturation) with which immigrants of Muslim origin are faced in French society, until Mourad's sharp intervention brings attention to Tartois' hypocrisy. The young teacher betrays his profound displeasure as he cynically summarizes the politician's tortuous discourse: 'Pour résumer votre pensée, Bernard, la France a un problème avec l'islam' (Guène, 2014: 283) (To summarize your thinking, Bernard, France has an issue with Islam). Any apologetic attempt falls on deaf ears and even aggravates Tartois' series of faux pas. In his defense, the politician uses 'les Dounias et les Mourads' (Guène, 2014: 285) (the Dounias and the Mourads) as models of integration and emancipation, which unlike their fellow coreligionists, perfectly know how to follow their adoptive country's rules and are not in danger of experiencing an identity crisis. Mourad's pertinent analogy with *Babar, the Elephant*, concludes the fictional social critique and entertaining verbal duel. Like the popular character in the children's book of the 1930s, Dounia and all the other "models of integration" so proudly displayed in the media or at carefully orchestrated social receptions will forever be referred back to their origins, despite stubborn and often painful attempts to configure illusory identities. The fact that the protagonist reached a certain degree of success and emancipation is symbolic of a young Maghrebi-French generation who has come a long way in their efforts toward social "integration."

In her novels, Faïza Guène portrays remarkable young characters that do not hesitate to take risks, motivate, and empower their loved ones. As they cast a critical look upon society, they understand the need to fight prejudices and, more importantly, their own ambiguities. While for Doria and Ahlème, building new identities seems to represent an inevitable step toward integration, Dounia is so determined 'to free' herself from the domineering family environment, that she becomes a puppet in the hands of skillful politicians who transform her into an artificial symbol of social success. Slowly and sometimes hesitantly making their way from the margins of society toward a more legitimate status within their community and their country, Guène's characters undoubtedly possess admirable resources for redesigning modern family values and for forging new and stronger identities.

Note

1 All translations are mine unless otherwise indicated.

References

Alquier, A. (2011). 'La Banlieue parisienne du dehors au dedans: Annie Ernaux et Faïza Guène,' *Contemporary French & Francophone Studies* 15(4), 451–8.

Boulard, S. (2012). 'Langage, tangage: Le vent de folie de l'écrire chez Faïza

Guène,' in N. Redouane and Y. Szmidt (eds), *Qu'en est-il de la littérature "beur" au féminin?* Paris: L'Harmattan.
Busnel, F. (2014). 'Un Homme ça ne pleure pas, prétend Faïza Guène,' *L'Express*. Web. May 25, 2015.
Guène, F. (2004). *Kiffe kiffe demain*, Paris: Hachette.
Guène, F. (2006a). *Du rêve pour les oufs*, Paris: Hachette.
Guène, F. (2006b). *Kiffe Kiffe Tomorrow*, trans. S. Addams, London: Definitions.
Guène, F. (2008). *Dreams from the Endz*, trans. S. Ardizzone, London: Chatto & Windus.
Guène, F. (2010). *Les gens du Balto*, Paris: Librairie Arthème Fayard.
Guène, F. (2011). *Bar Balto*, trans. S. Ardizzone, London: Chatto & Windus.
Guène, F. (2014). *Un homme, ça ne pleure pas*, Paris: Fayard.
Harzoune, M. (2014). 'Faïza Guène. Un Homme, ça ne pleure pas,' *Hommes et migrations*, 1306, 118–20. Web. May 25, 2015.
Lacoste-Dujardin, C. (2000). 'Maghrebi Families in France,' in J. Freedman and C. Tarr (eds), *Women, Immigration and Identities in France*, Oxford/New York: Berg.
Le Breton, M. (2012). 'Repenser l'identité et la citoyenneté françaises dans les romans *Dit violent* de Mohamed Razane et *Kiffe kiffe demain* de Faïza Guène,' in I. Vitali (ed.), *Intrangers (I) Post-migration et nouvelles frontières de la littérature beur*, Paris: L'Harmattan/Academia, 93–117.
Mechaï, H. (2010). 'Icônes de la diversité ou archétypes de l'imaginaire colonial?,' *Les mots sont importants*. Web. May 25, 2015.
Mehta, B. J. (2010). 'Negotiating Arab-Muslim Identity, Contested Citizenship, and Gender Ideologies in the Parisian Housing Projects: Faïza Guène's *Kiffe kiffe demain*,' *Research in African Literatures*, 41(2), 173–202.
Murdoch, H. A. and Donadey, A. (2005). *Postcolonial Theory and Francophone Literary Studies*, Gainesville, FL: University Press of Florida.
Naamane-Guessous, S. (1991). *Au-delà de toute pudeur: La sexualité féminine au Maroc: Conclusion d'une enquête sociologique menée de 1981 à 1984 à Casablanca*, Paris: Karthala.
Redouane, N. (2012). 'Pourquoi les filles des émigrés maghrébins en France prennent-elles la plume?,' in N. Redouane and Y. Bénayoun-Szmidt (eds), *Qu'en est-il de la littérature "beur" au féminin?*, Paris: L'Harmattan.
Sciolino, E. (2004). 'From Paris Suburbs, A Different Voice.' *New York Times*, E1, Regional Business News, Web. July 15, 2014.
Thomas, D. (2008). 'New Writing for New Times: Faïza Guène, *banlieue* writing, and the post-Beur Generation,' *Expressions maghrébines*, 7(1), 33–51.

4

The immigrant in Abdellatif Kechiche's cinematic work: transcending the question of origins

Emna Mrabet

Starting in the 1980s, filmmakers from Maghrebi[1] immigrant families began to represent themselves and their daily lives. They revealed the discrimination they experienced and the problems arising from an identity crisis within French society. They set out to reclaim their history, offering a competing narrative to the stigma they had so far been subjected to[2] (Tarr, 2005: 9). The 1980s signal a turning point in the history of the representation of people of North African origin. The new figure of the Maghrebi youth would now replace that of the immigrant worker, which dominated the films of the 1970s such as Ali Ghanem's film *Mektoub?* (1970) and Naceur Ktari's *Les Ambassadeurs* (1975). The famous filmmaker Costa-Gavras and his wife helped produce Medi Charef's work *Le Thé au harem d'Archimède*, which was released in 1985. Known in English as *Tea in the harem of Archimedes*, this was one of the first films ever made by a young man with North African immigrant roots to reach a wide audience. It paved the way for others, whose cinematic works testified to the real-life experiences of Maghrebi-French youth emerging at that time in the political and social sphere.

Filmmakers like Malik Chibane (*France* in 1994 and *Douce France* in 1995) and Rabah Ameur Zaïmeche (*Wesh wesh qu'est-ce qui se passe?* in 2002) produced their first works by choosing the *banlieue*[3] as the backdrop framing their film narrative. Labeled as *beur cinema* (*beur* being a somewhat derogatory term for people from the Maghreb), their works articulated common themes such as societal integration, racism, crime, identity crises, as well as problems linked to unemployment, drug addiction, and trafficking, which were rampant in the suburbs. This label, however, has often been criticized. For instance, as Will Higbee notes in his book *Post-Beur Cinema: North-African Émigré and Maghrebi-French Filmmaking in France Since 2000*

> the term Beur Cinema appears to function as a form of strategic essentialism, whereby a heterogeneous minority endorses an essentialised identity

in order to further their collective aims and combat the oppression or exclusion effected by hegemonic discourse. However, by identifying specifically with the difference of a particular social minority, such a strategic use of essentialist discourse inevitably carries the risk of isolating the very group it intends to empower. (2013: 13)

Furthermore, as Higbee highlights, the same term has been questioned and rejected by the very people it is supposed to designate. Maghrebi-French directors have been reluctant to accept a generic label that emphasizes a cultural and ethnic difference rather than the narrative content or aesthetics of their films.

Like the aforementioned filmmakers of the 1980s and the 1990s, Abdellatif Kechiche also seeks to portray people of North African origin in his cinematic work, but with an important twist. Born in Tunisia he came to France at the age of 6. His films *La Faute à Voltaire* (2001), *L'Esquive* (2004), and *La Graine et le mulet* (2007) respectively follow the lives of Krimo, Jallel, and Slimane, all three born to Maghrebi immigrant families, but from different generations. In this chapter, I will highlight the idiosyncratic ways and cinematic techniques used by the filmmaker to draw the portraits of three North African immigrants or Maghrebi-French youths, showing their personalities, their journey and their quest, and the communities in which they live.

Unlike the previous generations of Maghrebi-French directors, Kechiche chooses to create characters that stay away from clichés and stereotypes, while simultaneously managing to avoid the trap of communitarianism and to transcend the issue of origins, as will be shown in this chapter.

I will also examine the different cultural allusions deployed by the filmmaker, who chooses to anchor his characters in a composite intercultural field based on literary intertexts and allusions, which release the protagonists from the chains of ethnic clichés and open the door to an alternate reality.

In his first film, *La Faute à Voltaire*, Abdellatif Kechiche portrays Jallel, a young Tunisian man, who entered France without papers, thus living there illegally. He pretends to be of Algerian nationality and manages to obtain a temporary permit to travel freely across the French territory. He attempts to legalize his situation by engineering a fake marriage with Nassera, a young woman he meets in a bar. But she runs away on the day of their wedding, throwing him into despair and deep depression. In the psychiatric hospital where he ends up, he meets Lucie. While the young man seems to find a new stability in France through this relationship and the bonds of friendship and solidarity he develops in the homeless shelter where he lives, the law catches up with him, and he is suddenly arrested by the French police before being deported. In *L'Esquive*, Kechiche's second feature film, youngsters Lydia, Frida, and Rachid who all live in a housing project, rehearse a play by Marivaux, *Le Jeu de l'amour et du hasard* (*The Game of Love and Chance*) directed by their French teacher. Krimo, who lives alone with his mother, falls in love with Lydia and tries to approach her by "buying" Rachid's role as Arlequin. Finally, the third film, *La Graine et le mulet* (*The Secret of the Grain*), features Slimane, a migrant worker in the port city of Sète, who is unemployed because of his age. With the help of his children, his ex-wife Souad, and his stepdaughter Rym, he decides to restore a barge and open a couscous restaurant there.

These first three feature films portray people of North African origin, one of the director's favorite themes at the beginning of his career.[4] 'Je suis moi-même issu de l'immigration donc je m'intéresse à ce que je connais ... C'est une population très peu représentée et quand elle l'est, c'est d'une façon très caricaturale avec des clichés, des poncifs. La représentation a une importance dans l'idée même que l'autre se fait de vous' (Melinard, 2004) (I myself am from a migrant background so I am interested in what I know ... This is a largely underrepresented population and when it is represented, it is a caricature, rehearsing clichés and stereotypes. These clichés are significant because they shape the idea that others will have of you).[5] Therefore, it is worth examining how Kechiche's films present fresh and unexpected portrayals of immigrant characters which seek to counter the usual clichés.

An unusual portrayal of the immigrant

The originality of Kechiche's first two works compared to other films of the 1980s and 1990s portraying North African immigrants, resides mainly in the fact that the narrative bypasses the sociological dimension to focus on the progression of the narrative and the encounters and events affecting the protagonists. Each of these films is akin to an initiation story. They trace Jallel and Krimo's paths as the characters experience love and its torments and they discover new worlds – France as a country for Jallel and the theater for Krimo. They both end up disappointed and fail. The first one is sent back to his native country and the second comes to terms with the fact that he cannot play a part and disguise himself. Yet, as highlighted by Jacques Mandelbaum, *La Faute à Voltaire* is also a philosophical tale, in the way of Voltaire's *Candide* or Montesquieu's *Persian letters*,[6] French narratives which 'met[tent] en cause les travers de notre société à travers le regard d'un personnage prétendument innocent ou exotique. Cette rhétorique de la feinte et du faux-semblant court tout au long du film, depuis le mensonge qui permet à Jallel d'obtenir son entrée en France ... jusqu'aux méthodes destinées à apitoyer les gens dans le métro' (2001) (diagnose the failings of our society through the eyes of an allegedly innocent or exotic character. This rhetoric of pretense and deception runs throughout the film, from the lie allowing Jallel to set foot in France to the tricks used to make subway passengers feel sorry for him).

Furthermore, satire, allusions, and irony, rhetorical devices typical of philosophical tales, are used in the film and remind the viewers of Voltaire, the master of this literary genre (Tritter, 2008: 59). At the beginning of the film, Mustapha suggests that his friend Jallel boast about France during his interview to obtain a residence permit. Specifically, he is to overstate the merits of 'France comme pays des libertés; patrie de Voltaire et des droits de l'homme. Liberté, égalité, fraternité' (France as the land of freedoms, of Voltaire and human rights. Liberty, Equality, Fraternity.) This irony is repeated during the interview with the Préfecture employee, a scene where the camera dwells on a poster of the Declaration of the rights of man and of the citizen. The irony will reach a climax at the end of the film, when Jallel is brutally deported back to his native country, a conclusion suggesting that France's immigration policy falls short of the Revolutionary ideals which founded the French Republic.

Thus, in *La Faute à Voltaire*, the portrayal of the main character, together with the use of satire and irony, pulls away from the documentary style to emphasize the philosophical tale. In the course of the narrative, the filmmaker decides to leave aside some characters like Nassera, which leads to a disconcerting switch in the tale. In the second half of the film, Lucie leads Jallel to different adventures until his final arrest, bringing the spectator back to bitter reality and thus closing the loop of this contemporary tale.

Moreover, while the first scene takes place in a police station, the following sequences leave the administrative angle aside to focus on the protagonist's romantic encounters and his life in France. Jallel assumes several identities in order to overcome the obstacles inherent to his situation as a clandestine immigrant. He pretends to be Algerian in order to increase his chances of being granted asylum, then he calls himself Frank, the name of a friend from the homeless shelter where he currently lives, in order to secure access to psychiatric care. He also uses the driving license of another friend during a police check in a subway station. By intentionally pushing the administrative issue to the background, Kechiche gives primacy to the narrative at the expense of the demonstrative or denunciatory functions of his work: 'J'ai toutefois mis en avant le désir de raconter plutôt que la volonté de montrer ou de dénoncer. J'ai d'ailleurs essayé de la contenir, ce qui l'a peut-être fait ressurgir à certains moments comme à la fin, où je tenais à ce que la condition d'immigré clandestin que Jallel avait fini par oublier soit de nouveau mise en relief' (Lowry, 2001) (I have focused on the narrative desire rather than the wish to demonstrate or denounce. I also tried to subdue the tone of denunciation, but perhaps it resurfaces at certain times in the film, most notably at the end, where I wanted to highlight the predicament of an illegal immigrant, which Jallel had come to forget). Far from being simply revealed or emphasized, the immigrant status is a fundamental part of the narrative's construction.

So, the immigrant underdog's marginality is no longer a singular occurrence but is part of a broader picture of social exclusion in contemporary France. But this exclusion also comes with solidarity, which is exemplified when Jallel is seen with the residents of the homeless shelter on the one hand, the patients of the psychiatric hospital on the other, who support him, but even more so within the love story between Lucie and Jallel. As

Colin Nettelbeck rightly points out, 'through the highly individualized acting performances by Sami Bouajila and Elodie Bouchez, Kechiche avoids the danger of stereotyping. This is primarily the story not of *the* migrant and *the* Frenchwoman, but of two needy people brought together by circumstance' (2007: 309).

Similarly, instead of emphasizing sociological issues, the director develops the plot of *L'Esquive* around the love triangle between the characters Magalie, Krimo, and Lydia. If Kechiche briefly rehearses a class stereotype in the opening shots, he does so to overturn it in order to suggest a different perspective. While being torn between two women, Krimo discovers the world of acting. This allows Kechiche to sidestep the usual stereotype of Maghrebi-French youth living in low-rent housing in the suburbs, to focus instead on the world of theatre through the love intrigues in Marivaux's play, *Le jeu de l'amour et du hasard*, as they mirror Krimo's own love adventures: by playing Arlequin, a character who is in love with the servant Lisette (played by Lydia), Krimo can confess his feelings through the Marivaux text. In an interview to the French newspaper *La Croix*, the director noted, 'There is such a stigma about these neighborhoods. I wanted to talk about love and drama for a change' (Guignoux, 2004). Thus, he chose to portray the banality of everyday life in these young immigrants' plots. The intertext of Marivaux's play enables Kechiche to represent a teenager of Maghrebi origins in a new and different way, shifting the play's intrigue to a spatial–ethnic one. While in *Le Jeu de l'amour et du hasard*, the playwright explores class prejudices, by having masters and servants switch parts,[7] in *L'Esquive*, Kechiche crosses boundaries: Krimo occupies a physical place, the theater stage, where young men of Maghrebi origins are traditionally absent, confined as they are to the margins. Thus, like Marivaux who overturns class hierarchies and features the servants, the filmmaker chooses to focalize his narration on an under-represented social class. In *L'Esquive* as in *La Faute à Voltaire*, the filmmaker plays off our expectations to better confound them, replacing violence and precariousness with poetry and a taste for the unknown, which can be found at the margins.

Kechiche's first three films are dominated by male figures with distinct characterization that goes beyond the usual representations of Maghrebi-French immigrants. Jallel is presented as a sensitive and cultured man, who loves poetry and attempts to earn a living in France, despite his clandestinity. His literary culture is first revealed when he recites for Nassera a poem by Umar Ibn Abi Rabiah, a famous Arab poet (646–712) who celebrated courtly love (*ghazal*). By using this poem, Jallel is able to express his love interest in a subtle way, even though he and Nassera find themselves in the loud atmosphere of a bar, which is not conducive to intimacy and a love confession. In the second half of the film, Jallel gets in a relationship with Lucie and Ronsard's famous sixteenth-century poem 'Mignonne allons voir si la rose' takes center stage when it is performed in the unexpected setting of the Paris metro. The characters stage this public reading and then hand out roses to subway passengers, a playful and unusual strategy for earning a living. Filmed in a front view, Jallel pretends to recite this poem for the passengers although, in fact, his implicit love confession is intended for Lucie. Literary references serve to create in the viewer's mind an alternative view of the immigrant, who is therefore no longer to be considered a source of problems, an anonymous person in a mass of people haunted by despair and poverty, but an individual in love with France and its poetry.

After his plan for a marriage of convenience with Nassera falls through, Jallel goes through depression. Several shots followed by ellipses indicate his distress. He is shown alone in the metro, then lying on his bed and sobbing, surrounded by his shelter friends, who try to console him. Then we find him bedridden in a hospital, refusing to eat, until he is admitted to a psychiatric institution. Without resorting to dialogue, the filmmaker reveals the extent of Jallel's despair through this sequence. By focusing on his sensitive nature and his emotions, his friendships and love relationships while in France, Kechiche invites the viewer to look at the human complexity of the character, rather than rehearsing the stereotypical image of the immigrant conveyed by the media. As we empathize with Jallel, we find his final expulsion all the more unbearable.

The use of poetry is also an artifice used in *L'Esquive*. In Kechiche's second film Krimo uses the theatre and Marivaux's lines to reveal his attraction to Lydia. Thanks to stolen goods he buys his way into the role of Arlequin in order to get closer to the girl he wants. From then on, the classical play and the film diegesis echo each other, as in the first scene of the eighteenth-century play performed by Krimo in front of the class, where the dialogue allows Krimo (playing Arlequin) to express his budding love for Lydia (Lisette): 'Vous vous trompez, prodige de nos jours, un amour de votre façon ne reste pas longtemps au berceau, votre premier coup d'œil a fait naître le mien, le second lui a donné des forces et le troisième l'a rendu grand garçon. Tâchons de l'établir tout de suite et ayez soin de lui puisque vous êtes sa mère' (Marivaux: 2000, 51) ('You're mistaken, you miraculous being. Love such as you inspire doesn't stay long in the cradle. Your very first glance gave birth to my love, your second gave him strength, and your third made a fine strapping lad of him. Now we must marry him off as soon as possible. You're his mother, after all, so you must take good care of him') (Marivaux: 2007, 27). Like Arlequin who is enamored with Lisette, Krimo is in love with Lydia. Even if Krimo eventually fails to perform the role of Arlequin and abandons the theatre, he has discovered a new world much removed from his own, that of the theatre. As often in Kechiche's films, literature plays a part in constructing the main characters' development. In *La Faute à Voltaire* and *L'Esquive*, the filmmaker respectively calls on Arab literature and classical French drama to sidestep the stereotypes and clichés associated with the representation of Maghrebi immigrants. Through the use of art and poetry, he creates for his characters an escape into an *ailleurs*, a possible alternate reality.

In *La Graine et le mulet*, Kechiche's third film, the portrayal of Slimane, a character who embodies the figure of the migrant worker, is no less original. He is a faithful reflection of the first generation of Maghrebi to have immigrated to France and whom the film writer pays tribute to. Kechiche wants to film 'Slimane with his family problems, personal and sexual difficulties, avoiding the archetype of the immigrant' (Morice, 2007: 20). In this film, several characters are linked to the history of Maghrebi immigration: not only Slimane but also a group of musicians who are the protagonist's friends. Kechiche depicts their daily lives in their tiny hotel rooms and their attempts to recreate an environment reminiscent of their country of origin, for instance through the music they perform. Here, music, like the food tradition of couscous, maintains a permanent link with the immigrants' original culture.

The filmmaker certainly highlights the difficulties Slimane faces due to his immigrant status, when he is fired by his employer after thirty-five years of work or when he decides to open his own restaurant and is confronted with the administrative red tape and the condescension of Sète's upper class. Yet, unlike the immigrant worker characters in 1970s films (e.g. Ali Ghanem's *Mektoub?*), Slimane is not depicted as a victim but as a fighting character. Despite his inarticulateness (he does not speak French fluently) and his ignorance of social codes, he manages rather well to stand up to the various obstacles on his way, in order to reach his goal, with the help of his stepdaughter Rym.

Through Slimane, who is divorced and lives with his new girlfriend and her daughter, Kechiche depicts a recomposed Maghrebi family, firmly anchored in the city of Sète and in contemporary France. This family's problems are like that of any other "French" family: a deceiving son, a cheated wife, jealousies, and rivalries between Slimane's first and second families. But the film writer does not hide the singularity of Slimane's plot. The couscous dish seals the Sunday reunion. This emblematic food from Maghrebi culture plays a major role in the diegesis: Slimane wants to open a fish-couscous restaurant and the disappearance of the metal cauldron with the "grain" to be served to the first patrons forms the key element of the plot and a major obstacle to Slimane's success. This culinary specialty prepared by Slimane's ex-wife, together with the Arabic words spoken during the Sunday meal (*ayshik*/thank you; *basmillah*/in God's name; *mziya*/favor) and discussions about the proper use of Arabic, individualize this family living in the city of Sète. As Will Higbee points out

> What distinguishes Kechiche from earlier/other Maghrebi-French directors, though – and what marks out *La Graine et le mulet* as landmark film in the history of Maghrebi-French film-making – is that Kechiche fully acknowledges the difference of his Maghrebi-French and North-African immigrant protagonists without ever making this the determining or deciding factor surrounding their place within French society, or indeed their identification as 'other.' (2011: 224)

From cultural references to political commentary

Kechiche's filmwork often displays an abundance of cultural and artistic references which testify to his eclectic educational background and serve several purposes. As noted before, poetry and drama in *La Faute à Voltaire* and *L'Esquive* become vehicles for feelings of love, allowing the filmmaker to paint a unique portrait of immigrant characters. In *La Faute à Voltaire*, literary and artistic references are also used to give the film a denunciatory function. The title itself refers to two emblematic figures of French literature: Voltaire, the eighteenth-century author, Enlightenment philosopher, and defender of freedom and individual rights, and Victor Hugo, evoked through Gavroche's song from the 1862 novel *Les Misérables*. The references to these two humanists in the film are not accidental. They serve to emphasize the ideals of liberty, justice, and social protest which the two celebrated authors stand for, in stark contrast with some situations faced by immigrants today, who can be deported in an unfair and arbitrary manner.

Through a similar technique, the film shows a famous Paris monument located on *Place de la Nation*. This sculpture, which is part of a monumental piece named 'The Triumph of the Republic,' was built by Aimé Jules Dalou between 1889 and 1899 for the city of Paris to exalt the French Republican sentiment. It is used by the filmmaker as a metaphor to highlight two opposite facets of the French Republic. It first appears in the opening shot. Shown carrying flowers, the allegory embodies the bright promises and abundance of France – images that Jallel or any other immigrant can have in mind upon arrival in the metropolis. In the last sequence of the film however, the monument is shot from the back and comes to symbolize the darker side of the Republic, its injustice and lack of egalitarianism. Rather than offering an explicit and straightforward condemnation of French immigration policy, Kechiche inscribes his cultural and literary heritage in symmetrical scenes which echo each other to highlight the political implications of his work. As Colin Nettelbeck notes, 'using canonical artefacts of French culture as markers, these films expose the social, psychological, and cultural obstacles that can stand in the way of those who dream of integration into French society; and they demonstrate – with a lucidity all the more acute for being laced with humour – the ragged systemic flaws that lie not far below the surface of social life in France today' (2007: 308).

Marivaux's theater gives *L'Esquive* its political dimension and calls for a fresh view on young people living in rundown housing projects. The cultural and ethnic backgrounds of the protagonists are not revealed explicitly, as the director prefers to represent a population living at the margins of society rather than focusing on any single aspect of identity. The introduction of *Le Jeu de l'amour et du hasard* in the film allows to compare two language registers: the formal register of classical theater and the informal orality of contemporary familiar language, without ever establishing a hierarchy between them. Placed on the same level as the refined language used by Marivaux, *banlieue* language is therefore no longer to be understood as a marginal sociolect spoken by a minority but as a colorful and imaginative idiom, a source of linguistic renewal and creativity. As Kechiche points out, 'C'est un mélange culturel. La créativité de ce langage vient souvent du métissage dans lequel il évolue. Chacun va chercher dans sa culture de nouveaux termes, de nouvelles expressions; je trouve qu'il y a une très grande richesse dans ce langage. C'est une culture à part entière' (Melinard, 2004) (It is a cultural mix. The creativity of this language often comes from the métissage of the social context in which it is spoken. Each speaker borrows new words, new idioms from his/her culture. I find this language very rich. It belongs to a whole different culture).

Moreover, as Vinay Swamy claims, by transferring a canonical cultural text from the traditional and institutionalized places (theaters, university) to the marginalized suburbs, '*L'Esquive* puts into question the very divide between high and low cultures and the legitimacy of territorial distinctions traditionally associated with them' (2007: 57). The move from the center to the periphery reverses the protagonists' path in other films featuring the *banlieue* (*Le Thé au harem d'Archimède* or *Hexagone*), where the characters move out of the suburbs into the Paris city center, which is considered to be the bastion of hegemonic culture. Thus, 'in consciously choosing not to represent this all-too-common displacement, Kechiche signals a significant shift in *beur* and *banlieue* filmmaking. The very act of bringing so-called high art in the form of the play to the *banlieue* disrupts the one-way movement towards the (urban) centre(s) of power' (Swamy, 2007: 61).

The major role granted to Marivaux's play in the film allows Kechiche to avoid the usual clichés associated with representations of low-cost housing and the *banlieue*: drug problems, unemployment, and crime. Yet, the director does not hide the violence which plagues it. It is hinted at in the story of Krimo's father who sends drawings of sailboats from prison to his son, symbolizing his dream of escaping the restrictions and limitations of life in the economically deprived suburbs. This violence is revealed more explicitly in the relations observed between boys and girls, for instance in the scene where Fathi, Krimo's best friend, attacks Frida in order to force her to talk to her friend Lydia and pressure Lydia to return Krimo's love. Another example is when Lydia, her friends, and Magalie get together to oblige Magalie to admit that her relationship with Krimo is over and give Lydia a chance to decide whether or not she wants to be in a relationship with him. In the film, love affairs are controlled by the group, which leaves no room for individual freedom. Violence is further highlighted by a significant use of close-ups, one of the distinguishing feature of Kechiche's aesthetic, when the police assault Krimo, Lydia, and their friends. The filmmaker reveals the arbitrariness of the identification check, as the excess of police violence has no other justification than the fact that the young people find themselves in the marginal territory of the *banlieue*.

As I demonstrated above, Kechiche deconstructs the stereotype of Maghrebi-French youth living in low-rent housing in the suburbs. Yet, this particular scene emphasizes the determinism of the film, which is also suggested by Marivaux's play and revealed by the French teacher's comment, 'Ce que Marivaux nous dit, là les riches jouent les pauvres, les pauvres jouent les riches et personne n'y arrive, personne n'y arrive bien, ce qu'il nous montre, c'est qu'on est complètement prisonnier de notre condition sociale' (Marivaux shows us that here the rich play the poor and the poor play the rich, but nobody can do it successfully. He shows us that we're prisoners of our social class).[8] Thus, 'the police violence demonstrates that whatever their educational prowess, these young people continue to be contained by the gaze of those representing the power of the state' (Tarr, 2011: 135–6).

In *La Faute à Voltaire* as in *L'Esquive*, Abdellatif Kechiche anchors art and literature in his narratives. These references enrich the films, by offering deeper levels of interpretation and helping to paint a unique picture of immigration through an unusual technique. In *La Faute à Voltaire*, the allusion to great literary figures like Voltaire and Victor Hugo, which embody ideals of justice and liberty, allows the filmmaker to confront these ideals to the policies of contemporary France on illegal immigrants. In *L'Esquive*, the simultaneous presence of classical theater language and *banlieue* youth language allows Kechiche to highlight the richness and inventiveness of this popular idiom and shift his emphasis from the center to the periphery of the dominant culture. Those who are usually relegated to the margins are thus given a chance to reappropriate their culture and language. 'Both films [*La Faute à Voltaire* and *L'Esquive*] derive much of their dynamism from a tension between subversion of French cultural traditions and a quest to renew those traditions' (Nettelbeck, 2007: 308).

The importance of female figures

The predominance of strong female protagonists who are placed at the center of the narrative and move the plot forward is another feature of Kechiche's work. It contrasts with the figure of woman as metaphor of absence in many films by Maghrebi-French directors (with the exception of Malik Chibane's *Hexagone* and *Douce France*). As noted by Will Higbee, 'While Kechiche will remain true to the universe of the adolescent *banlieusard*, his film offers significant agency to the young female protagonists of the housing estate; a group that, with few previous exceptions, most obviously *Jeunesse dorée* (Ghorab-Volta, 2001) and *Douce France* (Chibane, 1995), have been systematically marginalized in the diegesis of the *banlieue* film' (2013: 105).

Far from adopting a passive position, in *L'Esquive*, Lydia, Frida, and Nanou assert their opinions in front of their male counterparts and use masculine phrases in their dialogues, thus appropriating men's vocabulary. They address each other using terms such as 'brother' or claiming attributes of the opposite sex when they use expressions such as 'm'en bats les couilles' (I don't give a fuck). 'The verbal agency granted to the female protagonists is further reinforced by their prominent physical presence in exterior spaces of the *cité*, where they congregate to exchange gossip, discuss their aspirations and even confront one another. This representational strategy is, again, rare in the *banlieue film*, where external spaces tend to be exclusively coded as masculine' (Higbee, 2013: 105).

Similarly, in *La Graine et le mulet*, Rym is a character distinguished by her dynamism and her proactive attitude. She functions as a sort of interface and intermediary between Slimane and French society. She speaks on his behalf when he lacks the verbal skills to try to pitch their restaurant idea to the relevant administrative authorities. The young woman also uses trickery to rescue her stepfather from his predicament when the cauldron with the couscous grain disappears during the opening of their new restaurant. To entertain the guests and make them forget the long wait for the couscous dish, Rym improvises an oriental dance. The use of oriental dance can be seen as a cliché of the oriental woman exposed to the colonial gaze, but Rym resorts to that dance as a trick to save the situation and transforms the cliché into an instrument of salvation. At the very same time, Slimane runs off in a desperate and frantic effort to retrieve his moped which has been stolen by some kids of the housing project. United in a desperate physical exertion, both protagonists are plunged in a trance, which works as a metaphor for the transition from the older to the younger generation. This theme is symbolically illustrated in the title, where the 'seed' (*la graine*) refers to Rym and the younger generation, and the mule (*le mulet*) represents Slimane and the older generation. In Kechiche's film, the offspring of the first North African immigrants are represented by a proactive youth which is in harmony with the older generation. This portrayal of Maghrebi descendants is very different from previous works (like *Le Thé au harem d'Archimède*, *Hexagone*, and *Douce France*), where Maghrebi-French youths have broken off ties with their parents and are shown to live in a social context characterized by unemployment, drugs, and racism.[9] With the oriental dance, intended here as a sacrificial ritual, however, Rym recovers what might be called the culture of her origins, not to retreat into cultural isolationism but rather to be able to play an active role in the narration and help Slimane earn his place within French society.

All the other North African female characters in *La Graine et le mulet* are strong and independent women. For instance, we watch Souad, Slimane's ex-wife, blaming him and claiming the alimony he owes her. Similarly, Slimane's daughter from his first marriage, Karima, talks about her active role in the strike at the factory. She reprimands her husband for being too passive and scolds Majid, Karima's brother, for his unfaithfulness. Finally, Latifa, Slimane's companion, owns the hotel where he and his immigrant friends are staying, and rules them with an iron fist. She represents a free and independent female figure in her sexuality and in her relationship with Slimane.

With an opus that now includes a total of five films,[10] Kechiche has developed a unique cinematography which focuses on building complex characters and on narrative development rather than cultural and ethnic identity. The diegesis is enriched by numerous literary and artistic allusions to dodge stereotypes and clichés and offer a fresh image of Maghrebi-French youths and immigrants. The filmmaker also shows unexpected facets of female immigrants and their daughters, giving them a new voice and endowing them with strong and independent personalities. They guide the plot and bring about key changes in the narratives of these films.

Abdellatif Kechiche's work is a milestone in the history of the representation of these disenfranchised groups. His film *La Graine et le mulet* was screened by over a million spectators and his work has often been acclaimed by critics, receiving numerous awards.[11] The reception of his films grants new visibility and recognition to Maghrebi-French filmmakers, confirming Kechiche's ability to transcend the issue of origins and to endow his characters with a universal dimension. Furthermore, by distorting symbols of the greatness of France, the filmmaker articulates an acerbic critique of French Republican ideals which, in the case of immigrants, has become pure utopia.

Finally, Kechiche's films both continue previous film traditions and break free from them, in the sense that they 'not only blur the boundaries between what center and margin mean in twenty-first-century France, they clearly provide a continuum to the preoccupations of the generations of the 1970s, 1980s, and even the early 1990s. Although still concerned with the critical issues and causes of marginalization, racism, unemployment, and state repression, these [Kechiche's] films rarely decry the torts of history, presenting characters that are complex agents, rather than victims, of their daily lives' (Esposito, 2011: 232).

Notes

1 The terms 'Maghrebi-French' and 'North African' will be used in this chapter without any pejorative or colonial connotations. They will allow me to avoid the term *Beur* which I will discuss later.
2 Special issues of *Cinématographe* (1985) and *CinémAction* (1990) testify to the emergence of this new cinematographic movement.
3 A space situated on the periphery of France's major cities where we can find *les cités*, usually called *les cités de banlieue* (housing projects).
4 Yet, it is worth noting that the national identity of the characters is never explicitly revealed or emphasized. We know that Jallel is Tunisian and must impersonate an Algerian to increase his chances of getting the legal paperwork, but this fact is not particularly foregrounded. Similarly, the viewer can guess that most of the young protagonists in *L'Esquive* (Krimo, Frida, Rachid, Fathi, and Nanou) are of North African origin, as a few clues

indicate this (for instance, raï music or television programs in Arabic which Krimo's mother watches), but the issue of national origin does not play an important role in the diegesis.
5 Unless otherwise referenced, all translations are mine.
6 Just like Candide in Voltaire's tale, Jallel leaves his country and is faced with several obstacles and hardships which confront him (and the reader/viewer) with a rough reality: injustice, the horrors of war, and starvation in Candide's case and the arbitrariness of immigration politics for Jallel. Like Voltaire, Kechiche traces the journey and the disillusionment of a character who finds himself out of his country – hence his *candid* gaze – in order to highlight the injustices of contemporary European society.
7 In the eighteenth-century play, Mr. Orgon asks his daughter Sylvia to marry his friend's son, Dorante. Sylvia, who is reluctant to obey, switches clothing with her maid Lisette in order to observe Dorante. Unbeknown to Sylvia, Dorante dons Arlequin, his servant's attire to test Sylvia. In spite of Dorante's lower-class disguise, Sylva falls in love with him, while Lisette finds love with Arlequin.
8 Marivaux's play ends with master and servant couples falling in love within their respective social class: the masters with the masters and the servants with the servants, despite their confusing disguises.
9 Malik Chibane, the film director of *Hexagone* and *Douce France*, resorts to humor to diffuse the drama of his narratives.
10 *La faute à Voltaire* (2001), *L'esquive* (2004), *La graine et le mulet* (2007), *Vénus noire* (2010), *La Vie d'Adèle chapitres 1&2* (2013).
11 *L'Esquive* and *La Graine et le mulet* were awarded four Césars respectively, and his latest film, *La Vie d'Adèle chapitres 1&2* was awarded the *Palme d'or* at the Cannes film festival in 2013.

References

Durmelat, S. (2008). *Fictions de l'intégration: Du mot beur à la politique de la mémoire*, Paris: L'Harmattan.
Esposito, C. (2011). 'Ronsard in the Metro: Abdellatif Kechiche and the Poetics of Space,' *Studies in French Cinema* 11(3), 223–34.
Guignoux, S. (2004). 'Tchatchez-moi d'amour dans le "neuf cube,"' *La Croix*, January 7.
Henebelle, G. and Schneider, R. (1990). *Cinéma Métis: De Hollywood aux films beurs*, Paris: Corlet-Télérama, Collection CinémAction, 56.
Higbee, W. (2011). 'Of Spaces and Difference in *La Graine et le Mulet* (2007): A Dialogue with Carrie Tarr,' in W. Higbee and S. Leahy (eds), *Studies in French Cinema – UK Perspectives 1985–2010*, Bristol, UK/Chicago: Intellect, 217–29.
Higbee, W. (2013). *Post-Beur Cinema: North-African Émigré and Maghrebi-French Filmmaking in France Since 2000*, Edinburgh: Edinburgh University Press.

Lowry, S. (2001). '"La Faute à Voltaire": Entretien avec Abdellatif Kechiche,' *Les Inrockuptibles*, February 13. Web. June 3, 2016.
Mandelbaum, J. (2001). 'Un héros clandestin naturalisé par une comédie grand public,' *Le Monde*, February 14.
Marivaux, P. (2000). *Le Jeu de l'amour et du hasard*, Paris: Pocket.
Marivaux, P. (2007). *The Game of Love and Chance*, trans. S. Mulrine, London: Nick Hern Books.
Melinard, M. (2004). 'Cette jeunesse n'a pas de place dans le paysage audio-visuel,' *L'Humanité*, January 7.
Morice, J. (2007). 'Propos recueillis d'Abdellatif Kechiche,' *Télérama*, 3022, December 12.
Nettelbeck, C. (2007). 'Kechiche and the French Classics. Cinema as Subversion and Renewal of Tradition,' *French Cultural Studies*, 18(13), 307–19.
Strand, D. (2009). 'Être et parler: Being and Speaking French in Abdellatif Kechiche's *L'Esquive* (2004) and Laurent Cantet's *Entre les murs* (2008),' *Studies in French Cinema* 9(3), 259–72.
Swamy, V. (2007). 'Marivaux in the Suburbs: Reframing Language in Kechiche's *L'Esquive* (2003),' *Studies in French Cinema*, 7(1), 57–68.
Tarr, C. (2005). *Reframing Difference: Beur and Banlieue Filmmaking in France*, Manchester: Manchester University Press.
Tarr, C. (2011). 'Class Acts: Education, Gender, and Integration in Recent French Cinema,' in S. Durmelat and V. Swamy (eds), *Screening Integration: Recasting Maghrebi Immigration in Contemporary France*, Lincoln, NE/London: University of Nebraska Press, 127–43.
Tritter, J.-L. (2008). *Le Conte philosophique*, Paris: Ellipses.
Williams, J. S. (2011). 'Open-Sourcing French Culture: The Politics of Métissage and Collective Reappropriation in the Films of Abdellatif Kechiche,' *International Journal of Francophone Studies* 14(3), 391–415.

Filmography

Kechiche, A. (2000). *La Faute à Voltaire*, Flach Film.
Kechiche, A. (2003). *L'Esquive*, Lola Films/Noé Productions Int.
Kechiche, A. (2005). *La Graine et le mulet*, Pathé Films/Hirsch.

5

Seeking paths to existence in Rachid Djaïdani's *Rengaine*

Mona El Khoury

Rengaine, Rachid Djaïdani's first feature-length film not only expands on 1980s and 1990s works by Maghrebi-French directors,[1] but is quite original in the themes it tackles.[2] Indeed, if Djaïdani's film shares 'a concern with the place and identity of the marginal and excluded in France' (Tarr, 2005: 3) which is typical of *beur* and *banlieue* films, it innovates through its focus on minority racism and its treatment of identity construction.[3] The original choice of telling a philosophical tale to discuss real and urgent sociocultural issues and bridge over cultural, religious, ethnic, and gender differences is a reflection of Rachid Djaïdani's personal and professional heterogeneous profile.

Born in 1974 in a Parisian *banlieue* slum to a large family of Algerian origin, Djaïdani is a trained stonemason and a competitive boxer. At the age of 20, he was hired as a stage-managing intern for the shooting of *La haine* (Kassovitz, 1995), a film that was to become the prototype of '*banlieue* cinema.' This first step into the cinematic world only increased Djaïdani's interest in film art (Kiner, 2011). With fake resumes and random castings, he was able to get small parts as an *épicier* (a storekeeper, typically of Arabic origin in France) or a delinquent, until realizing the political implications of the image he was projecting, namely the cliché of the subaltern or 'bad' Arab.[4] So he developed the desire to create his own roles in order to elude the stereotypes that essentialize Maghrebi-French men. Before he started directing films, however, his adventure continued on the stage. British theater director Peter Brook first spotted Djaïdani on a television set where Rachid was speaking about his first novel (Regnier, 2012). Brook then asked the young man to become a member of his theater company, where Djaïdani got his training.

After his experience on Kassovitz's movie set, Djaïdani started to write, because, as he said, 'je veux exister' (I want to exist) (Pivot, 1999). His first novel, *Boumkoeur* (1999), which dealt with life in the ghetto of *quartiers*, was a bestseller. Consequently, intellectuals and the media tagged him a '*banlieue* writer,' to which Djaïdani responded: 'Ecrivains de banlieue, okay, mais est-ce qu'on leur dit "écrivains bourgeois" ou "littérature de bourgeois" ou "littérature de fils de"?' (Mboungou, 2007) (*Banlieue* writers, okay, but do people say 'bourgeois writers' or 'bourgeois literature' or 'literature of the sons of'?). Djaïdani constantly questions classifications. His works specifically represent the suffocation resulting from categorization, in other words the dictatorship of identity, whether social, ethnic, cultural, or professional. For Djaïdani, identity is always in flux, and subject to constant negotiation.

With his second novel, *Mon nerf* (2004), he tried to distance himself from the label of *banlieue* writer by staying away from 'slum' stories, switching to a psychological–sexual plot.[5] Moreover, while writing his book, Djaïdani shot a documentary on the process of novel creation. Titled *Sur ma ligne*, this film is not just a response to the suspicions of plagiarism expressed by some critics and publishing houses, but also a demonstration of the authenticity of Djaïdani's talent and writer status (Reeck, 2012: 66). Additionally, the film reveals another transformation of the stonemason, boxer, actor, and writer, who becomes a director – the best possible demonstration of the problems of putting labels on identity. Djaïdani's third novel, *Viscéral* (2007), goes back to the slums to talk about ways to escape. The story is that of a boxing coach whose life is turned upside down by two encounters: a beautiful woman who makes him discover love, and a casting director who introduces him to art. As when he was a boxer, Djaïdani pursues a 'strategy' of eluding labels, all the while integrating autobiographical elements. This novel constitutes a *mise en abyme* of Djaïdani's life, and prefigures the plot of *Rengaine*, the filming of which started around the same time as the writing of the novel.

The shooting of *Rengaine* took place over the course of nine years and under extreme conditions: no budget, no professional actors other than the two main characters (the little-known Slimane Dazi and Stéphane Soo Mongo), no technicians, no script, and unauthorized shoulder camera shots in the streets of Paris, in natural light. Djaïdani stood up to the rejection of sponsors and made a movie 'à l'arrache' (with an intuitive feel), 'bancal plutôt que banquable' (shaky rather than profitable) (Kaganski, 2012). The film revives the themes of love and cinema, the two formative encounters in *Viscéral*, but from another point of view. *Rengaine* shows what prevents this personal and professional blossoming: intercommunity racism, rejection of the 'other' and of the other's difference. The plot is simple: Sabrina, a French woman of Algerian origin (Sabrina Hamida, Djaïdani's wife), and Dorcy (Stéphane Soo Mongo), a Black Christian actor, have been in love for one year and decide to get married.[6] Sabrina has forty brothers – an improbability accepted in the context of the tale and a number which recalls both the *Ali Baba* thieves and the days of Ramadan, thus immediately inscribing this film into the imaginary context of Islam. The eldest, Slimane, opposes this marriage and tries to rally the other brothers to his cause. Whereas in *beur* and *banlieue* films the focus was on white racism against ethnic minorities, Djaïdani breaks new ground by introducing an unusual topic in French cinema: racism between Arabs and Blacks (Kaganski, 2012). At the same time, the camera follows the professional misfortunes of Dorcy, an unlucky actor who is turned down for all the parts he tries to get, and therefore finds himself 'ghettoized,' professionally speaking, unable to switch roles and identities. As I will show, this double storyline reflects Djaïdani's particular story in an even more autobiographical way, while giving his film a universal scope. *Rengaine* offers a dialogue between the particular and the universal on multiple levels. Just like the camera, I will first follow Slimane's fall into 'particularism,' that is, the traditional family order marked by patriarchal domination. Next, I will analyze Dorcy's path toward the 'universal,' namely the subversion of any sectarianism. To conclude, I will discuss the friction of the two paths and the meaning of the 'tale' *Rengaine*.

'The path of deviation': Slimane's story or the question of tradition

The first ten minutes of the film are made up of unstable and unframed close-ups that convey the idea that we are entering the intimate space of the characters. The camera is positioned, sometimes awkwardly, as close as possible to the actors' skin and objects in order to underline the tension and fragility of life.[7] The first scene is a moving close-up that follows what the viewer finally manages to identify as a tricycle. The child's bike, which is seen rolling along an asphalt street, is guided by a long sleeve, which the camera progressively follows, revealing the person pushing the bike. It is Slimane, the eldest of the brothers. This initial shot offers a metaphor for Slimane's position with respect to his siblings, symbolized by the child's bike. He regards himself as a guide and a guardian of tradition who replaces the parents. In fact, Slimane's parents are not once mentioned during the film, an absence that sets *Rengaine* apart from *beur* and *banlieue* films, in which the immigrant parents generally represent 'tradition,' against which the children's generation defines itself.[8] As anthropologist Camille Lacoste-Dujardin (2000) explains, in traditional Maghrebi immigrant families, after the father, who is at the top of the familial hierarchy, the (eldest) son, not the mother, is the next authority figure – gender thus taking precedence over generation. Slimane is therefore portrayed as a traditional embodiment of patriarchal authority, the weight of which is reflected in the large number of brothers, who are, for the most part, under his influence.

Rengaine powerfully denounces the oppressive sexism from which Sabrina attempts to break free. As Carrie Tarr explains, this masculine domination is both a legacy of tradition and a masculine overcompensation resulting from a particular social condition:

> Thanks to measures enabling the police to stop and detain individuals suspected of being illegal residents,[Blacks and Arabs] also suffer from the

invidious *délit du faciès*, the crime of simply looking different, which makes them vulnerable to police harassment. In these circumstances, it is not surprising that young males may express their alienation through undesirable, antisocial and hypermacho behaviour. The shift of patriarchal authority from the father to *les grands frères* ('the older brothers') has also led to a notable regression in the situation of women in the *banlieue*. (2005: 7)

The shift in patriarchal power from the father to the elder brother is remarkably represented in the character of Slimane, who clearly looks older than his siblings.[9] He acts as a father figure, because he believes it is his responsibility to watch over his family: 'Je suis un mur, c'est ma tradition … Je suis un grand-frère, c'est mon métier … Je suis le père de mes quarante frangins, je suis le père de ma sœur' (I am a wall, in keeping with my tradition … I am a big brother, that's my job … I'm a father to my forty younger brothers, I am a father to my sister). The metaphor of the 'wall' emphasizes the idea that Slimane freezes 'identity,' prevents it from evolving and mixing, and it suggests that the respect of tradition induces petrification.

The 'wall' starts to crack down when Slimane learns, from an anonymous voicemail, that his sister is going to marry the man of her choice. This announcement undermines Slimane's moral authority. The voice message triggers a series of actions that describe a 'ligne de fuite' (line of flight) (Deleuze, 1977: 47), aiming to find a new stable 'ground,' that is, a way for Slimane to re-establish his authority.[10] To do so, Slimane marks out a new 'territory' – a milieu in which his domination can be effective – by gathering a group of brothers who side with him.[11] In Deleuzian terms, Slimane's line of flight, like any lines of flight, 'se reterritorialise' (reterritorializes itself) (Deleuze, 1977: 47).[12] Thus, under the pretext of finding the person who left him the message, Slimane starts on a quest, from brother to brother, with the same attitude (*la même rengaine*) and the same refrain (*rengaine*): 'Est-ce que tu savais que Sabrina allait se marier?' (Did you know that Sabrina is going to get married?), he asks each of them. The French word *rengaine* has several meanings which come into play throughout this chapter. First, a *rengaine* is a refrain in a song, so a motif which is repeated. In this regard, Slimane's question to his brothers sounds like a refrain. Figuratively, *c'est toujours la même rengaine* (it's always the same old thing, the same old song) conveys the idea of stagnation or the lack of change, in a negative way. Slimane's attitude pertains to such a 'blockage.' Finally, the verb *rengainer* means keeping one's words to oneself. We will see later how this last meaning applies to Slimane's story.

The one question Slimane asks to his brothers ('Did you know that Sabrina is going to get married?') is a sonorous 'ritournelle' (ritornello), a chorus that is 'une expression qui trace un territoire' (Deleuze and Guattari, 1980: 397) (an expression that traces a territory). The movie echoes the anthropological phenomenon of disregard of the traditional patriarchal authority in immigrant families confronted with a different, western culture

(Lacoste-Dujardin, 2000: 58–9). Yet Djaïdani takes the issue of the 'patriarchal system in question' to a new dimension (Lacoste-Dujardin, 2000: 57). First, it is not the father but his substitute, the elder brother, who loses his grip on his siblings. Second, the context is not a friction between minority and majority (national) culture anymore, but between two different immigrant minorities (Slimane's and Dorcy's).

Slimane's re-territorialization occurs within a specific geographical perimeter, not the *banlieue*, but rather the streets of the northern Paris neighborhoods.[13] Breaking away from the locations of '*banlieue* cinema,' *Rengaine* reclaims the Paris of *beur* cinema, namely the neighborhoods with a high density of disenfranchised immigrants. This return to familiar places emphasizes, through space, Slimane's quest for a lost patriarchal structure of *beur* communities. However, what is shown of immigrant districts in *Rengaine* differs from past movies. In *beur* films, most of the scenes often take place in cafés, whereas in *Rengaine*, the street is the main setting. In general, the omnipresence of this public space suggests both the appropriation of the city by the *Beurs'* children and a sense of persistent social exclusion of the third generation, which is relocated to the streets.[14] In this particular case, Slimane's wandering in the streets reflects his "existential" destabilization, in contrast with the more "stable" location of the café, shown in *beur* movies. Resulting from the lack of funding, shooting in the street is also an aesthetic commitment aiming to show the characters' most intimate preoccupations against the contrasting backdrop of public spaces.

Likewise, the temporal dimension of Slimane's re-territorialization is meaningful: it is during the month of Ramadan, which allows Djaïdani to engage with concerns about negotiating the role and place of religion for Muslims.[15] Shortly after the first ten minutes of the film, a sequence shows Kamel, one of the brothers, and a Black friend breaking the fast at the end of the day, while discussing Sabrina's choice. The friend admits he cannot understand Kamel's intolerance of his sister's marriage. Kamel subsequently explains that Dorcy is an 'Africain' and 'pas un frère ... pas un musulman' (not a brother, not a Muslim). The Black friend gets angry and responds that his own family, where Kamel broke the fast the night before, has always considered Kamel one of their own, implying that universal affiliations (based on love and friendship) take precedence over religious affiliations. The two friends fiercely argue and end up parting ways.[16]

This sequence is later echoed by another, in which Dorcy is drinking coffee with friends of Algerian origin, who call themselves Muslims. He explains to them his predicament and the two friends discourage him from marrying Sabrina, for the reason that he is not a Muslim. Yet, Dorcy replies: 'Moi elle m'aime, on s'aime, c'est ça qui compte' (She loves me, we love each other; that's what counts). He extols a universal feeling (love) against the particular social tradition of marriage within the community, a form of sectarianism shared by Dorcy's own mother, as she radically refuses to have a daughter-in-law who is not Black. The refusal of religious compromise in matters of love and marriage contrasts with the way other types of ritual are negotiated. For example, Dorcy makes his friends realize that they are drinking coffee in the middle of the day during Ramadan, a remark that greatly upsets the Muslims, who do not accept to be called out on their own contradictions and leave the café while insulting Dorcy.

By choosing to situate the plot of *Rengaine* in the middle of a religious *rengaine* (the rhythm and behaviors typical of the month of Ramadan), Djaïdani refreshes the way Islam is portrayed in *beur* and *banlieue* films, which is hardly ever discussed (Cadé, 2011: 41–57). Fundamentally, the film engages with the problematic denial of an ever-changing, multifaceted Muslim identity. The fear of the unknown is at the root of the brothers' rejection of difference. At one point, one of the brothers asks: 'T'as déjà vu un mélange rebeu-renoi?' (Have you ever seen the offspring of an Arab and a Black?), a genuine question to which a sibling half-jokingly responds: 'J'ai déjà vu un dragon!' (No, but I've seen a dragon!).[17] The joke around the idea of miscegenation between Blacks and Arabs is the sign of an idealization of 'racial' purity, never explicitly expressed, yet often alluded to, and which is based on a confusion between religion and ethnicity.

Slimane's anxiety about desacralizing tradition and his obsession with the idea of a "pure" identity reflect his refusal to recognize his own otherness. His enunciation of the *rengaine* ('did you know that Sabrina is going to get married?') highlights, like every ritornello, a problematic self-defining process. Indeed, what existential meaning can be given to this incessant return of the question, of this 'retour éternel' (eternal return) that evokes, like a portmanteau word, a 'ritournelle' (ritornello)? Slimane's ritornello only serves to protect the fantasy of a pure 'identity' and a determining origin – in other words, a 'simulacre' (simulacrum) (Deleuze and Guattari, 1980: 370, 431). Neither Slimane nor any of the brothers who rally around him have a valid argument to justify their opposition to Sabrina's marriage. The climax of Slimane's lack of reasoning is shown in his encounter with Sabrina, a scene where he has absolutely nothing better to say to his sister than his leitmotif, i.e. that she cannot marry Dorcy and that there will be no wedding. Slimane's rejection of Dorcy relies exclusively on tradition, erected as the ruling principle of life.[18]

Through a funny but significant sequence involving two other brothers, Slimane's *rengaine* is implicitly compared to that of a bad investigator who keeps trotting out insulting questions. The two brothers, idling near Gare du Nord station, are interrupted by Slimane who came to ask them his *rengaine* question. The brother who bragged of having dropped out of school is the one with the harshest words: he wants to 'séquestrer' (kidnap) his sister, 'la mettre dans un coffre' (put her in a trunk), and then 'la ramener au bled' (take her back to their Algerian village). Djaïdani implicitly suggests the need to educate the children of the *beur* generation, teach them the values of the French Republic, and combat sexism and violence against women.[19]

The exchange between the three brothers continues until it is interrupted by a journalist doing street interviews. He explains that he is administering a survey on 'les minorités urbaines dans l'espace public' (urban minorities in the public space). At first sight, this topic is ambiguous and insulting to the brothers, so Slimane immediately retorts 'quelles minorités?' (which minorities?). The journalist, who is quite naive but clearly embarrassed, responds: 'bah ... des gens comme vous qui traînez autour de la gare, quoi!' (Uh ... people like you, who hang out around the station, you know!). The scene is both hilarious and powerful. Djaïdani pokes fun at the cliché of young people, often of Maghrebi or African origin, frequently unemployed, whom the media tends to stigmatize. And he derides the hypocritical ('politically correct') use of the term 'urban minority' which barely hides the idea of 'ethnic minorities' or 'religious minorities.'[20]

The questions that the journalist asks, before Slimane chases him away, are insulting as they presuppose an essentialized difference that is immediately tagged as 'negative.' For example, Slimane is asked: 'Est-ce que votre délinquance de bande s'explique par votre non-mobilité?' (Can your gang delinquency be explained through non-mobility?), words presuming that Slimane is a delinquent. In the end, this whole scene is an ironic repetition of Slimane's *rengaine* about Dorcy not being a Muslim Arab: in both cases, the question presupposes an "other" who is not tolerated.

The symbolic violence carried by such a construction of identity and inflicted on the "others" is actually at the heart of Slimane's intimate life. Not only is he the guardian of tradition, but he is also its victim. In a dramatic twist around the middle of the film, the viewer learns that Slimane has been going out with a Jewish woman for a long time. This information renders Slimane's *rengaine* incoherent and hypocritical. The elder brother is, in fact, a man torn between two different desires, a man who affirms that he wants to 'briser les chaines' (break the chains) of communitarianism and get married, but at the same time confesses that he is 'blocked' because Nina is a 'feuj' (Jew).[21] While denouncing a form of cultural and familial anti-Semitism, Djaïdani shows the friction between the particular – the religious identity claimed by Slimane – and the universal – his feeling of love, which overcomes the limits imposed by his idea of what being a Muslim means. Slimane's view of identity, closed and one-dimensional as it is, is weighing down heavily on him: his hunched posture and crestfallen look convey his personal alienation. His existential schizophrenia is further reflected in the music which accompanies the Slimane scenes, as it alternates between traditional Oriental music with the zither and music resulting from an Afro-Occidental mixing, such as funk and jazz, hybrid styles which symbolically refer to Sabrina and Dorcy as a couple. Slimane is also the only character that switches between Arabic and French, his bilingualism resulting from a double culture he has trouble accepting.

Finally, while the suspense has dramatically grown with Slimane illegally purchasing a gun to kill or threaten Dorcy, one climactic sequence is decisive as it inflects Slimane's path. We see Slimane with the real eldest brother, who was "repudiated" from the family thirty years ago because he is gay. The sequence takes place in a dark cellar and gives rise to the most violent altercation in the movie. Slimane insults his brother, calling him a 'pute' (whore) and 'salope' (slut). Drawing on Bourdieu's *La Domination masculine*, Maxime Foerster notes the significant choice of feminine insults: instead of uttering offensive words for 'gay' (like the term 'faggot' he used when chasing away the journalist), Slimane's discourse reveals the deep link between homophobia and misogyny in a social structure based on traditional masculine domination (2014: 183). Through a 'stratégie d'inversion' (inversion strategy), the eldest brother manages to show that Slimane is the one who lacks 'couilles' (balls), whereas he and Sabrina have the courage to live their lives without shame (Foerster, 2014: 184).[22] This unbearable truth causes Slimane to react physically and threaten to kill his brother. But the eldest is not afraid and responds that he has been dead for thirty years already. In fact, the underground space connotes the idea of a tomb, and the gay brother's returning from the grave 'fait penser au défoulement du refoulement, à la remontée en surface d'un corps qu'on croyait noyé, d'une voix qu'on espérait éteinte pour toujours' (Foerster, 2014: 187) (reminds us of the abrupt return of the repressed, the resurfacing of a body that was believed to be drowned, of a voice that was expected to be forever silenced).

After the altercation with the eldest brother, Slimane remains dazed. While the gay man leaves the sepulchral space of the cellar, Slimane stays for a moment inside the gloomy walls, which recall the 'walls' of the tradition he pretends to embody. Just before he left, the brother said to Slimane: 'ce soir, c'est la nuit du destin, les portes du paradis sont ouvertes, je prierai pour toi' (tonight, it's destiny's night, the doors of heaven are open, I will pray for you). This hope is fulfilled in the final sequence of the film, which shows the gay brother's impact on Slimane's "path." Touching on a still-taboo topic in post-*beur* cinema, Djaïdani's film pioneers a reflection on homosexuality, a repressed aspect of human experience in Maghrebi-French Muslim culture, and provides visibility to gay Arabs in France.[23]

Djaïdani's criticism of racist and heteronormative discourse falls within the heated debate about the legalization of homosexual marriage in France. The same month when *Rengaine* came out, a powerful homophobic movement started to take actions against the reform promised by presidential candidate François Hollande and the proposed bill legalizing homosexual marriage. The homophobic movement's name – 'la Manif pour tous' (protest for all) – sounds like a bad echo of the bill, 'le mariage pour tous' (marriage for all), which was framed within the logic of republican universalism. *Rengaine* thus contributes to the sociopolitical cause seeking the recognition of 'all' love relationships as equal.

'The path of the righteous': Dorcy's story, or the search for universality

The first shot of Dorcy is the film's poster. He is shown hugging Sabrina on a grey pedestrian street, which is shot out of focus and could just as well be a part of a metal bridge. The sharp focus on the young pair (Black man and white woman) contrasts with the pale and smooth uniformity of the road. In a certain way, the poster immediately suggests that Dorcy and Sabrina's path is not 'determined in advance' but rather remains to be invented, its color being undetermined. As Sabrina says to Dorcy at a time when he is driven to despair by Slimane's attitude, it is necessary to 'évoluer, avancer' (evolve, make progress) with their lives together, even if the couple's love cannot change her brothers' attitude.

The first appearance of the two characters in the film provides a literal image of the couple's choosing to walk off the beaten path, since Dorcy and Sabrina are shown in the woods under a tree. The representation of the mixed-race couple in *Rengaine* often consists of a close-up of the two colors, black and white, which are intertwined. Shots of juxtaposed light- and dark-colored stones in the shape of a heart, of Dorcy and Sabrina holding hands, or of their hands playing on the piano keys intensify the idea of harmonious mixing. Just before the final scene of the film, a shot built on a strong light contrast symbolizes the two forms of otherness Dorcy is faced with. We see him sitting at night on the steps of the Sacré-Cœur basilica in Montmartre. The contrast between the lit-up white church and Dorcy's dark shadow recalls the overwhelming racism the young man is subject to, based on his skin color. Moreover, the domes of the Sacré-Cœur, evoking the architecture of a mosque, recall the problem of the religious difference between the two lovers.

In fact, the treatment of skin color tells the story of *Rengaine* from another point of view, that of Dorcy, to whom the stigma of black skin is attached. In his private life, Dorcy's love story with Sabrina is complicated by Slimane's opposition to Dorcy's religion (not a Muslim) and skin color (black). The sequence where the elder brother learns about Dorcy's identity is significant. He convinces a neighborhood child to tell him what he knows about Sabrina's boyfriend. The child provides him with Dorcy's name, his profession, and before anything else, he mentions two physical characteristics: the color of Dorcy's face, which is 'tout noir' (completely black) as well as his 'gros nez' (big nose). The child's words are accompanied by gestures, which mime a large, deformed face.

This description reiterates the stereotype of Black people, which Djaïdani plays on in order to undermine it. In the next sequence, Dorcy is seen wearing a bear mask while repeating a scene from Pierre Corneille's tragedy, *Cinna*, for a casting. The actor turned-animal literally embodies the Black stereotype. As Mireille Rosello points out in *Declining the Stereotype*, stereotypical representations of Africans have remained unchanged despite the protests of Aimé Césaire, Léopold Sedar Senghor, and others. They consist of an image of an 'endearing, childish, harmless, yet potentially rabble-rousing African,' and it is precisely what the mask turns Dorcy into: a teddy bear (Rosello, 1998: 4). But the costume worn in the context of *Cinna* does not make sense at all, and the whole picture is so ridiculous that it becomes laughable, thus undermining the stereotype, which literally does not stick to Dorcy's skin anymore, when it feels too hot for him and he takes off the mask.

Echoing Mireille Rosello's book title, Djaïdani 'declines the stereotype' according to the double entendre of the term 'declining,' taken in a semiotic meaning and in a social sense. Indeed, according to the 'politics of grammar,' to decline means to 'acknowledg[e] the various formal identities that one element of language must adopt depending on its position and role within a larger linguistic unit' (Rosello, 1998: 10–13), as with German, Latin, and Greek nouns. And this is precisely what Djaïdani does, not with linguistic but with visual units: one element in the shot is changed (i.e. the novelty of the mask on Dorcy's face, compared to his bare face) and takes on a different meaning. This formal declension has a socio-ideological impact, which is the second meaning of 'declining.' According to the 'grammar of politics,' 'to decline' refers to the refusal of an invitation. Declining the stereotype of Black people's alleged animalism through an ironic visual repetition, i.e. a literalization of the cliché, Djaïdani finds a way of 'depriving [the stereotype] of its harmful potential by highlighting its very nature,' which is a deforming and grotesque representation (Rosello, 1998: 11–13).

Practicing such a declension is an ambiguous gesture, because it involves both a refusal of the stereotype and a participation in its social circulation. The scene with the bear mask is so ridiculous that it does not leave much space for ambiguity but later in the film, another process of declining the same stereotype is more hazardous. While Slimane is wandering around a theme park, we see him standing for a long time before an automaton of King Kong, the giant movie monster resembling a colossal gorilla. He watches the mouth of the monster open and close repeatedly. However, a few sequences earlier, the camera showed us a close-up of Dorcy exaggerating the features of his face, stretching them as much as possible with his hands, and making with his mouth the same movement as the automaton.

Here, the viewer will understand that Djaïdani replaces Dorcy's image with a gorilla, pointing to the stereotype haunting Slimane. But, since there are several sequences between the one showing Dorcy's facial mimicry and the one in the theme park, there is a risk of establishing a loose but literal link between the two, thus reinforcing the stereotype. Yet the automated King Kong is itself a deformation of a famous film (by Merian C. Cooper and Ernest B. Schoedsack in 1933), which diffused the image of the monster. Unlike Slimane, the viewer is at a distance. *Rengaine*'s King Kong being a copy of a copy, the image of Dorcy making faces reinforces the mimicry which challenges the authority of the essentializing discourse. Dorcy 'mimics' King Kong, rather than 'represents' him, and this performance is an appropriation that debunks the cliché (Bhabha, 1991: 85–92).

Djaïdani does not treat stereotypes as the opposite of truth but, as Rosello puts it, as 'one of the narratives that a given power wants to impose as the truth at a given moment' (1998: 17). Several sequences show Dorcy being humiliated or poorly treated by stage directors. For example, in the sequence when Dorcy is being interviewed, the director provokes him by smacking and hitting him to see his range of emotions, as she explains afterwards. In another shot, an artistic director refuses to pay him after a photo shoot and threatens to turn him in for robbery if he continues to claim his money. Other sequences aim to show racism toward Black people in the art milieu, into which Dorcy is desperately trying to be accepted. They point to the necessity for an actor to be white-skinned in order to be allowed to stand in front of the camera.

During the same photo shoot, the artist-director spreads white foam all over Dorcy's body and face before she can film him as 'bien blanc' (really white). Her words to him, 'c'est bien, vous êtes bien blanc' (that's good, now you're really white), all the while making the scene grotesque and laughable, denounce the implicit racial norm. The absence of minorities, and in particular of Black people from French theater, cinema, and more generally, culture and the arts, is a subject of discussion within the film. In fact, like another repetition, or a real-life *rengaine*, actor Stéphane Soo Mongo has experienced in real life the discriminations denounced in the film (Soo Mongo, 2015). In *Rengaine*, one of Dorcy's friends explains that when it comes to innovation (from an ethno-cultural perspective), France is a 'suiveuse' (follower) and not a 'meneuse' (leader). He further advises Dorcy to try to get noticed abroad in order to succeed later in France.

A few sequences later, this idea is taken up once again by Dorcy's (Black) drug dealer. Dismantling the cliché of the uneducated loser, Djaïdani presents a dealer who knows how to cite from Racine's plays and understands power mechanisms in the cultural sphere. The dealer explains to Dorcy that if there is no French equivalent to Denzel Washington, it is because in France it is necessary to conform to the stereotypes attached to Black people. He ironically mentions the success story of Mouss Diouf, a Black actor who played a secondary role in *Julie Lescaut*, a French television series filled with racial clichés. In this popular program, Mouss Diouf plays the character of the "good" Black man recruited by the police force for his physical strength to assist and obey Julie, the police chief and a white woman.[24] In his début as an actor, Djaïdani personally experienced the constricting weight of these clichés, as I mentioned previously.

The film's concern with Black people's agency in French cinema would suggest that Djaïdani is aiming to convey a political message in favor of affirmative action. In the 'Special Features' added to the film, a scene cut from the final montage is particularly interesting. We watch Dorcy and his agent debating the idea of ethnic quotas in French cinema. While the agent thinks they are necessary and that positive discrimination would give visibility to Dorcy, the Black actor is opposed to them and defends universalism as the basis for the selection of talent. This difference in opinion reflects Djaïdani's own indecision. In the final version of *Rengaine*, however, Dorcy listens to his agent and seems to agree with him. This probably indicates Djaïdani's disappointment with the universalist ideal as it applies to the gentrified cinema industry, which did not give him a chance but left him on the margins of French production.

In several interviews, Djaïdani repeats what the final credits of *Rengaine* show. On the one hand, there is the desire to believe in the universalist ideal of the French Republic, represented, in the end credits, by the blue–white–red colors of the French flag, which frame each letter of the title *Rengaine* displayed on bulletin boards at the entrance of a public school, a symbol of the Republic par excellence. On the other hand, dropping from the final cut the sequences showing Dorcy debate over ethnic quotas is a sign of the limits of this ideal and its dysfunction, as conveyed by the sentences printed on the credits: 'Dans la foi du septième art, nous aurons fait notre voyage en marge. Neuf ans de traversée du désert pour atteindre sa lumière. Sauvage ou illégal le cinéma brûle en nous et je lui dis je t'aime' (For the sake of cinematic art, we completed our journey on the margins. Nine years crossing the desert to reach the light, finally. Wild or illegal filmmaking burns bright within us and I say 'Pictures, I love you').

The filmmaker's perseverance in his love of film and his insistence on making his own 'guerrilla-cinema' find their equivalent in the obstinacy of Dorcy and Sabrina's love. As a matter of fact, the main idea of *Rengaine* is that love is what gives the strength to transcend borders. In the end, even though Djaïdani deplores the lack of funding which affected his work, he is nonetheless proud of the success of *Rengaine*, which was selected at the 2012 *Quinzaine des réalisateurs* at the Cannes Film Festival. As he confirmed to Serge Kaganski of the magazine *Les Inrockuptibles*: 'Pendant neuf ans, j'ai cherché des mécènes et je n'ai vu que des miskins, des pingres, des producteurs qui ne mettaient pas un sou. Les films à l'arrache ne les intéressaient pas. Mais regarde aujourd'hui, frère ... Regarde où je suis, où est le film à l'arrache!' (Over a period of nine years, I searched for sponsors and those I found were nasty, stingy producers who didn't give me a cent. Films shot *à l'arrache*, impromptu and with very limited means did not interest them. But look at me now, man ... Look where I am now and where my film is!).

The surprise over the very positive reception of the film echoes the final dramatic twist of *Rengaine*. While Slimane becomes more and more threatening, Dorcy is more and more worried by the rumors of the brothers' anger. After romance and comedic sequences, the film becomes darker and begins to resemble a crime story. Slimane's and Dorcy's paths seem to converge through a succession of shots that suggest tragic fatality. Dorcy looks desperate: the music of the soundtrack is sad while he is wandering at night through the streets of Montmartre. After we see Slimane illegally purchasing a gun, the next sequence displays Dorcy being kidnapped at night in the street by three men wearing balaclavas. The next shot focuses on the young Black man tied to an electric chair, gagged and bleeding. We do not see the aggressor but the preceding scenes lead us to assume that it is Slimane, probably accompanied by some of his brothers.

The long and powerful torture scene showing a traumatized Dorcy whining and suffocating reflects the violence of his relation to Sabrina's brothers. After a long close-up lingering for over a minute on the character, the camera moves slowly away to reveal a scene of filming and then the technical and artistic team. The viewer now realizes that Dorcy is playing a part in a short film titled *Métaphysique de la chaise* (Metaphysics of the chair). The fictitious scene (the film within the film) is very successful, the technical team applauds, and the director congratulates the actor. In addition to being a pleasant surprise for the spectator, this scene is a triple *mise en abyme*. First, it physically repeats the psychological violence of Slimane hunting down Dorcy. Second, within the film's discourse on the lack of minority voices in cinema, the scene is a demonstration of this absence in French cinema, since the cameraman realizes that the whole sequence was filmed without a tape in the recorder. The Black community's lack of voice and subjectivity is suggested through Dorcy's voiceless presence. When he finds out about the technical mistake, Dorcy gets angry and leaves the studio, saying that he will not redo a very exhausting shooting. Finally, the scene constitutes a *mise en abyme* of the filming of *Rengaine* itself, insisting *not* on the difference between reality and fiction, but on their possible confusion. Indeed, by its singular conditions of production (no set, no professional actors, no script, etc.), *Rengaine* is a mix of fiction and real-life raw materials, close to a documentary.

This combination of hyperrealism and storytelling gives the ending of the film its full meaning. One of the brothers, a taxi driver, overhears Dorcy's address, through a coincidence that only pertains to fiction, when his passenger, who is also the director of the short film, mentions it during a phone conversation. The given address is, in reality, Rachid Djaïdani and Sabrina Hamidi's home address.[25] Fiction and reality are again interwoven. A few sequences later, the meeting between Dorcy and Slimane finally happens. We are left to guess that the taxi driver gave Dorcy's address to Slimane, who is waiting for Sabrina's fiancé on the street.

In Djaïdani's interview included in the DVD's special features, the director recalls that another ending had been planned for the film, which was initially to be called 'Quarante frères' (Forty Brothers). Although this first title emphasized the fictional aspect of the film, the original ending was meant to be more realistic. The sequence, which can be seen in the special features but was left out of the final cut, shows Slimane drawing his gun. He shouts at Dorcy and shoots him in the head. Djaïdani explains that he changed the ending after his daughter's birth – a happy event – the magic of which he wanted to inject in the film. In this way, the ending of *Rengaine* turns the film into a philosophical parable. As Djaïdani explains, at the beginning of the film, Slimane '*dégaine*' (draws his weapon) and at the end, '*il rengaine*' (he holsters it), while keeping his *rengaine* (refrain) to himself.

The shift to the second meaning of the word *rengaine* (to put away a weapon) is allegorized in the film's final sequence. It is night-time, when the two men cross paths. Slimane calls out, 'Dorcy?' and the latter responds, jaded: 'C'est moi, ouais' (Yeah, that's me). The two men stare at each other for a long time. The camera focuses on Slimane's damp eyes with a tear rolling down his cheek. Afterwards, the camera shows a close-up of Dorcy's face, nonplussed. A voice-over pronounces a prayer that Slimane is silently saying in Arabic. It is the first Surah of the Koran, called *Al-Fatiha*, or 'The Opening.' The film does not specify the source, but offers subtitles:

> Au nom de Dieu, le tout miséricordieux, louanges à Dieu, Seigneur de l'univers, le bien faisant, le miséricordieux, Maître du jour du jugement dernier, Toi seul nous adorons. De Toi seul, nous implorons le secours, Guide-nous dans le droit chemin, le chemin de ceux qui sont comblés de faveurs, pas de Ta colère. Pas le chemin des égarés. Amen.

> (In the name of God, the infinitely merciful, praise be to God, Lord of the universe, the compassionate, the merciful, Ruler on the Day of Reckoning, You alone we do worship. You alone we ask for help, Guide us on the straight path, the path of those who have received your grace, not your anger. Not the path of those who have wandered astray. Amen.)

Here the film suggests that Slimane, who 'has gone astray,' questions himself and searches for the voice of moral rectitude within himself, not within a 'blind' tradition. Djaïdani does not reject Islam as such, as causing the problem of intolerance, but rather, he denounces misinterpretations of Islam and imprisonment in intolerant traditions. A reinterpretation of the first Surah allows for the tolerance that Slimane demonstrates at the end of the film, which turns into a philosophical tale. Once the prayer is finished, Slimane speaks the final words, addressing Dorcy: 'Je vous demande pardon' (Please forgive me). Dorcy gives a slight movement of the head, seems to be on the verge of speaking, and then leaves. As Foerster remarks, recalling that the gay brother said he would pray for Slimane, 'il semble que de prière en prière, ce soit l'amour et le respect du prochain qui l'emportent contre le défoulement de la violence' (it seems that, from prayer to prayer, love and respect for the neighbor finally prevail over the unleashing of violence) (2014: 188).

Blocking the path of those who do not believe in love and tolerance

The film ends on this powerful scene of forgiveness, foreshadowed by the sequence where Dorcy plays Augustus in *Cinna*, Corneille's tragedy on the clemency of the Roman emperor. *Rengaine* discusses the three possible paths of existence evoked by the first Surah of the Koran and by the biblical Psalms: the 'way of the righteous,' the 'way of the wicked' (the sinners) and the 'way of the ungodly' (the non-believers). In a dialogue between Dorcy and his mother, she advises him to say a short prayer before going to a casting. She recommends that he recite Psalm 23 ('The Lord is My Shepherd'). Just like the opening Surah of the Koran, the Christian prayer speaks of the correct path to follow and the guidance offered by faith. Djaïdani does not reject or oppose Sabrina's and Dorcy's different religions. On the contrary, he highlights their common guiding principles of humility, tolerance, and the constant search for justice. The tale thus takes on all its meaning as a genre: Djaïdani's story aims to be exemplary. The film creates an imaginary and social space for the negotiation of values inherited from previous generations and/or deformed by ignorance. As Djaïdani likes to repeat, individuals can be social bridges between each other, but the film itself bridges social and cultural differences, both within and outside of the diegesis, between characters and between spectators.

The fundamental problem that *Rengaine* tackles concerns the essentialization – and subsequent stagnation – of culture and identity that suffocate individuals. The film raises the question of how to find the way to emancipation and self-invention, that is, each person's particular path to the universal humanity that we all share. The film's answer to this question is love, love between each other and the love of art. In his interview with *Les Inrocks*, Djaïdani confirms this idea, speaking of French *banlieue* life deterioration:

> L'épanouissement ne se fait pas tout seul ni en meute. Il se fait souvent à deux, en étant amoureux. S'empêcher d'être amoureux, c'est s'empêcher de grandir. Empêcher l'autre d'aimer c'est l'emprisonner ... Les vrais bonhommes ce sont ceux qui acceptent d'aimer et d'être aimés. C'est ce qui manque aujourd'hui en banlieue, et quand les mauvaises interprétations de la religion s'y mêlent.

> (Fulfillment is not achieved alone or in a pack. It is often done in pairs, by being in love. Stopping yourself from being in love is to prevent yourself from growing. Preventing others from loving is to imprison them ... True good men are those who accept to love and be loved. This is what is missing from the *banlieue* today, and when bad interpretations of religion are mixed up with it.)

In the end, Djaïdani's *Rengaine* is a summary of the film director's own adventure. Like Slimane, he is the eldest of his siblings and he ventured on hazardous paths. Like Dorcy, he fights to exist through art. Moreover, since he is himself of 'mixed-race,' he epitomizes Sabrina and Dorcy's future. With a Black Algerian mother of Sudanese origin and an Algerian Arab father, Djaïdani's hybridity is like that of Dorcy and Sabrina's future offspring.

The artist-filmmaker thus created a work that represents the principle of his own existence, his virtual childbirth. As Tarr writes, 'The desire for self-representation can be seen as symptomatic of [the artists'] need for self-affirmation as both social and artistic subjects' (2005: 11). Indeed, Djaïdani's fight stems from a lack of representation – artistic, historical, and political – that his novels attempted to fill to some extent. It is the same fight that he started in a more physical way in the boxing ring. The compulsive and impatient filming technique of his films recalls the boxer's head-on blows and his art of dodging. From a stonemason to a boxer facing his adversary, Djaïdani creates his existence through the art of pitting the particular against the universal.

Notes

1. The term 'Maghrebi-French' as used by Will Higbee refers to 'those French directors of Maghrebi-immigrant origin who were either born in France or moved there at an early age. These directors share this experience of having spent their formative years in France, while also being influenced to varying degrees by the North-African cultural heritage of their parents' (2013: 23). The designation 'Maghrebi-French' avoids the problematic terminology 'second generation of immigrants,' 'beur,' etc. … terms which do not take into account individual life experiences but establish categories based exclusively on generation or ethnic origin. For a discussion of these other terms, see Higbee (2013: 18–19).
2. The so-called *beur* films of the 1980s and the *banlieue* cinema of the 1990s were mainly "social realist narratives," like Rachid Bouchareb's *Bâton rouge* (1985) and Karim Dridi's *Bye-bye* (1995), at times with comic aspects, as in Mehdi Charef's *Le Thé au harem d'Archimède* (1985), the prototype of *beur* cinema. The very end of the 1990s and 2000s, on the contrary, showed a greater diversity in the genres of films shot by Maghrebi-French filmmakers, a change which Higbee analyzes as being one fundamental characteristic of the post-*beur* turning point. In addition to mainstream comedies (Djamel Bensallah, 1999: *Le Ciel, les oiseaux, et … ta mère!*), romantic comedies (Roshdy Zem, 1999: *Mauvaise foi*), action comedies (Zem, 2002: *Le Raïd*), war films (Bouchareb, 2006: *Indigènes*), thrillers (Bouchareb, 2010: *Hors-la-loi*), and historical dramas (Lyes Salem, 2013: *L'Oranais*), Maghrebi-French author-led films were more numerous and varied in genre and topic in the 2000s. Directors like Rabah Ameur-Zaïmeche and Abdellatif Kechiche have since acquired significant visibility – Kechiche being awarded the *Palme d'Or* at the 2013 Cannes Film Festival for *La Vie d'Adèle* (*Blue Is the Warmest Color*), a romantic drama on "white" feminine homosexuality. The English translation is the title of the graphic novel the film is based on.
3. My use of the terms '*beur*' cinema and '*banlieue*' filmmaking draws on Carrie Tarr's (2005: 2–3) definitions of these particular genres.
4. See the 'special features' section (*Compléments*) and the 'Entretien entre Sabrina Hamida et Rachid Djaïdani' on the DVD of *Rengaine*, and Kiner

(2011). In his novel *Viscéral*, Djaïdani recalls that one day his father scolded him for being a drug dealer, even though it was only a role that he had played in a television series. Similarly, his mother received a call from an Algerian relative who expressed her regret that Rachid had married an 'Asian.' In this case also, it was just a film role. The family's confusion between fiction and real life has profoundly influenced Djaïdani's reflection on representation. In his third novel, the main character clearly alludes to this: 'Vous me proposez un dealer en haut d'affiche, demain un rôle d'islamiste terroriste ... C'est ça votre cinéma? Vous les gens du show-biz, vous ne vous rendez pas compte des conséquences de vos histoires' (Today you put me in the limelight, casting me as a drug dealer, tomorrow you'll give me the part of an Islamic terrorist ... Is this your cinema? You show-biz people, you don't realize the consequences of your stories) (Djaïdani, 2007: 105).

5 Djaïdani attributes the lack of success of his second novel to the fact it did not deal with immigrant neighborhoods and he felt he had been typecast as a *cité/banlieue* writer (Kaganski, 2012).

6 The first name 'Dorcy' is uncommon in French and recalls the last name of Jane Austen's hero (Mr. Darcy) in *Pride and Prejudice*. Mr. Darcy's unconventional romanticism and complex love story find an echo in Dorcy and Sabrina's cross-cultural love.

7 As Rachid Djaïdani poetically expresses in the '*Compléments*' (special features) to the film: 'C'est pas la caméra qui bouge, c'est la vie qui bouge' (Think of it as the movement of life, rather than camera movement).

8 See, for example, Mehdi Charef's, *Le Thé au harem d'Archimède* (1985), Rachid Bouchareb's, *Cheb* (1991), and Djamel Bensalah's, *Le Ciel, les oiseaux ... et ta mère!* (1999) (Higbee, 2013: 4).

9 Slimane is probably between 40 and 50 years old. All the actors, except Slimane Dazi (Slimane) and Stéphane Soo Mongo (Dorcy), are Djaïdani's friends or family. This practice is common among directors working with a small budget or no budget at all (Tarr, 2005: 11).

10 The Deleuzian concept of 'ligne de fuite' (line of flight) represents the reaction to a destabilized situation, namely a series of actions – the 'fuite' (flight or escape) – supposed to lead to a new stable 'ground,' or milieu – a process that Deleuze calls a 'reterritorialisation' (reterritorialization) (Deleuze, 1977).

11 I borrow the concept of 'territory' from Deleuze and Guattari, who use it in a number of ways in their work. In my argument, 'territory' defines an original milieu in which a particular *ethos* (guiding values or ideals) is expressed. This ethological sense of 'territory' prevails in Deleuze and Guattari (1972).

12 Deleuze explains that 'territory' is created through the continual process of deterritorialization (that is, decontextualization, separation) and reterritorialization, through which a new coherence is sought. This ethological model hinges on the biological processes of deterritorialization, whereby milieu components are detached and given greater autonomy, and reterritorialization, through which those components acquire new functions within the newly created territory.

13 The elder brother begins his 'flight' toward Place Stalingrad, in the 19th arrondissement. Afterwards, several sequences take place on line 2 of the subway, an elevated line that crosses the northern and eastern arrondissements of the capital. The majority of the remaining shots take place between the 18th arrondissement (Barbès-Rochechouart, Pigalle, Abbesses), the neighboring 10th (the Gare du Nord railway station, the Canal Saint-Martin walkway), and 19th arrondissements (the Ourcq Canal and the Parc des Buttes Chaumont).

14 Although the two lovers are not unemployed, many brothers (including Slimane) seem inactive, and the camera shows them wandering in what looks like a ghetto inside the capital city. Djaïdani shows different fault lines that are somewhat hidden by the opposition *banlieue*/city.

15 Before *Rengaine*, Djaïdani produced a 'web documentary,' titled *Une heure avant la datte*, in which he interviewed Muslims on what Ramadan means to them.

16 There are multiple scenes where Djaïdani shows the paradox of ordinary racism at the heart of Black–Arab friendships. For instance, the violent rejection of the other, who is nonetheless a neighbor and close friend, is visible when the boxer brother hears the news of Sabrina's wedding from Slimane. The boxer feels free to physically express his violence against a punching bag, in the immediate presence of his Black trainer and friend, who overhears the conversation.

17 'Rebeu' and 'renoi' are backslang or *verlan* terms for Arab and Black (*noir*).

18 As Alec Hargreaves explains about Muslim tradition, 'because of the dominant role traditionally attributed to men, marriages between Muslim women and non-Muslim men are strongly discouraged and may not be legally recognized at all [in Islamic countries]. In France, daughters of Muslim immigrants marrying non-Muslims run a much higher risk of being shunned by their families than do sons who take non-Muslim spouses' (2007: 96–7).

19 *Rengaine* draws a subtle link between freedom of thought and social integration within the Republic. The three brothers who oppose Slimane head-on – the mechanic, the inspector, and the gay brother – are those who have built their own life and have a job and a family. This concern with the republican model is a new aspect of Maghrebi-French cinema (Higbee, 2013: 96–129). While opposing the victimary discourse of republican disaffiliation, Djaïdani underlines the share of responsibility of those who lock themselves up in sectarianism. Without denying the structural mechanisms leading to the exclusion of citizens of colonial descent, such as the social reproduction of institutionalized racism, *Rengaine* focuses on the sectarianism of those who are often displayed as victims.

20 It is worth noting that ethnic statistics are prohibited in France as the republican concept of the nation precludes the possibility of considering citizens in terms or ethnicity or religion (Hargreaves, 1995, 2007: 10–11).

21 Backslang for 'Jew' or 'Jewish.'

22 The eldest brother mentions the fact that Slimane never defended him when he was attacked and beaten by homophobic boys at school and that he

is hiding his Jewish girlfriend from his family. In this interesting reversal, Slimane, who first reproached his gay brother with being a 'frangine' (sister) rather than a 'frangin' (brother), now finds himself in the "feminine" position, since he never fought for his brother. Therefore, Slimane is also 'in the closet' (Foerster, 2014: 184).
23 In 2013, a year after *Rengaine* came out, Abdellatif Kechiche's *La vie d'Adèle* brought a lesbian story to the big screen. However, even though the director is Maghrebi-French, his film is not about Muslim or Maghrebi-French identity. Literature and films have nonetheless addressed the topic of Arab or Muslim homosexuality (Foerster, 2014: 189–91).
24 It is very interesting that the gender non-conformity of the series (where the major detective is a female and not a male as 'expected') is established at the cost of racial subservience. It reads as if the disruption of gender and racial clichés cannot go hand in hand.
25 In the special features, Djaïdani mentions the address '23 Rue André Barsac in Paris' as his place of residence. His neighbor is Stéphane Soo Mongo, whose collaboration on the film is due to their 'chance' meeting on this same street.

References

Bhabha, H. (1991). *The Location of Culture*, London/New York: Routledge.
Cadé, M. (2011). 'Hidden Islam: The Role of the Religious in *Beur* and *Banlieue* Cinema,' in S. Durmelat and V. Swamy (eds), *Screening Integration: Recasting Maghrebi Immigration in Contemporary France*, Lincoln, NE/London: University of Nebraska Press, 41–57.
Deleuze, G. and Guattari, F. (1972). *Capitalisme et schizophrénie*, vol. 2, Mille Plateaux, Paris: Minuit.
Deleuze, G. with Parnet, C. (1977). *Dialogue*, Paris: Flammarion.
Deleuze, G. and Guattari, F. (1980). *Mille Plateaux. Capitalisme et Schizophrénie 2*, Paris: Minuit.
Djaïdani, R. (1999). *Boumkoeur*, Paris: Seuil.
Djaïdani, R. (2004). *Mon nerf*, Paris: Seuil.
Djaïdani, R. (2007). *Viscéral*, Paris: Seuil.
Durmelat, S. and Swamy, V. (2011). *Screening Integration: Recasting Maghrebi Immigration in Contemporary France*, Lincoln, NE/London: University of Nebraska Press.
Foerster, M. (2014). 'Mon grand-frère n'a pas de prénom: L'homosexualité maghrébine à l'épreuve de la famille dans *Rengaine*, de Rachid Djaïdani,' *Contemporary French Civilization*, 39(2), 179–95.
Hargreaves, A. G. (2007). *Multi-Ethnic France: Immigration, Politics, Culture and Society*, 2n edn, New York: Routledge.
Higbee, W. (2013). *Post-Beur Cinema: North-African Émigré and Maghrebi-French Filmmaking in France Since 2000*, Edinburgh: Edinburgh University Press.

Kaganski, S. (2012). 'Rachid Djaïdani: "J'aimerais créer un truc qui reste,"' *Les InRocks*, November 15. Web. July 10, 2015.

Kiner, S. (2011). 'Une heure avant la datte. Portrait de Rachid Djaïdani,' *Arte Television Series on Ramadan*. YouTube. Web. July 10, 2015.

Lacoste-Dujardin, C. (2000). 'Maghrebi Families in France,' in J. Freedman and C. Tarr (eds), *Women, Immigration and Identities in France*, Oxford/New York: Berg, 57–68.

Mboungou, V. (2007). 'Rachid Djaïdani, "Viscéral,"' Afrik.com. May 2. Web. June 30, 2015.

Pivot, B. (1999). 'Rachid Djaïdani/Fruit de notre époque,' YouTube. Web. June 28, 2015.

Reeck, L. (2012). 'Lettre ouverte au monde des lettres françaises: *Sur ma ligne* de Rachid Djaïdani,' in I. Vitali (ed.), *Intrangers (I), Post-migration et nouvelles frontières de la littérature beur*, Sefar 2, Paris: L'Harmattan, 47–69.

Regnier, I. (2012). 'La vie sans mode d'emploi,' *Le Monde*, November 13. Web. July 15, 2015.

Rosello, M. (1998). *Declining the Stereotype: Ethnicity and Representation in French Cultures*, Hanover, NH/London: University Press of New England.

Sellah, S. (2012). 'L'Expression de la réclusion dans l'œuvre de Rachid Djaïdani,' in N. Redouane (ed.), *Où en est la literature beur?* Paris: L'Harmattan, 137–51.

Soo Mongo, S. (2015). 'Annonce de casting raciste: Acteur et noir, on m'a dit que j'étais "difficile à éclairer,"' March 25. *L'Obs. Le Plus*. Web. July 10, 2015.

Tarr, C. (2005). *Reframing Difference: Beur and Banlieue Filmmaking in France*, Manchester: Manchester University Press.

Filmography

Djaïdani, R. (2012). *Rengaine*. Haut et Court.

6

Beur and *banlieue* television comedies: new perspectives on immigration

Caroline Fache

On July 17, 2013, *Paris à tout prix* (Kherici, 2013), a comedy about immigration, was released and received mixed reviews, despite decent numbers at the box office. Two days later in *L'Express*, journalist and movie critic Xavier Leherpeur assessed the production of French films about immigration in an article titled 'L'immigration dans le cinéma français: un bilan mitigé' (2013) (Immigration in French cinema: mixed reviews). In his review, Leherpeur also analyzes 'la manière dont le cinéma français aborde l'immigration,' (the way in which French cinema addresses the issue of immigration) and eventually wonders what cinematic genre is best suited to represent immigration. On the one hand, as Leherpeur deplores, most comedies that deal primarily with immigration too often fall into 'clichés mielleux et consensuels' (easy and consensual clichés). On the other hand, comedy seems to be the ideal film genre to deal with polemical and divisive topics such as immigration and cultural differences: 'Populaire par principe, fédératrice par définition et optimiste par nature' (popular by principle, unifying by definition, optimistic by nature), it downplays the immigrant's tragic condition and resolves conflicts in a burst of laughter. Some directors explore the comedy genre in more critical and creative, albeit darker ways, like Aki Kaurismäki with his powerful film *Le Havre* (2011), a retro-provincial bittersweet comedy, in which an older man encounters a young illegal immigrant. Similarly, Mohamed Hamidi disrupts the easy clichés and turns of comedy in *Né quelque part* (2013), in which he reverses the perspective on migrations by sending the main character back to his homeland. Leherpeur eventually wonders if comedies do serve the immigrant's cause and if, after all, drama and documentary are not the only engaging and appropriate modes of expression.

The same question may be asked about the TV productions of the last ten years since, according to the box office and the *audimat* (audience ratings) for the Paysage Audiovisuel Français (or PAF, to designate French broadcasting in general), comedies about immigration, or produced by immigrants and their descendants, are thriving. Blockbuster comedies about the *banlieues*, immigration, or children of immigrants, such as *Les Kaira* (Gastampide, 2012), which had more than one million viewers, the pilot of the TV film series *Aïcha* (Benguigui, 2008), which set a record with more than five million viewers, and the TV movie pilot of *Fortunes* (Meunier and Cohen, 2011) show that the French audience is fond of this genre. In order to join in with this popular trend, respond to audience expectations, and satisfy political expectations (such as the equal opportunity law of 2006),[1] two public TV channels, France 2 and Arte, commissioned films about immigration in 2008. Both pilots were audience rating tests that confirmed a public desire to see more minorities on-screen, and the ensuing projects materialized respectively into two TV series: *Aïcha*, directed by Yamina Benguigui (four TV movies, including the pilot) which was broadcast between 2008 and 2011, and *Fortunes* by Stéphane Meunier (one season of eight episodes preceded by a TV movie pilot codirected by Bertrand Cohen), which aired in 2011–12.

In *Aïcha*, Benguigui introduces us to Aïcha Bouamazza, who, just like her brothers, sisters, and cousins, dreams of leaving the *cité* (or *banlieue* housing project) where she lives with her family and reach across the *Périphérique*, the Paris beltline. Meunier focuses his series *Fortunes* on Brahim Béchéri, a young real estate agent, who is trying to build his own business in the city of Tours, with his best friends' help. The two series were broadcast over the same period of time on public channels and introduce two distinct groups of youth, young women in one and young men in the other. Yet the characters are approximately the same age and their parents have all emigrated from the Maghreb. The lens through which French society is viewed and depicted makes both series particularly innovative. Indeed, the characters are no longer mere objects of study or powerless witnesses of the misery associated with immigration, but rather they are critical and active agents in their society.

This chapter proposes to address Leherpeur's concerns and to analyze whether or not TV comedies do serve the cause of the immigrants and people linked to immigration, what strategies are used to tackle the issue, and finally how they contribute to the representation of minorities on the PAF. Although post-*beur*[2] and *immigré* filmmaking is a field ever expanding and increasingly mainstream as demonstrated by Will Higbee's *Post-Beur Cinema: North-African Émigré and Maghrebi-French Filmmaking in France Since 2000*, few studies look at TV series, which are in fact a privileged window into the *immigré* world for a great number of people living in France (Blion et al., 2006: 101). Higbee reviews in depth the works of prominent directors such as Bouchareb, Bensala, and Allouache, but like other studies, he does not take into account TV visibility, although he includes the questions of production, reception, and distribution, and therefore visibility and access. My chapter takes a new perspective onscreen representations of immigrants and minorities because it focuses specifically on more popular forms of depictions such as TV films and TV series that commit to the lighter tone of comedy. Despite harsh critiques on these productions, I posit that they offer an alternative depiction of minority youth of North African descent because they move away from the stereotypical figure of the 'tragic immigrant' and that they are particularly meaningful, since public television remains the most popular and accessible media in France. This alternative representation is supported not only by each director's choice of characters and plots but also by their preference for the comic genre over drama and documentary and by the channels' political decision to produce and broadcast such programs. The two productions and the portrayal of the characters undoubtedly participate in the politics of representation (content and forms) and representativeness (numbers and visibility) of minorities on TV, as defined in the report on media representation of immigrants (Blion et al., 2006) by the national antidiscrimination agency called Fonds d'Action et de Soutien pour l'Intégration et la Lutte contre les Discriminations (FASILD).[3] I will first introduce the production and reception contexts of the TV series and clarify why choosing comedy increases the representativeness of minorities. Next, I will study the aesthetic strategies deployed to represent children of immigrants and their universe and show how these strategies transform the spectator's gaze. Finally, I will examine the strengths and limitations of the political and aesthetic strategies at stake and reposition them within the relevant televisual context.

Representation and representativeness in Aïcha and Fortunes

With Yamina Benguigui as a director, backed by her renown as an acclaimed filmmaker and by her fame as deputy mayor of Paris (2008–12) advocating for human rights and against discrimination, *Aïcha* was a sure success. In fact, it is certainly because of Benguigui's popularity and experience that in 2008, France 2 commissioned her to shoot a prime-time television film about immigration in today's French society. Thus, Benguigui filmed a *banlieue* comedy titled *Aïcha*, which focuses on a young woman living in the low-income housing neighborhood of Seine-Saint-Denis, north of Paris. As Carrie Tarr explains, *banlieue* film was an emerging genre in the 1990s, characterized by its organization around a specific space and resisting the negative general public perception and control of that space (2005: 13–19). The contested notions of *beur* v. *banlieue*, and the roles and categorization of members of the various communities they designate complicate the debate. Since the two terms are ethnically and geographically charged, they often limit the scope of Maghrebi-French representations and confine them to stagnant images (Hargreaves, 1999: 115–18). For the purpose of this study, I will use *banlieue* as a term referring to the space and communities ghettoized by their marginal status as underprivileged and underrepresented groups. The

Aïcha series can thus be considered to belong to the *banlieue* comedy genre because of its location, its classic happy ending, and the director's light and funny approach.

The *Aïcha* pilot tells the struggle of Aïcha Boumazza, the eldest daughter of the family, to leave her *cité* in order to fulfill her professional and personal dreams across the *périph'* while compromising with family and community expectations. Whereas her parents came from Algeria, Aïcha, her siblings, and cousins were all born in France. Some of them have had great success in their studies despite the typical difficulties they encountered as youths from the *cités* with immigrant parents. Even though the film uses timeworn clichés of the *banlieue* and of Maghrebi families (authoritarian father, run-down buildings, etc.), it nevertheless throws a different gaze onto the *banlieue* space, insofar as it is seen through the eyes of a strong-willed, optimistic, and open-minded young woman who embraces some stereotypical behaviors and rejects others. She is supported and challenged by her mother and her aunt, the noteworthy comical duet formed by the famous Rabbia Mokkedem and Baya Bouzar, known as Biyouna. The first scene of the film immediately foreshadows the intent to reverse the perspective on the *banlieues* since it ends on a shot of Aïcha, holding a camera and snapping a picture of the viewer after briefly introducing the women in her close family. The following establishing shot which constitutes the opening credits shows the beltway linking Paris to the suburbs, the housing projects where the Bouamazza family lives, and the disrepair of the buildings and neighborhood. Broadcast on May 31, 2009, *Aïcha* set the year's record for the public channel.

Following the success of the first *Aïcha* film, France 2 ordered three more episodes to constitute a series of four films between 2008 and 2012. The other three episodes follow the same pattern in which Aïcha overcomes obstacles and troubles in order to carry out professional, sentimental, family, and community projects. For instance, in *Aïcha, un job à tout prix* (episode 2), the young woman starts a career and tries to protect her job in the *banlieue* branch of a big Parisian fashion company, all the while putting out fires started by her cousin in the *cité*. The third episode, *Aïcha, la grande débrouille*, takes Aïcha on a mission to save from demolition the building in which her family lives, and the last episode to date sends her and her family on vacation in *Arcachon*, a small beach town in France, far from their usual Algerian summer vacations.

During the same time period, *Fortunes* appeared in a similar context, after the Arte channel commissioned a TV film, whose success also generated the commission of the subsequent TV series. Unlike *Aïcha*, the *Fortunes* series is characterized by its critical acclaim, its relative success with the viewers, and a premature cancelation. Indeed, the film received the award for best first fiction script at the Prix Europa festival in Berlin and the TV5 Monde award for best francophone film at the Festival International Cinéma Tous Ecrans de Genève in 2008, while the series received the jury prize at the Grand Prix RTL des Séries in 2012. According to Médiamétrie (French audience-ratings agency), the film was seen by over a million spectators the first time it aired on Arte and by 2.4 million viewers for its second broadcast on France 2, and the series was followed by an average 150,000 per episode on TV (Arte) and 75,000 online (Video on Demand), except for the last episode, seen by fewer than 90,000 viewers. Its trajectory is therefore different from *Aïcha*'s, which received harsher critiques, but whose audience rating success is unquestionable. Yet, *Fortunes* offers a representation of young descendants of immigrants who are both mainstream and more alternative than the people observed by Carrie Tarr (2005) or Edouard Mills-Affif (2004). Both series cease to conform to France's stereotypical views on the immigration 'issue.' In fact, they reposition their characters and plots on society's margin, which is defined as an active and productive periphery, foregrounding characters who strive to make economic and social contributions on a local, national, and global scale.

As Jonathan Ervine explains in *Cinema and the Republic*:

[T]elevision channels play a major role in supporting film production in France and have helped to fund several of the works studied here. French television culture is very important when it comes to how immigrants and *banlieue* residents are represented in the media. Certain films analysed here criticise television for its failings (for example, Christophe-Emmanuel Del Debbio's *Banlieues: sous le feu des médias*) whilst others demonstrate that it is also a medium by which it is possible to correct or challenge stereotypical discourses (for example, Philippe Triboit's *L'Embrasement* and Hugues Demeude's *93: l'Effervescence*). (2013: 4)

Even though French television culture has existed for a long time, TV channels activities have taken a new direction in France as in the rest of the world, since they have diversified their interests and now have tremendous impact on all film production. Consequently, TV productions should not be overlooked, in particular at a time when TV films and series dominate the audience ratings and influence the viewers' choices and tastes, as François Sauvagnargues, the director of Arte's fiction programs from 2003 to 2011, fully knew. Still, there are few prime-time TV series whose main focus is immigration or characters linked to immigration, even though other series address the topic of immigration using a more traditional format like the documentary. *Le choix de Myriam* by Malik Chibane (2009) and *On n'est pas des marques de vélo* (2003) by Jean-Pierre Thorn, respectively broach well-known topics such as single-parent families, delinquency, and drugs, and then salvation through art, hip-hop precisely, in a very serious manner.

Whereas France 2 prudently ordered only one TV movie from a well-known director and then three more once the pilot proved to be extremely successful, Arte's commissioning, programming, and eventual discontinuing of the series *Fortunes* constitute a problematic and even dangerous political move. Any artistic expression in the postcolonial realm represents a political statement, which can be subjected to various interpretations, as a desire to put diversity on a long-term, deep TV footing or a mere wish to increase the audience ratings in the context of the serial battle among the channels of the PAF. The channels' programming choices reflect an economic and social reality, whose pendants are discrimination and a certain form of censorship to silence unsettling voices, as Pierre Bourdieu deplores in his 'intervention' on television (Bourdieu, 2008: 14). In an article for *Slate*, Pierre Langlais quotes François Sauvagnargues incidentally acknowledging that Arte's series selection is aimed at an older audience, because 'notre public est plutôt soixantenaire, et il préfère les unitaires' (Langlais, 2010) (our viewers are mostly in their sixties and they prefer TV films to series). The Arte program director then concedes that his goal was to cast a broader net and reach a different type of spectators, and he states that he wanted to disrupt traditions and 'aller vers les univers les plus décalés et inattendus possible' (2) (move toward the edgiest and most unexpected spheres). Sauvagnargues' intent was therefore to break away from the usual and reductive images of immigration and the *banlieue*, made up of bloody battlefields, neighborhoods that are ablaze, and miserable and depressed housing projects.

It seems that Arte took a risk with a TV format (the TV series) that depends on continued and loyal viewership, a choice revealing a certain awareness that minorities are a long-term and important audience. France 2, however, made sure that minorities were a low-risk investment and with the format chosen (independent TV films) for *Aïcha*, it is understandable that the film series would only count a limited number of episodes. One is compelled to question the limited impact of *Aïcha* as a social phenomenon. The real but limited and disposable presence of minorities on-screen reproduces the erroneous idea of the immigrant as a transient guest, and that of a marginal population who plays a peripheral and secondary role in French society. Yet, Aïcha, Brahim, and their peers relentlessly repeat that they too are French, implying that they belong to French society and are not going anywhere. They too claim their right to belong and succeed in France, and affirm their status as citizens in their own right. Meanwhile, *Aïcha* and *Fortunes* also fulfill their primary mission to represent and contribute to the visibility of minorities on mainstream and public French broadcasting. Despite difficulties and issues in programming and deprogramming the series, France 2 and Arte's courage is remarkable, as few channels commit to showing such programs. Both channels did not solely rely on audience-driven, money-making shows but engaged in meaningful, potentially impactful, and socially responsible programming. They were the only ones taking the risk of presenting prime-time series about children of immigrants who are neither troubled nor threatening, but, rather, embody the richness of diversity against a credible and realistic background.

Edouard Mills-Affif demonstrates that immigration and any related topic are mostly presented in documentaries or reportage-type programs. In an inventory of more than 5,000 programs of all kinds from the mid 1980s onwards, he notes that between 1981 and 2003, only two TV films dealing with immigration can be found, which correspond to the comedy-drama genre rather than to drama per se (Mills-Affif, 2004: 7). The shift from the big to the small screen can be explained in part by the televisual renaissance that started in the new millennium and is driven by powerful TV networks, which invested abundant resources in high-quality series and created sustained loyalty and dependency among a very broad and diverse audience. The shift toward comedy is justified by blockbuster successes and by the need to explore ever newer, edgier modes of expression, and go against the grain of the typical tragic climate shrouding the issue of immigration. Comedies about immigration, such as *Aïcha* and *Fortunes*, though they take place in different urban contexts, fulfill the three functions identified by Xavier Leherpeur, namely, provoking laughter, conjuring up a sense of unity and optimism, and addressing serious questions.

If social misery (unemployment, lack of job security, precarious housing, racial and sexual discrimination, and violence) still prevails in the low-income housing projects around large and medium-sized French cities, directors of supposedly 'light' comedies displace both topic and locus. *Fortunes* is set in the "province," more precisely in Tours, while for *Aïcha*, social and geographical mobility and the subsequent relocation define the context of the story. The films are no longer just about watching the French suburb inhabitants struggling in their prescribed environment, but about uncovering their dreams and resources and reaching universal dreams. These films depart from a certain pessimism associated with immigration, which Alec Hargreaves evokes in 'No escape? From the "cinéma beur" to the "cinéma de la banlieue"' (1999); yet, they do not single out children of immigration or restrict them to the sticky *beur, banlieue*, and second-generation immigrant identity (119). The series' directors stress the importance of the ambitious and entrepreneurial individual who crosses national borders to reach the global market. For instance, in *Fortunes*, Brahim's business endeavors take him to Lebanon to negotiate with a Russian businessman in charge of an Emir's European accounts. He breaks free of the national social constraints and takes part in the global economy. His ethnicity is no longer the only defining social marker, but his ability to navigate between different cultures and find common ground becomes an essential asset for international business. If anything, international exposure and commercial success remain a challenge for directors and producers since a significant number of spectators can be found abroad in francophone spaces. Border-crossing characters reflect the filmmakers' awareness that their themes and France's productions must look beyond national boundaries to be relevant in today's world.

Transforming the gaze: aesthetics and comic strategies

In order to touch upon universal themes, *Fortunes*' director chose a rather simple plot: four friends are dreaming of making a fortune. The prequel to the series, an independent television movie released in 2008 where the spectator meets Brahim, his friends and girlfriend, was so successful that it was followed by an eight-episode series. It concentrates on the blooming romance between Brahim and Héléna and the difficulties they encounter as a mixed couple while following Brahim, his brother Fathi, and their two best friends, Driss and Mike, in their unsuccessful yet continuous efforts to run Brahim's real estate office and become rich. Brahim, who comes from a Muslim family, and his girlfriend Helena, whose mother is a devout Portuguese Catholic, recently had a son called 'François-Francisco-Farid,' a name that catalyzes the tensions between the various communities involved. The major contrast between the film and the series concerns the backdrop of the show, which shifts from the Brahim–Helena romance to the professional ploys of the group of friends. When Brahim's office finally signs its first major contract, a fierce Chinese competitor, Nicolas Chen, opens an office right across the street. The four associates quickly understand that they must overcome the administrative irregularities and skullduggeries from the town hall, which jeopardize the building permit for the plot of land in which Brahim has invested everything.

To allow the viewer to identify more easily with the characters in *Fortunes*, Meunier shifts into a semi-alternate universe and transports the viewer into the protagonists' fantasies. On-screen, this translates into a particular esthetic process meant to capture the characters' environment and to break with stereotypical characterization of young Maghrebi men, since all four friends are always shown wearing formal business attire. Furthermore, violence, which used to plague *banlieue* films, does not take place in France but abroad or in Brahim's imagination.

The treatment of violence in *Aïcha* is graver, since there is a clear difference between the suburbs of large French cities and those of smaller towns. In *Aïcha*, suburban blight and economic difficulties are exacerbated because of overcrowding, transportation issues, and lack of privacy in the *cité*, to which Aïcha refers as 'prison,' while in *Fortunes*, the male characters move about easily, do not depend on public transport, and travel regularly to the nearby countryside to buy land. Images of roads and metaphors of paths to success are expressed in similar ways in both series. However, the pace and markers that define the routes contrast with one another: slow and sinuous for Aïcha, and fast, open, and direct for Brahim, as he drives through a small town called 'Monnaie' (money) on his way to a business deal.

As stated in the title, *Fortunes* is about Brahim and his peers' great ambitions and dreams, but it is also about luck and wealth. The opening credits are carefully designed to convey the spirit of the series and thus start with a bird's-eye shot of Tours. This wide-angle aerial shot, which translates the protagonists' freedom and ambition, is intensified by the subjective camera mimicking the gaze of a bird of prey (sharp focus in the center and blurry contours): the characters have a specific goal and they will chase it methodically. The sense of freedom and dream is further supported by the ethereal and atmospheric soundtrack *For Agent 13* performed by Montreal band the Besnard Lakes. After a few seconds, the viewer realizes that the landscape shown is in fact a miniature-scale model of Tours, over which the title *Fortunes* appears, placed like a Monopoly pawn. The setting and themes are then set: a bid for wealth and achievement, for which one must take risk and sometimes wager just as one would when playing Monopoly. The opening credits ends with the four silhouettes, in dark suits, standing still on €500 bank notes, the letters OR of the title word lighting up in gold over the four individuals. The credits' scene comes to a full stop on the beeps and chimes of a slot machine. The spectator thus enters a world more or less coded by the characters' fantasy. This is also a transition to a dream world that allows for the characters' escape from reality, and consequently from social pressure and anxiety. The spectator enters this alternate universe with the characters and together they navigate unfamiliar spaces. In turn, this shared experience creates more empathy in the audience (Hargreaves, 1999: 122).

In *Aïcha*, rhinestones illuminate the title at the beginning of the opening credits, informing the spectator of the heroine's vocation since she is committing herself to a career in fashion. In both cases, the titles shine like their protagonists, who are full of promise, a cliché directly inherited from American soap operas. Nevertheless, Benguigui maintains a shadow of ambiguity over Aïcha's future since the credits, filmed in natural light (blue hue) and under a mantle of clouds, render a weighty atmosphere and view of the *cité* and Paris *périph'* (beltway), as seen from the Bouamazzas' kitchen window. The shot composition is both busy and static at the same time. In addition, apartment buildings rise before Aïcha's eyes, potentially blocking her view onto greener pastures. The character's heavy longing is abruptly interrupted with the contrasting loud and fast-paced breakfast at the Bouamazzas, in the bright green, tiny kitchen, in which Aïcha and her siblings move gracefully, twirling around one another. While they are eating, the father instructs Aïcha, her brother, who, according to his mother, goes to the 'Ministers' school,' and her sister, an amateur boxer, to come back home on time. Their little morning routine continues on a happy note as the father leaves for work and a neighbor arrives to help Madame Bouamazza to study for her driver's license test that she has failed countless times.

Shifting into a world whose references are no longer only contained within French boundaries allows Meunier's characters to move away from long-standing stereotypes like the idea that minorities have no other choice than stay in the projects, or have their referential universe defined by traditional French and North African cultures. Their quest for success is a rejection of the idea that children of immigrants are bound to integrate the lower social classes of French society. It also reflects reality since many French youths of African descent dream of leaving France to live the American dream. Brahim and his associates identify with the anti-heroes who have made an impact on them in their youth: the characters in *Reservoir Dogs* (1992) and *Pulp Fiction* (1994) from Quentin Tarantino's cinematic universe. They create an imagined community by mimicking and quoting their heroes, but they do not engage in political acts as the supranational communities described by Benedict Anderson do (2006).[4] In fact, their community is based on ideals and projections that are not founded on any common background or origin. There is therefore no sense of duty to a community outside their close group. The opening scene is a great intertextual homage to the American director's work: the four friends are standing in front of the city hall on the lookout for the employee who counterfeited their building permit application. The second episode's plot and title 'Reservoir Pulp,' confirm the reference: as the director recreates scenes from *Pulp Fiction*, the characters wear dark suits and remind the viewers of the hatchet men in *Reservoir dogs* (Mr. Pink, Mr. White, Mr. Black, etc.) and of even more emblematic characters like Vincent Vega (played by John Travolta) and Jules Winnfield (played by Samuel L. Jackson). The tone is set. The awkward team gets entangled in comical situations but adheres to a code of conduct that is as improvised as it is fleeting, except for the infallible loyalty and friendship they maintain within the group. *Fortunes*' director expands his references to American crime comedies directly and indirectly, using medium shots and American shots and skillfully playing with depth of field. He also relies on another important referential element, namely the soundtrack, which is cleverly composed of tracks such as Galt MacDermot's theme song 'Coffee Cold' from the famous film *The Thomas Crown Affair* (1968) and the more recent *What Have You Done?* by Naomi Shelton and the Gospel Queens (2009).

Intertextuality is also woven into the script. Leaning on Linda Hutcheon's *A Theory of Parody: The Teachings of Twentieth-Century Art Forms* (2000), I posit that, using intertextual and perhaps hypertextual references, the director and scriptwriters actively and deliberately encrypt image and sound as a form of self-derisory and critical mimicry. The opening credits, for instance, contain a direct reference to *Reservoir Dogs*' official film poster as an inverted image, where the standing protagonists are shot from the back, their shadows clearly delineated in front of them. Many spectators in their thirties and forties understand the nods to Tarantino's works, since they are generational pieces. Consequently, it allows a wide audience to identify with the characters through a referential universe they share as a generation and across French divides.

In *La Haine* (1995), Matthieu Kassovitz had already used references to American gangsters. One of his three protagonists, Vinz, looking at the mirror, asks repeatedly: "are you talking to me?" before pretending to draw a gun and pull the trigger. This is a direct reference to Martin Scorsese's *Taxi Driver* (1976), in which Robert De Niro's character, a mentally unstable Vietnam veteran working as a taxi driver in New York, was practicing the same dialogue in his apartment before drawing a real gun out of his sleeve. The characters in *Fortunes* look nothing like the protagonists in *La Haine*, but they share the same fascination for American gangsters. Brahim and his friends who indulge in activities that are borderline illegal, do so with enough distance or childish naivety to take on the role of their favorite American movie gangsters. Unlike Vinz, they see themselves as businessmen whose seriousness is performed through their perfect business attires, their elocution, and the way they carry business with an action plan, organized offices, and meetings. In so doing, they distance themselves from the stereotypical presumed offenders portrayed in *La Haine* and undermine the stereotype by choosing the type of "elegant" gangsters they want to be. The mimicry is critical in the sense that the four friends strive to remain within legal boundaries, and never commit a violent crime or even engage in physical altercation.

The car scene (season 1, episode 1) captures a dialogue between Driss and Mike, filmed in medium and close-up shots reminiscent of *Pulp Fiction*'s emblematic scene. In Tarantino's film, Vincent Vega and Jules Winnfield casually compare and contrast McDonald's sandwiches in France and in the US, as they are driving toward the apartment where they are going to kill their next contract. Similarly, in *Fortunes*, Driss and Mike are on a stakeout for the man who jeopardized their real estate deal. They discuss the strategies Driss employs to seduce more women, which leads Mike to advise Driss to improve his pronunciation of vowel sounds: /nikola/for Mike v. /nikulɒ/for instance. Mike's criticism stems from Driss' inquiry on how to attract more bourgeois women, whom his accent might repulse. After schooling him briefly and disagreeing, Mike concludes: 'Tu l'as bien dit bâtard, tu vois!' (See, you said it right, bastard). The comic effect comes from the discrepancy between the situation, the dialogue, and the ridiculous conclusion that negates the original intent: Driss wants to sound more eloquent by erasing pronunciation markers, but he does so by pronouncing profanity properly. Eventually, the targeted man leaves the city hall, and all four friends start chasing the employee. Whereas they seemed rather methodical in their close surveillance, their organization shatters once they begin to argue, push and slap each other, to establish who will catch the prey. The camera shifts from a static shot to a handheld motion that follows the pursuit, reinforcing the impression of chaos and including the spectator in the action. When the viewer expects an increase in violence with the next scene focusing on the employee bound head and foot, the rhythm is yet again disrupted with text appearing on the screen in the manner of a typewriter. Its casual language undermines the dramatic intensity of the scene: 'Le mec de la mairie' (the dude from the city hall). Unpredictability and discrepancies between speech and image, between image and subject, and between subject and linguistic register provide comic effects and subtly question caricatured categories too often imposed on characters like Brahim and his friends.

Benguigui does not break with comic traditions about Maghrebi characters, but comic effects also often come from the dialogues in her four films and from the interactions between Aïcha's mother and other women, including her aunt, Biyouna. On the one hand, Mrs. Bouamazza overtly expresses her prejudice on all sorts of society topics, including recent popular xenophobic concerns: 'En tout cas, moi, je veux être relogée qu'avec les Français, ni avec les Arabes, ni avec les Africains ... Je veux choisir mes voisins!' (episode 1) (In any case, I only want to be rehoused among French folks, not Arabs, nor Africans ... I want to be able to choose my neighbors!). On the other, Biyouna, a more tolerant and progressive woman, makes incisive remarks on the condition of women, the projects' residents, and she always contributes most improbable anecdotes on her past encounters. Among her friends, she names Bernard Montiel (episode 1), a favorite TV presenter among people her own age, and some man called Ionesco (episode 2). 'Ionesco' happens to be her former Romani lover who wrote her love poems and is a homonym of the famous French-Romanian author. Mistakes on names and Biyouna's mixing of reality and fantasy provoke the viewer's continuous wonder and laughter. The dynamic between both sisters triggers laughter because they represent the classic comedy duet based on opposite personalities, who remain complementary and united.

In fact, comedy unites through laughter because the audience experiences an emotion at the same time as the characters, which creates a sort of bonding complicity between the spectator and the characters (Bergson, 1914: 132–71). In both series, the characters joke, laugh, and hear aberrations about themselves. Aïcha smiles knowingly at the camera, when she understands the irony of a double-entendre situation, as when her father tells her that he will not let her marry a man who fears circumcision, while she knows he is only performing the role of the very traditional father to scare her unofficial boyfriend, Patrick. Moments later, Patrick, a non-Muslim, faints after hearing the description of the cutting procedure. In *Fortunes*, the discrepancy is between the intensity of the abduction scene and Driss' question, when he wonders why the victim's name is Nicolas. Nicolas argues that: 'De toute façon les Arabes ici en France, y'en a que pour vous! Vous êtes partout, dans les banlieues, dans les boulangeries, dans les épiceries. Même à la télé, on ne voit que vous!' (You Arabs get all the attention around here in France, you are everywhere, in the *banlieues*, in the bakeries, in the grocery stores. Even on TV, it's all about you!). Nicolas expresses an obvious irritation vis-à-vis his invisibility and the lack of interest for the Asian community. Brahim and his friends pause and burst out laughing, stunned by the resentment their favored position brings about. They identify with the '*Beurs*,' the 'Arabs,' and, more generally, with youths of immigrant origins (including Mike through his status as a stigmatized minority, negatively represented in the media).[5] It is inconceivable to them that another group would consider that they are overrepresented and that their situation could be enviable. Here, the director speaks to the fact that North Africans have gained visibility on the televisual landscape (FASILD), and that their presence is greater than it was; however one must not forget other minorities, which remain invisible in the French media. Besides, if some minorities are now visible, their presence is still rather rare in certain venues and genres, and they remain attached to the "issue" or "problems" of immigration, therefore continually associated with serious and tragic expressions.

Comic success rests on the audience's sympathy toward the characters. Both protagonists dream intensely. Brahim's nights are animated by phantasmal nightmares, while Aïcha daydreams, expressing her superstitions and wishes, in the hope they will be fulfilled by destiny. The characters' dreaminess and determination make them all the more likeable in the eyes of the spectator. However, most comical effects depend on the characters who interact with them.

Lisa, Aïcha's best friend, who cannot help eating large quantities of North African treats, embodies an uncanny clumsiness and naivety that make the spectator smile. Brahim's friends are full of surprises. Fathi, Brahim's elder brother, has a fiery temperament and keeps changing jobs, both because of his lack of professionalism and due to an affair with his boss' wife. Driss, Brahim's childhood friend, sometimes simple-minded and uncouth, sometimes brilliant, supports his friends and tries to break away from his very traditional family, who is pressuring him to get married. Mike, the 'Gypsy' friend who just got out of prison, is a clever and voluble smooth talker. Driss provides a perfect example of endless disruption and surprise in a character. After sabotaging one of Brahim's real estate opportunities by jumping in a grave during a funeral, Driss aggravates the situation when he promises a client that he and his associates will produce organic cheese. The farmer will be able to taste the bogus cheese before closing the deal on the farmland that Brahim wants to buy to build a housing development. When Brahim scolds him and inquires how he intends to bring this new project to life, Driss announces that he will go to the multimedia library. The discrepancy between the seriousness of the situation and Driss' infantile solution contributes to soften the characters' image and invites the spectator to laugh with and at the characters. In turn, this helps to relieve some of the tension that exists between immigrants' descendants and the other French communities.

Conflict does not stem from an identity crisis or from a clash with French society because of the marginalization of the immigrant population, but rather from structural problems which any citizen may be facing: the slowness of bureaucracy, pathetic bribes in the back rooms of the city hall, etc. Despite the issues, comedy provides a resolution to the main conflicts through laughter, and the proposed solutions are often more ridiculous than the original problems. In the first episode of *Fortunes*, after losing the deal on the building land, Brahim's next move is to sell an old castle to an Arab emir. Although the plan fails, the new client invites him and his associates to Lebanon to work on plans for a luxurious city. Once again, the deal fails, and as an amicable solution to the tricky situation, Brahim and his associates offer to find a great striker for the Emir's soccer team in exchange for a construction project in Argentina. The outlandish imbroglio continually morphs into a more problematic situation, yet the level of optimism, supported by promises of greater profit, remains undiluted.

Meunier's comedic strategy lies on repeatedly placing his characters in impossible and ridiculous situations. In the TV movie for example, the last solution to help fund the real estate agency consists in providing the Muslim community in Tours with sheep for Eid al-Kabir. With no experience in sheep keeping, Driss, Brahim, and Mike let the flock escape from the backyard in which the slaughtering is to happen. Although some of these comic effects resort to easy tricks, they still work in their respective contexts, because the strategies, rooted in French culture and humor, satisfy the spectators on the whole.

Comedy's strength and limitations in representing minorities

Although the audience ratings give us an idea of the series' success, one must also analyze the critical reception both among professional and amateur spectators. Yet it is important to remain cautious because if the audience ratings for *Aïcha* have set records, critiques were also harsher than those for *Fortunes*. The most positive reviews applaud the actors' comic performances in both series, by Sofia Essaïdi (as Aïcha) and Rabbia Mokkedem (as Biyouna) in *Aïcha* and by Salim Kechiouche (as Brahim) and Arnaud Ducret (as Mike) in *Fortunes*. Others praise the light and funny tone used to depict North African families, while the most negative ones relate to the use of clichés about the Maghrebi community, Muslims, and *banlieue* in France and dismiss the comedy genre altogether. On the *Mediapart* blog and in the television column of *Télérama*, critic Madjid Messaoudene calls the *Aïcha* series an embarrassment because the plot is very simplistic and uses gross coincidences. He criticizes the stereotypical, conservative, and even backward portrayal of the North African parents and the offensive clichés about the Gypsy community. Indeed, the Bouamazza parents refuse to let Aïcha date a non-Muslim man, while Ionesco, Biyouna's former Romani lover, is covered in jewels and bares a gold-ridden smile. This criticism is echoed by amateurs on the *AlloCiné* and *SensCritique* websites.

The criticisms are valid, but exaggeration and stereotypes are also part of comedy's structure. The suburb filmed in *Aïcha* is simulated, as much as the universe created in *Fortunes*, because the locations only display what is acceptable and useful to the plot. They appear unrealistically sanitized or disordered: there is relatively little cultural mixing, since immigrant communities (West and North African, Asian), and other minority communities (people of color from Guadeloupe, Gypsy) seem able to avoid all meaningful contact with other groups. They only interact with outsiders in forced and orchestrated contexts, as is the case during the awkward encounters between the protagonists' and their partners' families. These scenes, like the media discourse to which Bourdieu refers in his work, 'do things, generate fantasies, fears, phobias, or simply false representations' (2008: 8). Meunier's and Benguigui's depiction of an integrated community – it is integrated since it is aware of the stereotypes it is subject to – is harmful because it confines this population to an extreme communautarism that is not realistic. It seems, however, that the critics read Benguigui's and Meunier's works without taking into account the directors' intent to popularize minorities on-screen and the politics of production that drive the series programming.

As a matter of fact, one must credit both directors for their purposeful use of stereotypes, their sense of irony and various layers of humor, which can satisfy different types of audiences, including insiders,[6] and conjure up the idea of transnationalism and globalization. A good example is the first name Brahim and Héléna choose for their son, François, which is one of the most emblematic first names in French. This generates some tension between the two families since they have different origins. Each one claims the child as an heir to their culture, with Brahim's family choosing to call the child Farid, with Héléna deciding on Francisco. Transnational exchange is also manifest in Brahim and his associates' international business deals when they negotiate with a Saudi emir via his Russian middleman, and they travel beyond national borders. Their ability to navigate between different spheres allows them not to be confined to the *banlieues* like Vinz, Saïd, and Hub in *La Haine*, to travel outside of the locus attributed to Maghrebi youth in France, and to conduct business in Lebanon and Argentina.

As far as Benguigui's use of stereotypes is concerned, Aïcha's eccentric boss, Albane Granger, is not just a ridiculous character, but rather she is the protean caricature of the French upper-class socialite, who does not understand the world around her. Her character is so overloaded – she wears a patchwork of ethnic clothes, mispronounces foreign names when she name-drops, etc. – that the spectator must understand she embodies cultural ignorance and outrageous consumerism, and her contributions (like most of her lines) are ultimately superfluous and barren. Whereas Albane Granger fails in her attempts at cosmopolitanism and multiculturalism because she does not experience diverse cultures but consumes them, the youths and other characters like the mothers in *Aïcha* are much more composite characters who differ in their ability to contribute not only to the culture in which they live but also the global scene.

Aïcha discovers that women in her mother's generation were very familiar with Angela Davis, a symbolic figure of American civil rights activism. At first, Aicha is surprised at the feminist thread that brings together women of different origins and contexts, whom she believed to be completely disconnected from one another. Her mother and aunt even shared with Angela Davis a transnational moment of historical significance, as they were protesting during the Panafrican Festival of Algiers in July 1969, while listening to the American activist delivering a speech on the condition of men and women of color. During this scene an original recording of another famous Davis speech, the 1979 Black History Month convocation at Florida Agricultural & Mechanical University, is playing in the background, while the camera lingers on pictures of Angela Davis pinned to the wall in Aïcha's room. The superimposition of different historical moments and loci over the current situation in France raises the issue of the transmission of values, knowledge, and feminism beyond city and national borders, while placing Maghrebi women and their daughters in a global context. The intertwining of women's spheres, the intergenerational transmission, and solidarity give Benguigui's project a universal dimension and illustrate Michael Rothberg's *Multidirectional Memory* (2009).[7] By connecting Aïcha's *cité* to other historical supranational events, the filmmaker shows young viewers that their mothers took part in the struggle and that they all are legatees of women's struggle across space and time. The memories and histories of marginalized groups do not compete against one another. On the contrary, they inform and nurture each other, providing the next generations with the tools and critical apparatus required to ensure their success in a changing society to which they belong and contribute.

Conclusion

Arte and France 2 both rose to the challenge when deciding to program series about descendants of immigration at prime time. As public channels, it is their social and political responsibility to do so. The film directors they chose opted for comedy rather than drama or documentary, two genres that dominate the representation of immigration on-screen. One question still needs to be addressed: did they succeed in providing an alternative, popular, and entertaining image of immigrants' descendants, and if so, to what extent? Without a doubt both channels, which used different strategies, considerably contributed to representing minorities (Maghrebi in particular) and thus enhanced their representativeness. One measure of this success can be found in the increasing popularity of the main actors from both series and most notably in Kechiouche's acting career. Nonetheless, the series are also flawed, as noted by the critics, and their flaws cannot be defended easily. The criticisms are in fact very helpful since they challenge the ways in which TV programs can provide healthy and sustainable frameworks for the representation of minorities.

Representing immigration and its outcomes remains a thorny issue. Yet, the film and program directors discussed in this chapter decided to break away from the tragic figures of immigrants and their children. In fact, although some films of exceptional quality address immigration such as the documentary *Mémoires d'immigrés, l'héritage maghrébin* (Benguigui, 1997), the topic is often treated in a serious, even alarmist manner. Whereas sympathy and empathy for a group experiencing difficulties are powerful weapons toward a common awareness of injustice and disparities, it is sometimes necessary, particularly in times of social crisis, to present the concerned communities under a different light. Relief through laughter and sympathy toward funny and non-threatening characters cannot be the only strategy to balance the representations of immigration, but these depictions participate in the efforts to include and respect diversity. Numerous spectators, including immigrants, their children, and other communities, followed the series and appreciated being exposed to alternative representations at prime time, when audience exposure is much higher than in the movie theaters. Since ratings over one season cannot be fully indicative of audience behavior and opinion vis-à-vis the subject matter and the format chosen to convey it, it is deplorable that the series were cancelled hastily and prematurely, though the decision was justified by economic reality. Other channels and directors may reiterate the experiment, without falling into the pitfall of televisual communitarianism, where each community would have its own programs. It is hoped that they will produce constructive and positive programs that chronicle lives filled with hardship but also with happiness and hope. Despite a certain anemia and challenges surrounding the representation of immigrant communities and other underrepresented group, an increasing diversity has been noticeable on television screens in the last ten years, especially in variety shows, talk shows, and news broadcasts, as well as in the production of various genres of films on the topic of immigration.

Notes

1 In 2006, then minister of culture Renaud Donnadieu reinforced the role of the Conseil supérieur de l'audiovisuel (National Media Council) and the representation of minorities in the media through legislature. Article 47 of the Equal Opportunity Law of 2006 (Loi n° 2006–396 du 31 mars 2006 pour l'égalité des chances) stipulates that the media's programming must reflect France's diversity.
2 See Will Higbee's discussion on the loaded concepts of *beur* and *banlieue* cinemas (2013: 9–17).
3 The collective work set to question the policies instituted by the French authorities and various media outlets (television, radio, press, Internet, etc.), comparing and contrasting the situation in France with those in the United States, United Kingdom, and Germany. After a rather exhaustive examination of the state of representation and representativeness in France, the study applauded France Télévision's plan to include more diversity in all their programs but also deplored the lack of collaboration between general audience media and ethnic media, and the difficulty in the French media context of pushing for the presence of identified ethnic minorities. It finally suggested the need for more studies on the audience ratings and public opinion, the minority professionals working in all media including advertising because these forums reproduce an ideological stance. Progress has been made since the 1980s, but the media can still be accused of racism because of the notable absence of diversity in their programs unless they point at social problems specifically linked to the underrepresented minorities. The inequitable representation of the communities that make the fabric of a society and nation state constitutes an actual violation of democratic rights.

4 Although the concept of *imagined communities* was originally coined to describe the social construction of nations which are supported by people who perceive themselves as part of a group, it has since been used more broadly to describe communities of interest or awareness that transcend geographical borders. Brahim and his associates identify with the main characters of Tarantino's movie in the sense that they represent marginality and are successful at the same time while making money quickly.
5 Mike comes from a Gypsy family. Recently, the increased flow of Roma people from eastern Europe has triggered new and heightened tensions in France. Although Mike and his family are not Roma, but French Gypsies, they are still the target of discrimination and racism.
6 It is difficult to know to what community both amateur and professional critics belong unless they specify the resemblance to their families and experiences. However, these "insider" comments can be found and the reviews are mixed. On the one hand, some women found regrettable that in Aïcha, women are once again disenfranchised, on the other, some enjoy seeing the Maghrebi community portrayed in a comical manner.
7 Michael Rothberg demonstrates how the Holocaust has enabled the articulation of various stories of victimization, while at the same time, post-World War II events have brought the Shoah into public memory. Rather than creating a competition, histories of trauma inform one another and allow for a better understanding of processes of victimization and memory.

References

Anderson, B. (2006). *Imagined communities: Reflections on the Origin and Spread of Nationalism*, 2nd edn, London: Verso.
Banahamax. "Au menu couscous et crise d'hystérie: Avis sur Aïcha." *SensCritique*. July 27, 2013. Web. May 12, 2016.
Bergson, H. (1914). *Laughter: An Essay on the Meaning of the Comic*, New York: Macmillan.
Blion, Reynald et al. (2006), *La représentativité des immigrés au sein des média*, Paris: Fonds d'Action et de Soutien pour l'Intégration et la Lutte contre les Discriminations. Web. September 15, 2015.
Bourdieu, P. (2008). *Sur la télévision*, Paris: Raisons d'Agir.
Ervine, J. (2013). *Cinema and the Republic: Filming on the Margins in Contemporary France*, Cardiff: University of Wales Press.
Hargreaves, A. (1999). 'No escape? From the "cinéma beur" to the "cinéma de la Banlieue,"' in E. Ruhe (ed.), *Les Enfants de l'immigration*, Würzburg: Königshausen and Neumann, 115–28.
Higbee, W. (2013). *Post-Beur Cinema: North-African Émigré and Maghrebi-French Filmmaking in France Since 2000*, Edinburgh: Edinburgh University Press.
Hutcheon, L. (2000). *A Theory of Parody: The Teachings of Twentieth-Century Art Forms*, Champaign, IL: University of Illinois Press.

Langlais, P. (March 20, 2010). 'Arte, les séries pour rajeunir l'audience,' *Slate*. Web. February 15, 2015.
Leherpeur, X. (July 19, 2013). 'L'immigration dans le cinéma français: Un bilan mitigé,' *L'Express*. Web. September 15, 2015.
Mills-Affif, E. (2004). *Filmer les immigrés: Les représentations audiovisuelles de l'immigration: 1960–1986*, Bruxelles: Editions De Boeck Université.
Messaoudene, Madjid. 'Aicha, ou comment Yamina Benguigui qui n'est pas photographe, collectionne les clichés. Les Blogs,' *Médiapart*, September 8, 2011. Web. May 12, 2016.
Rothberg, M. (2009). *Multidirectional Memory: Remembering the Holocaust in the Age of Decolonization*, Redwood City, CA: Stanford University Press.
Tarr, C. (2005). *Reframing Difference: Beur and Banlieue Film in France*, Manchester: Manchester University Press.

Filmography

Benguigui, Y. (1997). *Mémoires d'immigrés, l'héritage maghrébin*, Bandits Production.
Benguigui, Y. (2009). *Aïcha*. Les Auteurs Associés, Les Auteurs Associés.
Benguigui, Y. (2011). *Aïcha, un job à tout prix*, Elemiah.
Benguigui, Y. (2011). *Aïcha, la grande débrouille*, Elemiah.
Benguigui, Y (2012). *Aïcha, les vacances infernales*, Elemiah.
Chibane, M. (2009). *Le choix de Myriam*, Nelka.
Gastampide, F. (2012). *Les Kaïra*, Save Ferris Entertainment.
Hamidi, M. (2013). *Né quelque part*, Quad.
Jewison, N. (1968). *L'Affaire Thomas Crown*, Mirish Corporation.
Kassovitz, M. (1995). *La Haine*, Canal+.
Kaurismäki, A. (2011). *Le Havre*, Sputnik.
Kherici, R. (2013). *Paris à tout prix*, Mandarin.
Meunier, S. (2011). *Fortunes*, Television series, Terence.
Meunier, S. and Cohen, B. (2008). *Fortunes*, TV Film, Adventure Line Productions.
Scorsese, M. (1976). *Taxi Driver*, Columbia Pictures Corporation.
Tarantino, Q. (1992). *Reservoir Dogs*, Live Entertainment.
Tarantino, Q. (1994). *Pulp Fiction*, Miramax.
Thorn, J.-P. (2003). *On n'est pas des marques de vélo*, Mat Films.

7

They had a dream: out-marching exclusion and hatred

Jimia Boutouba

La violence, c'est d'avoir 20 ans, pas de boulot et les flics sur le dos. Slogan

(20 years old, unemployed and harassed by the cops: that's violence)[1]

La première marche pour l'égalité et contre le racisme à l'initiative de S.O.S Minguettes a permis de réaffirmer que nous, jeunes, issus de l'immigration revendiquions le droit à l'intégrité physique, morale, politique et sociale. Notre droit à vivre ici ne se discute même pas … C'est le problème de l'acquisition des droits politiques qui est désormais clairement posé … Ce que nous voulons, la justice, l'égalité, le respect, nous n'irons pas le quémander, nous affirmerons clairement nos droits et toutes les forces politiques devront prendre leurs responsabilités … A nous de créer et de montrer notre force. A nous de lancer les Etats Généraux de la jeunesse issue de l'immigration. (Tract du Collectif Jeunes Paris et Région Parisienne)

(The first March for Equality and against Racism, initiated by SOS Minguettes, allowed us, the youth born in France to immigrant parents, to claim the right to bodily, moral, social, and political integrity. Beyond our indisputable right to live here … it's the issue of the acquisition of political rights that is now at stake … The justice, equality, and dignity we want, we won't beg for them. We will loudly and clearly state our rights and all the political factions will have to face their responsibilities … It's up to us to build and demonstrate our strength. It's up to us to launch the General Assembly of the youth born to immigrant parents)

Democratic politics lies in what one does rather than in what one receives or is entitled to. (Jacques Rancière)

In November 2013 Moroccan-Belgian filmmaker Nabil Ben Yadir released his second feature film, *La Marche*, to commemorate the thirtieth anniversary of the first national anti-racist movement in France. The six-week march was a historical touchstone event that mobilized over 100,000 demonstrators. It was described as France's equivalent of America's civil rights protests, a 500-mile march from Marseille to Paris, intended to awaken France to State racism, violence, and rampant discriminatory practices in its midst. This was 1983, a time when France witnessed with relative indifference and impunity the rise of hate crimes and police repression specifically targeting Franco-Maghrebi youths. Faced with this alarming situation, aggravated by the political leaders' lack of responsiveness, *banlieue* youths took matters into their own hands, creating a counterculture of protest. Some channeled their anger and alienation into spectacular urban "rodeos," car burning, and violent confrontations with the police. Urban turmoil escalated in the summer 1983, turning bloody in some segregated neighborhoods, like the cité des Minguettes on the outskirts of Lyon, which saw an unprecedented upsurge in rioting and clashes between the youths and the French police.

Yet the 1980s also witnessed the rise in political and civic activism in the form of graffiti, music, concerts, theatre, and increasing associative action, thereby demonstrating what philosopher Jacques Rancière (1999) defines as democratic politics. The 'hot summers' in the *Minguettes*, as the media called them, sparked new forms of civic and political engagement. Young men and women became massively involved in the fight against racism and for civil rights and for a new definition of citizenship which stressed socialization based on plural belongings, the promotion of sociocultural integration in the suburbs, and the mobilization against police brutality and judicial discrimination. One of the instigators of the 1983 March, Toumi Djaidja, had been very active with community groups and within the association he was presiding over, SOS Minguettes Avenir. During one of those hot summer nights, Djaidja was seriously wounded, shot in the stomach by a police officer, while attempting to free a youngster from a police dog. The then 21-year-old hatched a plan for what was to become the March for equality and against racism, as he lay in his hospital bed recovering. Inspired by Gandhi's non-violent movement and Martin Luther King's March on Washington, Toumi Djaidja was joined by a local priest, Christian Delorme, and a small group of twenty people. Together they launched a historic march across France. In this collective action, male and female marchers found ways to fight against a system that had consistently oppressed and excluded them. Speaking from a new subject positioning, they displayed banners and slogans to demand the right to have rights, the right to '*éga-liberté*' (Balibar, 2010), which implies 'the right to participate in political processes that aim, among other things, at the invention of new rights, new forms of inclusion and empowerment' (Ingram, 2015: 218). The protestors were not seeking a new classification but demanding that minority youths be recognized and treated as equal citizens. In marching, they engaged in an act of emancipation, thus performing what Jacques Rancière defines as 'active equality' (May, 2008: 142).

In examining how the long journey across the French hinterland is imagined as a space of intervention and how it is experienced as a liminal state where impermanence becomes a positive way of communal engagement, I will demonstrate how the film *La Marche* presents the youths' story as a troubled relationship with home and the march as political praxis and a metaphor for homecoming. As a group, the march connotes desired community and emotional togetherness. It claims anchoring visions of solidarity and connectedness across gender, class, race, and sex divides. As a metaphor, the marching group becomes a political mode of existence. In *La Marche*, Ben Yadir thus offers an oppositional gaze and a substantial project, defined as a narrative of mobility that departs from allocated places and the suppressed speech of the 'unaccounted for' and moves to formulated politics and discourse.

Framing exclusion, shooting difference: the part that has no part

Differing "communities" are increasingly imagined into being by a multiplicity of discourses in the press, in television coverage, and in narratives of social events, where the languages of "realism" become a naturalized encoding of the "real." In the past three decades, the discourses that have framed the French suburbs have carried connotations of widespread and recurrent violence, egregious looting, ransacking, rioting, and other socially disruptive behaviors. When riots erupted in 1981 in Les Minguettes, triggered by a feeling of exclusion among the youth, social deprivation, and growing tensions with the police (Jalouzi, 1992: 21–2), the political and media discourses insisted on the dangerousness of the *banlieue*, a site inhabited by immigrant masses that posed a growing threat to the integrity and the values of the French Republic. It was as if, suddenly, there was a qualitative change in the perception of delinquency (Dubet and Jalouzi, 1984). The stigmatization of the suburb and its dwellers, the conflation between criminality and immigration further exacerbated the public debate and contributed to reinforce the ethnicization of the *banlieue*. The mainstream media across the political spectrum spoke in one voice, unanimously representing a danger of alarming proportions:

> La vie quotidienne des habitants de ces cités, ce sont aussi les innombrables vols et déprédations, les agressions, les viols, les gestes et les propos insultants, les menaces. Un climat pourri propice à toutes les explosions, à l'engrenage de toutes les violences. (*Le Figaro*, September 5, 1981)

> (Daily life in these neighborhoods amounts to countless robberies, depredations, assaults, rapes, incivilities, and threats. A rotten atmosphere conducive to all kinds of social outbursts and breeding more violence.)

Dans les quartiers à forte densité maghrébine, la situation devient explosive. ... Le gouvernement en supprimant les expulsions d'individus douteux encourage les dévoyés! Aujourd'hui, les voyous n'ont plus rien à craindre. (*Le Figaro*, July 7, 1981)

(In neighborhoods with a large North-African population, the situation is critical ... In suspending the deportation of suspected individuals, the government has encouraged delinquents. Today, thugs have nothing to fear)

Un repaire de jeunes Arabes en colère, chômeurs et plus ou moins délinquants. (*Libération* 1981, cited in Rinaudo, 1999: 30)

(A lair for angry, unemployed, and more or less delinquent young Arabs)

Following the Minguettes incidents and the virulent debates they generated, the government ordered two official reports to investigate the situation in the *banlieue* and to shed a light on: 'Les jeunes d'origine étrangère, qui sont-ils? Combien sont-ils? (importance par rapport aux jeunes Français). Existe-t-il une délinquance spécifique à la condition des jeunes étrangers?' (Llaumet, 1982: 3) (Who are these foreign-born youths? How many are they? How do they compare to French youths? Is there a delinquency specifically tied to their condition?). The *banlieue* dwellers, mostly immigrant communities, have had to bear the weight of public scorn attached to living in spaces that are labeled as fearsome, no-go zones, rife with crimes and lawlessness. As Alec Hargreaves argues, 'the mass media have played a central role in this reconstruction, in the course of which they have disseminated and reinforced stereotypical ideas of people of immigrant origin as fundamentally menacing to the established social order' (1996: 607). In this sense, the *banlieue* has become 'commonplace to bring up the same spatial references ... when talking about issues such as "the problem of integration of immigrants," the republican model of integration, social fracture, violence, and insecurity. Furthermore, it has become possible to evoke all of these issues at once by a simple reference to "the *banlieue*"' (Dikeç, 2007: 124). Magnified by the media craze, this sudden heightened visibility in the public sphere also propelled to the forefront of the political stage a new kind of political discourse which translated into an anti-immigrant vote with the first electoral 'victory' of Jean-Marie Le Pen, founder and president of the extreme right party Le Front National. The 1983 municipal elections took place in a context of growing dissatisfaction with unemployment, blamed on the 'surplus' of immigrants and perfectly illustrated by the (in)famous slogan Le Front National had coined five years earlier: 'Un million de chômeurs, c'est un million d'immigrés de trop! La France et les Français d'abord!' (One million unemployed people is one million immigrants too many! France and French people first!)[2]

Drawing upon sociologist Pierre Bourdieu's theories, Abdellali Hajjat argues that:

> Ceux qui sont les plus démunis de capital culturel, comme les jeunes des cités, forment un 'groupe parlé.' On voit leurs actes mais on n'entend pas leur parole. Ils sont 'parlés' par des individus ou des groupes détenant du capital culturel (journalistes, militants, acteurs politiques …) qui peuvent en parler positivement (qualification) ou négativement (disqualification). (Hajjat, 2013: 66)

> (Those who are dispossessed of culture, like the young people living in suburban areas, constitute a 'spoken' group. Their acts are visible but their voices are not heard. They are 'spoken' by individuals or groups who possess cultural power (journalists, militants, politicians …) who can speak of them positively (qualification) or negatively (disqualification)).

Hajjat reformulates the problem of domination and exclusion by drawing attention to socio-symbolic constructs whereby social boundaries are redeployed and enforced. Behind this constant characterization of the *banlieue* as a site of delinquency, violence, lack of order, and/or disrespect for social order, lies a long history of the French State's discriminatory policies toward immigrant population from former colonies and a systemic oppression shrouded in national distortion and amnesia. This systemic violence which translates into social exclusion, geographical confinement, and discriminatory policies, is further accented by accrued police surveillance and brutality, 'une police aux réflexes coloniaux [qui] sans presque de transition … est alors passée de la chasse aux fellagas' (terme utilisé pendant les guerres d'Afrique du Nord pour désigner les combattants indépendantistes) à la poursuite des jeunes délinquants d'origine étrangère' (Delorme, 2013: 102) (a police force still entrenched in colonial attitudes that moved, with scarcely any transition, from hunting down 'fellagas' (term used for North African militants in the wars of independence) to hunting down delinquent youths of foreign origin). This violence remains deeply rooted in a repressed colonial past, haunted by the ghost of the Algerian War of Independence that saw an unprecedented surge in violence both in Algeria and France.

Increasing police brutality and repression by private citizens culminated in the assassination of hundreds of immigrants. In a chilling account, journalist Fausto Giudice (1992) chronicles a host of what he terms 'Arabicides' from 1970 to 1991, concluding that in post-'68 France one may kill Arabs with impunity. The year 1982 and the summer of 1983 were particularly bloody with more than forty hate crimes targeting mainly young Arab males (Ben Jelloun, 1984: 27–32). 'Although North Africans represented no more than 40 percent of the population, between 1980 and 1993 they accounted for 78 percent of all officially recorded racial crimes' (Derderian, 2004: 11).

In bringing this suppressed history onto the screen, Ben Yadir's priority is to unveil the everyday drama of systemic, physical, and symbolic violence within the social and cultural perimeters of the Republic. The director deliberately moves from a politics of representation to performative processes, supported by the film's neorealist aesthetic. By its topic (the civic struggle of a disenfranchised category), its source (sociological documentation), its style (documentary inflected), and its focalization (the youth), Ben Yadir's film presents many interesting aspects that point to a neorealist inspiration. The aesthetic forms of realism that he adopts have a particular impact, as they establish codes of representation anchored in the verisimilitude of lived experience. *La Marche* thus subscribes to an aesthetic that views cinema as a medium endowed with a unique ability to reflect (on) the past and an aesthetic resource through which the filmmaker can expose, confront, and grapple with the legacy of a violent past.

Historian R. C. Raack contends that film can address and represent some aspects of the past least perceptively reflected in traditional history. 'Traditional written history does not accurately mirror the multi-dimensional world we daily encounter'; film, on the other hand, with its 'quick cuts to new sequences, dissolves, fades, speed-ups, slow motion, and the importance of sound' offers a way of 'sensing the past' (Raack, 1983: 416). *La Marche* offers a visual history that seeks to recover the liveliness of a multidimensional world by reconstructing the way historical people witnessed, understood, experienced, and sensed the past. This empathetic reconstruction of the past is sustained by Ben Yadir's 'neorealist' aesthetic, which brings engaging narrative techniques to bear upon sociohistorical issues. Martin O'Shaughnessy argues that 'the real is that which is normally unseen but hurts ... Cinema's role is to bring this uncomfortable and disruptive real to visibility' (2003: 194). The new realist codes in *La Marche* offer an immersive experience of duration and gestation featuring extended sequence shots and a restlessly inquisitive probing camera (often handheld), whereby the spectators are brought into direct touch with the characters, their inner worlds, aspirations, struggles, emotions, and language. This is magnified by Ben Yadir's most crucial film grammar, the close-ups, which create a visual counterpoint and bring us into close intimacy with the characters' emotional journey.

The filmic performance of violence confronts the spectator with a grim environment, replete with menace, aggravated assault, and lynching. Graphic imagery of violated bodies, not a substitute stylized rendition of violence, thus documents a culture heavily saturated by racist killings and senseless beatings. The montage aesthetic serves a social agenda, in that it makes the viewer sense the traumatic impact of real social and physical violence. By using graphic imagery, Ben Yadir places the filmic representation of violence into proper synchronicity with the era. The first sequence is particularly powerful in its depiction of violence, offering a glimpse of the world in which the socially marginalized youths are forced to live. A documentary-style pan sets the geographical context at the start. The camera tracks a still undefined space while framing in a medium long shot four dark silhouettes sitting on the front steps of a rundown building. Facing them, in sharp focus, stands a dark row of squarely shaped buildings that obstruct the view. As the camera moves closer to the group, the shot changes from that particular medium shot to an eyeline-matching shot, in which the viewer sees the characters' surroundings through their eyes, and is thus able to sense the claustrophobic environment.

As the camera cuts to a different angle to face the characters, space begins to close in on them and on the spectator as well. The dark palette of colors and the low-key lighting reinforce the gloomy atmosphere of entrapment and create an ominous feeling of imminent danger, as if an undefined threat is lurking in the dark. The film thus uses a kind of hyperrealist claustrophobia to dramatize persistent but arrested motion which leaves the viewer ill at ease. The camera then approaches the young men, bringing them closer to the spectator in a medium close-up shot. We hear three of the characters engaged in a casual conversation; the fourth one, Sylvain, sitting slightly behind the others, seems removed from the scene and absorbed by his music. The camera's closeness draws us into their inner world, slowly unveiling the way each one of them deals with his socio-spatial environment. Farid copes through excessive eating, the fourth unnamed young man states that nothing will ever change and invokes violence as the only possible response. Mohamed, who is shown reading a newspaper, offers an intellectual approach to social change, emphasizing the power of associative action and non-violence, while Sylvain remains taciturn and shuts the world out with his headphones plugged into his ears. Yet his face betrays intense emotions and repressed anger, soon to be confirmed when the music he plays on his Walkman fills the air and we hear Renaud's 'Hexagone,' a political song that vehemently criticizes persistent State violence. Suddenly, the idle moment is shattered as a young man chased by a vociferous black dog runs through the scene, setting the whole group in motion. The four young men quickly dash through the oppressive night and the dark alleys of the dormant *cité*, to rescue the youngster, who is viciously mauled by the police dog. Crucially, the camera is not fixed in this scene, but handheld and constantly moving, as if in response to the characters' physical movements and emotional turmoil. In this move from the arrested static shots to the broadly chaotic movement, we are placed on direct par with the characters. There is no static frame or use of shot/counter-shot formation to freeze the multi-perspectival, circular flow. The *mise-en-scène* and the subjective points of view add to the anxiety, while the camera tightly frames the characters and dispenses with the contextual landscape, to bring us closer to the characters' raw emotions: panic and fear in the face of danger and relentless violence.

Mohamed is the first to catch up with the dog and its victim. As he wrestles to set the young man free, the music abruptly stops. The diegetic sound of the dog's barking in conjunction with a tight close-up of its wide-open jaws heightens the intensity of the moment. The dog suddenly becomes quiet, propelling Mohamed and the viewer into another fearful moment, powerfully captured by the close-up of his terrified expression as he glances over his shoulder. Slowly turning around, he is confronted with a gun pointed at him. The low-angle camera shot accents his crushing feeling as he realizes the lethal danger he faces. Hand held out open, Mohamed is begging the police officer not to shoot. Seconds later, a gunshot tears through the night and Mohamed collapses to the ground. In this dramatic scene, the spectator's identification with the youth, which is achieved through narrative focus and points-of-view shots, is not so complete that s/he loses all critical distance. The film skirts the spectator's location within the story to allow him/her to confront the unremittingly harsh social conditions and relentless violence, bound to erupt at any time. The viewer is thus able to experience how the youths are constantly assaulted by uncertainty – an uncertainty that feeds on the fear of violence.

A thread runs through the film, in the form of a series of scenes staging intense violence. One of the central scenes in the movie depicts a gruesome attack on one of the female marchers. The scene opens with a blurred and dark-silhouetted shot of Mounia approaching a group of men. The shot slowly fades out as she starts a conversation with them, then the camera cuts to the next shot closely following her as she staggers back and collapses before her friends. The camera zooms to reveal the swastika that was carved into her back with a knife. While the actual assault remains off-screen, its impact on Mounia and the entire group becomes a defining moment in the politicization of the march and its fight against biological racism.[3] Other terror attacks punctuated the march, including the shooting death of a nine-year old boy and the ordeal suffered by Habib Grimzy, a 26-year-old Algerian tourist, beaten and stabbed by three French Foreign Legion recruits on a night train and thrown to his death from the window, an attack all the more horrific as no passenger on the train intervened to rescue the young man.[4] Because of the shocking nature of these senseless killings, and to honor the memory of the victims, Ben Yadir chose not to fictionalize these terrifying events but rather to inscribe them as 'raw historical material,' embedding archival and news footage in the film narrative. The use of archival footage inscribes the movie into a historiographical moment, creating a heterogeneous text that weaves a new relationship between present and past.

The film thus works through history and aesthetics, combining archival material and fictional re-creation, to model a new form of historical knowledge appropriate to these violent stories, which are quickly forgotten and dissociated from national memory.

The filmic discourse registers a pervasive political reality and replaces the discursive framing of the *banlieue* as a violent and lawless wasteland by a long list of victims and their dislocated bodies. The filmic narrative turns their severed stories into a haunting presence and a text that disrupts and puts into crisis the political language attached to the modern French nation.

Political dissensus: the account of the unaccounted for

The discursive framing of the *banlieue* as a lawless wasteland and the ensuing heated public debates fueled by the media, were not just political ploys. The different actors involved in these public debates conveyed similar ways of perceiving and framing problems and ordering space, thus configuring and legitimizing a particular regime of representation, what philosopher Jacques Rancière would call a 'police' ordering. According to Rancière, the police, in its original sense of government organization, rests on an inegalitarian ordering of society's parts.

> The police is thus first an order of bodies that defines the allocation of ways of doing, ways of being, and ways of saying, and sees that those bodies are assigned by name to a particular place and task; it is an order of the visible and the sayable that sees that a particular activity is visible and another is not, that this speech is understood as discourse and another as noise. (1999: 29)

The police are thus based on a particular regime of representation, which he refers to as 'the partition of the sensible' and defines as the manner in which 'a relation between a shared common (*un commun partagé*) and the distribution of exclusive parts is determined in sensory experience. This latter form of distribution ... itself presupposes a distribution of what is visible and what [is] not, of what can be heard and what cannot' (Rancière, 2010: 36). It is a perceptual configuration of society that discloses at once the existence of a common (i.e. the whole to be governed) and the partitions that define the respective places and parts in it. The partition of the sensible orchestrates times and spaces, arranges the sensual and material world: what is in or out, central or peripheral, audible or inaudible, visible or invisible. 'What a police order seeks is to put everything in its place, through allotment and justification ... There are those who are in charge of allotment and those who are not, those who make decisions and those for whom they are made ... This has two effects: it excludes the recipients from political involvement and covers up that exclusion with the illusion of wholeness or completeness' (May, 2008: 47–8). Police ordering is thus a 'sensible,' that is, a perceptual configuration of society that frames and reduces the field of experience. The police not only assign to each body certain norms, roles, and occupation, but also affix status, identity, rank, and value.

Rancière explicitly distinguishes police from politics, defining the latter as 'an extremely determined activity antagonistic to policing' (1999: 29). Political activity thus refers to a mode of acting that perturbs the police ordering and subverts hierarchy by introducing *dissensus* into an inegalitarian partition of the sensible:

> Political activity is always a mode of expression that undoes the perceptible divisions of the police order by implementing a basically heterogeneous assumption, that of a part of those who have no part, an assumption that, at the end of the day, itself demonstrates the sheer contingency of the order and the equality of any speaking being with any other speaking being. (1999: 30)

The 'part that has no part' refers to those groups who are not equally included in the sociopolitical order. Symbolically and materially disqualified by the police, they are deprived of *logos*, i.e. of the capacity to express claims of justice and injustice through audible speech. Politics arises, however, when the excluded groups enunciate and stage a right to equality and liberty. In so doing, they become the instigators of political *dissensus*. When it takes place, this political praxis aims to 'shift a body from the place assigned to it … It makes visible what had no business being seen, and makes heard a discourse where once there was only place for noise' (Rancière, 1999: 30). By introducing political *dissensus*, the excluded groups demonstrate that they are equally capable of entering into public life. Politics is the event when those who have no proper place in the political community forcibly partake in that community. Rancière's concepts of politics and the partition of the sensible allow us to understand both how the police distributes power and legitimizes social hierarchy and how the 'unaccounted for' can challenge and rupture police domination on the basis of the principle of equality.

In light of Jacques Rancière's political thought, we can read the 1983 march as a political praxis that aims at disrupting the police order. It is the enunciation of the right to equality and liberty and the staging of an egalitarian demand, one that exposes the existing sociopolitical order in order to disrupt it. The march embodies that demand of the right to equality, made visible and audible. It is a political act in that it disturbs the established police order and creates a new political space of intervention. It is also a transformative process in that it turns into qualified political subjects those whose voice has been only regarded as noise by the police order. As a site of political mobilization and a mode of 'subjectification,' the march emphasizes democratic practices, those very same practices and concepts that the French Republic purportedly stands for and yet has consistently denied the *banlieue* youths (Rancière, 1999: 35). As Loïc Wacquant notes, 'the very idea of relegation to a separate space of *institutionalized social inferiority and immobility* stands in blatant violation of the French ideology of unitarist citizenship and open participation in the national community' (2008: 179). The march thus maps a geography of the political that allows 'the part that has no part' to reject the prevailing social distribution of roles and places and to become visible and audible as political subject.

Mapping space, performing place: the practice of democratic politics

In Ben Yadir's film, the cinematic image focuses on political *dissensus*, showing how the excluded subjects gradually deregulate all representations and participate in a new distribution of the sensible. As the group of permanent marchers embarks on an uncertain journey, the camera remains attuned to their trajectory and internal turmoil, giving shape to, and making visible, their multiple and fragmentary rebellions. The six-week journey is met with many obstacles, ranging from tight government's surveillance, to physical assaults on the marchers, racist attacks, illness, and internal dissent. Tensions erupt and threaten to dissolve the group. Violent confrontations oppose the priest (recast as Christophe Dubois in the film) to an uncompromising and combative Kheira. Opposing a fierce resistance to everything and everyone, this strong grassroots activist is anxious to act, leaving all fears aside to jump into the cause with unusual passion. Romance between Kheira's young niece Mounia and Sylvain adds to the tension. Overprotective of her niece, whom she brought along to initiate her to associative grassroots work and raise her political consciousness, she disapproves of her relationship with Sylvain. Mounia herself grapples with conflicting feelings, exacerbated by internalized racial barriers, when she tells Sylvain that their biracial romance has no future and that it will end with the march. Another marcher, Yazid, remains haunted by a violent past, having served a two-year prison sentence for the aggravated beating of a police officer. Claire, the Canadian reporter, attempts to negotiate a new positioning and make sense of her world after her left-wing liberal parents rejected her because of her sexual orientation. Hassan, a drug addict who joins the march, threatens the cohesion of the group but Christophe Dubois, the priest, insists on his staying, as he sees the march as Hassan's redemption. Along the way, Mohamed, mastermind and leader of the march, has to fight fear and uncertainty in order to keep the group together, the march on track, and the 'dream' alive.

While the protagonists are introduced as a heterogeneous group, their bodies are still bound, carrying the weight of invisible shackles and chains. As marginalized individuals, these wounded souls are all haunted by violence and exclusion. René Leduc, the van owner, and Christian Dubois, the priest, embody two father figures walking alongside the youths. Christophe Dubois is invested with a moral, organizational, and personal authority, while Leduc remains a silent, but not passive, observer, as the historical march painstakingly takes shape and unfolds. René, who has no narrative relationship to the central figures, serves as a point of reference, a spectator/witness. Oftentimes, the camera lingers on his face, revealing his contemplative gaze. His witnessing of the march constitutes the 'taking place of' the event.

Following in the marchers' steps, the camera circulates on the nation's roads gathering the traces of localized resistance, weaving together flux and encounters, making visible 'le réel de proximité' (Jeancolas, 1997: 57) (proximate realism). 'At the same time, close attention to social dynamics means that the marginalized are not exoticized but are connected to social dysfunction in a way that can push up towards a political rather than a voyeuristic relation to the image' (O'Shaughnessy, 2003: 195). The film thus positions the viewer as a co-traveler experiencing different types of spaces and sensing history as it unfolds.

To map this performative space of political intervention, Ben Yadir turns to the road-movie genre, which he recasts as a powerfully politicized genre staging the spatial movement as the domain of heterogeneous sociopolitical forces. Through its reinterpretation of this genre, his film invites a rethinking of the geography of the political. Hegemonic power exercised by those in positions of authority actively produces and reinforces differences through modes of social and spatial division. Enclosed in an imposed territoriality (an ethnicized '*cité*'), difference is thus produced and contained in real and imagined spaces. In Michel Foucault's terms, space plays an essential role in 'any form of communal life; space is fundamental to any exercise of power' (Foucault, 1984: 252). If space is taken as integral to the exercise of power and is fundamental to communal life, then space can also be productive of political subjectivities leading to self-forming subjects. The film's tactics in moving from filmic discourse to filming performative practices adds to its political edge, reinforced by its unique treatment of space. It cleverly emphasizes a cartography of mobility that challenges and overturns the physical and ideological containment of minorities, which Foucault might include in his concept of 'state racism' (2003: 82). Those who are thus subjugated can resist and thwart the state of imposed 'otherness' to which they have been relegated, in favor of a space of openness, symbolized by the open road they travel. The racial and social partitioning of space we witness at the beginning of the movie gives way to a new dynamics which takes shape in movement, crossing, encounters, and exchange, thus creating a fluid network that, in turn, enables the forging of new subjectivities. The move from an essentialist to a more fluid identification is rendered in the film's zooming out the concept of 'roots' to bring into focus that of 'routes.'

In classic road movies, the open road and travel reflect a fundamental belief in 'the freedom to move upward and outward' (Eyerman and Lofgren, 1995: 55). The characters' freedom of movement is positively opposed to the stifling values of a stable society. The road offers a liberating potential; it is characterized by fluidity and open-endedness, serving as an extended metaphor of quest and discovery. In Ben Yadir's film, however, the construction of space does not tend toward a mythical conception of the road, with the landscape operating as a canvas against which the characters can achieve self-realization. Here the road and trajectories play a vital role in remapping new political and cultural spaces. The road, and by extension the march itself, provide a different mode of political engagement and discernment. From a group without *logos*, dispossessed subjects who cannot partake in the sociopolitical order, the marchers are now recast as those who constitute the political by repartitioning the spaces they cross and within which they act. The filmic narrative engages with the idea of space as a process. As the marchers progress geographically, the filmmaker exploits all elements of the changing landscape, offering a visual journey from the dark alleys of the *cité* to little-traveled roads and uncharted spaces, deserted fields, and muddy country roads. The film's focus on these landscapes thus offers a different 'heritage' vision of the nation. Ben Yadir does not idealize or rhapsodize the French landscape; nor does his film project the territorial mapping of the French landscape as a classic quest for identity. Emphasis on a mobile camera eye embodies the way the characters discover their surroundings in a "real," non-idealized dimension. It translates the desire to explore beyond prescriptive borders, fixed cultural boundaries and consecrated spaces. Instead, the camera journeys through an unglamorous landscape, vast rural spaces, small village roads, and open fields. City centers, monuments, famous landmarks are intentionally glimpsed out of focus, remaining in the background, or kept off-screen altogether.

The portrait of the traversed landscapes is magnified by cinematic strategies emphasizing the characters' experience of the landscape via the use of the traveling point-of-view shots. The scenes alternate between objective shots of the marchers and subjective shots of their experience of the spaces they cross. The roads are typically filmed in long or medium long shots, with minimal camera movements and with the shots focused on the characters. The marchers are thus shown as a group occupying or crossing a point in space. In using static wide shots, the characters' movement is emphasized in that it is not the spaces that scroll across the frame but the characters themselves who move through the frame. The camera moves only to the extent that the characters move. Ben Yadir thus delineates the space his characters occupy or move through. In this cartographic filmmaking, we get a sense of space as perceived and experienced by the marchers. The still shots in which the characters are not marching generally stress some specific action. They function as a kind of punctuation in the marchers' long journey, capturing scenes of encounters, difficult dialogues, heated confrontations, or celebratory gatherings and communion, mostly taking place in liminal spaces (gymnasiums, immigrant *foyers*, meeting halls, classrooms). These marginal encounters away from main roads, consecrated spaces, and official buildings, play a significant role in cementing a fragmented nation and suturing relations. Peripheral, transitional spaces become the stage for encounters and dialogue across the nation and are transformed into a new public site of political engagement and creativity.

The march endorses processes of change and (re)generation, as well as a belief in the shared experience of collective spaces that generates comradeship and solidarity. As a locus of metamorphosis, the road extends beyond the marchers to the communities touched by them. The political also arises through community transformation. From the one-man committee on the marchers' first stop in Salon-de-Provence to the massive crowd headed by political dignitaries in Paris, the march advances through human and social networking. Every step of the way and every meeting turn into a 'contact zone,' the proliferation of which along the road, within and between cities, constitutes a nodal geography that features a micro-politics of sociocultural redefinitions. Mary Louise Pratt coined the term 'contact zones' to talk about social spaces where disparate cultures meet, confront and grapple with each other, often in highly asymmetrical relations of domination and subordination – like colonialism and its aftermath. Pratt adds that 'a contact perspective emphasizes how subjects are constituted in and by their relations to each other. It treats the relations among colonizers and colonized ... not in terms of separateness or apartheid, but in terms of co-presence, interaction, interlocking understandings and practices, often within radically asymmetrical relations of power' (1992: 7).

Contact zones, as featured in the film's numerous encounter scenes, subvert asymmetrical relations of power by enabling communication and communicability across previously unbridged differences. They play with mobility across the threshold between symbiosis and separation, exclusion and inclusion, hospitality and hostility. Since contact zones also bear a corporeal dimension, the co-presence, the shared moment in time and shared bodily space, make (ex)change and discursive transformation possible.

In one of the early town hall meetings held by the marchers, Mohamed states: 'we are told that people are indifferent. But people are not indifferent. Extreme racism is social. It has no color.' In stating this, Mohamed displaces the discourse from a restricted field perceived as a 'foreign' category to an internal problem, thereby inviting everyone to critically examine the impact of State racism and the issue of social progress, or lack thereof, within the nation. By displacing the discourse from the periphery back to the center (the nation), from foreign to domestic spaces, he calls attention to the urgent need to address not an immigrant problem foreign to the constitution of the nation, but a thorny ethical question that has fragmented the national body. This particular sequence begins with an establishing long shot of the marchers and the priest, Christian Dubois, sitting across a scattered group in a small meeting hall. A close shot follows as the conversation starts. A series of close-ups and medium close-ups show the marchers' and the crowd's mutual uneasiness as they face each other. As the lines of communication become more open and dialogue more fluid, the rapid shot/reverse-shot that follows binds the marchers and the audience by framing them together. The way the crowd responds to the marchers in face-to-face encounters thus creates the impression of a reconstructed collective body. As individuals come together and bodies commingle in a shared space, they allow a redefinition of social integrity, associated with empathy, contact, and commitment.

Another such moment happens in Lyon, where the marchers hold their first large rally, just two weeks into the march and soon after Mounia's shocking assault. The high-angle shot shows the group on a stage, standing behind Mohamed, as he approaches the microphone to address the cheering crowd. Looking over his shoulder, the subjective point-of-view camera reveals the presence of the marchers' parents in the crowd, the very same people who, at first, adamantly opposed the idea of the march. 'We are more determined than ever,' Mohamed tells the crowd. 'We face racism every single day. But despite their hatred, despite their violence, we have the solidarity of all the people giving us support and welcoming us in their homes.' The tight connection between the eye of the camera and the crowd brings into focus an associative visual, aural, and emotional experience. In so doing, it shows how the march has given rise to a collective mo(ve)ment.

Ben Yadir's film *La Marche* represents the marchers' journey as an opportunity for the discovery and exploration of new possibilities within a socio-geographical territory, a cognitive mapping of the nation space. By meandering from south to north, the characters embrace a territory and reconstruct their own experience and narrative of the nation. Visually and symbolically the road expresses a new national imaginary. Typically, in the road movie genre, roads and cine-maps are used to anchor the filmic diegesis in specific geographical locations and to spatialize the narrative journey that unfolds in the film. *La Marche*, however, adopts a more performative function of mapping, one that informs understandings of place and space as cultural, perceptual, and cognitive processes. The geographically fragmented groups and communities become active participants in conceptually remapping relations. Such a process also emphasizes a plurality of loci of enunciation, that is, 'the geo-political and body-political location of the subject that speaks' (Grosfoguel, 2007: 213). Cast as a new site of the national 'imagined community' (Anderson, 1983), images of the road and narratives of youth groups emerge, as the former 'unitary' portraits of the nation become increasingly fragmented. The unraveling of previous narratives and images of national identity also brings into the limelight new sociocultural dynamics and representations which express the different vocabularies of modernity, embodied in the public debates held by the youths, their slogans, tracts, banners, drawings, and Farid's travelogue which is symbolically addressed to Gandhi. Music plays an essential role in the emergence of a new communal political experience insofar as it interacts with wider feelings, informing notions of collective identity and community. In this film, soundscape, much like landscape, plays a part in the characters' positioning, providing a sense of a shared place and present.

The sociopolitical journey that *La Marche* dramatizes, anchors the film in memory and allows for forgotten stories to resurface. Yet Ben Yadir's filmic narrative does not lead to a conception of history that is monumental; nor does it turn memory into memorial. Rather, the film's fictionalization of the 1983 march raises the question of the relevance of this march to contemporary France, highlighting the continuing struggle along the contentious lines of race, gender, sexuality, and religion. The film's ability to represent more open spaces destabilizes boundaries between self and other, insider and outsider. It articulates a repartitioning of the field of political experience, as France's invisible minority and internal periphery engage in acts of 'political subjectification' (Rancière, 1999: 35). The 1983 march constitutes a foundational event and a model of a micro-political challenge to State police, whereby marginalized characters become political subjects by disrupting the litigious distribution of places and roles.

Yet, thirty years later, this historic march has turned into a historical footnote, almost forgotten, rarely celebrated and/or commemorated. Nabil Ben Yadir's filmic re-enactment of the six-week journey, which President François Hollande watched at a special screening at the Elysée palace, helps dispel the collective amnesia over the events of 1983, thus inviting us to re-examine the meaning and the place of this event in national history. The filmic discourse is all the more significant, as today's France is caught in yet another tide of discursive and systemic racialization of its public space, exacerbated by populist discourses.

Notes

1 All translations are mine unless otherwise indicated.
2 In 1980, the slogan was updated to read '2 millions de chômeurs, ce sont 2 millions d'immigrés en trop! La France et les Français d'abord!' (2 million unemployed people is 2 million immigrants too many! France and French people first!). Two years later, there was another update, with '2 million' becoming '3 million.'
3 Biological racism is opposed to 'cultural racism,' which Balibar also calls 'Racism without races,' whose dominant theme is not biological but pertains to the insurmountable dimension of cultural differences.
4 The French Foreign Legion is a military branch of the French Army made up of foreign nationals willing to serve in the French Armed Forces.

References

Anderson, B. (1983). *Imagined Communities: Reflections on the Origin and Spread of Nationalism*, London: Verso.
Balibar, E. (1994). *Masses, Classes, Ideas: Studies on Politics and Philosophy before and after Marx*, trans. J. Swenson, New York: Routledge.
Balibar, E. (2010). *La Proposition de l'égaliberté*, Paris: Presses Universitaires de France.
Ben Jelloun, T. (1984). *Hospitalité française: Racisme et immigration maghrébine*, Paris: Seuil.
Delorme, C. (2013). *La Marche: La véritable histoire qui a inspiré le film*, Montrouge: Bayard.

Derderian, R. (2004). *North African in Contemporary France: Becoming Visible*, New York: Palgrave Macmillan.
Dikeç, M. (2007). *Badlands of the Republic: Space, Politics and Urban Policy*, Oxford: Blackwell.
Dubet, F. (1987). *La Galère: Jeunes en survie*, Paris: Fayard.
Dubet, F. and Jalouzi, A. (1984). 'Une nouvelle politique de prévention: Le cas de l'opération été 1982,' *Revue Internationale d'Action Communautaire*, 11(8), 151–62.
Eyerman, R. and Lofgren, O. (1995). 'Romancing the Road: Road Movies and Images of Mobility,' *Theory, Culture and Society*, 12(1), 53–79.
Foucault, M. (1984). 'Space, Knowledge and Power,' in P. Rabinow (ed.), *The Foucault Reader*, New York: Pantheon, 239–56.
Foucault, M. (2003). *Society Must Be Defended. Lectures at the Collège de France 1975–76*, New York: Picador.
Giudice, F. (1992). *Arabicides: Une chronique française 1970–1991*, Paris: La Découverte.
Grosfoguel, R. (2007). 'The Epistemic Decolonial Turn: Beyond Political Economy Paradigms,' *Cultural Studies*, 21 (March), 211–23.
Hajjat, A. (2013). *La Marche pour l'égalité et contre le racisme*, Paris: Editions Amsterdam.
Hargreaves, A. G. (1996). 'A Deviant Construction: The Media and the "Banlieue,"' *New Community*, 22(4), 607–18.
Ingram, J. (2015). 'Democracy and its Conditions: Etienne Balibar and the Contribution of Marxism to Radical Democracy,' in M. Breaugh, P. Mazzocchi, R. Magnusson, and P. Penner (eds), *Thinking Radical Democracy: The Return to Politics in Postwar France*, Toronto: University of Toronto Press, 210–34.
Jalouzi, A. (1992). *Les années banlieues*, Paris: Seuil.
Jeancolas, J.-P. (1997). 'Une Bobine d'avance: Du cinéma et de la politique en février 1997,' *Positif*, 434, 56–8.
Llaumet, M. (1982). *Les jeunes d'origine étrangère*, Paris: Centre d'Information et d'Etudes sur les Migrations.
Marange, J. and Lebon, A. (1982). *L'insertion des jeunes d'origine étrangère dans la société française*, Paris: La Documentation Française.
May, T. (2008). *The Political Thought of Jacques Rancière: Creating Equality*, Edinburgh: Edinburgh University Press.
O'Shaughnessy, M. (2003). 'Post-1995 French Cinema: Return of the Social, Return of the Political?,' *Modern and Contemporary France*, 11(2), 189–203.
Pratt, M. L. (1992). *Imperial Eyes: Travel Writing and Transculturation*, London: Routledge.
Raack, R. C. (1983). 'Historiography as Cinematography: A Prolegomenon to Film Work for Historians,' *Journal of Contemporary History*, 18(3), 411–38.
Rancière, J. (1999). *Disagreement*, trans. J. Rose, Minneapolis, MN: University of Minnesota Press.
Rancière, J. (2000). *Le partage du sensible*, Paris: La Fabrique.

Rancière, J. (2010). *Dissensus: On Politics and Aesthetics*, London: Continuum.
Rinaudo, C. (1999). *L'Ethnicité dans la cité: Jeux et enjeux de la catégorisation ethnique.* Paris: L'Harmattan.
Wacquant, L. (2008). *Urban Outcasts: A Comparative Sociology of Advanced Marginality*, Cambridge: Polity Press.

8

Narrativizing foreclosed history in 'postmemorial' fiction of the Algerian War in France: October 17, 1961, a case in point

Michel Laronde

The larger question of institutional violence and its erasure from public consciousness by the manipulation of the representation of violent events in collective memory has been brought to the forefront of postcolonial studies for some time now. More precisely, in the specific domain of immigration studies in France, understanding how camouflaged acts of State violence surface naturally or forcibly in, and through, cultural representations, has become a significant trend in the academic research of recent years. The present chapter hopes to contribute to an ongoing interest in the area, as an introduction to a longer project that examines the place occupied by history when it is present as traces and fragments in the literature of immigration produced in France since the early *beur* novels of the 1980s. My project approaches this question through the case study of a single significant date of the Algerian War in metropolitan France, known as October 17, 1961. This specific event has been the object of many inscriptions in postcolonial fiction, starting with several *beur* novels in the 1980s and their ramifications in today's urban literature. My objective is to focus on the formal presentation of the various inscriptions of the historical event in texts (its many textualizations in terms of size, location, and style) and to analyze how the aesthetic presentation of the event in fiction has evolved over the past twenty years. The inscription in the present of French culture of memorial fragments of past events, which have been excluded from the nation's collective history, may have formal consequences on narrative techniques. Conversely, differences in the aesthetic presentation over time may point to an evolution of the postcolonial mentality in reference to traumatic experiences tied, in this case, to the war in Algeria. It may yield valuable information on the potential role of postcolonial fiction in the healing of collective traumas inherited from the past through the practice of postmemorial writing as a way to bring back the past.

My approach ties in with the process of 'historicizing' and its intimate affinities with fiction writing, which Michel de Certeau analyzed at length in *L'Écriture de l'histoire* (1975). It also raises the question of new forms of narration (such as Dominique Viart's 'archaeological' novel: see note 4), which may modify the role of fiction as an articulation between the discourse of history and the practice of literature. Among the questions which may be addressed regarding the role played by the inscription of specific fragments of colonial history in postcolonial fiction, one of my interests is to ask if a change in mentality can be detected in the development of a postmemorial writing style in fiction by the descendants of North African immigrants and by mainstream French writers not intimately linked to immigration; or, conversely, if the variations in the ways the event is inscribed in different texts have the capacity to put traumatic history in a new perspective that needs to be assessed. Such observations may reveal an evolution of the mentality of French culture vis-à-vis the traumas embedded along the fault lines that mark the divide between the colonial and the post-colonial periods.[1] Rather than keeping history and fiction separate, my working hypothesis is that the potential of immigration fiction as a vehicle to decipher and rehabilitate pieces of history that have been repressed, ignored, manipulated, or silenced by the State, needs to be observed at the junction of history and its inscriptions in fiction narratives. It is hoped that this intersection will lead to explorations that will open new directions for a closer examination of the methodological, aesthetic, and didactic aspects of the practice of writing history in fiction. This specific articulation, which shifts the boundaries between history and literature perceived as two distinct fields of cultural knowledge, has become more pronounced over the past twenty years in the Arabo-French corpus of postcolonial literatures in France.[2]

Postmemorial writing has to be understood through the larger perspective of the development of a North African immigrant community in France in the 1950s and 1960s. Starting with the generation of *beur* writers in the 1980s, the articulation between the fields of history and literature takes a particular form, both new and perhaps different from the practice of mainstream French fiction, a trend confirmed with the 1990s Arabo-French fiction inherited from the early *romans beurs*. Extending over the entire period of postcolonial writing in France, postmemorial writing is based on Marianne Hirsch's umbrella term of postmemory. It refers to the specific ways in which bits of colonial history are presented in the novels. Therefore, postmemorial writing also refers to the techniques that mark the inscription of the memory of the past in present postcolonial French culture. Different facets of the history of the colonial empire have been a frequent source of inspiration for francophone literature in general, which took hold during the period of decolonization sixty years ago. Colonial history is indeed present in the postcolonial discourse of immigration fiction, but the writers' focus is more often on questions of silence, forgetting, remembrance and memory, all of which are symptoms of a postmemorial attitude and frame of mind that can be traced back to some of the earlier *beur* novels of the 1980s and seems to be specific to the culture of North African immigration. In some ways, these novels are concerned with the larger question of 'historicizing' the present discourse of French culture by integrating into fictional narratives the silences and distortions of the official history written by State-controlled institutions during the sensitive decolonization period of the 1950s and 1960s. Ultimately, my interest in the process of 'historicizing' will include the examination of postmemorial writing as a practice that may raise the question of new forms of narration. For example, could the substitution of new forms of narration for the chronological mode characteristic of the nineteenth-century's classic historical novel reveal a significant variation of the message between 'second-generation' *beur* writers of the 1980s and the 1990s generation of post-*beur* authors I have identified as Arabo-French writers? Can this evolution still be traced in today's urban literature? Postcolonial writers in particular have increasingly integrated practices of postmemorial writing in their fiction as a result of their quest for a corrective process to both fill in, and make up for, the silences and blanks of history by searching for traces, interrogating personal memories, collecting witness accounts and calling on archival resources for concrete information.[3] One of my objectives, therefore, is to investigate whether they do so by disrupting the chronological mode of the classic historical novel. In that context, does the fiction follow the path of a memorial quest that adopts the narrative strategies of an investigation of the past by starting from a position in the present? If so, does it use a retrospective approach that may well be enough to redirect the linear historical novel toward the type of novel presented as 'archeological' by Dominique Viart?[4] Can the phenomenon of the 'retroversion' of history, the end of historical temporality and the 'chaotisation du temps' (chaotization of time), a concept proposed by Jean Baudrillard in *L'illusion de la fin* (1992), suggest modes of writing where various processes for the *mise en abyme* of ingredients in fiction that have historical value would question the limits between history and fiction? In situations where the *mise en abyme* concerns an aborted historical event that has been officially minimized, modified, and consequently distorted, silenced, forgotten, or clearly negated, does the writing style, which is at the junction of history and fiction, echo the status of myth, a situation that would be disconnected from the reality of a past event? If anything, my probes seem to suggest that the intersection between history and literature offers rich possibilities for postcolonial readings of the *beur*, Arabo-French, and contemporary literature of North African immigration. It is also an invitation to investigate the ramifications of my hypotheses not only for other francophone literatures, but also for mainstream French literature, since immigration cultures in the post-colonial context are necessarily and intimately tied by history both to the present and past of hexagonal culture, in a privileged interactive dynamic with its former colonies which deserves closer attention. Since it refers to a post-colonial period inherited from a colonizer–colonized relationship, North African immigration also occupies a privileged intellectual and aesthetic position as a new set of cultural practices generated by the points of contact between (at least) two mentalities for the writers, that of the culture of their origins, as well as that of the culture of their lived experience as sons and daughters of immigrants in France.

What seems to warrant a new assessment of the literature that established immigration studies within France with the advent of the 1980s *roman beur*, is the mere passing of time that has extended the post-colonial period by thirty years and is gradually being transformed into historical time by the succession of generations. During that same period, the body of texts has grown steadily through a regular flow of annual publications. In retrospect, immigration literature approaches French collective memory as a process of sedimentation which opens, today, a significant perspective onto the presence of a postcolonial mentality inherited from the painful fractures between France and its colonies, a period culminating in the last war of liberation, the 1954–62 Algerian War of Independence, and the last and most violent act of this war on French soil, the massacre of October 17, 1961 in Paris. In that extended perspective, the *roman beur* of the 1980s can be framed today as a literary phenomenon including the semi-autobiographical first novels of self-trained young men and women of Maghrebi origins, born and educated in France, or (less often) born in their parents' country of origin, mostly Morocco and Algeria. Their desire to dramatize and fictionalize North African immigration in France is motivated mainly by their situation as 'second generation immigrants' acculturated in the urban setting of many French cities. As the first group of writers to be identified according to ethnic criteria and to have produced a body of literature that can be recognized based on its content, these young writers want to ground their fiction in their own experience as a first generation of French nationals or residents raised in France's shantytowns and high-rise buildings and educated in French schools in the 1960s and 1970s. In the same breath, they also fictionalize their parents' experience of migration, often presented as a combined traumatic displacement in space and a dramatic distortion in time. These two characteristics carry within them the ingredients that become the symptoms and ferment of the postmemorial writing practices that have expanded after the 1980s: silences and *souvenirs*, recollections and remembrances, memories and memory, rememory, transcription, and re-presentation. With time, these ingredients have evolved into the signifiers of a full-fledged awareness of postmemorial writing whose latest stage seems to be marked by a desire to bridge larger gaps in the mending process that is ongoing during the post-colonial period. With the passing of time, the turn of the twenty-first century sees the publication of several novels that take the need for healing one step further, suggesting that the state of amnesia may be coming to an end and that new steps toward anamnesis continue to take place, moving progressively toward reconciliation through dialogue and recognition.[5]

The sixty-year span that corresponds to the post-colonial period between France and its former colonies constitutes a historical continuum that starts symbolically with the end of the War in Algeria in 1962. During the past thirty years, immigration literatures have made the presence of a postcolonial mentality within France a reality that began with the publication of the first *beur* novels in the 1980s, following an interval of silence concerning the traumatic events tied to the last war of liberation from the French Empire. This period of silence between 1962 and the early 1980s was a time of forgetfulness, perhaps a conscious act of forgetting, that lasted about twenty years and marked a discontinuity in terms of the longer historical stretch formed by the colonial and post-colonial periods together. After the fracture of the war and the ensuing years of silence, the act of tying together the strands that would make history seem continuous between past and present over a twenty-year historical void, began as early as the first *beur* novels. Initially, it takes the form of scattered souvenirs, bits of memory, incomplete recollections, and partial reconstruction; integrated in the fiction, these echoes from a disrupted and disruptive past initiate the process of recreating a collective perception of the continuity of history.

The concept of postmemory (Hirsch, 2012) that has emerged during the thirty-year presence of a postcolonial literary discourse within France, is crucial to reach back to some of the earlier texts, such as Nacer Kettane's *Le sourire de Brahim* in 1985, or Mehdi Lallaoui's *Les Beurs de Seine* in 1986, and bring a different quality and richness to certain allusions, scenes, or entire sections of the novels that integrate historical ingredients into the narration. In this perspective, the many buried or aborted memories that were silenced during the period of public denial and collective amnesia between 1962 and the early 1980s are reactivated through the process of naturalization of certain historical ingredients, which is the active principle of fiction writing (I will expand on this in the next section). Therefore, it is not necessarily the documentation selected by politicians and historians that generates collective history, but rather the blanks of a public discourse once they are filled by the multiple experiences and reconstructive memories of individuals. Silences serve to correct fragmentary or falsified historical accounts when they are allowed to resurface through fiction. Imagination, then, becomes a key principle in the process of mending the chronological continuum of history that was interrupted by the many silences caused by a succession of personal and collective situations of trauma which have dotted the war and post-war periods. In Algeria, the Sétif and Guelma massacres (May 8, 1945), the *Toussaint Rouge* attacks (Red All-Saints Day) (November 1, 1954), the battle of Bab-el-Oued (March 23– April 6, 1962), the Oran massacre (July 5–7, 1962), and the assassination of the monks of Tibhirine (March 26, 1996) are some of the visible high points of the forever incomplete post(-)colonial memory of the traumatic history between France and Algeria. In France, the Paris massacre of October 17, 1961 and the Charonne metro station massacre of February 8, 1962 are pregnant references to situations of collective traumas tied to the silences of the war. As the post-colonial era expands, a growing number of personal accounts grounded in more general post(-)colonial situations such as the 'repatriation' of pieds noirs, the plight of *harkis*, or the French veterans' post-war syndrome, make it clear that various forms of personal remembrance disclose undetected silences which contribute to fill more – and often unsuspected – blanks in the fabric of collective history, in an unending process of repair.

Postmemorial writing, as conceived of in this chapter, has its roots in the early literary production identified as *roman beur* and continues to expand in the 1990s with Arabo-French literature and beyond. Consequently, one has to look for indications of a postmemorial frame in the early novels and pay attention to the symptoms, or signs, of that mindset that can be detected in the texts. A systematic study of the different clues, which point to a specific traumatic event in the history of relations between France and Algeria across the corpus since the 1980s, can yield crucial information to help understand how postmemorial writing works technically. In addition, what it says on the role of literature in a collective search for a process of healing and reconstruction follows to some extent the path of what Mireille Rosello has described as the 'reparative' in narratives (2010: 1).[6] Keeping this in mind, the next section of this chapter outlines the main methodological tools that allow me to generate meaning, in my search for the reparative potential of postmemorial writing, through the observation of the various inscriptions of one single traumatic event in a significant number of French novels, postcolonial and others, that have been written since the first *romans beurs* of the 1980s. It is hoped that this structured probing will uncover new angles to enrich the reading of the postcolonial immigration literature generated in the aftermath of *roman beur*, in at least one area, that of its role in the ongoing process of mending the historical disjunctions that linger on between France and Algeria.

October 17, 1961: a methodology

> Certes, on sait bien que les mémoires ne sont pas forcément l'Histoire. Mais elles la nourrissent. Bien sûr, chaque témoignage n'est qu'un regard individuel, partiel et partial. Car, on le sait, chaque témoignage recueilli a subi le travail de l'oubli. Mais chaque témoignage est comme pour les archéologues un précieux fragment d'une pièce historique. Plusieurs pièces permettent, sinon de reconstituer toute la pièce, toute la scène, toute l'histoire, du moins de faire des hypothèses, en les rapprochant, en les comparant. (*Ajir*, 2006)

> (Indeed we know that bits of memory are not necessarily History. But memories keep history alive. Of course, each individual account is incomplete and partial. As we know, the collected testimony has undergone the pressure to forget. But each testimony is, as with archeology, one precious fragment of a larger segment of history. And although they may not make it possible for us to reconstitute the entire piece, the whole scene, the complete story, several fragments put together may at least allow us to come

up with hypotheses, by comparing the various pieces and connecting them together.)[7]

My contextualization of the issues raised by the practice of postmemory writing is historical and spatial, as well as textual. Politically and ideologically, the general context is that of the extension of the war in Algeria to the Hexagon. As a result, France, and more precisely its capital city, become the locus of the displaced conflict, where antagonistic communities are forced to interact with, and confront, each other in a space characterized by the intrusion of the marginalized space of the colonized (the war in Algeria), within the conventional space of the colonizer (the Algerian War in France). Historically and spatially, the 'event,'[8] is a postcolonial geo-historical relocation of an instance of severe colonial violence, transported this time onto metropolitan soil and causing a major situation of collective trauma.[9] In this liminal space, the unwanted and contested event that forced the official silence of the State is very strictly delimited as one day in Paris during the Algerian War, on October 17, 1961.

My examination of the form and function of postmemory writing in the context of the literature of immigration is organized around that single, historically significant event. The date is now well known for the massacre of an unknown number of Algerians during a peaceful march on October 17, 1961, where thousands of unarmed protesters demonstrated in favor of Algerian independence and protested the curfew imposed by Maurice Papon, the Paris chief of police at the time. The version of '3 dead, 64 wounded' announced in the media the day after the march (Einaudi, 1991: 183) became the official matrix that would impose silence on the documented realities of the event for many years afterwards. Institutionalized as the result of an imposed silence rather than a consensus, this official version endured for decades in its original form. Although dead bodies were discovered for several weeks after the event, it had no corrective effect on the initial announcement endorsed by the State. With time, however, the official withholding of information intended to render the event invisible has forced other forms of discourse into playing an alternative role as channels of knowledge: public investigations, eyewitness testimonies, victims' personal accounts, historians' work, declassification of police archives in October 2011 (Brozgal, 2014) and other forms of documentation, all led to an estimated number of victims comprising between a few dozen and possibly several hundreds. In literature, for instance, the event has resurfaced in novels at an increasing rate since the 1980s. It justifies the focus of this project, exclusively centered on the role played by fiction in representing this event that was precluded from becoming history at the time it happened. My method of investigation is organized around a fragment of text I call an *ekphrasis*, present in a number of contemporary French novels that carry traces of the foreclosed reality of the massacre.[10] The goal is to observe the epistemological function of the repetition of different types of references to the event when it is embedded in different fictional texts. These multiple inscriptions can vary in size from a mere allusion, to entire chapters, to the event being at the core of the novel. The wide range of *ekphrases* constitutes a test case to observe one specific manifestation of 'postmemory' writing in postcolonial literature in France.

In this section of the chapter, I will briefly outline a method of textual analysis organized around the recurrence of the event in the form of a matrix inscribed in a number of novels, with each new fictionalization serving as a symbolic anchor of the event. Present in two early *romans beurs*, as a self-contained opening chapter in Nacer Kettane's *Le sourire de Brahim* in 1985 and an embedded discussion in Mehdi Lallaoui's 1986 novel *Les Beurs de Seine*, the event is also the central motivation in Didier Daeninckx's 1984 novel *Meurtres pour mémoire* (*Murder in Memoriam*). In this project, I have chosen not to take into account representations or echoes of the situation found in a number of fiction films and documentaries inspired by historians' work or other sources of information. One of the main reasons for limiting the representation of the event to fiction writing is that novels are a specific mode of communication producing a distinct discourse on culture (as do films, plays, and non-fiction productions on their own terms). Logically, then, this single object of study (October 17, 1961), as it is inscribed in postcolonial culture through one clearly identified mode of production (the novel), may be considered as part of a paradigm that would include other discursive modes. It can also belong to a second paradigm around historical situations which have been foreclosed and it can be put in parallel with other anchors of the traumatic French-Algerian history. Together, these situations embedded in fiction will constitute a larger pattern of the reconstructive narrative that corresponds to the 'age of memory' identified by Henri Rousso in *The Haunting Past* as 'an unprecedented attention paid to the tragedies of the twentieth century' through a 'sensitive, affective and even painful relationship with the past' (Rousso, 2002: 1, quoted in Rosello, 2010: 2).

The methodology for observing how the officially truncated version of the October 17, 1961 event is corrected follows a two-step process. First, I document how the event is 'narrativized,' that is to say how this cultural ingredient with historical value, which was barred by the French State from becoming part of the collective narrative at the time it happened, is circulated in French culture through fiction writing, a discursive form that is different from the conventional production of a politico-historical discourse. This first step where the event is 'naturalized' in fiction as an ingredient from reality through the process of narrativization, is familiar to all fiction readers. What needs to be described in more detail, then, is the central articulation of the process that explains the modalities of the passage from the discourse of fiction to the discourse of history. This key concept will be named the 'denaturalization' of the event. Prior to presenting the process of analysis that leads to the transfer of the event from fictional to historical discourse, I will identify as the *ekphrasis* the place where the event has been narrativized and is inscribed in fiction as a naturalization of the event, before it can be taken out of the context of fiction through an operation of denaturalization. Let me now sketch out the process briefly.

1. The *ekphrasis*. As the reader of a number of novels where the event is present, my obvious first move is to identify as the *ekphrasis*, the textual space where a reference to October 17, 1961 is found. Ignoring the aesthetic function assigned by classical rhetoric to an *ekphrasis*, I give it the role of 'authentifier le "réel"' (authenticating the 'real'), '"le réel concret"' ('concrete real') (Barthes, 1984: 185). To do so, I pay attention only to its formal aspect as a descriptive insert that can be lifted from its immediate textual environment and detached from the context of a specific fiction in which the event has been previously "naturalized" by way of the *ekphrasis*.
2. The naturalization. The event is naturalized when the author includes it in the discourse of fiction. The naturalization of elements from the real world in a novel is therefore a rhetorical gesture that creates a link between history and reality (where statements are considered true or false) and fiction (where statements are neither true nor false). With this first step, the movement goes from reality to fiction through the act of writing. Elements of the real are 'de-realized,' i.e. stripped of their referential quality to a concrete reality, and inserted in the closed world of one specific text where their function is discursive. Certain aspects of reality are transformed into elements of fiction by analogy: from that moment, the borrowings from reality have to be interpreted as facts which take place in the domain of fiction and no longer in that of 'concrete' reality. At that point, it is important to realize that the process of naturalization through fiction writing offers different ways to *imagine* the same piece of reality. When one single reality (the event being examined here), is reimagined and naturalized in different novels, each naturalization becomes an autonomous reference to the event because it is produced in the unique and closed world of one specific fictional text. One can easily anticipate the benefit that will be drawn from the repetition of this particular event once it is naturalized in a number of autonomous fictions written by different authors. As a result, the different naturalizations become multiple references to the event, 'resulting in a canonization – or archive – of sorts' (Knox, 2014: 390), and will ultimately combine together to form a *discourse* on the event.
3. Denaturalizing the event. The next step is a process of *transposition* whereby an ingredient from reality that has been naturalized in a work of fiction is transferred from the domain of literature to the domain of history, where it gains historical status. As with any act of reading, the process is partly tautological: it goes first from the event to the text (naturalization and narrativization), then from the text to history: it is taken out of the world of fiction, it is somehow defictionalized, to become

integrated as an act of speech in the discourse of history. The gesture is therefore a dynamic process whose objective is to contribute to the revision of a historical situation that has been officially truncated. The act of denaturalizing the event does not mean its nature is modified. Once the event is detached from a work of fiction, denaturalized, and given a new function in the world of reality, it metonymically acquires certain characteristics of the real world (the sign 'becomes' the signified, it is no longer neither true nor false, it is now either true or false). As the official record of the historically significant event in the discourse of State culture was initially manipulated, partially deformed, and silenced, the act of denaturalizing takes on an active role to correct falsified reality. The false, or distorted, presentation of the event in its authoritative version, which was officially inscribed in culture as a matrix with historical value ('3 dead, 64 wounded'), is now called into question. What is at stake, then, is no longer the initial process of denaturalization, in the sense that the inscription of the various deviations from the matrix in different works of fiction (its different naturalizations) serves to verify the lack of authenticity of this matrix, whose official form is the one that is made to conform to reality, identified by Pierre Laborie as '*mémoire convenue*' ('convenient memory') and presented as the only authoritative one, the one that warrants credibility.[11] Verifying the authenticity of the matrix calls it into question, and calling the officially established version into question results from the matrix being repeated with variations in form (the extent of its spatial presence in novels) and in content (the extent of the 'traces' of reality found with each naturalization).

4. Historicizing. My expectation is that the layers of new clues provided by the confrontation of bits of information gathered from the accumulation of singular *ekphrases* in distinct works of fiction, will serve to correct the initial matrix. In combination with the information collected in official archives and other sources used by historians, journalists, and other investigators, postmemorial writing will help me to come ever closer to imagining a more accurate representation of the event. The final step of the transposition process is to reintroduce the corrected narrative of October 17, 1961 into a different discourse, that of history and culture, with the purpose of rewriting a foreclosed situation, a situation of the past which is being 'historicized.'

Why 'postmemory'?

And yet, postmemory is not a movement, method, or idea; I see it, rather, as a *structure* of inter- and transgenerational return of traumatic knowledge and embodied experience. It is a *consequence* of traumatic recall but (unlike posttraumatic stress disorder) at a generational remove. (Hirsch, 2012: 6, italics in text)

Borrowing the term 'postmemory' from Marianne Hirsch's work on memory of the Holocaust and adapting this concept to the October 17, 1961 project needs to be justified and its nuances contextualized. Besides the fact that the term has already been applied to the field of immigration studies in recent research, my choice is reinforced by Hirsch's affirmation that 'other contexts of traumatic transfer … can be understood as postmemory' and that it may provide further understanding of 'the process of intergenerational transmission' at large (2012: 18).[12] Hirsch announces her intention to examine 'how the break in transmission resulting from traumatic historical events necessitates forms of remembrance that reconnect and re-embody an intergenerational memorial fabric that is severed by catastrophe' (2012: 32). The inscribing of the October 17, 1961 event as an e*khrasis* in a number of postcolonial novels also results from a 'break in transmission' that takes the form of the repressed narrative of a traumatic event (a peaceful march ends as a massacre perpetrated by the Paris police) with a historical potential (the extension of the Algerian War on mainland France). Twenty years later the sons and daughters of first-generation immigrants break the official silence when they embed fragments of this event (as well as of others) in fictional narratives to open channels of communication between their parents' generation and their own, in an effort to repair the individual fractures experienced in 1961. Their work also reaches to the rest of the French population, mostly unaware of the situation, thus initiating the slow process of mending collective trauma.

The first step in my investigation is to observe this single event of the Algerian War on French soil that was silenced by the official history written by State-controlled institutions. I start with the assumption that the present of postcolonial French culture is 're-historicized' (the official war history is being revisited) by integrating fragments of this specific repressed memory into a number of postcolonial fictional narratives. In the sense that the event inscribed in the fiction of North African immigration as early as the 1980s is still an active drive in postcolonial French literature today, the project resonates with Hirsch's reading of 'second-generation writers' that may 'share certain qualities and symptoms that make [them] a *postgeneration*' (Hirsch, 2012: 4). The concept of 'postmemory' allows me to investigate 'the continuities and discontinuities between generations' (Hirsch, 2012: 6) as they take the form of the intergenerational movement between the 'first' and 'second' generations (1960s–1980s), and beyond, of post-colonial North African immigration in France.[13]

My project gains momentum when Hirsch's concept of postmemory is transposed from the reality of an intergenerational situation between children and parents to the imagined representations of October 17, 1961 in literature across more than two generations. At that point, while I still conceive of the notion of 'postgeneration' as a marker of time and space in real life (hence, post-generation), symbolically it also comes to represent a continuum of texts of fiction that cover the entire post-colonial period since the 1980s.

Therefore, it goes beyond the physical reality of an experiential transmission over two generations and suggests that the clearly marked divide between the first and second generation will gradually fade into a post-immigration situation of blending. However, over that thirty-year period, the span of three generations as it is imagined in fiction will provide the specificities of the concept of postmemory as it applies to the history of North African immigration in France. Since '"postmemory" describes the relationship that the "generation after" bears to the personal, collective, and cultural trauma of those who came before' (Hirsch, 2012: 5), the event of October 17, 1961, once inscribed in a number of postcolonial novels, becomes a special mediator between the past of the writers' parents or grandparents and their own present, and between them and the overall French population. Therefore, as a chosen anchor in the traumatic past of the Algerian War, the event of the massacre functions as a probe or 'point of memory' into a process of historicizing the present by utilizing the medium of fiction as an 'imaginative investment, projection, and creation,' in order to mediate 'postmemory's connection to the past' (Hirsch, 2012: 5). I expect that extending the notion of 'postgeneration' to cover the entire post-colonial period in France will provide more material for analyzing the workings of postmemorial practices in this context. It is my hope that the longer perspective of two or more generations of characters in novels that reactivate this event from the past will yield precious insight into the evolution of the process of recovery from a historical trauma through inter- and trans-generational communication. Leïla Sebbar's *La Seine était rouge* offers an excellent example of the capacity of the concept of postmemory to generate a discourse that links the imagined circulation of the event between three generations to the real-world experience of it. As historical distance increases with time, one may expect that more writers with direct, remote, or indirect connections to the event will renew the narrative techniques of postmemorial writing, making the reinscription of the event in the memory of individuals, in the collective memory of certain groups, and in the institutionalized memory of French culture more sophisticated. Gérard Streiff's *Les caves de la Goutte d'Or* convincingly demonstrates how easily and efficiently fiction can integrate the memorial work done by historians and recirculate its message as a transitional discourse between history and fiction.

Another reason for adapting the concept of postmemory is that the repetition of the October 17, 1961 event in novels constitutes a succession of individual voices that feel the need to participate in a collective act of filling 'the gaps in knowledge' (Hirsch, 2012: 6). Repetition is at the core of the process of 'repairing' the fractures of an incomplete postcolonial historical narrative. It is the principle that will disclose how the silences that have surrounded a traumatic experience in the particular context of immigration are given the power to speak. Since the *ekphrasis*, the clear textual reference to the event, is repeated in narratives spanning an extended period (thirty years) and several generations of writers (ten years representing one generation) and since it is recontextualized by writers from North African origins as well as from mainstream French culture, it becomes a powerful tool to observe the dynamic of different modes of reappropriation, correction, and transmission of foreclosed historical situations. Repetition is a dynamic re-enactment which gives the event extension (it takes slightly different forms each time the *ekphrasis* is recontextualized) and creates a momentum: each repetition turns silence into a speech act that contributes to a discourse generated by the infinite variations between individual speech acts. That momentum becomes a convincing structure to circulate the objects of our connectedness with the past: souvenirs, recollections, remembrances, memory, rememory, all interact in various ways to make postmemory a powerful multifunctional tool that is capable of generating different layers of meaning. Commenting on images of the Holocaust, Hirsch concludes that 'repetition itself [is] a specifically postmemorial response to an inherited trauma,' thus supporting my hypothesis (Hirsch, 2012: 108). Here, as in Hirsch's study, 'repetition connects the second generation to the first, in its capacity to produce rather than screen the effect of trauma,' with the awareness that the mending process through works of fiction will increasingly circulate between more than two generations (2012: 108). This is where my deliberate choice of examining *ekphrases* embedded exclusively in fictional narratives is made clear. The process of representing the event (of imagining a representation of the event) by a choice of fragments that are intimate to individual writers, and of re-presenting them (of presenting them again) in new contexts, acts like a phenomenon of crystallization. For the critic, time and distance turn individual creativity into a conscious collective initiative. Each isolated re-creation of the event, using slightly different bits of reality framed in the self-contained world of an individual novel, functions on the collective level as a performance that is constantly being re-enacted and modifies the conventional official discourse. Through the work of time marked by the growing number of contextualizations of the event, every new piece of information gathers around the core I have identified as my initial matrix ('3 dead, 64 wounded'). Acting as a magnet for corrective history, the core attracts new pieces of information that form progressive layers of sedimentation by adding new knowledge to the core and by slowly assembling the scattered particles into a concretion of coherent, stable elements. This concretion is the ever-provisional final product, a reconstitution of the partially silenced, incomplete event, through the aggregation of particles of information that have corrective powers. It offers the possibility to repair distorted historical memory, but only partially, ever so slightly with each inscription in a new text, through bits of information gathered from the mosaic of separate narratives, knowing that their restorative capabilities are forever incomplete, that they cannot come together into a finite historical discourse. It is well known that '*the* reparative *in* narratives' (Rosello, 2010: 1) is a never-ending task of approximation. In that sense, each new text is another safety valve allowing the healing power of narration to continue its 'postmemorial working through' (Hirsch, 2012: 122) of the traumatic past in a present impeached (in its general and legal sense) by unresolved layers of silences in the fractal historical fabric between France's and Algeria's colonial and post-colonial pasts. Wedged at the intersection of memory and history, the massacre of October 17, 1961 is the object of a continuous act of translation in, and through, postcolonial fiction, forever confronted with the impossibility of being woven into a final, common, master narrative, which could be detached from the present, tucked away in its respective national historical contexts – France's and Algeria's – and preserved as the newest official record of the event.[14] This is precisely what the flow of partial rewritings of the October 17, 1961 massacre in fictions will prevent: the fossilization of the event into an official myth that has been debunked by the 1980s *beur* generation and is the object of a continued performative activity keeping the restorative power of fiction alive.

Notes

1 I have always considered the distinction between post-colonial with a hyphen and postcolonial as one word as pertinent to mark a significant difference between a reference to historical time and a concept (Murdoch and Donadey, 2005: 176–7). Of course, the difference of meaning does not exclude the concomitant presence of the concept and the temporal marker, as suggested with post(-)colonial. I believe that applying this distinction to the question of postmemory ('post-memory' as a marker of time, 'postmemory' as a concept) will allow me to refine my analysis along the same line as 'post(-)colonial.'

2 For a genesis of the evolution of immigration literatures in France since the 1980s, see Laronde (2014: xxvii–xxx; 2005: 175–92). While postmemory writing in the postcolonial period clearly had its origins in the *roman beur* of the 1980s, it marks the Arabo-French corpus of the 1990s as well, which serves as a link to the present. It is significant that the Afro-French literature from that same period did not develop along the line of what I call postmemory writing, although research certainly exists that ties in easily with the same dialectic (Dauge-Roth, 2010).

3 Lia Brozgal explores the role played by the archive or by its absence. Her remark that the absence of the archive is particularly efficient in 'bring[ing] to the fore the role of the literary text in representing that which cannot be seen or experienced, and in producing a new form of archive, one that slips the bounds of state control' (2014: 35) is of great interest to me since it clearly ties in with my project. Her article 'excavates and analyzes the alternative forms of epistemological activity at work during, and in spite of, the fifty-year period of archival silence imposed by the French government' (2014: 35). She argues that 'literature has filled in an epistemological void and, in so doing, created an alternative to the official archive' (2014: 38). Also related is Katelyn Knox's article 'Rapping Postmemory, Sampling the Archive; Reimagining 17 October 1961.' As an illustration of both trends, Gérard Streiff's 2001 novel, *Les caves de la Goutte d'Or*, makes ample use of

archives, while Leïla Sebbar relies on the power of fiction alone to pursue the same goal of excavating the past through a process of reconstructive postmemorial writing.

4 I could have started my chapter with this quote from Dominique Viart's entry on the novel in *Encyclopædia Universalis*:

A travers les "récits de filiation" et les "fictions biographiques," le sujet contemporain, orphelin des valeurs qui présidaient à l'existence de ses aînés, cherche en effet à comprendre un temps qui lui échappe, et à prendre en charge le legs du passé. Aussi, au moment où se referme le "court vingtième siècle" (1914–1989), laissant derrière lui un sillage de désastres et dépouillant le présent de ses récits de légitimation, les romanciers procèdent-ils à une véritable réhistoricisation de la conscience subjective. Mais ils ne le font guère à la façon du roman historique, pas même en imitant les rares romanciers des années 1960–1970 – Marguerite Yourcenar, Michel Tournier ... – qui s'y sont essayés. Selon les modèles offerts par Claude Simon et Patrick Modiano, c'est à partir du présent qu'ils envisagent ce passé, substituant dans le corps du livre le récit de la recherche et de l'enquête à la narration chronologique des événements proprement dits. Car le modèle fondateur du roman historique, lié, comme le rappelle Lukacs, à une période d'expansion, est désormais caduc: ce sont les traces et les archives, les récits insatisfaisants et tronqués, les zones d'ombre et d'incertitude que traque désormais un roman que l'on dirait plus justement "archéologique" qu'historique. (2002)

(Through his 'narratives of filiation' and 'fictional biographies,' the postmodern subject, deprived of the values that governed the existence of his elders, is trying to understand a time that eludes him and to take charge of the legacy of the past. So, at the close of 'the short twentieth century' (1914–1989), which leaves behind a string of disasters and robs the present of its narratives of legitimacy, the writers proceed to a complete rehistoricization of our subjective consciousness. But they do not proceed the way the historical novel did, not even by imitating the few novelists who have tried their hand at it in the 1960s and 1970s – Marguerite Yourcenar, Michel Tournier ... Following Claude Simon's and Patrick Modiano's examples, they approach the past from their position in the present and substitute in the body of their texts the narrative of the quest and the investigation for the chronological narration of the events themselves. Since the original model for the historical novel, which is tied, as Lukacs reminds us, to a period of expansion, is no longer viable, traces and archives, unsatisfactory and incomplete accounts, areas of shadow and uncertainty are what the novel that should be more appropriately called "archeological" rather than historical is looking for) [translation is my own]

What Dalila Kerchouche calls her 'quête harkéologique' (harkeological quest) in her book *Mon père, ce harki*, takes the form of an investigation into her father's past. Although the text is not a novel but a documented account of her years growing up in different *harki* camps in France, the neologism is obviously one such extension of the metaphor of the 'archeological' in fiction writing.

5 In his introduction to *Memory, Empire, and Postcolonialism*, Alec Hargreaves alludes to one important step in that progression when he reminds us that 'far from fading, memories of empire seemed to strengthen as the generations who had experienced the colonial venture advanced in age ... Today, those who fought in the war are nearing old age and a growing number have become anxious to unburden themselves of secrets which they have kept for almost half a century' (2005: 3). As Susan Ireland points out in 'The Algerian War Revisited,' the three works of fiction she briefly examines, Maïssa Bey's *Entendez-vous dans les montagnes ...* (2002), Akli Tadjer's *Le porteur de cartable* (2002), and Zahia Rahmani's *Moze* (2003) 'illustrate the desire to move forward by refusing to "différer le travail collectif de mémoire et de toujours retarder l'occasion de la réconciliation" (2005: 204) (put off collective memory work and defer the possibility of reconciliation). Some of the other texts that contribute to postmemorial work by using anamnesis as a narrative technique, but with a radically different approach, are Leïla Sebbar's novel *La Seine était rouge* and Dalila Kerchouche's autobiographical search for her father's past in *Mon père, ce harki*.
6 Both Mireille Rosello and Marianne Hirsch use the concept of the 'reparative' and acknowledge that the source of the metaphor is found in Eve Sedgwick's work. With her title, Rosello insists that '[her] study ... is not about reparative narratives but about *the* reparative *in* narratives' (2010: 1, italics in text) and that 'the reparative in narratives is less an object (a type of narrative) or even a practice (reparative reading) than the encounter between the two' (25). For Hirsch, '"reparative reading" offers alternative ways of knowing' (2012: 24). I will pay particular attention to the functional variations of the concept when I use it in the context of postcolonial fiction.
7 All translations are mine unless indicated otherwise.
8 I use the term "event" to refer to October 17, 1961 in its full historical sense, as a set of facts that correspond to a situation and lead to an outcome, to an evolution. In this context, "event" has often been used as a euphemism, with the intention of minimizing the brutality of the situation. In the case of the decolonization and independence of Algeria, the war was first referred to, in France, as *les troubles* (the unrest), then as *les événements* (the events), and finally as *la guerre* (the war), a term that would slowly prevail with the passing of time and the working through of the process of anamnesis. To describe October 17, 1961, historians and journalists chose terms that are much stronger than 'event': '*massacre*' (Einaudi, *Octobre 1961: Un Massacre à Paris*); '*tragédie*' (Brunet, *Police contre FLN: Le Drame d'octobre 1961*); '*crime*' (Le Cour Grandmaison, *Le 17 Octobre 1961: Un Crime d'Etat à Paris*). The proliferation of terms only shows the unclear status of the event and the intricacies of the process of working through the situation in language.
9 In his introduction to Marcel and Paulette Péju's 1962 manuscript, *le 17 octobre des Algériens*, Gilles Manceron puts the event in a global historical perspective by recalling Jim House and Neil MacMaster's remark that, 'même s'il [cet épisode] est rarement reconnu comme tel, il s'agit, dans toute l'histoire contemporaine de l'Europe occidentale, de la répression d'Etat la

plus violente et la plus meurtrière qu'ait jamais subie une manifestation de rue désarmée' (even though it is rarely acknowledged as such, in the entire contemporary history of western Europe, this episode of State suppression is the most violent and bloody to have ever been suffered by an unarmed street demonstration). Manceron insists on the enormity of the massacre by adding that 'le nombre de ses victimes est supérieur, par exemple à celui de la répression de la place Tiananmen à Pékin en 1989 par les autorités chinoises, un événement qui, lui, avait eu immédiatement un retentissement mondial. C'est assurément un événement unique dans l'histoire de la France et de sa capitale' (the number of victims, for example, was higher than that of the suppression at Tiananmen Square in Peking by the Chinese authorities in 1989, an event that had an immediate global impact. It is obviously a unique event in the history of France and its capital). In a note, he adds that the number of victims was greater than the Champs de Mars shooting on July 17, 1791, which killed about fifty (2011: 7). Even the November 13, 2015 terrorist attacks in Paris which killed 130 people do not compete with the likely death toll of October 17, 1961.

10 So far, I have identified eighteen novels where the event is present.

11 Just as the terms '*mémoire convenue*' or '*mémoriellement correct*' (memorially correct) indicate the 'right' way to think of the German Occupation and the Vichy government, camouflaging the extent of the October 17, 1961 massacre, points to the 'correct' way of thinking of the Algerian War in France.

12 *A Practical Guide to French Harki Literature* is a good example of this recent development. In her contribution to the book, 'Harki daughters' "Righting" Narratives,' Geraldine Enjelvin also feels the need to integrate the concept of postmemory to the field of immigration studies when she discusses the 'testimony writing' of four second-generation French women writers whose fathers were harkis (2014: 93).

13 This scope justifies using postmemory with a hyphen (post-memory) to refer to a temporal and spatial marker similar to my use of "post-colonial" to designate a hiatus between two historical periods. I hope that transferring my distinction between the 'post' of 'post(-)colonial' with or without a hyphen, to the term postmemory, will add a layer of meaning to the concept of postmemory. Post-memory with a hyphen, then, would signal the temporal disruption of the linear continuity between generations in the process of memory-building ('an uneasy oscillation between continuity and rupture,' Hirsch, 2012: 4) and highlight the movement of 'working through' the past on a cycle of two generations; postmemory without a hyphen becomes the sign of a mentality which is part of, and functions along the same lines as, a postcolonial mind frame where the temporal fracture between past and present is resolved in the inclusion of the past in the present. I hope this distinction between temporal (historical) time and a generational practice of recalling the past (archeological time tied to the present), thereby signaling a tighter connectedness of the concept of postmemory with that of the postcolonial, will better refine the specificities of the concept of postmemory when it is transferred to the domain of the literatures of immigration in France.

14 The study of postmemorial writing could branch out in a new direction if one were to consider the place of the October 17 event in fiction from Algeria. It would be most informative to investigate how the event has been represented in the new national literature from Algeria after the cultural discontinuity brought about by the country's independence in 1962, knowing that the year 1961 in France is the critical articulation signaling the end of the French colonial empire. In that sense, the October 17 event is intricately linked to the traumatic chiasm that marks the end of the colonization era, heralding both the beginning of a post(-)colonial culture in France and the advent of a new national literature in Algeria.

References

Ajir. Pour les Harkis. (2006). Web. November 17, 2015. web.archive.org/web/20090215232126/http://harkis.com/article.php3?id_article=31
Barthes, R. (1984). 'L'effet de réel,' *Le bruissement de la langue*, Paris: Seuil, 179–87.
Baudrillard, J. (1992). *L'Illusion de la fin ou la grève des événements*, Paris: Galilée.
Bey, M. (2002). *Entendez-vous dans les montagnes . . .*, La Tour d'Aigues: L'Aube/Barzakh.
Brozgal, L. (2014). 'In the Absence of the Archive (Paris, October 17, 1961),' *South Central Review*, 31(1), 34–54.
Brunet, J.-P. (1999). *Police contre FLN: Le Drame d'octobre 1961*, Paris: Flammarion.
Certeau, M. de (1975). *L'Ecriture de l'histoire*, Paris: Gallimard.
Daeninckx, D. (1984). *Meurtres pour mémoire*, Paris: Gallimard.
Dauge-Roth, A. (2010). *Writing and Filming the Genocide of the Tutsis in Rwanda: Dismembering and Remembering Traumatic History*, Lanham, MD: Lexington Books.
Einaudi, J.-L. (1991). *La Bataille de Paris: 17 octobre 1961*, Paris: Seuil.
Einaudi, J.-L. (2001). *Octobre 1961: Un Massacre à Paris*, Paris: Fayard.
Enjelvin, G. (2014). 'Harki Daughters' "Righting" Narratives: Resistance Identity and *Littérature Naturelle?*,' in K. Moser (ed.), *A Practical Guide to French Harki Literature*, New York: Lexington Books, 83–99.
Hargreaves, A. G. (ed.) (2005). *Memory, Empire, and Postcolonialism: Legacies of French Colonialism*, Lanham, MD: Lexington Books.
Hirsch, M. (2012). *The Generation of Postmemory: Writing and Visual Culture after the Holocaust*, New York: Columbia University Press.
Kerchouche, D. (2003). *Mon père, ce harki*, Paris: Seuil.
Kettane, N. (1985). *Le Sourire de Brahim*, Paris: Denoël.
Knox, K. E. (2014). 'Rapping Postmemory, Sampling the Archive; Reimagining 17 October 1961,' *Modern and Contemporary France*, 22(3): 381–97.
Laborie, P. (2011). *Le Chagrin et le venin: La France sous l'Occupation, mémoire et idées reçues*, Paris: Bayard.
Lallaoui, M. (1986). *Les Beurs de Seine*, Paris: L'Arcantère.

Laronde, M. (2005). 'Displaced Discourses: Post(-)coloniality, Francophone Space(s), and the Literature(s) of Immigration in France,' in A. Donadey and A. Murdoch (eds), *Postcolonial Theory and Francophone Literary Studies*, Gainesville, FL: University Press of Florida, 175–92.

Laronde, M. (2014). *Rethinking Reading, Writing, and a Moral Code in Contemporary France: Postcolonializing High Culture in the Schools of the Republic*, Lanham, MD: Lexington Books.

Le Cour Grandmaison, O. (2001). *Le 17 Octobre 1961: Un Crime d'Etat à Paris*, Paris: La Dispute.

Manceron, G. (2011). 'Préface: Une publication nécessaire,' in M. and P. Péju, *Le 17 octobre des Algériens*, Paris: La Découverte.

Moser, K. (2014). *A Practical Guide to French Harki Literature*, Lanham, MD: Lexington Books.

Murdoch, A. and Donadey, A. (eds) (2005). *Postcolonial Theory and Francophone Literary Studies*, Gainesville, FL: University Press of Florida.

Péju, M. and Péju, P. (2011). *Le 17 octobre des Algériens*, Paris: La Découverte.

Rahmani, Z. (2003). *Moze*, Paris: Sabine Wespieser.

Rosello, M. (2010). *The Reparative in Narratives: Works of Mourning in Progress*, Liverpool: Liverpool University Press.

Rousso, H. (2002). *The Haunting Past: History, Memory, and Justice in Contemporary France*, trans. Ralph Schoolcraft, Philadelphia, PA: University of Pennsylvania Press.

Sebbar, L. (1999). *La Seine était rouge*, Paris: Thierry Magnier.

Streiff, G. (2001). *Les Caves de la Goutte d'Or*, Paris: Baleine-Le Seuil.

Tadjer, A. (2002). *Le Porteur de cartable*, Paris: Jean-Claude Lattès.

Viart, D. (2015). 'ROMAN – Le roman français contemporain, Ecrire l'Histoire: Le roman archéologique,' *Encyclopædia Universalis* [n.d.]. Web. January 24, 2015.

Viart, D. and Vercier, B. (2005). *La Littérature française au présent: Héritage, modernité, mutations*, Paris: Bordas.

White, H. (1973). *Metahistory: The Historical Imagination in Nineteenth-Century Europe*, Baltimore, MD: Johns Hopkins University Press.

9

Unearthing the father's secret: postmemory and identity in *harki* and pied noir narratives

Véronique Machelidon

Interviewed by Thierry Leclère in *La Guerre des mémoires: La France face à son passé colonial*, renowned French historian Benjamin Stora summarized his life's work as an attempt to 'dresser des passerelles entre deux mémoires différentes [de la colonisation française] et de trouver des espaces mémoriels communs' (2011: 37) (bridge two different memories of French colonization and find common memorial spaces). In an earlier article titled 'Quand une mémoire (de guerre) peut en cacher une autre (coloniale)' Stora deplores that 'une sorte de cloisonnement, de communautarisation du souvenir par une position victimaire s'est installée dans une compétition du statut de la meilleure victime. A partir de là les différents groupes de mémoire déjà à la périphérie de la société ne demandent pas à l'Etat ou aux responsables politiques de rendre des comptes, mais le demandent à l'autre communauté' (2006: 66) (a sort of cloistering and memory appropriation by communities taking on the role of victim has set in, resulting in a competition between different communities for best victim status. From then on, the various memory groups already located on the margins of society do not hold the State or political representatives accountable but instead turn against each other). In turn, this attitude reinforces the 'colonial fracture' (Bancel and Blanchard, 2006: 13)[1] and France's amnesia regarding its colonial past, which has severe consequences for its present and future, as postcolonial subjects, the ghosts of the French Republic (Barclay, 2011: 22), feel socially excluded, and an 'important segment of French society' still rejects Algerian immigrants (Stora, 2005: 65).

In the first decade of the twentieth century, however, a memorial reawakening occurred. In the wake of the 2003 celebration of the *Year of Algeria* in France and following the production of postcolonial studies in the Anglo-Saxon world, there has been a recent blooming of critical works on both sides of the Atlantic, dedicated to the study of the "*harki* experience" from the point of view of history or literature.[2] Yet Stora's appeal for building bridges between different groups and their cloistered memories of the Algerian War of Independence (1954–62) and its sequels has found overall little echo among today's literary critics. Susan Ireland's article 'Creating Shared Memories in Three Harki Narratives' is a notable exception. Instead of comparing works written exclusively by members of the *harki* community, she studies novels by different actors of the Algerian War: a pied noir, a *harki* daughter, and a veteran French soldier. Not only do these works diegetically engage in a comparison of the 'perspectives of memory carriers representing two or more different constituencies,' but Ireland herself establishes bridges between writers that belong to opposite sides, that of the colonizer (the pied noir, the military) and that of the colonized (the *harki*-s) (2014: 102).³ In so doing, Ireland also suggests that the production of '*harki* narratives' is not the exclusive prerogative of the *harki* community but that they may be generated, surely with different emphases and sensitivities, by representatives of other groups involved in the war.

My own reading of Dalila Kerchouche's *Mon père, ce harki* (2003) and Thierry Galdeano's *Pieds-noirs, Harkis, nos cœurs orphelins* (2012) follows in Ireland's footsteps by comparing works from different postcolonial constituencies, one by a *harki* daughter and the other by a pied noir son.⁴ Produced by descendants of different actors in the Algerian War of Independence, both have at their core the search for the father's secret linked to his role in the war. The fathers' silence and denial can be seen as resulting from trauma exacerbated by France's (self-)imposed colonial amnesia. The discovery of the father's mystery takes each of the two narrators on a memorial quest that ultimately results in psychological and emotional growth, helping the *harki* daughter and pied noir son find their identity and place in French society. Each narrative attempts to heal to some degree the wounds of war and expatriation, particularly for the 'postgenerations' but only the pied noir son as protagonist and narrator performs and enacts the reconciliation between separate, *harki* and pied noir, community experiences, pointing to the creation of memorial bridges recommended by Stora.⁵

Odd bedfellows: a transgeneric comparison

Before discussing each of the postmemorial and identity quests, it is helpful to establish the validity of a comparison between works belonging to seemingly different genres. *Mon père, ce harki* is a well-known, much-read example of what Giulia Fabbiano defines as the paradigm of 'Harki literature' in that it 'talks about and revisits the main memorial topoi upon which [*harki*] feelings of collective belonging are constructed: life in Algeria, enrollment, post-independence, internment in France and life in the camps, forgetfulness, and the identity quest' (2014: 26). In the first part of the narrative titled 'France, la traversée des camps' (France, from camp to camp), Dalila Kerchouche, a journalist for the weekly French magazine *L'Express*, commemorates the fortieth anniversary of her parents' arrival in France in 1962 by retracing her family's expatriation from Algeria and wanderings through French internment camps. In the second part, her genealogical inquiry into her roots takes her to Algeria on a quest for her father's past.

Kerchouche's book has been described as a composite, intergeneric work combining 'le réel et le fictionnel, le roman et l'autobiographie, le reportage journalistique, l'étude socio-anthropologique et ethnologique, l'analyse historique' (Elbaz, 2012: 208) (reality and fiction, novel and autobiography, journalism, socio-anthropological, and ethnological study, historical analysis). It will not identify itself as a novel because 'la fiction, à elle seule, aurait tendance à dissoudre cette vérité incontournable dont veut nous faire part l'écrivain' (Elbaz, 2012: 209) (fiction by itself would tend to water down this major truth that the writer wants to share with us). Indeed, Kerchouche establishes her authority by quoting a variety of official and scholarly sources that support, confirm, and generalize her account of her family's experiences. Yet, despite this effort to demonstrate the veracity of the facts and stories she has compiled from her relatives' and other witnesses' testimonies, Kerchouche 'blends traditional journalistic research methods with literary techniques.' As noted by Kenneth Olsson, she aims to 'resuscitate the past. In order to make this project come to fruition, she endeavors to enter into a sort of time warp, letting places and various histories transform her into a vessel for "voices" of the past' (2014: 150).

Thierry Galdeano's *Pieds-noirs, Harkis, nos cœurs orphelins*, on the other hand, is a much lesser-known work that is structured along two plots. One follows the Galdeano family's arrival from Algeria to France in 1969, describing their struggle to integrate French society and achieve modest professional stability. The other narrative strand traces a *harki* couple's repeated attempts to escape internment, in order to reunite with the man's brother in the southern French city of Montpellier. The book advertises itself as a 'novel' on the title page, qualifying this by adding that 'certains passages de ce roman sont librement inspirés de faits réels' (2012: 4) (some passages of this novel are free renditions of real events). The author's dedication of his work to his wife, children, and his late father's companion and the concordance between certain "facts" of the autodiegetic narrator's fictional life and the author's biographical data, as posted on his personal webpage, encourage the reader to interpret this work of fiction as semi-autobiographical, particularly since the main protagonist of the novel has the same first and last name as the author (Thierry Galdeano). Similarly, the first-person narrator's wife and children in the novel are named after the author's real-life family, and his career at the end is the same as the author's actual profession (348). Presenting itself as fiction, *Pieds-noirs, Harkis, nos cœurs orphelins* is in part an autobiographical testimony written for 'tous les enfants, petits-enfants des Harkis et des Pieds-noirs' (all children, grandchildren of *harkis*, and pieds noirs) in a generalizing gesture evoking Kerchouche's collective postmemorial duty: 'Alors qu'au départ je ne pensais écrire qu'une histoire individuelle, je me rends compte que ce récit ressemble au parcours de milliers d'anonymes. Que des milliers d'enfants de harkis auraient pu réaliser le même voyage que moi' (187) (Initially I thought I was writing an individual's story; now I realize that this story is also that of thousands of anonymous people. Thousands of *harki* children could have gone on the same journey as I).[6]

Although Galdeano's novel does not aim at scientific or scholarly accuracy as Kerchouche does, it is nevertheless firmly anchored in identifiable historical reality. The 1954 visit of interior minister François Mitterrand to Algiers, the Evian accords of March 1962, which paved the way for Algerian independence, the massacre of pieds noirs and *harkis* in the Algerian city of Oran on July 5, 1962, the various French presidential elections, and the economic and construction boom of the 1970s provide a realistic historical framework for the fictional adventures of the Galdeano family and their questionable progress after their 1969 "repatriation."

The generic hybridity of these two works, Kerchouche's, which presents itself as non-imaginative, and Galdeano's not-quite-fictional narrative, becomes more easily understandable if both are interpreted as presenting postmemories, in the sense established by Marianne Hirsch:

> "Post-memory" describes the relationship that the "generation after" bears to the personal, collective, and cultural trauma of those who came before – to experiences they "remember" only by means of the stories, images, and behaviors among which they grew up. But these experiences were transmitted to them so deeply and affectively as to *seem* to constitute memories in their own right. Postmemory's connection to the past is thus actually mediated not by recall but **by imaginative investment, projection, and creation**. (2012: 5, emphasis added)

Postmemory as personal urgency

Kerchouche's postmemorial quest, which results in the narrator's series of shifting identifications, is triggered by the father's reticence to tell the event which is the 'ground zero' of *harki* experience, namely his "choosing" the French side by enlisting as an auxiliary of the French Army in the Algerian War of Independence. As Giulia Fabbiano explains

> l'enrôlement pro-français est un événement central de l'histoire familiale, parce que fondateur d'un nouveau cours; à partir de ce moment, rien ne sera plus pareil pour les membres de la famille et une rupture généalogique spatio-temporelle se consommera entre l'avant/maintenant et l'ailleurs/ici. L'enrôlement n'inaugure pas seulement une nouvelle lecture de l'histoire ... mais pris au sein d'un plus vaste processus post-colonial, participe en tant qu'ethnogenèse, de la fabrication d'une nouvelle posture identitaire et surtout sert de principe explicatif de l'existence. Le passé, le présent et

l'avenir sont lus à la lumière de ce qui est malencontreusement nommé "engagement" aux contours tellement douloureux qu'il est parfois, voire presque toujours impossible d'en parler. (2010: 99)

Enlisting on the French side is a defining moment in family history, because it sets a new course; from then on, nothing will be the same for the family members, and a spatial and temporal genealogy rupture will occur, dividing before and now, back there and here. Enlisting with the French does not simply generate a new reading of history ... but within the larger postcolonial process, it contributes as ethnogenesis to the building of a new identity and serves as a principle explaining one's existence. Past, present, and future are read in the light of a misnamed pro-French "engagement," which causes so much pain that it is sometimes, or even almost always, impossible to discuss.

Kerchouche's emotional investment in the belated transmission of the past is reflected in the pressing questions inaugurating her narrative and setting her off on a pilgrimage through France and Algeria to fill in the gap of the father's silence (13). These questions return in key places of the narrative, for instance between the end of the first, longer section, and the second part, which takes the narrator back to Algeria, the source of the family's drama: 'Pourquoi s'est-il engagé aux côtés de la France? Pourquoi a-t-il renoncé à son pays? Je ne sais toujours pas. Il ne m'a encore rien dit ou à peine ... Plus je m'approche de lui avec mes questions, et plus il fuit, se rétracte, m'échappe, prétextant fatigue, heure du journal télévisé ou de la prière, courses à faire ... Pourtant c'est là-bas que la vie de ma famille a basculé. Là-bas que mon père est devenu harki' (201) (Why did he enlist on the French side? Why did he give up his country? I still don't know. He has not told me anything or hardly ... The closer I come to him with my questions, the more he runs away from me, withdraws, evades under various pretexts, like tiredness, the television news or prayer times, errands to do ... Yet my family's life was turned upside down back there and back there my father became a *harki*). The repetition of 'là-bas' (back there) emphasizes the colonial 'ethnogenesis,' which created a fractured, postcolonial identity. What Fabbiano designates as a 'malencontreusement nommé engagement' (misnamed engagement) Kerchouche first describes equally awkwardly as the father's 'choice' in a Manichean paradigm that opposes treason to loyalty, thus replicating hegemonic national myths in Algeria and France.[7]

In contrast with Kerchouche's inaugural interrogations about the father's past, Antoine Galdeano's war experiences are delayed to the end of the first third of the novel and they are initially raised not by his son Thierry, but by a third-person heterodiegetic narrator who describes Antoine's sleep disorder: 'Antoine vociférait dans son sommeil. Bien plus éveillé que sa femme, il insultait l'ombre de ses bras. Projetés par la lumière de la pleine lune, des serpents se cabraient et ondulaient sur les murs de sa chambre' (124) (Antoine was shouting in his sleep. Far more awake than his wife, he was yelling at the shadows cast by his arms. Illuminated by the full moon, snakes were writhing and slithering on the bedroom walls). The pied noir's apocalyptic nightmares, where he mumbles about shootings, killings, misinterpreting orders, and running for his life, are associated by the narrator with Antoine's volcanic temperament, his resistance to orders, his disrespect of authority, his instability, and his frequent bouts of anger against outsiders and family, including his son Thierry.

Instead of the nostalgic evocation of Algerian colonial life (*nostalgérie*) typical of much pied noir literature,[8] the third-person narrator traces Antoine's "post-traumatic stress disorder" back to his Algerian past, 'lambeaux de vie déchiquetés par les *barbelés* de son inconscient?' (158, emphasis added) (pieces of a life in tatters, ripped apart by the *barbed wires* of his unconscious). Like the *harkis* corralled behind camp fences and into national oblivion, Antoine cannot overcome the trauma of the Algerian War. Half-way through the novel, Thierry's voice takes over as a first-person autodiegetic narrator, and his interest in the father's repressed war experience heightens, particularly after discovering Antoine's loaded pistol hidden in his parents' bedroom (204). Now speaking as a 'je,' Thierry tries to piece together the disjointed bits of memorial information that Antoine blurts out during the nightmares which haunt father and son, narrator and reader, at increasing frequency. The shift from third- to first-person narration indicates the personal urgency for Thierry of uncovering the father's buried secret, which poisons their relationship and stunts the son's personal growth. This relationship now becomes the main focus of the novel.

In her work on postmemory and the Holocaust Marianne Hirsch emphasizes the subjugating power of postmemories on the "generation after":

> To grow up with overwhelming inherited memories, to be dominated by narratives that preceded one's birth or one's consciousness, is to risk having one's own life stories displaced, even evacuated, by our ancestors. It is to be shaped, however indirectly, by traumatic fragments of events that still defy narrative reconstruction and exceed comprehension. These events happened in the past, but their effects continue in the present. (2012: 5)

Yet, as both Kerchouche and Galdeano suggest, reticence, the fathers' repression of the trauma of war and decolonization, produces equally devastating effects and urges the postgeneration to repair the violence of the past and the (self-)enforced silence through telling and writing. The pied noir son's family narrative in *Harkis, pieds-noirs, nos cœurs orphelins* and the *harki* daughter's imaginative reconstruction of her parents' past are both love messages to the paternal figure who has been silenced by what Bourdieu called the '"symbolic violence" … exercised through the construction, by the dominant ruling class, of an official narrative of the past that refuses to hear and integrate the "voice of the other"' (Enjelvin, 2014: 84). Benjamin

Stora completes this analysis by situating collective silencing within France's postcolonial amnesia:

> Après l'indépendance algérienne de 1962, l'histoire de l'empire colonial français semble avoir brusquement disparu des récits scolaires. Nécessaire oubli après la période de guerre, besoin de tourner la page sans doute. Mais aussi refus d'assumer les exactions commises et les inégalités du temps colonial. Dans les années 1970, la société française voulait oublier la colonisation, on ne l'enseignait plus, on ne transmettait plus cette histoire. La France, tournée vers l'Europe, voulait oublier le Sud. (2011: 33)[9]

> After Algerian independence in 1962, the history of the French colonial empire seems to have suddenly vanished from school textbooks, probably as a result from the need to forget, the need to turn the page after the war period surely, but also as a refusal to take responsibility for colonial crimes and inequities. In the 1970s French society wanted to forget colonization, this history was no longer taught in schools, it was no longer transmitted. France had turned toward Europe and wanted to forget the South.

Uncovering the father's past and the source of his trauma is presented as a prerequisite for the son's material, social, and psychological autonomy. While acceptance of the past through memory will not radically improve the Galdeano parents' life in France, it will help the "postgeneration" learn from their parents' experiences and develop different identifications. Thierry's plot from childhood through early adulthood develops as a reflection of his father's uncontrolled temper and rejection of authority. While Antoine evades reality through scuffles with local gangs and late-night parties with friends and occasional mistresses, his son makes up for the humiliations of French school by fleeing into reading fiction, watching movies, and running into a variety of life-threatening adventures. When he sets off on a path mirroring that of Antoine Doisnel, François Truffaut's asocial hero in the film *Les 400 coups*, Thierry's diegetic fate appears hardly promising.

It is only after hearing his father's story that Thierry can trust in his own powers and is mature enough to pursue graduate studies in England and France, which are crowned with a more rewarding job as a 'commercial au sein d'une agence immobilière' (real estate agent) to support his own growing family (348). Liberated by his confession, Antoine finds peace before dying a few months later. As the narrator concludes, 'les hommes et les femmes ont besoin de savoir leur passé, leur histoire pour construire leur avenir' (men and women need to know their past and their history in order to build their future) (375).

The narrator of *Mon père, ce harki* would certainly agree with this conclusion, although her quest is motivated by identity construction, not economic needs. Thanks to her parents' sacrifices and to her own efforts she enjoys professional stability as a journalist. Her efforts to uncover the father's role in the Algerian War of Independence are motivated by a search for personal wholeness and self-respect. As Zinel Ali-Ben Ali remarks, 'souvent les enfants de Harkis se réclament d'une double, voire d'une multiple appartenance' (2010: 120) (*harki* children often claim double, or even multiple, community identifications). The father's story, pieced together across the Mediterranean, will allow the narrator to reconcile her diverse cultural identities, as *harki*, Berber, Algerian, and French and to overcome the feelings of shame and guilt that she has inherited from him.

Postmemory as a collective and political undertaking

Through their respective mnemonic work, both Kerchouche's and Galdeano's narrators seek to humanize the father and with him the collectivity he represents, whether *harki* or pied noir. They attempt to restore the dignity he was deprived of during his lifetime (Ali-Ben Ali, 2010: 121; Elbaz, 2012: 208). In both works the postmemorial quest is at once individual and collective, as the restored fathers' "honor" falls back on their children and their communities (Redouane, 2012: 231). Thus, the narrator's inquiry in *Mon père, ce harki* is structured along a sort of narratorial anaphor: it begins with the letter "h" like *honte* (shame), proceeds to the "h" of *haine* (hatred of France and of her father) and ends up with 'un grand h' (a capital-letter "h") like *honneur* (276). This neat progression appears to undo the irony of the title *Mon père, ce harki*, which Susan Ireland has correctly identified as a takeoff from Gérard Lauzier's 1991 film *Mon père, ce héros*, and it simultaneously highlights the political dimension of Kerchouche's narratorial project (2009: 304). In Galdeano's novel, a similar generalizing intent is expressed in the postface, where the author presents himself as a spokesman for 'Harkis et … Pieds-noirs. Ces hommes et ces femmes (qui) ont gardé leur pudeur, leur dignité, et un peu de joie' (375) (*harkis* and … pieds noirs, these men and women who have retained their dignity, self-respect, and a bit of joy).

As noted by several readers, Kerchouche's inquiry into her father's past is initiated by yet another letter "h," standing for *harkeology*, a neologism she has coined to designate the historic and genealogical quest which takes her to Algeria, unbeknownst to her parents. The second part of the book combines information about the family before and during the War of Independence (1954–62). In processing all the historical and biographical information centering on the father's Algerian story as a *harki*, the narrator is implicitly led to revise her initial belief in choice and intentionality. The father's decision to support the French Army and enlist as auxiliary on the French side is found to be the result of circumstances, clan pressure, and economic necessity, not ideological commitment.[10] This important fact is validated by a local witness of the war, her cousin's uncle, who is of the same generation as Kerchouche's father and who recognizes that 'L'indépendance de l'Algérie, ce n'était pas notre priorité. On ne pensait qu'à survivre dans un pays où la guerre augmentait le risque de famine' (221) (Our priority was not Algeria's independence. All we cared about was to survive in a land where war was increasing the risk of famine). He adds that in a given family brothers would split and side with opposite factions (the FLN independentists or the French military) in order to protect their families from both camps and maximize their chance of survival. This was also the case in the Kerchouche family, where the narrator's father served the French, whereas his brother Latrache supported the insurgents. The father is further exonerated from guilt when the narrator finds out that he used his position in the French forces to protect the villagers (249).

Framing the multilayered discovery of a complex and ambiguous history

The final revelation of the father's war story is carefully staged and framed by the narrator's visit to the mausoleum of a pre-Islamic saint, Sidi Youcef, who is locally venerated as a prophet and protector of the Kerchouche family. The narrator's cousin Tayeb functions as the oracle who initiates the solving of the riddle. Tayeb's questions to the main (extradiegetic) narrator (Kerchouche) introduce an intradiegetic narrative, as if the history of the Algerian War and particularly that of the *harkis*, is so convoluted, controversial, and deeply buried, that the mystery can only be approached indirectly and patiently peeled off, as it were, one layer at a time: 'Est-ce que ton père t'a raconté la guerre? Ton père ne t'a rien dit?' (256) (Has your father told you about the war? Hasn't he told you anything?). Faced with Kerchouche's denial, Tayeb proceeds with his tale, as would the embedded narrator of a nineteenth-century French novel: 'Viens, assieds-toi là, je vais te raconter' (257) (Come over here, sit down, I'm going to tell you). But instead of quoting Tayeb's words in direct speech inside her own narrative, Kerchouche transcribes and appropriates them in her own voice, using the first-person possessive ('quand *mon* père rentre chez lui'). This shift to free indirect discourse, reveals the process of postmemory and shows how a witness testimony becomes the daughter's own, essential truth grounding her complex identifications and her life from henceforth.

From cousin Tayeb, the narrator finds out that her father, while serving in a French artillery regiment, became progressively converted to the cause of Algerian independence and helped the FLN as a double agent, by secretly furnishing ammunition to the insurgents.[11] While this discovery restores the father's honor from the "Algerian" point of view, it also complicates the narrator's understanding of the war, where the lines between friends and foes became muddled. Anti-French guerrillas disguised themselves with French military uniforms, Muslim natives supported both sides simultaneously, the FLN racketed and terrorized the Algerian people, and the French military turned against the Secret Armed Organization (OAS), which fought to keep

Algeria French despite the signing of the Evian Accords.[12] The narrator modestly concludes: 'Je comprends à ce récit qu'il n'y eut pas une guerre d'Algérie, mais *des* guerres d'Algérie: l'une algéro-algérienne, l'autre franco-française' (266) (From this narrative I understand that there was not *one* Algerian War, but several: one war pitting Algerian against Algerian, another pitting French against French). As the demarcation between different sides becomes blurred, between the French and the native insurgents, between various competing Algerian independentist factions, and between pro- and anti-colonization French, the father is absolved of guilt, responsibility, and treason. Instead, accusations of betrayal are redirected toward France, which disarmed and abandoned its Muslim auxiliaries, toward the local clan leader or Bachaga, who fled to France, and toward the new Algerian government, which did not abide by the Evian accords: 'Je suis déçue par la France autant que je le suis par l'Algérie. Les deux pays ont trahi leurs idéaux … Les traîtres ne sont pas ceux que l'on croit' (270) (I am disappointed as much in France as in Algeria. Both countries betrayed their ideals … The traitors aren't who you think they are). Ironically, the father's honor is restored when the narrator establishes the indignity of past political opponents and the messiness of decolonization, which defies simplistic binary judgments and undermines the construction of national master narratives on both sides of the Mediterranean.

The narrator's sobering realization of the ambiguities of the political struggle leads the reader to a deeper understanding of the reasons behind the *harki* father's silence and his denial of his double-agent role in the war (273–4). His testimony would undermine France's amnesia, forcing the nation to openly recognize that their Algerian "allies" did not really support them, just as it would question the official Algerian myth that all "true" Algerians were rebels and all *harkis* "traitors." As the father recognizes at the end of Kerchouche's narrative, these muddy truths cannot yet be spoken.

The revelation of the father's military past leaves the narrator caught in an uncomfortable *no (wo)man's land* of "neither … nor." Yet this dis-identification changes, as her genealogical inquiry broadens and expands into the clan's distant past and the narrator's observations of present Algerian life. When she witnesses gender role inequality and restrictions on women's freedom in rural Algeria, she feels reconciled with her French heritage, the guarantee of women's rights, and emancipation.[13] The narrator witnesses the devastating effects of a more recent war, the Algerian Civil War of the 1990s, which opposed governmental forces and extremist Islamist groups. The violence of Islamic terrorism hit all villagers and especially women, who must now be veiled to go out and who do so at their own risk. She hears eye-opening accounts of women being kidnapped and raped and of villages once again pillaged and racketed, this time by the Islamist rebels. As she realizes the physical danger, gender inequality, and divisiveness prevailing in modern Algerian society, the narrator is grateful to her parents for their sacrifices: 'Voilà la vie que j'aurais eue si mes parents n'avaient pas quitté l'Algérie. A cet instant je me sens française, définitivement française' (239) (This is the kind of life that would have been mine if my parents had stayed in Algeria. At this very moment I feel French, definitely French).

The narrator's acceptance of displacement and of her dual roots (Algerian and French) takes a positive turn and expands, as she uncovers another, more distant layer of her family's and her clan's history. Through earlier research she has found out that her ancestors were Berbers of the Beni Boudouane tribe and that they were forced to give up their language, their culture, and their religion during the Arabic colonization, which predated the French arrival. Thus, the French colonization, which deprived the clan of its fertile lands, repeated an earlier expropriation and socio-symbolic disempowerment, when the tribe was obliged to speak Arabic and convert to Islam:

> Cette révélation m'a bouleversée, parce qu'elle désensablait tout un pan de mon histoire. Je suis donc berbère ... Je me sens rassurée, rassurée parce qu'il y a déjà eu un changement culturel dans ma famille. De Berbères nous sommes devenus Arabes. Et d'Arabes aujourd'hui nous devenons français. Comme moi mes ancêtres ont changé de langue, de coutumes, d'identité. En basculant dans l'Islam, ont-ils eu le sentiment de 'trahir' leurs origines, comme j'ai pu l'avoir en devenant française? Apparemment non, cela dédramatise mon histoire. (214)

> This revelation was eye-opening for me, because it excavated a whole segment of my history. So I am a Berber ... I feel reassured because there was a cultural switch in my family history before. We were Berbers and then became Arabs. And today we're becoming French. Like me, my ancestors had to adopt a new language, new customs, and a new identity. As they switched to Islam, did they have the feeling of betraying their origins, as I did when I became French? Probably not. This makes my own history much less dramatic.

Thus, the narrator moves beyond the dual alternative of either Algerian or French to accept her multiple ethnic and cultural roots, and she understands personal and collective change as required by adaptation to historical, social, and political circumstances. Not only is she absolved, like her father, of betrayal of a fantasized monolithic pre-colonial identity, but she reclaims the prestige of her ancestors, who presided courts of justice, cultivated the arts, sciences, and letters, and stood on good terms with the Ottoman Empire. As the narrator moves further back in time, she understands that (de)colonization is a part of a long and complicated process exceeding the opposition France/Algeria, North/South, and belonging to the larger spatial and historical framework of the relations between the Middle East and the West. The identifications generated by this long and expansive history represent complex adjustments and personal negotiations that go well beyond individual agency and control.

Familial and affiliative postmemory: bridging cloistered memories

In *Pieds-noirs, Harkis, nos cœurs orphelins* Thierry's quest for the father's secret, which is the precondition of his own social, emotional, and psychological growth, remains geographically and historically circumscribed. It does not take him back to his parents' native land, the palm oasis of Béchar in western Algeria, but it is an equally complicated process of postmemorial detective work. When Thierry moves to Montpellier with his young wife Valérie to start a family of his own, he is haunted by Antoine's nightmares, the broken puzzle of his past, and the phantoms of Algerian life: 'A force de mettre ses rêves et ses cauchemars bout à bout, je suis parvenu à construire quelques bribes de phrases. Je cherche le sommeil chaque nuit et tente de reconstituer le puzzle ... Par ricochets je fais de ma vie une traçante de la vie d'Antoine. Il est le canon qui m'a projeté avec toutes ces questions. Des questions sur lui, des questions sur tout' (316) (As I piece together his dreams and nightmares, I manage to reconstruct bits of sentences. Each night, as I try to fall asleep, I seek to put the puzzle back together ... As a result, I turn my life into a mirror of Antoine's. He is the cannonball that hit me with all these questions. Questions about him, about everything). An hourglass containing sand from the Sahara Desert functions as a metonym, indicating the urgency of retrieving Antoine's buried Algerian story, as it foreshadows his imminent death.

During a visit to Angers, Thierry confronts his father about his role in the Algerian War. Perhaps less inhibited than the *harki* father in *Mon père, ce harki*, the pied noir volunteers an incomplete story, which is later confirmed by an external source, other repatriated pieds noirs acquaintances from Béchar. As Antoine's intradiegetic narratee, Thierry finds out that his father served during the war in a small military unit composed of soldiers, supported by a *harki* guide, and led by an ineffectual French captain. During a routine patrol in the Algerian mountains, they found the bodies of six French soldiers tortured and slaughtered by the "rebels." The captain set out to punish the murderers. But while his orders were to capture the Algerian fighters and bring them back for interrogation, the French commanding officer acted on impulse and massacred innocent shepherds, their wives, and children. Antoine, who was in charge of covering his unit, stood watching helplessly. When the French realized their fateful mistake, they were chased by the independentists. It is only thanks to the *harki* guide that the French soldiers returned to base camp unharmed.

Antoine's disturbing narrative illustrates France's deliberate ideological construction of a 'mono-vocal master narrative' of history extolling the commanding officer's bravery at the expenses of dissonant truths, the 'contending voices of ... other memory groups' (Enjelvin, 2014: 85). Only the officer's version was recorded by military hierarchy and went down to posterity, while the soldiers' discordant testimonies were silenced. As a result, the irresponsible French captain was decorated for his "bravery," in spite of having massacred innocent civilians and endangered the lives of his men and his native guide, who was later executed by the FLN. Although Antoine's testimony to the French military hierarchy was censored and he could not save the *harki* friend from the "fellaghas," he promised that he would find and protect the *harki* family. Unfortunately, he was able to locate only the daughter named Aicha, whom he saved from the July 5, 1962 massacre in Oran and brought back to their native town of Bechar.[14] Her mother was never found.

Antoine's narrative, like Kerchouche's description of the Algerian struggle for independence in *Mon père, ce harki* is an unspeakable tale about the messiness of colonial war, where appearances can be deceptive, and military or governmental authority is not to be trusted. Antoine's later disrespect of professional hierarchies in his French construction company and his disregard of orders in general make new sense after the reader understands the tragic consequence of military obedience and laissez-faire during the dramatic episode in the mountains. Thus, his bankruptcy in French metropolitan society is directly linked to the lesson learned during the war. His instability, his propensity for repeatedly getting into trouble, and his rebelliousness become endearing qualities that humanize him in the narrator's and the reader's eyes. Furthermore, Thierry comes to understand that what he interpreted as his father's lack of love and indifference was a desperate attempt to honor the past. Antoine's refusal to attend his son's wedding is explained by his traumatic recall of past tragedies, as Thierry got married on the very same day commemorating the Oran massacre.

The pied noir father's dignity is further restored in Thierry's description of Antoine's funeral, which emphasizes the theme of collective remembrance. The ceremony is attended by a multi-ethnic crowd, who think of Antoine with fondness, amusement, and gratitude. Like his past dream of owning an inclusive bistro, the multicultural assembly reflects his diverse roots and his unusual ability for bringing together people of vastly different origins. Portuguese, Spaniards, Tunisian Jews, Muslim construction workers, former restaurant patrons, French and Arab friends, a Moroccan housecleaner, pied noir neighbors from the Angers housing projects, a French gendarme, war veterans, descendants of Italian settlers in Sète, who took him fishing, all gather to honor a life whose richness Thierry never suspected (335). The spontaneous tribute to the pied noir's generous and impulsive character leads both narrator and reader to view Antoine's supposed failures and idiosyncrasies under a kinder and more tolerant light. As Thierry ponders his father's parting words at their last meeting, he finds reassurance in Antoine's promise that his son will have a very different and happier life. Thus, it is through personal and narratorial recollection and commemoration that Thierry can distance himself from his father's ghost.

Although the final salute of French veterans at the funeral would appear to put Antoine's traumatic past to rest, it signals an almost opposite effect in the plot, for Thierry is unknowingly entrusted with a new mission: completing his father's work of transcultural, postcolonial reconciliation and fulfilling his past promise to the *harki* guide, who lost his life because of French military aberration. While Kerchouche symbolized her Algerian journey as a new form of archeology, i.e. of exhuming the relics of the individual and collective past, Thierry's postmemorial duty is represented in the metonymy of a locked casket, 'une boîte en métal gris, assez lourde' (a fairly heavy grey metal casket), the father's only material inheritance (336). Thierry first puts it aside because it is 'désagréable par le souvenir qu'elle m'évoque' (it awakens unpleasant memories). But Antoine's legacy is not to fall into oblivion, as indicated by the quixotic exhumation and forced transfer of his remains to his wife's family vault in Angers: 'De sa tombe forcée, Antoine martèle mon remords, me reproche ma défaillance' (348) (From his unchosen tomb, Antoine hammers home my remorse and points out my failing).[15]

The full restoration of the pied noir father's story, which is now inextricably linked with the fate of a *harki* family at the diegetic level, becomes the son's task, taking him on a second, more concrete postmemorial quest. It does not lead Thierry back to Algeria on a genealogical search like Kerchouche; instead, the autodiegetic narrator imports his father's Algerian past to France. This requires a complicated narrative technique to verify the buried truth of the father's double-sided role in the war, on the colonizer's side and as the friend of an Algerian native. At this point the two narrative strands, the Galdeano script and the *harki* plot, which had so far moved side by side without much interconnection, converge to unite two constituencies of the Algerian War of Independence, the pieds noirs and the *harkis* and undermine the divide between colonizer and colonized.

The episodes of the pied noir family life and the interspersed scenes of the *harki* couple, Rachida and Abdel, who wander across southern France, seek to escape internment, are driven back over and over again to the Rivesaltes camp, and end up parked for twenty years in a *cité de transit* in Montpellier, are diegetically reunited at the end of the novel under Thierry's agency. While the *harki* plot consisted mostly of dialogues between the two refugees or between the refugees and the French population and of narration by a third-person omniscient narrator, Thierry's voice now takes over as the single, first-person narrator of both narratives. As Thierry assumes Antoine's moral inheritance and accepts his appointed mission of protecting and reuniting the *harki* family, the son not only completes his familial tribute to the father but he (and the author through him) initiates and performs a sort of *affiliative* postmemorial bridging (Hirsch)[16] or *restitution des mémoires plurielles* (Benjamin Stora). This process is symbolized by the metal casket with *harki* family pictures, which Thierry finds buried behind a pile of old cardboard boxes in his Montpellier cellar.

When Thierry decides to relocate to Angers in February 1994 on his mother's request, the puzzle grows. With the accidental rediscovery of the grey metal box, he unearths relics of Antoine's past, a visual proof of his role in the Algerian War. Thierry scrutinizes three old photographs and newspaper articles relating to the July 5, 1962 massacre of pieds noirs and *harkis* in Oran. The sepia-colored photographs show the tortured body of the *harki* guide now identified by name as soldier Bel-Kacem. They raise questions about the survival of his daughter, Aicha/Fatiha, who is shown on her wedding day, and of his unidentified wife, who is missing altogether from the family photography album of sorts. Linked to textual evidence, family pictures are privileged forms of expression in the aftermath of trauma. Quoting Jill Bennett, Hirsch explains how family pictures promote identification and sympathy across ethnic, religious, and cultural differences. She notes that sight 'is deeply connected to "affective memory": "Images have the capacity to address the spectator's own bodily memory; to *touch* the viewer who *feels* rather than simply sees the event, drawn into the image through a process of affective contagion"' (2012: 39). As the *harki* mystery thickens, the filial protagonist's affiliative postmemorial identification across space and time increases, but despite this new "turn of the screw," the two plots are left hanging in the air, and resolution is delayed.

It takes an additional twelve years of narrative time for Antoine's puzzle to unravel and Thierry's own "genealogical" and transcultural quest to be completed, when fiction merges with history, and the first-person narrator hears the news on French television of *harki* protest in the *La Grappe* neighborhood of Montpellier in February 2006. A French journalist is interviewing the spokesperson of AJIR 34, an interest group opposing city mayor Georges Frêche, who has called the local *harki* community 'sous-hommes' (subhuman) and seeks to evict them.[17] The historical framework of postcolonial racism and *harki* resistance, the "colonial fracture" analyzed by Blanchard, Bancel, and Lemaire, gives a public platform to the fictional AJIR 34 leader to narrate her story, her capture by the FLN in Algeria, her flight to France, and her escape from the camp with a male companion, who has since died.[18] When this intradiegetic narrator identifies herself as Rachida Bel Kacem, Thierry is finally able to put together all the scattered pieces of the puzzle and to complete his mission of (post)memorial reconciliation on the fictional level.

As Thierry visits Rachida in Montpellier and locates her daughter Aicha in Algeria through the Internet, he paves the way for the reunion of *harki* mother, daughter, and granddaughter, symbolically repairing the errors of the French government, which had sought to split apart refugee Algerian families and break down clan solidarity. By honoring his father's oath, the pied noir son also gives the Algerian mother her past identity and honor back. Rachida, who had changed her name for fear of retaliation by other Algerian immigrants in France, can proudly reclaim her identity as Radidja Bel Kacem, the wife of a soldier who was a hero for the *harki* community. The number tattooed in her flesh and identifying her as a *harki* is no longer a sign of shame, as it was for the Jews during the Holocaust, but a symbol of her sufferings and her humanity: 'Ce jour-là elle s'est sentie vivante, femme, harki, libre et presque française. Radidja n'a plus jamais pleuré et son cœur s'est irrigué de tout l'amour d'une famille' (370) (On that day she felt alive, a harki woman, free and almost French. Radidja stopped crying, her heart nurtured by all the love of her family). As Thierry completes the full circle of his father's mystery, he, too, is released from the burden of the past and his new freedom enables him to contemplate the future, as he confidently promises 'Je retournerai à Béchar' (370) (I shall return to Béchar).

Affirming the singularity of *harki* memory

In Galdeano's novel, the pied noir son's postmemorial search helps dignify both the pied noir father and the *harki* mother and bridge the cultural and colonial divide through affiliative remembrance. Does Kerchouche's narrative and patient exploration of her parents' (his)story lead to a comparable reconciliation between different constituencies of the Algerian War of Independence? Clearly, the pied noir experience does not interest the narrator of *Mon père ce harki* and postmemorial reconciliation between colonizer and colonized is shown to be impossible. In its portrayal of *harki*–pied noir relations, Kerchouche's text tends to display what Stora called 'une sorte de cloisonnement, de communautarisation du souvenir par une position victimaire' (2006: 66) (a sort of cloistering, a memory appropriation by a community taking on the role of victim). The most significant pied noir figures that appear in her book are the camp leaders, impersonally designated by their initials, A. B. in Mouans-Sartoux and C. D. in Bias. They held military and administrative supervisory positions in the Algerian colony, where each headed a *section administrative spécialisée* or SAS, 'une section qui s'occupait du renseignement et de l'encadrement administratif et social des "indigènes"' (137) (a section which was in charge of intelligence as well as administrative and social supervision of the "natives"). They are described as dictators, applying the worst practices of the ex-colonies to the camps which they run like ghettos. An objective witness, a doctor formerly working at the camp in Bias and quoted by Kerchouche, confirms that this was a generalized experience:

> Bias, c'était un état dans l'état. Le ministère avait engagé exclusivement des pieds-noirs parce qu'ils parlaient l'arabe. J'étais quasiment le seul métropolitain. Ils ont recréé l'Algérie de papa, avec l'anisette, la kémia et tous les poncifs de là-bas. Les pieds-noirs traitaient les harkis comme des indigènes. Ils les dépréciaient, les manipulaient, les humiliaient. Ils étaient ravis d'avoir ramené un morceau d'Algérie coloniale avec eux, d'avoir rapatrié leurs fellahs. Les uns dominaient les autres, c'était la logique du système (160).[19]

> Bias was a state within the state. The ministry had hired pieds noirs exclusively, because they spoke Arabic. In the camp, I was practically the only

Frenchman from the metropolis. They had rebuilt daddy's Algeria, with anisette, the kemia, and all the trite stereotypes from over there. Pieds noirs would treat harkis as they had the natives. They put them down, manipulated and humiliated them. They were delighted to have repatriated their fellahs, and preserved and brought along with them a piece of colonial Algeria. This was the logic of the system: the dominance of some, the submission of the others.

When the main narrator confronts the cruel A. B., the pied noir has a completely different interpretation of the past, articulated along the lines of the "mission civilisatrice de la France" (France's civilizing mission), an ideology which served to justify the French colonial enterprise from the end of the nineteenth-century onwards (Bancel and Blanchard, 2006: 40). The pied noir camp leader explains his violent practices by his goal, which was to maintain order and integrate the North African "barbarians." To achieve this, French first names were given to *harki* newborns, women were forbidden to practice their cultural traditions, Muslim students were sent to mandatory Catholic catechism, and children obliged to take weekly baths.

What the narrator calls 'assimilation forcée' (forced assimilation), the pied noir supervisor defines as legitimate methods to integrate and civilize primitive people and give their children the chance of success in French society through education. As Bancel and Blanchard note, 'le concept de "mission civilisatrice" se forge dans la représentation d'une unicité de la France et dans la croyance en un lien particulier entre la France et le monde, matérialisé par sa mission universelle d'"éducation"' (2006: 40) (the concept of a "civilizing mission" is forged through the idea of France's unicity and the belief in a special bond between France and the rest of the world, materialized in its universal mission of "education"). A. B.'s actions are motivated by a blind faith in the unicity of French civilization, which leaves no room for postcolonial points of view or practices. For Kerchouche there is no possible bridging between the experiences of the former colonized and those of the ex-colonizer, racist representatives of the French government, who remain trapped in their military past. And the impossibility of (post)memorial reconciliation between *harkis* and pieds noirs, as attested by the verbal confrontation between the narrator and A. B., results from the French government's (and society's) continuing refusal to face its colonial past. As the Bias doctor remarks: 'Ce règlement, C. D. ne l'a pas inventé, il suivait les ordres. C'est le gouvernement qui en est responsable. C'est lui qui a mis le système en place' (161) (C. D. did not invent these regulations, he was simply following orders. The government is responsible. It put the system in place).

More likeable, kinder, and open-minded pieds noirs appear in Kerchouche's narrative, but they are not given a voice. Kerchouche's historian friend Jean-Jacques Jordi, who is listed in the acknowledgments, shows her the place in the harbor where her parents landed. But although the Jordi and Kerchouche families arrived in France only one day apart (35), the narrator does not interview him, or pursue any comparison between their two families' respective experiences beyond her brief conclusion that 'ces deux destins, très différents, se rejoignent et se séparent ici (dans le port de Marseille)' (35) (their very distinct destinies join and split apart here, in Marseille's harbor). Kerchouche seems unable to accept the fact that at least some pieds noirs were also the victims of French decolonization and Algerian independence.

While Kerchouche insists on the singularity of the *harki* experience and denies the existence of a common memorial ground with pieds noirs and their offspring, she is much more interested in the possibility of a transnational Algerian reconciliation between different constituencies: the *harkis* who left to save their lives and their Algerian counterparts, who stayed in their native country but do not necessarily support Algeria's contemporary politics. She shows that the myth of *harki* betrayal has been conveniently crafted and entertained by government officials, including President Bouteflika, who compared *harkis* to pro-Nazi French collaborators during World War II. Thus, the myth of national pride and unity is inscribed in the names of Algiers' streets and in its monuments to war martyrs, shaping the minds and feelings of young Algerians, while the wiser generation of war veterans continues to hold an open hand to the *harkis* and their descendants. It is this *déformation de l'histoire*, a duplicate of France's erasure of its colonial past, that Kerchouche seeks to correct through her work, in the hope of bringing closer the point of view of *harki* immigrants and that of Algerian nationalists.

The above comparison between *Mon père, ce harki* and *Pieds-noirs, Harkis, nos cœurs orphelins* reveals that both works are closely related in their representation of the pied noir son's and *harki* daughter's postmemorial inquiries into the past. Both fathers' memories and voices have been muted by forms of collective "amnesia" on both sides of the Mediterranean, enabling the construction of "master narratives" of war, decolonization, and independence that conveniently silence dissonant truths. The *harki* father was silenced by France's willful forgetting of its colonial defeat, of its convenient betrayal of its Muslim allies, and of its refusal to recognize the ambivalent feelings of colonial auxiliaries and indeed of most Muslim Algerians. His voice is also censored in Algeria, a nation unified by the FLN myth of a unified insurgency against the French colonizer. The pied noir father is the victim of France's myth of war heroism and denial of responsibility for its military errors, in particular the massacre of Muslim civilians and auxiliaries.

By investigating the past beyond and against the grain of French and Algerian national myths, both narrators reconnect with their fathers and with their own history. In this process, each finds new personal strengths and develops an autonomous identity which is liberated from the ghosts of the past (Thierry) or integrates multiple heritages (Kerchouche). By accepting the messiness of decolonization and their father's double-sided roles in it, the two narrators find greater self-assurance and critical insights to face the future, while restoring dignity and humanity to the previous generation, who had been locked in trauma, denial, repression, and self-contempt. Through 'affiliative postmemory' (Hirsch), the 'restitution des mémoires plurielles' (restoration of plural memories) advocated by Stora takes place in Galdeano's novel, which performs an extensive and complex trans-Mediterranean, trans-colonial reconciliation between pied noir and *harki* memories at the levels of plot and narrative technique, in its title and postface. It is unfortunate that the different font sizes on the title page of *Pieds-noirs, harkis, nos cœurs orphelins* give less prominence to the second term (*harkis*) and appear to establish a hierarchy between both groups, which may not express the author's real intention. Kerchouche is unable to envisage a peaceful dialogue between *harki* and pied noir memories and prefers to point to the urgent need for a reconciliation between *harkis* and other Algerians and for governmental appeasement in Algeria.

Galdeano's novel appeared almost a decade after the initial publication of *Mon père, ce harki* in 2003. Perhaps it is the pied noir son's response to Kerchouche's representation of pieds noirs and *harkis* in the continuing roles of colonizer and colonized, of oppressor and victim, even after decolonization. Galdeano is also trying to deconstruct French metropolitan racism toward his own community, which was indiscriminately regarded as a group of colonial profiteers and wealthy landowners, whose arrival endangered French values and caused competition on the metropolitan job market. By emphasizing his family's struggle and limited resources, Galdeano undermines French prejudice and offers a more realistic view of Algerian pied noir society.[20] Antoine's bonds of friendship with *harkis* and North African expatriates is grounded in historical reality, for pied noir expatriation resulted in an 'inversion of colonial society because the repatriated French became strangers in the metropolis (and) they tended to get closer to those they knew before, those with whom they were familiar, namely the Arab immigrants, who were also foreigners in France. The feeling of exile brought together these two sides of colonial society' (Esclangon-Morin, 2007: 94).

It is true that this rapprochement between ex-colonizer and ex-colonized is in keeping with a long tradition of pied noir appropriation of the *harki* cause for ideological and political gains. According to William Cohen:

> History has been the locus of pied-noir concern. Having lost everything, they saw their final redemption in history ... Pied-noirs have tried to fix an image of harmonious relations between them and the Muslim population in the last few years by expressing concern for the Harkis ... By viewing the loss of Algeria through the prism of the fate of the Harkis, the (French) Left might, Pied-noirs probably hope, better understand the harm done by granting Algeria independence. (2003: 131–4)

By including *harki* associations and their representatives in their various manifests, pied noir spokespeople have managed to reinforce their demands on different French governments for material reparations and for an open recognition of the French authorities' responsibility in the past tragedy which affected all North African expatriates. A March 2007 proclamation or *charte nationale* issued by the Comité de liaison des associations nationales de rapatriés and signed both by pied noir and *harki* representatives, finishes its long list of requests with the creation of various monuments honoring the French presence overseas, the refusal of any 'repentance on the expansion of the French presence overseas during the 19th and 20th centuries,' 'objectivity in the teaching of French expansion overseas,' and the 'valorization of the French African Army and its history' (Calmeyn, 2012: 177–8). Thus, the alliance between some pied noir associations and some *harki* interest groups is directly founded on the defense of French colonization.

Galdeano's overall intent is to pay tribute to the long sufferings of the *harkis* in France and give them a visible platform to claim recognition for their sacrifices and their rights as human beings and as citizens. Nevertheless, his postface unites *harkis* and pieds noirs in a joint patriotic salute to French soldiers in Algeria, with Antoine as a metaphorical flag bearer: 'Si Antoine avait été un drapeau, autour de lui se seraient serrés tous les soldats français, dont les harkis' (375) (Had Antoine been a flag, all French soldiers, including the *harkis*, would have closed rank around him). Thus, the novel concludes with a final gesture to honor the father, as does *Mon père, ce harki* when the narrator proudly proclaims: 'Oui, je suis une fille de harkis. J'écris ce mot avec un grand H. Comme Honneur' (277) (Yes, I am a *Harki* daughter. I write it with a capital H, like Honor). In this context of postcolonial literature, is the semi-fictional pied noir father less honorable than the *harki*? Still, Galdeano's inclusion of the *harkis* under the (French?) flag may also be interpreted as an unwitting colonial appropriation which denies the divided loyalties and internal conflicts of many *harkis* and other Muslim Algerians. Seen in this light, Kerchouche's reluctance to bring in pied noir memories of the Algerian War and expatriation may well be in part a firm refusal to compromise with pied noir ideology and its belief in an idealized colonial society.

Notes

1 In their introduction, Blanchard, Bancel, and Lemaire define France's colonial fracture as 'la tension et les effets de la postcolonialité' (the tension and effects of postcoloniality). They note the uniqueness of France's two-faced attitude to its colonial past, which is based on nostalgia and institutional denial. Through the 1990s, French national history has been amputated from its colonial past. As a result, 'les mémoires coloniales sont devenues illégitimes et mutilées' (2006: 13–17) (colonial memories have become illegitimate and mutilated).

2 See, for instance, Besnaci-Lancou and Manceron (2008); Besnaci-Lancou,

Falaize, and Manceron (2010); *Harkis 1962–2012*, special issue of *Les Temps Modernes* 666 (November–December 2011); Moser (2014).

3 The term *pied noir* appeared during the war, at the end of the 1950s. It became widely used in France after the conflict to designate Europeans colonizers in Algeria. They were also called 'Français d'Algérie' (French from Algeria). After 1830, European settlers came in large numbers from a variety of countries and regions: France, Spain, Italy, Malta, Switzerland, Germany, Greece, Ireland, the Balearic Islands, German-occupied Alsace, and Corsica. Over one million European settlers were living in Algeria in 1962 and were considered French citizens (Calmeyn, 2012: 19–20). The term pied noir also loosely applies to Jewish inhabitants of Algeria, who had established themselves in North Africa long before French colonization. They acquired French citizenship through the Crémieux decree in 1870. As Cohen notes, the term pied noir was initially discriminatory and 'it was accepted, albeit reluctantly, by the European population only after their arrival in France in 1962' (2003: 129). Throughout this chapter, *harki* is used in its usual colonial and postcolonial meanings. As noted by Manceron, at the end of the War of Algerian Independence, it 'became a generic term to designate all the Algerian auxiliaries of the French army.' Manceron estimates that 'nearly half a million Algerians were at some time between 1955 and 1962 paid by the French army as auxiliaries' (2010: 26). After the war, the term took a broader, postcolonial meaning. According to Giulia Fabbiano, 'in post-Algerian France, the Harkis … are a post-ethnic, national minority that includes theirs spouses and descendants, spanning several generations' (2014: 17).

4 According to the novel, the Galdeanos had French and Spanish roots.

5 Enjelvin defines 'postgenerations' as 'the offspring of those who have personally lived through traumatic events' (2014: 93).

6 By contrast, historian Abderahmen Moumen insists on the great diversity of experiences among the *harkis*: 'on constate que la diversité [de situations] se poursuit dans le contexte de l'après-guerre: des supplétifs sont engagés ou pris en charge par l'armée avant l'indépendance alors que d'autres sont désarmés et abandonnés du jour au lendemain par des militaires français; des supplétifs ont été victimes de représailles alors que d'autres n'ont pas été inquiétés … des supplétifs ont transité de camps en camps alors que d'autres n'en ont jamais connu ou seulement durant un temps très limité' (2010b: 59) (we find great differences [in *harki* situations] and these continue in the post-war context: some auxiliaries are hired or taken in charge by the army before the independence, while others are disarmed and abandoned by the French military from one day to the next; some auxiliaries suffered reprisals, while others were unharmed … some auxiliaries moved from camp to camp, whereas others never experienced camp life or only for a very brief period of time).

7 Loyalty and treason are of course subjective concepts. Loyalty to France, the *harki* position, would mean treason to Algeria. But the issue is more complex, as French communists, for instance, despised the *harkis* and identified the Algerian independentists as their only true "friends."

8 See William Cohen: 'Since 1962 there has been a far larger literary output by Europeans from Algeria than in the entire preceding 132 years spanning the era from French conquest to Algerian independence. And while the writings do not all address the war, they reflect the desire to create and hold on to a memory, to recapture the world that was lost, existing prior to the fall of *Algérie française* (French Algeria)' (2003: 129). Also see Calmeyn for a list of writers celebrating nostalgeria or 'algérianisme de l'exil' (2012: 45).

9 In *Mon père ce harki*, the father's favorite motto 'li fat met' (the past is dead) expresses his belief that the Harki voice and story cannot be 'heard' on either side of the Mediterranean.

10 The local leader of the Beni-Boudouane clan, the Bachaga Boualem, invited men of his tribe to enlist on the French side. This native colonial administrator expatriated to France after the war and is known for authoring the first works of *harki* literature, titled *Mon pays la France* (1962), *Les Harkis au service de la France* (1963), and *L'Algérie sans la France* (1964). According to Fabbiano, it 'represents one of the original sources of memorial work undertaken thirty years later' and it can 'be considered (a) foundational text that … opened the path for structuring narratives focused on the "don du sang"' (2014: 21).

11 FLN: Front de Libération Nationale. It was founded in November 1954 as an underground, nationalist, pro-independence movement. It believed in military action in North Africa and in France to achieve Algerian independence. It successfully wiped out its main rival, the Mouvement National Algérien at the end of a long internecine struggle. Through its military arm, the ALN (Armée de Libération Nationale) (National liberation Army), the FLN was the major actor in the war against colonial France. It negotiated the ceasefire and the conditions of independence from France at Evian-les-Bains in March 1962. From 1962 through February 1989 it was the sole legal party in Algeria. The current Algerian President, Abdelaziz Bouteflika is a member of the FLN.

12 OAS: the Organisation Armée Secrète (Secret Armed Organization) was founded in February 1961 as an underground military group claiming to defend the European settlers in Algeria. It was headed by General Salan. In the name of 'French Algeria,' the Organization opposed the policy of Algerian 'disengagement' led by President de Gaulle. Its agenda was to destabilize the French government through violent terrorist actions both in Algeria and in metropolitan France and to break off the peace negotiations between the French government and the FLN. It sponsored several attacks on de Gaulle, such as the failed assassination attempt at Petit Clamart in August 1962 (Stora, 2001: 81–2).

13 Régis Pierret has shown the effect of gender on the *harkis*' process of identity formation (2014: 51–3).

14 On July 5, 1962 a crowd from the Muslim neighborhoods gathered in Oran to celebrate the newly proclaimed independence. Shots were suddenly fired, by unidentified snipers. Soon after, a manhunt erupted, where pieds noirs and their alleged Muslim "supporters" (*harkis* and civilians) were hunted down,

kidnapped, and massacred in reprisal. An estimated ninety-five people, Algerians and Europeans, were killed and 161 injured, while the French military stood by, watching. It seems that the French Army had received specific orders to stay away from what was now regarded as a strictly internal Algerian problem (Calmeyn, 2012: 222). Many people were abducted and their bodies were never found. Officially 365 Europeans went missing. This bloody episode accelerated the European settlers' flight abroad (Stora, 2001: 105; Vallaud, 2005: 125–6; Calmeyn, 2012: 221–2; Ferracci, 2012: 133–43). The Oran massacre is what Pierre Nora and Abderahmen Moumen call a *lieu de mémoire*, a key event in pied noir memory, emotionally invested and grounding their collective claim for recognition of their sufferings and reparation by the French government (2010a: 135).

15 Burial rites are an important and sacred topic for many expatriates. The pied noir community has been deeply affected by the neglect and profanation of Christian tombs in Algerian cemeteries after decolonization. One of their recurrent demands to the French and Algerian governments is the preservation of 'all Christian and Jewish cemeteries in Algeria and Tunisia, their restoration, maintenance, and protection' (Calmeyn, 2012: 177).

16 For Hirsch, *familial* and *affiliative* postmemory are 'two structures of transmission,' where the former designates 'an intergenerational vertical identification of child and parent occurring within the family,' and the latter an 'intragenerational horizontal identification that makes the child's position more broadly available to other contemporaries' (2012: 36). Thierry's identification with his father is familial postmemory, his sympathy for the plight of the *harki* family and search for the missing daughter are affiliative.

17 AJIR 34 was a *harki* defense group headed in 2006 by Mohammed Haddouche. In February 2006, some 300 *harkis* and pieds noirs demonstrated in Montpellier to protest mayor Frêche's 'injurious and defamatory speech which calls for racial hatred' (*L'Obs Société*). George Frêche belonged to the French Socialist party. When he called the *harki* activists 'sous-hommes,' he was using a racially offensive terminology harking back to Nazi ideology. However, his speech also targeted and denounced an earlier demonstration organized by the French right to support the controversial law of 2005 which affirmed the 'positive effects' of French colonization and in which some members of AJIR34 participated.

18 Rachida was interned in the Rivesaltes camp. As Abderahmen Moumen notes, this camp was used for *harki* widows, orphans, war invalids, and other maimed or physically handicapped men. These individuals were deemed 'inclassables, incasables, voire irrécupérables' and detained together. The French authorities considered them unfit for integration into metropolitan society (2010b: 57).

19 As Howell notes, Kerchouche's representation of camps like Bias was controversial (2006: 422). For Denise Bourgois, a French social worker at Bias, who knew the Kerchouche family well, the camp was 'certainly not the hell that Kerchouche depicts' (Lasserre, 2007).

20 In the total European population of colonial Algeria, only 3 percent had a

higher economic status than the average in metropolitan France, 25 percent had the same economic status, and 72 percent were poorer (Calmeyn, 2012: 20).

References

Ali-Ben Ali, Z. (2010). 'Porteurs de mémoire. Quand la littérature est attente d'Histoire,' in F. Besnaci-Lancou, B. Falaize, and G. Manceron (eds), *Les harkis, mémoire et transmission*, Ivry-sur-Seine: Editions de l'Atelier, 115–23.
Bancel, N., Blanchard, P., and Lemaire, S. (2006). *La Fracture coloniale: La société française au prisme de l'héritage colonial*, Paris: La Découverte.
Barclay, F. (2011). *Writing Postcolonial France: Haunting, Literature, and the Maghreb*. New York: Lexington Books.
Besnaci-Lancou, F., Falaize, B., and Manceron, G. (eds) (2010). *Les Harkis: Histoire, mémoire et transmission*, Ivry-sur-Seine: Editions de l'Atelier.
Besnaci-Lancou, F. and Manceron, G. (eds) (2008). *Les Harkis dans la colonisation et ses suites*, Ivry-sur-Seine: Editions de l'Atelier.
Calmeyn, M. (2012). *Les Français d'Algérie: 50 ans après*, Friedberg: Edition Atlantis.
Cohen, W. (2003). 'Pied-Noir Memory, History, and the Algerian War,' in A. Smith (ed.), *Europe's Invisible Migrants*, Amsterdam: Amsterdam University Press, 129–45.
Elbaz, R. (2012). 'Dalila Kerchouche et la quête "harkéologique" ou l'occultation historique des Harkis' in N. Redouane and Y. Bénayoun-Szmidt (eds), *Qu'en est-il de la littérature "beur" au féminin?*, Paris: L'Harmattan, 207–17.
Enjelvin, G. (2014). 'Harki Daughters' "Righting" Narratives: Resistance Identity and Littérature Naturelle?,' in K. Moser (ed.), *A Practical Guide to French Harki Literature*, New York: Lexington Books, 83–99.
Esclangon-Morin, V. (2007). *Les rapatriés d'Afrique du Nord de 1956 à nos jours*, Paris: L'Harmattan.
Fabbiano, G. (2010). 'Enrôlements en mémoire, mémoires d'enrôlement,' in F. Besnaci-Lancou, B. Falaize, and G. Manceron (eds), *Les harkis, mémoire et transmission*, Ivry-sur-Seine: Editions de l'Atelier, 98–114.
Fabbiano, G. (2014). 'Writing as Performance: Literary Production and the Stakes of Memory,' in K. Moser (ed.), *A Practical Guide to French Harki Literature*, New York: Lexington Books, 83–99.
Ferracci, J.-B. (2012). *L'Adieu. 1962: Le tragique exode des Français d'Algérie*, Paris: Les Editions de Paris.
Galdeano, T. (2012). *Pieds-noirs, Harkis, nos cœurs orphelins*, Editions Les 2 Encres.
Hirsch, M. (2012). *The Generation of Postmemory: Writing and Visual Culture after the Holocaust*, New York: Columbia University Press.
Howell, J. (2011). 'Sur les traces d'un père: "La quête harkéologique" de Dalila Kerchouche,' *Contemporary French and Francophone Studies*, 15(4), 415–22.

Ireland, S. (2009). 'Facing the Ghosts of the Past in Dalila Kerchouche's *Mon père, ce harki* and Zahia Rahmani's *Moze*,' *Contemporary French and Francophone Studies*, 13(3), 303–10.
Ireland, S. (2014). 'Creating Shared Memories in Three Harki Narratives,' in K. Moser (ed.), *A Practical Guide to French Harki Literature*, New York: Lexington Books, 101–23.
Kerchouche, D. (2003). *Mon père, ce harki*. Paris: Editions du Seuil.
Lanzmann, C. (ed.) (2011). *Harkis 1962–2012. Les mythes et les faits*. Special Issue of *Les Temps modernes*, no. 666 (November–December). Paris.
Lasserre, L. (2007). 'Le camp de Bias n'était pas l'enfer qu'elle décrit,' *La Dépêche*. November 15. Web. May 21, 2015.
Moser, K. (ed.) (2014). *A Practical Guide to French Harki Literature*, New York: Lexington Books.
Moumen, A. (2010a). 'Les Lieux de mémoire du groupe social "harki." Inventaire, enjeux et Evolution,' in F. Besnaci-Lancou, B. Falaize, and G. Manceron (eds), *Les Harkis: Histoire, mémoire et transmission*, Ivry-sur-Seine: Editions de l'Atelier.
Moumen, A. (2010b). 'La Notion d'abandon des Harkis par les autorités françaises,' in F. Besnaci-Lancou, B. Falaize, and G. Manceron (eds), *Les Harkis: Histoire, mémoire et transmission*, Ivry-sur-Seine: Editions de l'Atelier.
Olsson, K. (2014). 'In the Name of the Father: In the Voice of the Other,' in K. Moser (ed.), *A Practical Guide to French Harki Literature*, New York: Lexington Books, 145–67.
Pierret, R. (2014). 'From the Colonization of Algeria to the Repatriation of the Harkis,' in K. Moser (ed.), *A Practical Guide to French Harki Literature*, New York: Lexington Books, 37–56.
'Propos de Frêche: manifestation à Montpellier' (February 18, 2006). *L'Obs Société*. Web. May 21, 2015.
Redouane, R (2012). '*Fille de harki* de Fatima Besnaci-Lancou: Histoire occultée et mémoires blessées,' in N. Redouane and Y. Bénayoun-Szmidt (eds), *Qu'en est-il de la littérature "beur" au féminin?*, Paris: L'Harmattan, 219–38.
Stora, B. (2001). *Algeria 1830–2000: A Short History*, Ithaca, NY: Cornell University Press.
Stora, B. (2006). 'Quand une mémoire (de guerre) peut en cacher une autre (coloniale),' in P. Blanchard, N. Bancel, and S. Lemaire (eds), *La Fracture coloniale: La France au prisme de l'héritage colonial*, Paris: La Découverte, 59–67.
Stora, B. (2011). *La Guerre des mémoires: La France face à son passé colonial*, La Tour d'Aigues: Editions de l'Aube.
Vallaud, P. (2005). *La guerre d'Algerie. II. 1958–1962. La marche à l'independance*. Paris: Acropole.

10

Representations of the *harkis* in contemporary French-language films

Susan Ireland

After the signing of the Evian Accords on March 19, 1962, which officially ended the Algerian War of Independence, thousands of *harkis*, the Algerians who had worked for the French Army during the conflict, were killed by angry compatriots who viewed them as traitors. Many of those who managed to flee to France found themselves isolated in temporary housing camps, felt abandoned by the French, and were often rejected by Algerian immigrants who had supported the Front de Libération Nationale (FLN). This painful severance from the homeland made the *harkis* a 'communauté de destin' (Besnaci-Lancou, 2005: 13) (a community of destiny),[1] and the term *harki* soon became an 'identité transmissible' (Charbit, 2006: 63) (a transmittable identity), a kind of ethnic marker, which applied to the family as a whole and was passed down from one generation to the next. At the same time, the *harkis* found themselves erased from both the French and Algerian national narratives of the war. On the one hand, the construction of the founding myth of the Algerian nation, that of a people united in the struggle against the colonizer, served to demonize the *harkis*, who were seen as unpatriotic. On the other hand, they were excluded from the official French story of the war since they had come to represent France's national shame. Consequently, the subject of the *harkis* remained 'le tabou des tabous' (Hamoumou, 1990: 26) (the taboo of all taboos) for many years on both sides of the Mediterranean. When the silence surrounding the community was finally broken on the individual and national levels, the emerging corpus of historical, sociological, and literary works referred repeatedly to wounds, scars, trauma, and exclusion. The small body of documentaries and fiction films which appeared alongside the literary texts addressed similar issues and provided a further means of explaining the reasons for the *harkis*' migration to France. As such, these films constitute interesting examples of 'counter-heritage cinema,' a type of cinema which, as Will Higbee argues, proposes an alternative version to the dominant narrative of French colonial history (2013: 71).

Scholarly analyses of films depicting the war of independence routinely draw attention to the fact that, although a substantial number of films broached this topic between the 1960s and 1990s, the general impression was one of silence, a paradox encapsulated in the title of Raphaëlle Branche's 2008 chapter, 'Une impression d'absence: l'Algérie et la guerre d'Algérie au cinéma et à la télévision française depuis 1962.' This sense of absence has been attributed to a variety of factors including censorship, lack of interest, willful amnesia on the part of the government, and the fact that the war had not become part of French collective memory (Stora, 1997: 175). In the case of the *harkis*, who were already associated with invisibility and silence, and who would later be described as 'les oubliés de l'histoire' (the people forgotten by history),[2] the absence was very real, and they rarely appeared in fiction films made before 2000.

The presence of the *harkis* in France first manifested itself in the public arena in other domains. First, the media reported widely on a series of riots that broke out in the housing camps in summer 1975 in protest against poor living conditions and lack of opportunity in areas such as education and employment.[3] Subsequently, throughout the 1980s and 1990s, activism in the political and legal spheres on the part of second-generation *harkis* sought to redress injustices affecting the community and led to the filing of several suits against the French government, most notably in 2001. Finally, the placing of a plaque in the Invalides and the establishment of an annual Journée d'hommage national aux harkis (Day of National Homage to the *Harkis*) marked the end of official amnesia and ushered in a phase of memorialization and memory work. On the occasion of the first national commemoration on September 25, 2001, for example, President Chirac recognized France's debt to the *harkis*, asserting that they should not remain 'les oubliés d'une histoire enfouie' (the forgotten people of a buried history), but should become part of French national memory (cited in Enjelvin, 2004: 62). The gradual shift from invisibility to presence, and from silence to voice, is reflected in the emergence and evolution of a corpus of *harki* literature. During the period of silence (the 1960s and most of the 1970s), the *harkis*, many of whom were illiterate, were for the most part spoken for by other groups such as military officers and the pieds noirs (Moumen, 2014: 1). Nonetheless, three volumes written in the 1960s by former colonial administrator the Bachaga Said Boualam[4] shed light on many aspects of the *harkis*' experiences and would later be considered the foundational texts of *harki* literature (Fabbiano, 2014: 21). Likewise, very few literary works were published during the main period of militancy (the 1980s and 1990s), with the most notable exceptions being Saïd Ferdi's *Un enfant dans la guerre* (1981) and Brahim Sadouni's *Français sans patrie* (1985), both of which provided first-hand accounts of life as a *harki* in Algeria (Moumen, 2014: 3).[5] It was not until the 2000s, after the official acknowledgment of the important role played by the *harkis*, that a significant number of autobiographical and fictional works appeared.[6] In contrast with the activists of the earlier decades, the authors of these texts seek, as Giulia Fabbiano argues, 'to understand (not to denounce) and to foster a dialogue (not to accuse)' (2014: 26). In particular, they participate in the creation of collective memories, strive to heal the wounds of the past, and contest the reductive national scripts that assign them predetermined roles. In this sense, their work can be described as a form of counter-narrative that has much in common with counter-heritage cinema as defined by Higbee.

The presence of *harkis* in films made before 2000 reflects the different phases of *harki* activism and literary production and presents interesting parallels with the nature and evolution of films on the Algerian War in general. Historian Benjamin Stora's typology of films depicting the conflict, for example, identifies three main periods: the 1960s, the 1970s, and the 1980s and 1990s (Stora, 1997: 176, 196–202). During the 1960s, which were characterized by silence, censorship, and the army's monopoly on images of the war,[7] few films portrayed the war directly, thus contributing to the impression of absence. While a small number of overtly oppositional documentary shorts were shown illegally at that time (Dine, 1994: 219), the conflict was mostly portrayed as a painful memory associated with a distant place, as in classic films such as *Le Petit Soldat* (1963), *Muriel* (1963), and *Les Parapluies de Cherbourg* (1964) (Frodon, 2004: 75). The *harkis* do not appear in these films, but they were occasionally featured on the television news magazine *Cinq colonnes à la une*, which showed some of the first images of their lives in France.[8] A short segment ('C'étaient les harkis') of the program which aired on June 7, 1963, for example, focused on a group of *harkis* who had moved from the housing camp at Rivesaltes in the Pyrénées Orientales to an abandoned village in the Aude region.

Although self-censorship and collective amnesia continued throughout most of the next decade, this era saw the release of a few pioneering documentaries on the war, as well as a small number of anti-war films such as René Vautier's *Avoir 20 ans dans les Aurès* (1972) and Laurent Heynemann's *La Question* (1976), which began to draw attention to the realities of what would become known as the 'dirty' war (Dine, 1994: 228).[9] During this period, which saw the first riots in the housing camps and during which the second generation had not yet fully emerged as the voice of their community, the *harkis* were still mostly spoken for, as was the case in the field of literature. In *La Guerre d'Algérie* (1972), one of the best-known documentaries of the 1970s, Yves Courrière and Philippe Monnier created a montage of photos, newspaper headlines, and footage from French and foreign news programs in order to provide one of the first chronologies of the events of the war, but they made little reference to the *harkis*. The *harkis'* situation in France was, however, brought to light in a more sustained fashion in 1976, soon after the 1975 riots, in an episode of the weekly current affairs television program *Les Dossiers de l'écran*, which addressed the treatment of the *harkis* fourteen years after their arrival in France and, through the extensive use of interviews, provided a venue in which the voices of the community could be heard.

In the 1980s and 1990s, during the period associated with the end of amnesia, several significant documentaries brought the experiences of the *harkis* to the fore, either alongside those of other groups involved in the war or in programs devoted entirely to their story. One of the first of these, Denis Chegaray's three-part television documentary *Mémoire enfouie d'une génération – guerre d'Algérie* (1982), used a combination of interviews and archival images to provide information on the experiences of constituencies such as the pieds noirs, French conscripts, and the *harkis* (Stora, 1997: 199). A decade later, *Les Années algériennes* (Bernard Favre and Benjamin Stora, 1991), which sought to give a nuanced, comprehensive account of the war, drew attention to the controversial abandonment of the *harkis*, a subject also referred to in Bertrand Tavernier's *La Guerre sans nom* (1992).[10] Other documentaries, especially in the 1990s, began to focus more extensively on questions related to the children of *harkis*, who had become an increasingly visible presence in France. Eric Deroo and Alain de Sédouy's important three-part television series on the *harkis* (1993–94), for example, traced out the trajectory that had led to the plight of the second generation and examined their quest to define their identity and find their place in France.[11] Similarly, at the end of the 1990s Farid Haroud, the son of a *harki*, made a short documentary titled *Fils de harkis*; this was followed in 2001 by a second documentary, *Le Mouchoir de mon père*, which was inspired by his father's story. At the same time as the *harkis* themselves were making their voices heard in the political and legal domains, then, these documentaries started to incorporate them into a French history of the war, thereby legitimating their presence in France and identifying them as significant memory carriers in the context of immigration.

Few fiction films depicting the war were made in the 1980s and 1990s, and the *harkis* generally played only a very minor role in those produced by majority-French directors. For example, in Pierre Schoendoerffer's *L'Honneur d'un capitaine* (1982), which addresses the French Army's use of torture and summary executions, *harkis* appear briefly in just a small number of episodes, mostly as translators, in scenes where French soldiers interact with villagers, but also as witnesses of violence, as when an adolescent is tortured in a river or the bodies of dead Algerians are exhibited to the local population. As regards Maghrebi-French directors, Higbee pertinently argues that they made only a small number of films on the war during these two decades because they were 'more preoccupied with social realist narratives that dealt with issues of immigration, integration, racism and exclusion in the here and now of contemporary French society than in the colonial past' (2013: 69). Despite their emphasis on immigration, these directors generally did not address the *harkis*' position in France as a distinct community. Even Malik Chibane, who was the first Maghrebi-French director to place a *harki* family at the center of a film (*Douce France*, 1995), focuses primarily on concerns that the *harki* community has in common with other families of Maghrebi descent, including discrimination in the workplace, intergenerational conflict, gender roles, and arranged marriage. The fact that Chibane does not directly address issues which are specific to the *harkis* probably explains why little attention has been given to this aspect of the film. Most scholarly analyses either do not mention the fact that the main protagonist (Moussa) is the son of a *harki* or make only passing reference to his identity.

Sylvie Durmelat, however, discusses Chibane's portrayal of Moussa's father at some length. As she aptly observes, brief but significant shots of a few symbolic objects serve to establish the father's identity – his framed military medals, the portrait of de Gaulle hanging on the wall of the house, and the framed document attesting to his service with the French Army – but these indirect allusions to his past do not give rise to an indictment of France's treatment of the *harkis*. In Durmelat's words, Chibane's film 'offers … no claims for a political rehabilitation of the *harki*, no virulent critique of France's abandonment of its *harki* troops, and no denunciation of the FLN regime's repression and stigmatization of the *harki*' (2011: 99). Similarly, a small number of scenes evoke the legacy of shame handed down from one generation to the next, but they do not bring out the impression of the son's being indelibly marked or branded by the father's past as forcefully as the literary works do. In each of these scenes, a drunk Maghrebi client at the café run by Moussa calls him or his father a traitor, affirming on one occasion, 'vous êtes harkis de père en fils dans la famille' (you're *harkis* from father to son in your family). By way of an explanation for these insults, Moussa succinctly tells his friend Jean-Luc, 'pendant la guerre d'Algérie, mon père a choisi la France' (during the war of Algeria my father chose France), while Jean-Luc's short response, 'Ah, c'est pour ça que tu es sur la liste rouge' (So that's why you're blacklisted), constitutes the only reference to enmity within the Maghrebi immigrant community.

Besides these brief allusions, Chibane does not dwell on the transmission of stigma or on the tensions between the *harki* family and FLN supporters and their descendants, preferring instead to explore the commonalities of their experiences in France and highlighting the themes of integration and interethnic friendship. Likewise, the portrayal of the two daughters in the family serves to raise general questions related to gender, agency, and the wearing of the headscarf. Indeed, intergenerational trauma and the rehabilitation of the father do not emerge as prominent themes in the aesthetic domain until the early 2000s, when second-generation authors such as Dalila Kerchouche (*Mon père, ce harki*, 2003) and Fatima Besnaci-Lancou (*Fille de harki*, 2005) bring them to the fore in their autobiographical narratives.

The first years of the 2000s, which have been described as a turning point in the production of films on the war of independence, saw the release of a significant number of fiction films on the conflict and its aftermath, including Philippe Faucon's *La Trahison* (2006), Laurent Herbier's *Mon colonel* (2007), Medhi Charef's *Cartouches gauloises* (2007), Florent-Emilio Siri's *L'Ennemi intime* (2007), Rachid Bouchareb's *Hors-la-loi* (2010), and Alain

Tasma's *Harkis* (2006). When discussing this new corpus, Martine Beugnet argues that this decade signals the end of cinema's 'long-lasting silence' on 'France's "dirty war"' (2007: 227), while Stora speaks of the beginning of 'l'ère d'un questionnement plus mûr sur la guerre d'Algérie' (2008: 38) (the era of a more mature examination of the Algerian War). Unlike many of the earlier cinematic portrayals of the conflict, these films directly confront the unpleasant realities of the war and encourage the viewer to reflect on its psychological effects on those who participated in it.[12] As Beugnet notes, this corpus depicts 'the complex situation of the alienated protagonists of a dirty conflict, inviting identification with unexceptional men and women torn between contradictory allegiances' (2007: 227). *Harkis* appear in all of these films and play a central role in several of them, particularly *La Trahison* and *Harkis*. While most of the films are set in Algeria and portray the circumstances that led to the *harkis'* uprooting from their homeland, Tasma's *Harkis* focuses on their experience of immigration in France. Taken together, they shed light on the trans-Mediterranean dimension of the *harkis'* lives and identity and illustrate the painful consequences of their deracination.

In *La Fracture coloniale*, Nicolas Bancel, Pascal Blanchard, and Sandrine Lemaire posit that the 2000s have seen a significant upsurge of interest in colonial and postcolonial history, a phenomenon they describe as a 'retour du refoulé' (2005: 10) (return of the repressed). France's controversial use of torture and its treatment of the *harkis* constitute two of the issues brought to the fore during this period, and both feature in the new generation of films. *Mon colonel* and *L'Ennemi intime*, for example, unflinchingly confront the subject of torture and use recurrent images of horror and violence to suggest the return of the repressed. Both films focus on the moral disintegration of an idealistic new recruit who ultimately engages in acts of brutality and dies when he can no longer live with what he has done. In this fashion, both contest the mythical image of the colonial soldier whose '"masculine" traits, such as bravery, honour, duty and youthful vigor' made him 'a bastion of honourable values, leading the civilising mission by example' (Mossman, 2013: 75). Adapted from a novel by Francis Zamponi, *Mon colonel* centers on the relationship between Colonel Duplan, a strong supporter of French Algeria who wants torture to be carried out within the rules in his jurisdiction, and the young lieutenant Rossi, a former law student whose role is to advise the colonel on the legality of his actions. The perspective presented in the film is, however, entirely French and, much as they had in *L'Honneur d'un capitaine*, the *harkis* remain an occasional presence in the background – a *harki* serves as translator in a scene in which a woman is forced to lift up her veil in order to have her photo taken, and when local business owners participate in a general strike, a translator informs them that their shops will be blown up if they do not open them.

Harkis play a more substantial role in *L'Ennemi intime* which, as a secondary theme, begins to evoke the experience of the Algerian (*harki*) Other. Inspired by a book by Patrick Rotman,[13] this film portrays the complex relations between the alienated Sergent Dougnac and the idealistic Lieutenant Terrien, who gradually loses his humanity and becomes a torturer. Director Florent-Emilio Siri, who has been described as 'glor[ying] in gore as no other French filmmaker before him' (Jeancolas, 2007: 46), and whose film has frequently been compared to Oliver Stone's *Platoon*, graphically depicts a relentless cycle of violence and reprisals and underscores the brutality on both sides of the conflict. If, as Philip Dine has observed, the figure of the '*barbare*' is 'the most enduring image of the FLN combatant' (1994: 183), *L'Ennemi intime* emphasizes that the war engendered 'barbarians' in both camps. Despite the recognition at the very end of the film that an estimated 300,000 to 600,000 Algerians died in the war, the perspective is again primarily French, and the Algerians are most often depicted as a target, a corpse, or a wounded or tortured body.

The representation of the *harkis* constitutes a notable exception to this portrayal. Although the abandonment and the massacres, two of the foundational events in the formation of *harki* identity, are not explicitly evoked, several characters are more fully developed and stand for different forms of engagement with the French Army. Sayeed, a regular soldier, is associated with faithful service, his loyalty symbolized by the huge scar from wounds he received at Monte Cassino during World War II. Indeed, Dougnac pays tribute to the colonial troops, remarking that it was thanks to men like Sayeed that the battle was won. Sayeed also serves to evoke the origins of the enmity between *harkis* and FLN families living in France: when Dougnac decides to spare an Algerian prisoner, Sayeed executes him in retaliation for the fact that the FLN had killed his wife and three children. The theme of animosity between the two groups is reinforced through the figure of Rashid, who used to be on the side of the FLN. The film conveys the local population's hostility toward the *harkis*, for example, when Rashid accompanies a group of French soldiers into a village looking for arms, and a boy angrily tells him that his brother will kill him. At the same time, and perhaps most importantly, the film depicts Rashid's grief when he is shown in tears beside the body of his dead cousin, next to a room full of villagers who have been massacred by the FLN. This brief but striking portrayal of the pain of the Other recurs in the sympathetic treatment of Rashid's own death; in particular, the image of his tortured body underlines the idea that the war was a traumatic experience for the *harkis* as well as for the French, and indirectly evokes the massacres that would occur after the proclamation of independence. Finally, an Algerian boy who is the sole survivor of the massacre in his village is again associated with the theme of trauma, and his life during the war is contrasted with photos of Terrien's happy-looking six-year-old son. Found hiding in a well, the boy represents the children and adolescents taken in and recruited by the French Army. In particular, the viewer is often aware of the boy's forlorn gaze, as he sees prisoners being tortured, for example, or when he looks at the charred landscape and burned bodies after the French use napalm to wipe out their enemies. In a broader sense, the parent–child relationship

Terrien tries to foster with the boy recalls the paternalistic colonial order, and the boy's ultimately abandoning the French Army camp after the climactic scene in which he pleads with a frenzied Terrien to stop torturing an old man, serves to indict the dehumanizing colonial regime.

In a 2003 interview, Stora observed that films on the war generally do not portray 'la parole et la douleur de l'autre' (2003: 11) (the voice and the pain of the other), but are rather made for specific audiences. Elsewhere, he calls for writers and filmmakers to engage in the 'restitution des mémoires plurielles' (1997: 190) (restitution of plural memories) that he deems necessary if the wounds caused by the war are to be healed. Although the emphasis is on the French soldiers' experience, *L'Ennemi intime* in a very modest way suggests that suffering took many forms and was shared by the *harkis*. Two other films of the 2000s, *La Trahison* and *Cartouches gauloises*, go much further in the depiction of shared trauma. Indeed, Guy Austin remarks that in *La Trahison*, 'we see French cinema finally starting to engage with the trauma not just of stock figures such as the white French soldier or the FLN-sympathizing French journalist, but of the ethnic Algerian' (2009: 124). Adapted from Claude Sales' autobiographical narrative of the same name, *La Trahison* focuses on the relationship between Lieutenant Roque and a group of four *harki* soldiers, especially Corporal Taïeb, as they work together in a remote part of eastern Algeria in 1960.[14] Midway through the film, Roque is informed that the four men are suspected of being involved in a plot to kill him and to allow the FLN to take over the camp. Throughout the film, Taïeb and Roque, the two main characters, are portrayed as equals caught up in a tragic war, and all of the *harkis* are given agency and a voice. Like Sales in his autobiographical text, Roque tries to understand Taïeb's motivations and concerns rather than condemning him for his implication in the plot. In addition, recurrent images of the Algerian people's distress reinforce the impression of shared suffering, while repeated shots of the *harkis* witnessing the manner in which villagers are displaced from their homes by French soldiers underscore the difficulty of their position.

As the title suggests, the film centers on the theme of betrayal, a notion that has served to stigmatize the *harkis* and which has become one of the primary markers of their identity in Algeria and in the context of immigration. Virtually all of the works written by the children of *harkis* in the 2000s refer to the highly charged terms 'trahir' (to betray) and 'traître' (traitor) in order to draw attention to the transmission of a stigma that makes a 'fille de harki' (the daughter of a *harki*) a 'fille de traître' (the daughter of a traitor) (Kerchouche, 2006: 50). The persistence of this unwanted identity is also evident in the fact that in the Bou Saada region of Algeria, where the film was made, it was difficult to find extras who were willing to play the role of *harkis* (Branche, 2008: 110). Like authors such as Kerchouche and Rahmani, Faucon problematizes the question of betrayal, which is evoked in several different contexts over the course of the film. Rather than focusing primarily on the local population's view that the *harkis* have betrayed their compatriots,[15] the film addresses the reasons why the four *harki* characters choose to betray the French Army and, as many literary works do, characterizes France's failure to protect the *harkis* as a further form of betrayal.

The unspecific nature of the title effectively evokes the general atmosphere of suspicion depicted in the film and highlights the idea that the traitor/patriot dichotomy was often not clear cut, thus conveying Sales' characterization of the war as 'grise' (grey) on both sides, rather than 'en noir et blanc' (black and white) (1999: 87). On the one hand, the betrayal plot serves to emphasize mutual distrust and reflects the army's concerns about the loyalty of some *harkis*. As historian William Cohen points out: '*Harkis* were suspected of contributing part of their wages to the FLN, of avoiding battle with FLN troops, and of showing insufficient zeal in rounding up FLN suspects' (2006: 165). At the same time, Faucon suggests why the *harkis* had good reason to have no confidence in France. When Roque is asked to swear that France will never abandon the *harkis*, he answers that it would not be honest for him to do so because he is not de Gaulle, a response the *harkis* find evasive and unsatisfactory. Likewise, a leaflet Roque finds in the *harkis*' room warns of the possibility of their being let down by the army: 'Ne croyez pas que la France vous récompensera. Elle se servira de vous et vous abandonnera comme elle a abandonné ses partisans en Indochine' (Don't believe that France will reward you. She will use you and abandon you, just as she did her supporters in Indochina).[16] Finally, many scenes depicting interactions between *harkis* and other Algerians suggest the *harkis*' recognition of, and sympathy for, the misery of the villagers, whose homes have been burned down and who are forced to move to an army camp. One of the *harkis*, for example, recounts that he is haunted by the uncomprehending expression of an elderly woman who reminds him of his mother.

The intertwining of memories and perspectives on the war is reinforced by the denouement of the film, which slightly modifies Sales' account of events. Sales, who did not see Taïeb again after his arrest, but heard that he had escaped, concludes his narrative with a final meditation on the motivations and preoccupations of a man he had always viewed as 'un homme à part entière' (1999: 60) (a full human being). By contrast, in the film, Roque sees Taïeb one last time, when he leans out of an army truck and shouts 'Vive l'indépendance, mon lieutenant, vive l'Algérie' (Long live independence, lieutenant, long live Algeria). This more dramatic ending with its strong anti-colonial statement, along with Roque's continuing desire to understand rather than to condemn the *harkis*, again places the blame for their situation on France, as is evident in Roque's last words: 'on les a piégés. On les a mis dans une position qui n'avait pas d'issue pour eux' (We trapped them. We put them in a position where they had no way out).

The depiction of shared trauma takes a very different form in *Cartouches gauloises*, which illustrates what Higbee characterizes as the 'historical turn' made by Maghrebi-French directors who, in the 2000s, began to re-examine 'a shared Franco-Maghrebi history' (2013: 4) rather than focusing primarily on the 'here and now' of French society (2013: 69), as in Chibane's *Douce France*. When discussing the compartmentalization of memories of the war of independence, which constitutes an important part of Franco-Maghrebi history, Stora poses the question, 'Quel film peut donner tous les points de vue?' (2003: 11) (What film could portray every point of view?). Charef takes up this challenge in *Cartouches gauloises*, which portrays the final months of the war and includes all of the constituencies involved. Throughout the film, Charef juxtaposes short scenes which convey an impression of shared suffering through their depiction of the violence that affected everyone – summary executions and torture carried out by the French, the FLN's killing of pied noir families, the beginning of the massacre of the *harkis*, and the FLN's purge of prostitutes, for example. These atrocities are all presented from the point of view of Ali, an 11-year-old newspaper delivery boy who has access to the various groups depicted and who is frequently portrayed witnessing events. His impartial, unemotional gaze, which unifies the scenes, seems to represent Charef's desire to provide 'a comprehensive and balanced view' (Durmelat, 2011: 106) and to record events in a neutral fashion.[17] At the same time, Ali's relationship with his pied noir friend Nico, which is foregrounded in many of the vignettes, highlights the intertwining of destinies and reinforces the theme of shared memories. As many critics have noted, the cabin the two boys have built symbolizes Algeria and complicates clearcut ideas of what it means to be French or Algerian.

As one of the constituencies portrayed in the film, the *harkis* appear in a variety of scenes, many of which poignantly evoke their fate. Algerians are seen insulting them; the pied noir station master refers to their being killed when independence is declared, and a *harki* tells a French officer that, while the French recruits will go home whatever the outcome of the war, for his men, the stakes are higher, since the only options are victory or exile. Several episodes explicitly depict France's abandonment of the *harkis* and its consequences. The figure of Djelloul in particular serves to illustrate the anguish of feeling betrayed and fear of popular justice. In one scene, a group of *harkis* are pushed away from a French Army truck that is about to leave and are told that there is no room for them. When Djelloul points out to a French officer that the *harkis*' families will be in danger if they are left behind, the lieutenant replies that he has received no orders to take them, a response that prompts Djelloul to shoot him.

At the end of the film, Ali symbolically finds Djelloul hiding in the cabin he and Nico have built, thus raising the question of what the *harkis*' place will be in an independent Algeria. The answer is provided in the following scene in which a group of villagers set off toward the cabin to hunt him down. The final image of a *harki* in the film is that of Djelloul's despairing gaze as he envisages his probable death at the hands of angry compatriots. Although none of the *harki* characters are well developed, as they were in *La Trahison*, *Cartouches gauloises* conveys the importance of 1962 as a pivotal moment in which the markers that would make the *harkis* a community of destiny came together – abandonment, the massacres, exile, and being branded a traitor. In this sense, *Cartouches gauloises* portrays the situation which sets the stage for the events portrayed in Tasma's *Harkis*.

First shown on France 2 in October 2006, *Harkis* is the only film to date to focus entirely on the *harkis*' experiences in France. Although a few other films contain some references to their lives in the *métropole*, the *harki* characters in them play only a minor role in the development of the plot or main themes. Yasmina Benguigui's *Aïcha*, for example, employs the stereotype of an Algerian family not wanting their daughter to marry a *harki*'s son, while Rachid Bouchareb's *Hors-la-loi* refers briefly to the use of *harki* units in Paris during the war of independence. *Harkis*, which stars well-known actors Smaïn and Leïla Bekhti, and whose screenplay was co-written by Dalila Kerchouche, portrays the life of the Benamar family at Bias, the sixth housing camp they have lived in since they arrived in France. Tasma's realistic, somewhat didactic approach emphasizes the interrelated topics of displacement, trauma, and marginalization, which are conveyed through the depiction of the spaces and functions of the housing camp. Like the Maghrebi-French directors discussed by Higbee, Tasma explores the consequences of a shared Franco-Algerian history by dealing with questions that are at once 'local, national and transnational' (Higbee, 2013: 5).

Throughout the film, the isolated Bias camp (the local) is associated with images of imprisonment, which serve as a metaphor for the aftermath of trauma. Repeated shots of closed gates and barbed-wire fences in particular evoke a sense of confinement and enclosure, and the *harkis* are portrayed as being locked in prisons of various types – in the camp itself, in silence, in unwanted stigmatizing labels, and, in the case of the young female protagonists, in undesired gender roles. At the same time, the camp represents exclusion and marginalization on the national level. Its location in a remote area recalls the idea that the *harkis* had come to embody the nation's dishonor and constituted a reminder of 'la mauvaise conscience et l'échec de la France' (Besnaci-Lancou, 2005: 104) (France's guilty conscience and failure), an idea conveyed by the many shots of *harkis* working in secluded areas of the woods. In this sense, the camp is presented as an in-between space, a kind of transnational no-man's land that is neither fully French nor Algerian. Indeed, Régis Pierret describes the *harkis* as 'une communauté intersticielle' (interstitial community), arguing that 'Etre harki, c'est justement n'être ni totalement l'un ni totalement l'autre' (1993: 99) (Being a *harki* means exactly that, being neither completely one nor the other). The fact that the majority of the *harkis* in the film spend most of their time in the confined space of the camp reinforces the notion of their marginalization.

Furthermore, several scenes emphasize the 'double rejet' (double rejection) that the *harkis* experience in France, where they are often treated as Arabs by the French but are also rejected by other Algerians (Pierret, 1993: 89). Sociologist Vincent Crapanzano attributes their impression of being 'ostracized and exiled' to this 'interstitial marginality' (2011: 175).

In *Harkis*, the eldest daughter in the Benamar family (Leïla) is subjected to racist taunts at school when an Algerian pupil calls her 'fille de harki, fille de traître' (daughter of a *harki*, daughter of a traitor); a French café owner insults her father Saïd, saying that he does not serve Arabs, and Leïla refers explicitly to the double rejection when she angrily retorts, 'la France se protège de nous parce qu'on est des Arabes. Et même les Arabes nous détestent' (France protects itself from us because we're Arabs. And even the Arabs hate us).

In addition, the Bias camp director embodies the paternalism and racism of the colonial system, which was often perpetuated in the camps. Many of the literary works too refer to this aspect of the *harkis*' lives. Besnaci-Lancou, for example, comments, 'Mis ainsi à l'écart, les adultes se sont sentis parqués et condamnés à rester des sous-citoyens, Français de seconde zone, traités comme s'ils n'avaient pas été décolonisés' (2005: 103) (Marginalized in this way, the adults felt penned in and condemned to remain sub-citizens, second-class French people, as if they hadn't been decolonized). In *Harkis*, the director of Bias is depicted as authoritarian and patronizing, pulling off Madame Benamar's headscarf in one of the opening scenes and telling the newly arrived family that his job is to turn them into 'des Français civ-ilisés' (civilized French people), thus echoing colonial discourse regarding France's civilizing mission. His main requirement for successful integration into camp life is, as he puts it, 'l'obéissance aveugle et sincère' (blind, sincere obedience), and his infantilizing attitude is further evident in the affirmation that, 'tout ce que fait le chef de camp est bon pour les harkis' (everything the director of the camp does is good for the *harkis*).

As Keith Moser contends in his analysis of *Harkis*, the director's approach to running the camp, with its emphasis on strict discipline, recalls the dis-ciplinary power structures described by Michel Foucault (Moser: 2014). In the director's punitive regime, any infractions are severely punished in order to discourage dissent, and any signs of subversion are immediately quashed. Leïla's uncle Ahmed, who had written to the government asking for the situation in the camps to improve, is taken to a psychiatric hospital (La Candélie) and thus represents the practice of sending rebellious *harkis* from Bias to this institution; he later returns to the camp a broken man, reduced to the state of a zombie. Other transgressions are punished by creating hardship or through public humiliation. Saïd is paid half his usual salary after asking why Ahmed has been sent to La Candélie; his son Kader is shamed in front of his classmates; the family's coal allocation is reduced to almost nothing when Leïla begins to show signs of rebellion, and Saïd is barred from work-ing for a month when he later defends his daughter.

Alain Tasma uses generational differences to suggest the nature of the *harkis*' resistance to this disciplinary environment. In the first part of the film in particular, Saïd and his wife, who represent the parents' generation, are associated with voicelessness, obedience, and fear of the world outside the camps. They have little contact with the local French population and hesitate to venture out of Bias, feeling safer in the camp community. In contrast, their daughter Leïla, who stands for the next generation of *harkis*, serves as the primary figure of rebellion against the status quo. Her resistance takes three main forms: her role in the demand for material reparations, her desire to put an end to her marginalization in French society, and her challenging traditional gender roles. First, when Leïla discovers that the *harki* families are not receiving the full 300 francs of their family allowance, she goes to talk to the camp director, seeking 'notre argent et la justice pour les harkis' (our money and justice for the *harkis*); she then successfully encourages a group of women to ask the state to give the allowance directly to them rather than to the director. Here, Leïla's struggle for justice clearly represents the activism of the children of *harkis*, who often acted on their parents' behalf. It is interesting to note, however, that Kerchouche's novel *Leïla*, which was published in the year the film was released (2006), goes much further in its portrayal of the second generation's collective rebellion, and culminates in a description of young people in the camps symbolically tearing down the barbed-wire fences that signify their exclusion.

Second, Leïla's friendship with Juliette, a sympathetic French character who stands in sharp contrast to the camp director, suggests the possibility of a supportive relationship between the *harkis* and the local population and counters Saïd's initial view that all French people are racists. Indeed, Leïla tells Juliette, 'je ne savais pas qu'il y avait des Français comme vous' (I didn't know there were French people like you). As the film progresses, Leïla's father too begins to find a voice and looks beyond the world of the camp, encouraged by his daughter. In one of the longest exchanges in the film, as part of what could be described as the father's rebellion, Saïd stands up for Leïla in defiance of the director, stating firmly when he is asked to leave, 'non, maintenant je parle' (no, now it's my turn to speak). During the ensuing conversation, in which Saïd does most of the talking, he evokes many of the main issues that have affected the *harkis*' lives. He accuses France of breaking its promise by abandoning the *harkis*, describes the horrific nature of the massacres, explicitly associates the French Army with betrayal and dishonor, and makes an impassioned plea for the children of *harkis* to be treated fairly: 'J'ai tout perdu en Algérie, ma famille, mon honneur; moi, je suis mort, mais pas mes enfants, ils sont vivants. Ils méritent autre chose que ce camp … de vivre comme tous les enfants en France' (I lost everything in Algeria, my family, my honor; I'm a dead man, but my children are alive. They deserve something better than this camp … they deserve to live like all children in France). The denouement of the film further highlights the need to end exclusion, as the Benamar family leave the camp to live near Juliette and her husband Lucien, who continue to provide them with hospitality and support. Similarly, the final scene of the film, that of Saïd driving Leïla to her first class as she starts her training to become a nurse's aide, underscores the theme of healing and suggests the beginning of another stage along the road to independence and integration.

Finally, Leïla's rebellion in the area of gender relations resembles that of many of the Maghrebi daughters portrayed in *beur* fiction. In Kerchouche's novel *Leïla*, the protagonist refers explicitly to feeling limited by cultural expectations regarding women's behavior, commenting 'Les traditions m'enferment autant que les barbelés. Deux fois prisonnière' (2006: 46) (Traditions imprison me just as much as the barbed-wire fences do. A prisoner twice over). Like the novel, the film addresses the gendered nature of Leïla's confinement and suggests that being a *harki* woman requires the negotiation of a second set of restrictions. Many scenes reminiscent of episodes in *beur* novels evoke generational conflict over the issue of gender roles. Leïla expresses her rebellion by secretly meeting Juliette's grandson Jerôme and occasionally allowing him to kiss her, but when a friend's brother sees her smile at Jerôme at school, he assumes the traditional patriarchal role of guardian of the Benamar family's honor and threatens to kill Jerôme if he goes near Leïla again. In addition, Leïla's father beats her, calls her a 'salope' (slut), and sets up an arranged marriage in order to bring her into line, a marriage she rejects by running away.

Like many *beur* protagonists, then, Leïla is depicted as being torn between two cultures and as not yet having managed to combine them into a unified identity. The question of how to reconcile the French and Algerian sides of her identity is particularly evident when she tells Jerôme that their relationship cannot work because of their different ethnicities: 'T'es Français; je suis Arabe. Ça ne marchera pas, tu le sais' (You're French and I'm Arab. It won't work and you know it). Jerôme's response, which counters her suggestion that the two cultures are mutually exclusive, seems, however, to offer a more optimistic perspective by appealing to their shared Frenchness: 'Ton père, il s'est battu pour la France, il peut pas refuser que sa fille sorte avec un Français' (Your father fought for France, he can't forbid his daughter to go out with a Frenchman). The central theme of a potential interethnic relationship thus emphasizes the need to go beyond oppositional discourses, while concomitantly suggesting that negotiating a new identity at the confluence of two cultures will not necessarily be easy.

In her discussion of the representation of *harkis* in the graphic novel, Jennifer Howell concludes, 'Despite the growing number of scholarly investigations relative to this community, its history, and collective memory, it would appear that the Harki, as a marginalized figure, remains on the fringe of all French cultural production' (2014: 190). Howell's observation applies very well to fiction films, in which *harkis* still occupy only a very small place. Furthermore, most of the films from the 2000s that do feature *harkis* are set in a much earlier period – *L'Ennemi intime* in 1959, *La Trahison* and *Cartouches gauloises* in 1960 and 1962 respectively, and *Harkis* in 1972 – and hardly any of them portray a *harki* in a context other than that of the war or the camps.[18] Paradoxically, it is Chibane's *Douce France* (1995), with its focus on a *harki* family living in a Parisian neighborhood in the 1990s, which departs the furthest from these scenarios and in this sense appears the most forward-looking in terms of its presentation of the *harkis'* experience of immigration. It remains to be seen whether any films made in the coming years will propose alternative scripts or delineate different ways of being a *harki* in France.

Notes

1. All translations are mine unless indicated otherwise.
2. This is the title of Michel Roux's historical study *Les Harkis ou les oubliés de l'histoire*.
3. Further riots occurred in 1987, 1991, 1992, and 1997, and protesters held hunger strikes in 1997 and 2000.
4. *Mon pays la France* (1962), *Les Harkis au service de la France* (1963), and *L'Algérie sans la France* (1964).
5. This period also saw the publication of Mehdi Charef's *Le Harki de Meriem* (1989), the first novel depicting a *harki* family to be written by an author who was not part of the *harki* community.
6. Some of the best-known of these include: Fatima Besnaci-Lancou's *Fille de harki* (2005), Zahia Rahmani's *Moze* (2003) and *France, récit d'une enfance* (2006), Hadjila Kemoum's *Mohand le harki* (2003), and Dalila Kerchouche's *Mon père, ce harki* (2003) and *Leïla: avoir dix-sept ans dans un camp de harkis* (2006).
7. Filming in Algeria was difficult because the army had a monopoly on images of the war and used its own production service, the Service Cinématographique des Armées (SCA) (Mossman, 2013: 76).
8. *Cinq Colonnes à la une* ran from January 1959 until mid 1969 and was known for its coverage of the war (Mossman, 2013: 71–2).
9. The 1970s also saw the appearance of some films made with a specific audience in mind, such as pied noir Alexandre Arcady's *Le Coup de Sirocco* (1979).
10. This four-hour documentary is composed of Patrick Rotman's interviews with conscripts from the Grenoble area and uses first-person testimony in order to illuminate the enduring emotional and psychological impact of the war.
11. The titles of the three episodes underscore the main phases of this trajectory: *Les Harkis: l'enrôlement, Les Harkis: l'abandon, Les Harkis: les fils de l'oubli*.
12. It is interesting to note that these films appeared in the same decade as the first major body of literary works written by the children of *harkis*, many of whom adopt a confrontational stance with regard to France's treatment of their families. Stora attributes the renewed interest in the past to the appearance of a new generation which includes 'les petits-enfants de l'immigration algérienne' (2008: 39) (the grandchildren of immigrants from Algeria), who wish to learn more about their heritage. References to this generation appear in the literary corpus, too. Fatima Besnaci-Lancou, for example, associates her coming-to-writing with a strong desire to put an end to the transmission of stigma and shame: 'Pour mes enfants, il me faut donc regarder ce passé

... Je ne veux pas que mon fils soit "petit-fils de harki"' (2005: 17) (For my children's sake, I have to look at the past ... I don't want my son to be called 'a *harki*'s grandson').
13 Rotman's book, which is based on archival research and the testimony of noncommissioned soldiers (including a *harki*, Rachid Abdelli), describes their encounter with 'la violence extrême: torture, exactions, sévices, viols, exécutions sommaires' (Rotman, 2002: 8) (extreme violence: torture, abuses of power, cruelty, rape, summary executions), all of which are portrayed or evoked in the film. Rotman also made a documentary titled *L'Ennemi intime* for France 3 (2004).
14 The screenplay was co-written by Philip Faucon, Soraya Nini, and Claude Sales.
15 This idea appears, for example, when boys throw stones at Ali in a village, calling him a *harki*, and when an FLN combatant retorts, 'Vous les Harkis n'êtes que des traîtres' (You *harkis* are only traitors).
16 The film also alludes frequently to the prejudice and racism encountered by the *harkis*, and to their isolation within the army.
17 The film does not examine the potentially traumatic effects on children of their witnessing horrific acts of violence. See Higbee for a discussion of this point (2013: 96–100).
18 The continuing focus on the camps in Kerchouche's scenario for *Harkis* can perhaps be explained in part by the fact that they constitute an integral part of the community's identity and collective memory, even though most *harkis* spent very little time in them (Cohen, 2006: 177).

References

Austin, G. (2009). '"Seeing and Listening from the Site of Trauma": The Algerian War in Contemporary French Cinema,' *Yale French Studies*, 115, 115–25.
Bachaga Boualam, S. (1962). *Mon pays la France*, Paris: France-Empire.
Bachaga Boualam, S. (1963). *Les Harkis au service de la France*, Paris: France-Empire.
Bachaga Boualam, S. (1964). *L'Algérie sans la France*, Paris: France-Empire.
Besnaci-Lancou, F. (2005). *Fille de harki*, Paris: Editions de l'Atelier.
Beugnet, M. (2007). 'Blind Spot,' *Screen*, 48(2), 227–31.
Blanchard, P., Bancel, N., and Lemaire, S. (eds) (2005). *La Fracture coloniale*, Paris: La Découverte.
Branche, R. (2008). 'Une impression d'absence: l'Algérie et la guerre d'Algérie au cinéma et à la télévision française depuis 1962,' in E. Savarese (ed.), *L'Algérie dépassionnée: au-delà du tumulte des mémoires*, Paris: Syllepse.
Charbit, T. (2006). *Les Harkis*, Paris: La Découverte.
Charef, M. (1989). *Le Harki de Meriem*, Paris: Mercure de France.
Charef, M. (2005). *1962, le dernier voyage*, Paris: L'Avant-Scène Théâtre.
Cohen, W. B. (2006). 'The Harkis: History and Memory,' in P. Lorcin (ed.),

Algeria and France 1800–2000: Identity, Memory, Nostalgia, Syracuse: Syracuse University Press, 164–80.

Crapanzano, V. (2011). *The Harkis: The Wound That Never Heals*, Chicago: University of Chicago Press.

Dine, P. (1994). *Images of the Algerian War: French Fiction and Film, 1954–1992*, Oxford: Oxford University Press.

Durmelat, S. (2011). 'Re-visions of the Algerian War of Independence: Writing the Memories of Algerian Immigrants into French Cinema,' in S. Durmelat and V. Swamy (eds), *Screening Integration: Recasting Maghrebi Immigration in Contemporary France*, Lincoln, NE/London: University of Nebraska Press, 93–111.

Enjelvin, G. (2004). 'Entrée des Harkis dans l'histoire de France?,' *French Cultural Studies*, 15(1), 61–75.

Fabbiano, G. (2014). 'Writing as Performance: Literary Production and the Stakes of Memory,' in K. Moser (ed.), *A Practical Guide to Harki Literature*, Lanham, MD: Lexington Books, 17–35.

Ferdi, S. (1981). *Un enfant dans la guerre*, Paris: Seuil.

Frodon, J.-M. (2004). 'Le Film de guerre n'existe pas: De l'Algérie au Vietnam,' *Cahiers du cinéma*, 593, 74–6.

Hamoumou, M. (1990). 'Les Harkis, un trou de mémoire franco-algérien,' *Esprit*, 24–45.

Higbee, W. (2013). *Post-Beur Cinema: North-African Émigré and Maghrebi-French Filmmaking in France Since 2000*, Edinburgh: Edinburgh University Press.

Howell, J. (2014). 'Reconstructing Harki Sites of Memory in the Graphic Novel,' in K. Moser (ed.), *A Practical Guide to Harki Literature*, Lanham, MD: Lexington Books, 187–207.

Jeancolas, J.-P. (2007). 'French Cinema and the Algerian War: Fifty Years Later,' *Cinéaste* (Winter), 44–6.

Kerchouche, D. (2003). *Mon père, ce harki*, Paris, Seuil.

Kerchouche, D. (2006). *Leïla: avoir dix-sept ans dans un camp de harkis*, Paris: Seuil.

Kemoum, H. (2003). *Mohand le harki*, Paris: Anne Carrière.

Moser, K. (2014). 'An Exploration of Foucauldian Disciplinary Power in Alain Tasma and Dalila Kerchouche's Film *Harkis*,' *Pennsylvania Literary Journal*, 6(3), 57–70.

Mossman, I. (2013). 'Conflicting Memories: Modernisation, Colonialism and the Algerian War *Appelés* in *Cinq colonnes à la une*,' in F. Barclay (ed.), *France's Colonial Legacies: Memory, Identity and Narrative*, Cardiff: Cardiff University Press, 71–89.

Moumen, A. (2014). '1962–2014: The Historical Construction of Harki Literature,' in K. Moser (ed.), *A Practical Guide to Harki Literature*, Lanham, MD: Lexington Books, 1–15.

Pierret, R. (1993). 'Les Enfants de harkis, entre triple appartenance et double rejet,' *Hommes et Migrations*, 1276, 88–101.

Rahmani, Z. (2003). *Moze*, Paris: Sabine Wespiesier.

Rahmani, Z. (2006). *France, récit d'une enfance*, Paris: Sabine Wespiesier.
Rotman, P. (2002). *L'Ennemi intime*, Paris: Seuil.
Roux, M. (1991). *Les Harkis ou les oubliés de l'histoire*, Paris: La Découverte.
Sadouni, B. (1985). *Français sans patrie*, Rouen: Copie Plus.
Sales, C. (1999). *La Trahison*, Paris: Seuil.
Stora, B. (1997). *Imaginaires de guerre: Algérie – Viêt-nam, en France et aux Etats-Unis*, Paris: La Découverte.
Stora, B. (2003). 'L'Absence d'images déréalise l'Algérie,' *Cahiers du cinéma* (February), 7–13.
Stora, B. (2008). 'La Guerre d'Algérie dans les médias: l'exemple du cinéma,' *Hermès*, 52, 33–40.
Zamponi, F. (1999). *Mon colonel*, Arles: Actes Sud.

Filmography

Arcady, A. (1979). *Le Coup de sirocco*, Les Films de l'Alma/Alexandre Films.
Benguigui, Y. (2009). *Aïcha*, Les Auteurs Associés Elemiah.
Bouchareb, R. (2010). *Hors-la-loi*, Tessalit Productions.
'C'étaient les harkis,' (7 June 1963). *Cinq colonnes à la une*, RTF.
Charef, M. (2007). *Cartouches gauloises*, K.G. Productions.
Chegaray, D. (1982). *Mémoire enfouie d'une génération – guerre d'Algérie*, France 2.
Chibane, M. (1995). *Douce France*, Alhambra Films.
Courrière, Y. and Monnier, P. (1972). *La Guerre d'Algérie*, Reggane Films.
Demy, J. (1964). *Les Parapluies de Cherbourg*, Parc Film/Madeleine Films/Beta Films.
Deroo, E. and de Sédouy, A. (1993–94). *Les Harkis: l'enrôlement, Les Harkis: l'abandon, Les Harkis: les fils de l'oubli*, France 3.
Faucon, P. (2005). *La Trahison*, Kinok Films/Créations du Dragon/Diba Films.
Favre, B. and Stora, B. (1991). *Les Années algériennes*, INA/France 2.
Godard, J.-L. (1963). *Le Petit Soldat*, Les Productions Georges de Beauregard/Société Nouvelle de Cinématographie.
Haroud, F. (1998). *Fils de harkis*, Aster – France 3.
Haroud, F. (2001). *Le Mouchoir de mon père*, Aster – France 3.
Herbiet, L. (2006). *Mon colonel*, K.G. Productions/Les Films du Fleuve.
Heynemann, L. (1977). *La Question*, Little Bear/Rush/Z Productions.
Resnais, A. (1963). *Muriel ou le temps d'un retour*, Argos Films/Alfa Production/Eclair/Fils de la Pléiade/Dear Films.
Schoendoerffer, P. (1982). *L'Honneur d'un capitaine*, Bela Productions/TF1 Films Productions.
Siri, F.-E. (2007). *L'Ennemi intime*, Les Films du Kiosque/SND Films.
Tasma, A. (2006). *Harkis*, France 2/Image & Compagnie.
Tavernier, B. (1992). *La Guerre sans nom*, GMT Productions/Little Bear/StudioCanal+.
Vautier, R. (1972). *Avoir 20 ans dans les Aurès*, Unité de Production Cinématographie Bretagne.

11

'L'oued revient toujours dans son lit': Franco-Maghrebi identity in Hassan Legzouli's film *Ten'ja*

Ramona Mielusel

The question of identity, in all its complexity, has always been the center of interest of Franco-Maghrebi literature and cinema.[1] The hybrid identities of these writers and filmmakers translate into artistic explorations of identity performed by the characters they create. It is also the main subject in *Ten'ja*, a 2004 film by Franco-Moroccan director Hassan Legzouli.[2] After a few short- and medium-length features,[3] he became known in francophone[4] cinema with the long feature film *Ten'ja*[5] (a title meaning 'Tangier' in Arabic, which was translated into French as *Le Testament*).[6] *Ten'ja* received numerous awards and was on the program of important festivals.[7] This fact proves a certain interest in the international film community for such topics.

Ten'ja follows the narrative structure of a road movie. The film tells the story of Nordine, a young Franco-Maghrebi man, forced to go to Morocco in order to bury his father, who died in France. After having spent more than thirty years working in the mines of northern France, his father's only verbal 'testament' was to be buried in his native village, Aderj. Nordine's journey is not only a return to his parents' native land and roots, but also a personal journey of cultural initiation. In the course of his journey, he meets two young Moroccans, Mimoun and Nora, who become his friends, and he gets to know the inhabitants of the village where his father was born. The trip to Aderj, the father's native village in the Atlas Mountains, is a transformative experience for him.

This chapter attempts to outline the key moments in Nordine's transformation and initiation from denial to acceptance of his double-sided identity as an essential understanding of his Franco-Maghrebi status on both sides of the Mediterranean. In order to map out this process, I will first focus on the main protagonist's relationship with his father and the impact of the father's death on his sense of identity. I will continue with an examination of the young man's hybrid, Franco-Maghrebi identity as it is revealed to him during his journey. Nordine successfully reconciles his multiple identities by the end of his experience as a conclusion to his transformative journey. The final point of this chapter is to see how Legzouli depicts the journey of transformation of Franco-Maghrebi characters in comparison to other films of the same genre.[8] The movie, by his structure and chosen topics, is a typical road movie, but Legzouli's twist at the end of his production distinguishes it from previous movies in the field.

The road movie genre and the importance of the journey in Ten'ja

The road movie is not a European invention, and it would not naturally appear among the choices of European producers. In his book *Driving Visions: Exploring the Road Movie* (2002), however, David Laderman notices a reinvention of the American genre in European films. According to him, in American films, the exploration of violence and danger is emphasized more than the journey itself (2002: 2). The American movies focus on the runaway journey, which an outlawed couple undertakes in order to escape social norms (e.g. *Bonnie and Clyde* in 1967 and *Thelma and Louise* in 1991), or on 'cowboy like' heroes seen as semi-nomads who tame wild nature and restore order based on the social customs of a specific community (e.g. *Gun Crazy* (1950), *Badlands* (1973), or *Wild at Heart* (1990)). The European road movie genre, on the other hand, explores the spiritual, emotional, and psychological status of the journey. The main goal of European road movies is introspection into the character's self-(re)discovery.

Furthermore, in Laderman's opinion, the European producers' choice of this genre is a means to explore the national culture, the traditions, and the cultural specificities of a particular country or area. Since distances in Europe are less significant than in North America, the European road movies provide a more detailed depiction of the national and cultural differences between the various places the characters explore in their quests. In contemporary society, which is undergoing political, sociocultural, and ethnic transformation, the filmmakers' displacement and movement from one place to another is facilitated through free border crossings and the freedom to travel.[9] Nevertheless, the road movies simultaneously depict a forced displacement and a continuous movement that are dictated by financial, social or political necessity, personal safety, or exile. The two themes, relative freedom of movement and forced displacement, coexist in the choice of subject in the movies made by Franco-Maghrebi filmmakers.

Migrant and diasporic film writers,[10] more than any other European filmmakers, have chosen the road movie genre for their interest in the journey itself. For them, it offers an opportunity to explore their own identity while representing characters who are constantly in search of their roots and culture. For Hamid Naficy (2001), the cinema of mobility, fragmented narratives, and multilingual dialogue belongs to the category of *accented cinema*.

It is a cinema produced by diasporic, migrant, and exilic filmmakers. In other words, the common trait is that the cinema of mobility is produced by displaced filmmakers who find themselves in continuous movement across countries, borders, genres, and languages, like the characters in their movies. *Accented* films are often based on quest journeys and displacement as well as numerous crossings of territorial, geographic, cultural and identity borders. The emphasis in these films does not necessarily come from the linguistic accents of the characters in the movie, but it expresses the directors' dislocation from their cultural roots, meaning their particularity in style. Moreover, accented cinema is a multilingual film production. The theme of displacement is identified not only in the film narratives, but also, as Naficy observes, in the multifaceted construction of their characters. Occasionally they metaphorically reproduce biographical characteristics of the filmmakers or of real people they have met during their life in the native country, their journeys, or their exile: 'Accented filmmakers are not textual structures or fictions within their films; they also are empirical subjects, situated in the interstices of cultures and film practices, who exist outside and prior to their films' (Naficy, 2001: 1).

The originality of accented films is their narrative hybridity, their cultural diversity, and their focus on the vision of the "Other," the displaced. Accented cinema becomes, therefore, a distinct form of expression that offers a new perspective on the ethnic minorities and immigrant/diasporic communities in contemporary society; a perspective that integrates at the same time the traditional forms of the national cinema of the countries where the filmmakers now reside.

Clearly, Legzouli's full-length production is closely related to both the road movie genre and to accented films. Since he is a migrant director, the focal points of his movie are the journey of initiation and the quest for identity. In the diasporic road movies, the journey undertaken by the main character is not just a straightforward itinerary, but rather a complex and challenging maze. In Nordine's case, the crossing of the geographical borders of France and Spain with Morocco as a final destination becomes a psychological and cultural exploration of identity. The travelling adventures along the way not only change the meaning and the trajectory of the journey, but they also radically transform the young man. Legzouli's road movie always keeps in the background the idea of Nordine's return to France, yet it also offers the prospect of Nordine's future return to Morocco (he left the door open to a new encounter with Nora later in time), a place he now discovers and perceives with new eyes.

Nordine's journey in *Ten'ja* is ultimately an identity quest. During this adventure, he is transformed by territorial displacement and the discovery of the Other. This Other is the Moroccans, who were foreign to him and whom he then came to know. At the same time, he discovers himself as being different from the Moroccans, as being the Other to them. Nordine's transformation would not have been complete in any other context than that of his identity quest and encounter with contemporary Moroccan culture. He reconnects with his roots and his parents' culture through memories of his father, who, although absent, facilitates Nordine's transition to the different stages in his identity transformation. Without the symbolic presence of the father in the film, the journey would not have had any psychological depth. Moreover, this feature film reveals the complexity of the father–son relationship, which represents the foundation of my analysis.

Nordine's relationship with his father

Even though Nordine's father is dead at the very beginning of the movie and only appears in his son's memories through numerous flashbacks, his physical and spiritual presence is evoked throughout the narrative. Nordine's journey to Morocco can also be viewed as a process of spiritual renewal undertaken together with his father. The viewer can grasp the functional relationship between the two characters in this movie as it is emphasized from the first scene of *Ten'ja*. The first few minutes show a close-up of Nordine in his vehicle inside a carwash. The camera frames his facial and body profile. The very brief discussion he carries on over the phone is followed by a deafening silence, which creates suspense. The following scene shows him comforting his mother before beginning his trip to Morocco in his SUV, his father's coffin tucked in the back of the car. The spectator can deduce that the father–son relationship was not very close during the last years of the father's life. The son feels pressured by his moral duties toward the family and toward the father more specifically, for he is reluctant to fulfill his father's request at first; he has misgivings about his father's choice of 'burial.' Out of respect, he undertakes the trip, even though he does not understand the meaning of this action. He does not feel worthy of accomplishing the task at hand when he realizes that the drive is demanding and that there will be many obstacles. Speaking on the phone with his mother from the Moroccan border, where he first gets into trouble with the authorities, he shows his disagreement with the father's decision: 'Je n'y peux rien. Je vais rentrer. Il ne m'a pas demandé mon avis'[11] (There is nothing I can do. I'm coming back. He did not ask for my opinion). Legzouli's film seems to show, at this point in the narrative, a "clash" between the first generation of North African immigrants in France and their offspring. The children have lived in their native/adoptive country apparently without keeping too many ties to their parents' native culture.

As Begag and Chaouite clearly explained in their book, *Écarts d'identité* (1990), an identity gap (*écart d'identité*) could be noticed between the second-generation immigrants and their parents in the 1970s and 1980s. Members of the second generation did not have a close connection with their families' roots and at the same time, their position in France prevented them from establishing a special bond with the French identity also.[12] Differences in the memories and histories of fathers and offspring may have been a cause of opposition between these two generations of immigrants in France. The younger generation did not share the lifestyle or values of their parents. The perception of their roots evolved depending on their place at different points in their lives. Yet, at the same time, Legzouli's film shows that the second generation is more flexible in terms of identification. Their ease in adapting to different social situations and the porosity of the territory where they grew up (in constant negotiation of borders and boundaries) make them more mobile and more receptive to change. Therefore, the young Franco-Maghrebi are more likely to compromise regarding their identity and their position both in North Africa and in France. It is easier for them to adapt to their situation, as their life is a continuous adaptation. For the younger generation, the "homeland," the place where they feel at "home," is France, not the Maghreb, whereas for their parents, the Maghreb is their "homeland" and France is simply "a home," a place to live, as seen in the case of Nordine and his father.

We could then say that Nordine distances himself from his father's ideas and thoughts without opposing them entirely. Even though the father, 'n'était pas trop vacances au bled' (was not too much into taking trips back home), as Nordine confesses to Nora, his 'guide' in the Moroccan Atlas Mountains, he nourished a deep hope to return to the native country and pass on to his son the desire to discover his roots. Yet the transmission of Moroccan culture and identity is not easily accomplished by immigrant fathers, as they lack the language to convey their knowledge. Their wisdom is reinstated in their children's memory later on, when they internalize what the parents wanted to pass on to them.

In this context, death becomes a trigger in the film. Nordine's trip to bury the old man in his native village is the equivalent of a true encounter between the main character and his father. Prior to the son's initiation and his discovery of Morocco, both of them were experiencing 'l'absence de mots' (a lack of words); they were missing the means to communicate with each other. Throughout the journey, the father's symbolic presence teaches Nordine that a return to his origins is a necessary life experience and process of self-discovery, especially if he does not intend to confine himself to a fixed place. The main character's mobility between identities, cultures, and countries, reconnects the loose ties between father and son and reduces the gap between them.

Memory constitutes another way by which the son brings the father back to life and makes him an integral part of the journey. The film contains flashbacks that show Nordine's childhood, his attachment to his father and the ease of communication between the two at that point in time. The son remembers the happy times when he was together with his siblings awaiting the father's return from the mine. The ritual of washing the miner's feet[13] after they had taken off his shoes indicates their respect for him and their appreciation of his efforts to provide for his family. Moreover, Nordine mentions the life lessons that his father taught them by using North African proverbs and traditions. His words of wisdom carry a great value for Nordine, who wants to preserve them in his recollections of dialogues with his father. For example, he remembers the scene when, at the beginning of adolescence, he missed the chance to go to Morocco on a school trip. He was torn by a setback related to his identity status in France.[14] In this delicate situation, the father did not show anger about the injustice inflicted upon Nordine, but instead offered him a life lesson through a single sentence: 'D'où vient cette branche? De cet arbre' (Where does this branch come from? From this tree). It was the father's way of saying that, in spite of his complicated legal status in both countries, Nordine was bound to know his roots and that he would sooner or later understand who he was and where he came from.

At the beginning of the movie, the young man seems to be passing through his father's country as a tourist, without any specific expectation. Nevertheless, the viewer discovers that Nordine goes beyond being a foreigner in Morocco, as he also carries throughout his entire journey the 'memory'[15] of his father's land, contained in the father's box of 'souvenirs.' At the beginning of the journey, his father's memories appear to be isolated objects without any specific meaning for the young man. A duplicate of the coffin, which holds the father's body, the box holds memories that, little by little, come to create a bond of identity between father and son. The box contains the memories of a man who left his country a long time ago (a newspaper article, an old record, and so on), but who maintained a strong connection with the land where he was born and lived until adulthood. This bond is henceforth transferred to the son, who carries the parental memories back to the father's birth country.

Later on, however, Nordine begins to understand the importance of the objects his father kept in the memory box: they are identity symbols as well as history markers of North African immigration to France. The song contained on the father's record and played in the film's soundtrack, highlights the heartbreak of those who went to work in the *métropole* in the 1950s and 1960s and were filled with nostalgia for their native country, a homeland kept alive in their thoughts through popular traditions. It is a Kabyle love song that speaks of the return to the beloved. In the context of the film, it metaphorically suggests the promise of the return of North African immigrants to their native land: 'Je te fais la promesse de ne pas t'oublier … de revenir un jour' (I promise never to forget you … to come back one day).

The newspaper article (with a picture of the father shaking hands with Mitterrand during the president's visit at the mine) vouches for the history of the first generation of North African workers in France and their social status ('invisible' low-class citizens contributing to the building of modern France). By understanding this history, Nordine becomes conscious of the reason why his father became silent during the last years of his life and why any exchange between them was impossible. The father's conversations with Nordine about his native country are difficult. The old man has feelings of betrayal and attachment for his native country, which Nordine does not share, as he is primarily focused on integration in the country of adoption. He finally gets to realize how painful it was for his father to articulate his suffering and how much it mattered to him that Nordine take this trip to Morocco.

To fulfill Nordine's transformation, the father must be laid to rest. In other words, he is not actually dead as long as he is not buried in the land of his childhood, or brought back to his roots and his home. After the completion of this spiritual task, Nordine realizes how much he resembles his father and how many things unite them. Legzouli's movie, unlike other Franco-Maghrebi films, shows how the main character becomes the father's alter ego, a keeper of the parental memory and a link between the immigrants in France and the Moroccans. The immigrants' memory has not vanished, but keeps surviving in their children's, as in Nordine's case.

Nordine's transformation

During his trip to Morocco, Nordine is facing a double lineage. He must justify the choice of his identity several times throughout his journey. From the time the young man sets foot in Morocco, the custom officer asks him: 'Vous êtes Marocain?' (You are Moroccan?). To avoid giving him a precise answer, one that he may very likely not know himself, Nordine refers to the official document he did not have with him during his adolescence trip, that is, his passport. Clearly enough, his accent betrays him and attracts the suspicion of the customs agent. He feels that his accent is unlike that of the Moroccans who live in Morocco, so the agent treats him as a foreigner.

Nordine's very identity is questioned on more occasions during the film. Nora tries to explain to him that he is the son of a Moroccan immigrant and that he has 'l'accent des immigrés' (the immigrants' accent), a typical way of speaking that was learned in the French suburbs, through contact with other immigrants' sons in the HLM (low-cost housing), with whom the youth mixes every day. Nordine can in no way hide his ethnic origin either to the French, who consider him an immigrant's son, an Arab, a foreigner to France, or to the Moroccans who discern in his speech the distinctive accent that betrays his 'Frenchness.'[16]

The main character is not only alienated because of the linguistic barrier, he is viewed as a foreigner, an *outsider*, as far as Moroccan culture is concerned. Several cultural details differentiate him from the country's nationals as well, which we will come to understand through the different encounters he makes along his journey. For instance, he learns that listening to music in the car in the presence of a dead body is culturally unacceptable. Nora explains to him that this is perceived as a sin in Morocco; she tells him that this gesture is equivalent to dancing on his father's grave. If for her, the gesture was culturally inappropriate in such a situation, for Nordine it represented the joy of listening to his father's favorite song and being finally able to find someone who could tell him the meaning of the lyrics.

Nordine meets many Moroccans on his way: customs agents, imams at the morgue, medical examiners, merchants and so on. Yet his journey to the village in the Atlas Mountains and then back to France is marked by the two key characters in the narrative: Mimoun, the *fou-sage* [wise fool] of Tangier and a potential illegal alien, and Nora, a college graduate who ironically affirms that being an educated, but unemployed young person, 'c'est la spécialité d'ici' (this is the specialty here).

These two characters take him under their protective wings and "initiate" him to the Moroccan lifestyle. Hence, Nordine learns to internalize his difference and to recognize in himself the characteristics of his father's culture. He learns to look at the Other as an integral part of himself, as a part of his own existence, while being viewed at the same time by Moroccans as the Other and the self. This idea is also conveyed by Kapuscinski (2006), who speaks of the close relationship between identity and Otherness. Just as Bakhtin previously theorized the concept of Otherness in *The Dialogic Imagination* (1982), Kapuscinski believes that the individual finds himself in a dialogic relationship with the Other. This relationship with Otherness affects both participants in the speaking act, where each one becomes the Other for the others and vice versa: 'Il est certain que l'Autre m'apparaît, à moi, différent; mais il en est de même pour lui. Pour lui, je suis l'Autre' (Kapuscinski, 2006: 14) (Certainly the Other appears, to me, different; but it is the same for him. To him, I am the Other). Nordine is the Other for the Moroccans just as the Moroccans are the Other for him; nonetheless, this division is erased once they start to know each other and he integrates a part of Other(ness) into his Self. For Legzouli's main character, this reflection becomes a crucial moment in his transformation as he can now put things in perspective. He realizes that, at different points in time, all individuals are Others for the people surrounding them. This is a normal position in a globalized contemporary world and it is not a specifically Franco-Maghrebi matter. In *Soi-même comme un autre* (1990), Paul Ricoeur reinstates the idea of defining oneself by constant reference to the other as a binary and reciprocal relation: one can always discover one's otherness by distinguishing one's identity from the other person. By the same token, Nordine can better understand himself after this experience because he discovered otherness (his Moroccan-ness) in France, the same way he discovered his French-ness while pursuing his journey in Morocco.

Legzouli offers an original view on Franco-Maghrebi identity because he presents Nordine as a special character who (re)discovers certain traditions and customs that were present somewhere in his mind, that his family had passed on to him, but that had remained hidden in his mind. Even though he grew up in France, his family transmitted these cultural traditions through daily practices and behaviors that his memory had absorbed without him noticing. The young man realizes his privileged status of feeling like the

Other and the same at once, while learning how to accept his difference and turn it into an asset.

The first 'adjuvant'[17] in his tale-like journey of initiation to Moroccan culture is Mimoun. He stands as a representative of Moroccan knowledge, who opens the doors of Paradise to Nordine. He is, to a certain extent, the representative of the 30-year-old generation, who grew up in a generational void and did not leave its mark in the Moroccan nation.[18] For them, the idea of the individual does not exist, as they keep defining themselves in relation to the community, the clan, and the family. The young Moroccan does not have a social status or promising future in Morocco. His only dream is to leave the country for a better life elsewhere. He is *burning* with desire to leave; [19] he wants to bypass the process of legal immigration, which is very difficult to achieve in a country like Morocco. Mimoun dreams of illegally going to Australia in order to join his beloved, Joony, a tourist he met in Tangier. The only souvenir he has of her is a photograph they took together before her departure. From Hassan Legzouli's personal point of view, this character becomes a reflection of 'une véritable revendication d'individualité chez les jeunes générations' (Loosen, 2004) (a genuine claim of individuality among the young generations) in Morocco. This demand creates an individual consciousness, as Mimoun desires to free himself from Moroccan social and community expectations which he cannot openly oppose. He struggles to assert his individual difference from the group in order to make his own choices in life: seek his freedom elsewhere, live in a place where he is a separate entity and he does not solely exist in relation to his community. Mimoun may equally be perceived as a representative of a new generation of young Moroccans who have become aware of their own value and of their ability to change the order of things in traditionalist Moroccan society.

The friendship between Mimoun and Nordine, characters representing the two 'lost' generations (the possible 'illegal' Moroccan immigrant and the Franco-Maghrebi in search of his identity) happens, symbolically, at the Tangier harbor prior to Nordine's return to France. Nordine and his Moroccan friend watch the sunrise and the lights of the European cities being extinguished across the Mediterranean Sea. The two worlds are so far apart, yet at the same time so close. There is always the possibility of encounters between the two generations, as in the case of Nordine and Mimoun, generations who have more in common than one would think. They are both going through an identity quest and a desire to be recognized in the society in which they live.

The second adjuvant, Nora, represents the image of the young Moroccan woman searching for points of reference. She is young, beautiful, and intelligent, but with no job prospect in Morocco. A return to the native village is also out of the question because of the shame she feels toward her family after leaving them for a better life in the city, which proved to be a failure. She is Nordine's guardian angel, for she takes part in his journey and in his father's burial preparations. She also embodies the image of the emancipated young woman who is gradually looking for her independence and for the right to make her own decisions. Even if she feels a lot of affection for Nordine, and the feelings are mutual, she decides to part ways with him after the father's burial and returns alone to Casablanca in order to think through her plans for the future. After the experience of the journey with Nordine, she finds herself stronger and more determined to change her social status, take charge of her life, and become a new person. She understands that she cannot let men provide for her for the rest of her life and that she must not put herself in a position of inferiority in relation to them. She noticed that Nordine showed appreciation for her qualities as a person and not just for her physical attributes, which caused her to rethink her interactions with the opposite sex. Through Nora's character, Legzouli shows the evolution in the social status of young Moroccan women compared to the previous generation. Today's young women are more liberated and closer to western values than their mothers and grandmothers. They cherish their freedom, but they are aware that they must still fight for financial independence.

Legzouli indicates that through these two very important encounters, Nordine has a 'rencontre avec l'Humanité' (Loosen, 2004) (an encounter with Humanity), that is, with the inhabitants of his father's village and the Moroccan people. He becomes an active participant in a life-changing adventure that he can only experience while being in his father's country. As cited by Kapuscinski in his article, Bronislaw Malinowski argues in *Les Argonautes du Pacifique occidental*: 'Pour pouvoir juger il faut être sur place' (Malinowski, 1963: 46) (In order to be able to judge, one must be on site).[20] In order to make comparisons between cultures and discover similarities and differences between social communities, the individual must maintain a direct contact with the other cultures in relation to which his 'I' is defined.

Nordine could therefore not feel a strong attachment to his father's country without his being there. No one can experience a day in a souk or in a *caravanserail*, if one is not present in these specific places. Even for the mint tea drinking ceremony in Morocco, a whole ritual needs to be observed. Nordine learns this from his friend Mimoun, who suggests that the tea should be poured from above to give it time to cool and for the fragrance of the mint to fill the air.

The main character is also taught the rituals of Moroccan hospitality and burial in the village. His world view changes after all these experiences. Once he returns to France, his life will never be the same. Nordine will have understood who he is and why this trip was so important to his father. He will no longer hesitate to say he is Moroccan when going through the customs again on a future trip to Morocco. He knows that he will be able to answer affirmatively and with conviction, just as he will be able to answer that he is French at the French border. His life experience in France will not prevent him from feeling both French and Moroccan. After this voyage, he can finally understand the advantage he holds over Franco-French citizens (*Français de souche*) and Moroccans, having a multicultural identity and heritage and being proud of them. He definitely feels good about being Franco-Maghrebi, about being able to mix both identities at the same time in order to create a new and fluid identity that gives his life an added value: being the Same (French) and the Other (Moroccan) at once. Experiencing the otherness becomes for him the sign of a new identity that is in the process of creating itself in contemporary society, a hybrid identity where ethnic, cultural, and social identities blend in together.

Conclusion

Hassan Legzouli's film *Ten'ja* facilitates the French audience's understanding of the North African immigrants' cultural origins, as well as their children's identity or identification struggle. We could conclude that there is nothing innate in the history of one's origins. A person is the result of an accumulation of life experiences, because in them, the encounters are fundamental to the development of the individual's life. The director conveys the message that the multifaceted identity of immigrant offspring is not a separation from tradition or family roots.

On the contrary, this multiple cultural heritage represents an asset for the Franco-Maghrebi individual and a tremendous advantage for the adoptive culture, as Legzouli affirms in one of his interviews: 'Je considère que le rapport aux origines n'est pas une déchirure, c'est un plus, une valeur ajoutée en quelque sorte. Les racines ne sont pas automatiques, et [ne] doivent être que source d'enrichissement, et non de conflit' (Loosen, 2004) (I believe that the relation to one's origins is not a rupture, it is a plus, a sort of added value. The discovery of your roots is not automatic and should result in enrichment rather than conflict).

The new nation thus created is culturally enriched with elements introduced by nationals from the immigrant community in France. For Legzouli, today's 'French identity' has become an identity in transformation, emanating from the diverse origins of its citizens, with numerous waves of migration bringing cultural richness to France. The weaving of different cultures and the cultural interactions between them can bring the communities closer, instead of pulling them apart. This new vision is definitely a step forward in Franco-Maghrebi cinema and other immigrant/diasporic cinemas, going beyond the discussion about the struggle of integration of "first- or second-generation immigrants" in France and their difference from Franco-French citizens.

After his journey of initiation, Nordine understands that he has added other layers of culture and identity to his own personality in a way that is not incompatible with his previous values and beliefs. The popular Moroccan proverb, pronounced by a character in the film, reminds us that there is an immutable attachment between the individual and his primary origins: 'L'oued revient toujours dans son lit' (The wadi always comes back to its source). In other words, Nordine has established such a strong bond with his native land that it cannot be undone.

Yet, Hassan Legzouli's film offers an open ending; the viewer does not know Nordine's destiny, what Nora's new beginning will be, or whether Mimoun's dream of leaving the country will come true. It is not made clear whether they will see one another ever again. What is certain is that Nordine has found his life's point of reference. After this experience, he will be able to live at peace with his origins. Through this journey of initiation, he succeeds in reconciling Moroccan roots and traditions with his French identity.

Notes

1 When I speak of Franco-Maghrebi writers and filmmakers, I am referring to the young generation of authors living in France, who were born of North African parents and raised outside of France, as in Hassan Legzouli's case. I purposely avoid using the term "immigrant authors/filmmakers" or "(post) colonial authors/filmmakers," for, in my opinion, these designations refer to other categories of directors and writers as well as to different cultural contexts. According to literary and film critics and theoreticians such as Michel Marie, Will Higbee, Peter Bloom, and Alec Hargreaves, the immigrant filmmakers that fall into the category of immigrant cinema would be mostly the representatives of the second generation of North African origin in France, born of immigrant parents and raised in the *Hexagone*, like Mehdi Charef, Yamina Benguigui, and Malik Chibane, for instance. Since the invention of the term in the 1980s, they are known as the "*beur* generation." I could also mention other names like Rachid Bouchareb or Tony Gatlif, who were not born in France and therefore are not second-generation immigrant filmmakers, but who belong to the same period as Charef and Chibane and deal with very similar topics. Regarding the term "(post)colonial" authors/filmmakers, I think of the colonial period and the years following the independence of the North African countries. Authors such as Tahar ben Jelloun, Assia Djebar, and Driss Chraibi have been very active in France, but their universe is strongly influenced by memories of their native country, even though they have immigrated and settled in France. While being conscious of the ambiguity of the term, for the purposes of this chapter, I therefore choose to keep the expression "Franco-Maghrebi' in order to distinguish Legzouli from a "Franco-French" filmmaker.
2 Born in 1963 in Aderj, Morocco, Legzouli has lived in Lille since the 1980s, when he came to study mathematics but went for cinema instead. He continued his film studies in Brussels, where he received his film director's degree from INSAS (Institut National Supérieur des Arts du Spectacle) in 1994. He returned to France to pursue a career as a film director.
3 *Ailleurs et ici* (1990), *Coup de gigot* (1991), *Le Marchand de souvenirs* (1992), *Là-bas si j'y suis* (1993), *L'Ère du soupçon* (1994), *Chronique d'un deuil ordinaire* (1998), *Quand le soleil fait tomber les moineaux* (1999).

208 Reimagining North African immigration

4 By francophone cinema I am referring to all movies produced entirely or partly in French under French financing by immigrant and diasporic filmmakers and that focus on the development of migrant/diasporic themes. This is the reason why I include Legzouli in this category and not in the category of French cinema.
5 Since 2004 Legzouli has produced a new movie titled *Le Veau d'or* (2012), a film that was shown at the 60th edition of the International Film Festival in San Sebastian in 2012 and at the 15th National Film Festival in Tangier the same year.
6 Will Higbee offers two alternate translations of the Arabic title: 'the land is here' or 'the land has returned' (2013: 135), but I have not encountered this translation anywhere else in my research. The French and English titles are totally different from the original Arabic, which shows the complexity of the matter. The Arabic title, *Ten'ja*, makes reference to the port of Tangier (Morocco), a point of departure for Moroccan immigrants to Europe and an important page in French and western-world immigration history. The harbor's name in the Arabic title relates to the destiny of first-generation immigrants in France and that of their children, as they find themselves 'harbored' between two cultures, two places, and two languages. The French title, *Le Testament*, underlines the importance of the Maghrebi legacy that the first generation passes on to their children, whereas the English title evokes for the viewer the idea of return to, and discovery of, the "homeland" by the second generation born, or raised, abroad and lacking a strong tie to their parents' native land.
7 It was part of the *Sélection officielle* at the Cannes Film Festival in 2005, and it represented Morocco at the Marrakech Film Festival the same year. It also won the *Prix spécial du jury* at the 24th International Film Festival of Amiens. Additionally, in 2004, it won the *Bourse du film du Sud* of the Agence de la Francophonie, an €80,000 award which served to fund the director's next production.
8 As Higbee noticed in his book, there was an emergence of journey quest and road movies at the end of the 1990s and the beginning of the 2000s, which focused on the idea of the 'return' of Franco-Maghrebi protagonists to their parent's country of origin, such as *L'Autre monde* (Allouache, 2001), *La Fille de Keltoum* (Charef, 2002), *Exils* (Gatlif, 2004), *Il était une fois dans l'oued* (Bensalah, 2005), and *Bled number one* (Ameur-Zaïmeche, 2006).
9 Although for western travelers, movement is still unlimited and a mere formality, we need to acknowledge the "migrant crisis" that started immediately after unrest in the Middle East, especially the war in Syria and Afghanistan. This resulted in the closure of some European borders, the rise of xenophobic feelings in some countries and in restrictions that will continue to affect freedom of movement within Europe.
10 Since 2000 many theoreticians and critics have focused on the theorization of cinema produced by immigrant filmmakers in Europe. For greater clarification of the concept of migrant cinema, or transnational cinema in relation to European national cinema, see Berghahn and Sternberg (2010), Ezra and Rowden (2006), and Higson (2000).

11 Transcription from the movie *Ten'ja* (2004) by Hassan Legzouli. All the transcriptions as well as the translations are mine.
12 For a more detailed analysis of the complex relationships between the first and second generations of immigration in France, see Hargreaves (2007) and Mielusel (2013).
13 This common scene in miners' lives refers to the biblical episode when Jesus washed his disciples' feet as a testimony of his love and communion with them, but also as a sign of forgiveness and coexistence with others. In Muslim culture, this gesture is a sign of respect and love for an older person coming from a trip or just returning from a long day of work. The washing of the feet before prayer (the *tahara*) represents a purification of body and soul. All these spiritual details show the importance of the ritual that Nordine and his siblings use to honor the father upon his return from work.
14 During the 1960s and the 1970s many North African immigrants went to work in France. In 1974 the government passed a law – *Le Regroupement familial* – which allowed the families of immigrants to join them in France. The succeeding governments made changes to the immigration and integration laws, changes which affected immigrants' wives and children in France. These changes complicated the situation of first-generation immigrant families. A large number of immigrants' offspring, those generically called 'the second generation,' held an uncertain status in France until the age of 18, when they had to decide on their nationality. Before that, they only had a resident card (*carte de séjour*) as an official document and no proof of their North African nationality, whether Moroccan, Tunisian, or Algerian. This probably explains the problem that Nordine faced with the immigration agents who prevented him from leaving France during the school trip.
15 According to Higbee (2013: 136), the items in the box represent only a 'selective' memory 'inherited' from the father's culture, such as certain photographs, articles from newspapers, or fragments of Arabic or Berber language, which constitute a 'cultural myth' for the young man without any connection with the actual reality of the Maghreb. In my opinion, they constitute more than a selective memory, as shown in my analysis.
16 On the dual social and cultural status of second-generation immigrant children in France (also known as *Beurs*), see Laronde. He considers them as hybrid individuals 'ni Français, ni Maghrébins' (neither French nor Maghrebi), yet at the same time 'Français et Maghrébins' (French and Maghrebi) (1993: 11).
17 This term is one of the six facets (actants) used by Greimas in his actantial narrative scheme when he analyzes the structure of a story: sender, object, receiver, helper (adjuvant), subject, and opponent.
18 The Moroccan youth has numerous characteristics in common with what is known as 'generation X' in the western world. According to William Strauss and Neil Howe, generation X is a sociological theorization of the children born between 1960 and 1989, between the decline of colonial imperialism and the fall of the Berlin Wall, which marked the end of the cold war and of totalitarian regimes in eastern Europe. Likewise, today's young Moroccans

represent a cultural group that finds itself in a period of social transition. Born at the end of the French Protectorate on Morocco, in a period of economic and social instability, they are part of the community of young college graduates who have lived through informational technology development and have acquired knowledge about the western world, but are restricted to a living space strongly marked by North African traditions and patriarchy.

19 The reference to the verb *brûler* (to burn) in the film must be read in close association with Merzak Allouache's movie *Harragas*, that premiered in 2009. The French translation of the film title is *Les brûleurs* (Those who burn). A *harraga* is a migrant stowaway who takes to the sea from North Africa, Mauritania, and Senegal with some *pateras* (unseaworthy boats) to reach the Iberian coasts, Gibraltar, Sicily, the Canary Islands, the Spanish enclaves of Ceuta and Melilla, the island of Lampedusa, or even Malta. This word comes from the North African Arabic dialect حراقة *ḥarrāga*, *ḥarrāg*, 'qui brûlent' (who burn) (the papers). This explains the reference in Legzouli's film to Mimoun's clandestine trip and to the smuggler in whom Mimoun places all his hope of leaving the country. On this, see Chapter 13 in this volume.

20 The book is about the discovery of Otherness in the Pacific islands as well as of other non-western cultures with their traditions and their languages in relation to the western cultural canon, but it can be easily applied to Nordine's situation.

References

Bakhtin, M. (1982). *The Dialogic Imagination: Four Essays*, trans. M. Holquist, Austin: University of Texas Press.

Begag, A. and Chaouite, A. (1990). *Écarts d'identité*, Paris: Editions du Seuil.

Berghahn, D. and Sternberg, C. (2010). *European Cinema in Motion: Migrant and Diasporic Film in Contemporary Europe*, New York/London: Palgrave Macmillan.

Ezra, E. and Rowden, T. (eds) (2006). *Transnational Cinema, the Reader*, New York: Routledge.

Hargreaves, A. (2007). *Multi-Ethnic France: Immigration, Politics, Culture and Society*, 2nd edn, New York: Routledge.

Higbee, W. (2013). *Post-Beur Cinema: North-African Émigré and Maghrebi-French Filmmaking in France Since 2000*, Edinburgh: Edinburgh University Press.

Higson, A. (2000). 'The Limiting Imagination of National Cinema,' in M. Hjort and S. MacKenzie (eds), *Cinema and Nation*, London: Routledge.

Howe, N. and Strauss, W. (1991). *Generations. The History of America's Future, 1584 to 2069*, New York: William Morrow.

Kapuscinski, R. (January 2006). 'Rencontrer l'étranger – cet événement fondamental,' *Le Monde diplomatique*, 14–15.

Laderman, D. (2002). *Driving Visions: Exploring the Road Movie*, Austin: University of Texas Press.

Laronde, M. (1993). *Autour du roman beur: Immigration et identité*, Paris: L'Harmattan.
Loosen, A. E. (2004). 'Hassan Legzouli parle de *Tenja*,' [interview]. *Africultures*. November 24. Web. June 8, 2016.
Malinowski, B. (1963). *Les Argonautes du Pacifique occidental* [1922], trans. A. and S. Devyver, Paris: Editions Gallimard.
Mielusel, R. (2013). 'La place des groupes micro-identitaires en France: Le cas des générations issues de l'immigration,' *Les Cahiers du Grelcef*, 4, 59–77.
Naficy, H. (2001). *An Accented Cinema: Exilic and Diasporic Filmmaking*, Princeton, NJ/Oxford: Princeton University Press.
Ricoeur, P. (1996). *Soi-même comme un autre*, Paris: Editions du Seuil.

Filmography

Allouache, M. (2009). *Harragas*. Distribution Jour de fête.
Legzouli, H. (2004). *Ten'ja*. Pierre Grise Distribution.

12

Rewriting the memory of immigration: Samuel Zaoui's *Saint Denis bout du monde*

Mireille Le Breton

In the 1980s and 1990s, a movement erupted on the French literary scene: the descendants of first-generation Maghrebi immigrants started to write autobiographical or semi-autobiographical novels in order to voice their *mal-être* in a society that did not seem to acknowledge they were French, endowed with the same rights as any citizen living in the French Republic.[1] Their narratives also incorporate stories of their parents' generation, people who had left for France during the waves of labor immigration.[2] These, however, appear only briefly as fragments or vignettes, and are not the focus of this new literary trend.[3] The old generation of *chibanis* remained the 'unassimilable faces of French society' (Sajed, 2013: 54). The word *chibanis* means the 'old man' or 'white hair' in Darija, the Arabic dialect spoken in the Maghreb. It refers to the population of aging Maghrebi immigrants, who left everything behind to come work in France during the post-war economic boom, when the country needed a labor force to rebuild itself.[4]

Until recently, the literature portraying the *chibanis*' lives in France told a story of marginalization, quasi-citizenship, exclusion, and of their identity slowly being erased over time (Ireland, 2011: 78).[5] Nasser Djemaï refers to these people as '*les Invisibles*.' They are voiceless, powerless, and isolated, dispossessed of their rightful belonging to a homeland, whether in Algeria or in France: 'ces Chibanis qui ne sont plus d'aucun monde – Invisibles – ici en France, et dans leur pays d'origine' (Djemaï, 2015) (*chibanis* no longer belong to either world – Invisible – both here in France and in their homeland).[6]

In the late 1990s, Yamina Benguigui devoted a study to the fathers, mothers, and children of the first wave of immigrants in France, and asked: 'Qu'avez-vous fait à mon père? Qu'avez-vous fait à ma mère? Qu'avez-vous fait de mes parents pour qu'ils soient aussi muets? Que leur avez-vous dit, pour qu'ils n'aient pas voulu nous enraciner [en France] sur cette terre où nous sommes nés?' (Benguigui, 1997: 9–10) (What did you do to my father? What did you do to my mother? What did you do to my parents to reduce them to silence? What did you tell them that dissuaded them from raising us as people of this land [France] where we were born?). Benguigui was among the first to bring to life the memory of the *chibanis* and *chibanias* and to give them a face and a voice. For the *chibanis*, the idea of returning to their native land was already firmly established when they arrived: they would work for only a few years in France and then return to Algeria.[7] They were *travailleurs provisoires* (temporary workers) as described by Abdelmalek Sayad (1980: 90). However, returning home became a myth, especially after the 1974 *regroupement familial* laws, which allowed some of them to be reunited with their wives and children in France. From then on expectations shifted, transforming a working population that was far from being settled, into a durable settlement (Benguigui, 1997: 10).

Consequently, since the 1980s the myth of returning has become a literary trope in the narratives written by the descendants of these early Maghrebi immigrants. The recurring image of their incapacity to settle in France is embodied in the metaphor of the large suitcase sitting on top of the living room cabinet, forever waiting to be packed for the final voyage home.[8] Literature of this period portrays the *chibanis* as characters evolving in narratives of loss (Coleman: 1998; Ireland: 2011), whose only salvation was to be found in their dream of returning to their native land, at best once they reached retirement. Historically, many of them never returned 'home,' and most of those who were able to did so when it was too late: their bodies were sent back in coffins to Algeria, where they would find their final resting places. The mothers, however, tended to choose their burial grounds in France, the land where they had raised their children: 'Les pères, morts prématurément, sont enterrés au village; les mères … seront enterrées dans le pays de leurs enfants, là où ils sont nés, le pays de leur vie, la France; c'est ce qu'elles souhaitent' (Sebbar, 2005) ('The fathers, who died prematurely, are buried in their native villages … The mothers' wish … will always be to be buried in the country where their children were born and where they spent their lives: France).

Later, at the turn of the twenty-first century, the forgotten generation of *chibanis* carved a new space within literary history. Sebbar remarks that 'l'actualité des pères et mères de la première génération dans la représentation littéraire et photographique est récente' (Sebbar, 2005) (The day-to-day reality of the first generation's immigrant parents is recent in literary and photographic representations). For instance, the title of the book, *Chibanis, Chibanias: portraits d'une génération sans histoire* (2003), plays on the double meaning of the French expression *sans histoire*, which refers both to those who never caused any trouble to society or led a quiet life, and to those who are without history: without a past. Samuel Zaoui's novel *Saint Denis bout du monde*, partakes of the literary turning point that conveys the faces and voices of this invisible generation. For the first time in fiction, a plot features a young French woman, Souhad, born to Algerian parents, who interacts with three old Algerian men, and travels with them. In the novel, Souhad observes them, listens to them, and takes snapshots of their lives, collecting their memories during their journey from France to Algeria. Souhad will make a reality of their dream to return to their native land, allowing the novelist to give new meaning to the trope of the 'myth of returning' found in migrant literature at that time.

The title of Samuel Zaoui's novel, *Saint Denis bout du monde* (2008), has a double meaning. *Saint Denis* is an impoverished suburb, north of Paris.[9] It is the '*bout du monde*' (end of the road) for migrant workers, who spend their entire lives there, working poorly paid jobs. Indeed, after barely surviving precarious housing conditions and loneliness, they are often unable to afford to return to their homeland in their old age. Thus, the title suggests the persistence of the mythical dream of a 'return to the native land' that is rarely fulfilled by impoverished workers. The novel describes how three Algerian immigrants, Hachimi, Malek, and Mustapha, survive their dull existence in Saint Denis, as they reach the evening of life. They are portrayed as silent, visionless, resigned, and misplaced elderly men in the opening pages. When they arrived in France between World War II and 1965, before and after Algerian independence, they dreamed of climbing the social ladder. After disembarking in Marseille, they lived in numerous French cities, traveling north in search of better working conditions. Yet, the characters failed at all points of their journey, only to land in Saint Denis in the 1970s as middle-aged men, just as *les Trente Glorieuses*, the glorious thirty-year economic boom, was ending. Thirty-five years later, with the three *chibanis* reaching retirement, this ghettoized area literally seems to be the end of the road for them. The title also bears an ironic dimension: this 'end of the road,' Saint Denis, actually becomes the starting point of new beginnings in the main characters' lives.

This chapter examines how the encounter between the three old Maghrebi men and the main protagonist, Souhad, disturbs their socially preordained, negative trajectory. She embarks with them on a 'road trip' to retrace their steps by traveling from Saint Denis to Algeria via Marseille. Souhad decides to depart in search for answers to her family's history. Her absent father never told her about Algeria, nor did he narrate the 'récit de son histoire de France' (Zaoui, 2010: 64) (the story of his French trajectory). She retraces the path of her father's immigration with the old men. These characters, old and young, travel in space, time, and memory to the loci of their individual and collective suffering. They trace their 'road trip' on a map of France, with carefully selected stops in the French cities that the three Maghrebi workers had once inhabited (space). This brings them back to the time when they arrived in France as young workers (time), and the harsh reality of immigration crushed their dreams of the promised land (memory).

Zaoui's fictionalized oral history, à la Jacques Le Goff,[10] explores the trope of the return to the ancestral land and the simultaneous journey of self-discovery: *revenir pour devenir* (coming back to become). It also explores Souhad's encounter with the father figure embodied in these three men. Through her discovery of places, faces, and voices, Souhad is able to reconstruct the 'truncated' part of her family history and thereby assemble the missing pieces of her family memory: *le puzzle de la mémoire* (the puzzle of memory). Finally, this chapter asks how the contemporary French novel rewrites memories of immigration in France to focus on new possibilities for reconciliation, as the genre itself may become a 'place of memory,' or what Pierre Nora calls a *lieu de mémoire* (1984: 1004).

Samuel Zaoui was born in 1967 in Paris, to a Sephardic Jewish father and a Kabylian mother. His first novel, *Saint Denis bout du monde* was published in 2008, shortly followed by a detective novel, *Omnivore*, in 2009. In *Saint Denis bout du monde*, Souhad, a young descendant of Algerian immigrants, seems to be perfectly integrated into French society; she is a well-established professor of classics and lives with her partner, Bruno. She teaches in Saint Denis, but for the longest time, she has neither seen, nor spoken to, her father, who lives in the neighborhood. She seems to have cut off all ties with her distant past, to avoid triggering memories of her family's trauma. Yet, in preparation for his journey back to Algeria for the first time in thirty years, Souhad's father calls to ask her to water the plants in the very house where she grew up, in Saint Denis. Her symbolically absent father leaves France, without meeting her again or giving her any explanation. Her daily life becomes unsettled as she is unexpectedly caught up in her family history and her origins. She loses the points of reference that had given her life meaning so far. Indeed, the walls she had built year after year to protect herself from her traumatic past suddenly fall apart, reviving her history and her memory. She ponders her past and realizes it has not been laid to rest. The three migrants, who will travel with her and are close to her father's age, will lead her on the path to rebuild her history and discover her personal story. Will the reconstruction of the characters' intricate and diverse histories allow them to recast the collective memory of their common immigration, as they embark on a quest for individual memory?

Not at peace with the past: *le passé qui ne passe pas*

Every character's past reflects a personal story that is painful and cannot be laid to rest. The characters' individual histories are grounded in personal trauma that can only be voiced in silence, retained as loss, and disclosed in isolation. Two unskilled workers, Malek and Mustapha, came to France after World War II. Hachimi, the third worker, arrived on French soil in 1965, shortly after the end of the Algerian War of Independence. The three men are considered to belong to the first wave of immigration and are derogatively called the *Sonac*, short for the *Sonacotra*, state shelters for young migrant workers.[11] They built their identity on the isolation that unfolds from silence. Unable to express themselves in French, two of them, Malek and Mustapha, have lived their entire life in France without being able to communicate properly. Hachimi, on the contrary, was educated and became a union leader in his firm, but in spite of his language skills, he did not dare to speak in public for fear of sounding different. The novel portrays him as being confident in writing, but not in speaking, where his accent would betray his origins. He explains: 'quand on l'écrit, l'accent ne s'entend pas' (Zaoui, 2010: 26) (when I write, no one can hear my accent).

They all have capitulated. When they encounter Souhad at the sunset of their lives, the three *chibani* immigrants spend time together, walking in the park of the *Légion d'Honneur* in the Saint Denis neighborhood near their shelters. But they do not talk to each other at all, not even in their common North African language. This absence of communication in French, in their Algerian dialect, and in standard Arabic has been ruling over their worlds for too long. In order to remain in France, they have sacrificed their families, who stayed back home in Algeria. They no longer communicate with them, except by sending them money. Their stay in the host country has led them to resign themselves to their fate as they journey on the path of loss and isolation, stripped of decent living conditions in France and cut off from their Algerian roots. They live with memories, their only remaining ties to reality: 'Souhad ne trouve plus rien à dire. Des photos à la place des enfants. De l'argent à la place des mots. Des souvenirs à la place de tout' (Zaoui, 2010: 125) (Souhad has nothing to say. Pictures instead of children. Money instead of words. Memories instead of everything).

Their memories can no longer be put into words and shared with anyone; they are fading away. Besides, France and Algeria blend together in their minds, leaving them alone to face a truncated memory. They are awaiting death quietly and see their dream of returning to the motherland vanish in time. The novel first borrows from the narrative of loss, a tradition noted in the opening pages and which conveys a sense of seclusion and powerlessness. These pages portray some sad, painful, but often very realistic, truths pertaining to the *chibanis*' daily lives. However, the novel departs from traditional tropes found in migrant literature when the encounter between the *chibanis* and Souhad takes place. Indeed, the young woman appears to be able to '*faire basculer le destin des vieux*' (Zaoui, 2010: 106) (dramatically upend the old men's destiny). Encouraged by Souhad to leave the *foyer Sonacotra*, the *chibanis* plan a journey with her, which takes them back to the places that have shaped their lives and memories in France.

Before her encounter with the old migrant workers, Souhad had built her personality around trauma caused by the loss of her younger brother, or rather, his unpunished murder. Souhad nurtured resentment and hatred against her father, because he forced his family into silence and oblivion, asking her and her two brothers never to mention the crime again in his presence. The narrator, Souhad, remembers:

> L'enquête, l'autopsie, les avocats, ça a duré trois ans. On l'avait trouvé dans la descente de la cave, le crâne enfoncé et un oeil crevé. (Zaoui, 2010: 91–2)

(The investigation, the autopsy, the lawyers… It lasted three years. He had been found in the basement staircase, with his skull crushed and one eye punctured.)

And she concludes:

> A la fin, au bout de trois ans, ma mère est partie. Elle est rentrée en Algérie… Mon père est resté. Pour nous. Je ne vois pas d'autres raisons. Alors on a fait comme il voulait, on n'a plus reparlé de Jaouad, jamais, on a tous oublié, profondément. (Zaoui, 2010: 93)

> (After three years, my mother left. She went back to Algeria. … My father stayed for us. I don't see any other reason. So we did what he said, we never spoke about Jouad again, ever. We all were driven to forget this.)

When Souhad lost her little brother, she lost her parents as well: her mother, who went back to Algeria, and her father, whom she could no longer understand. Her little brother's death has become a hole in Souhad's memory, her *trou de mémoire*. She had to build her identity on oblivion. In his article, 'Histoire ou mémoire?,' which follows in Paul Ricoeur's footsteps, Denis Collin mentions the importance of oblivion in the relationship between memory and identity construction. He talks about a necessary form of oblivion: 'La mémoire présuppose l'oubli comme son indispensable complément. Je ne peux me souvenir qu'en sélectionnant ce qui doit être oublié. Mais l'oubli est comme le fond nécessaire à partir duquel peut émerger la mémoire' (Collin, 2001) (Memory requires oblivion as its necessary complement. I can only remember insofar as I select what needs to be forgotten. But oblivion is like the necessary ground from which memory can emerge). Yet, in extreme cases like Souhad's story, oblivion can become a pathology and create an identity crisis. Indeed, at the age of 7, when the familial drama takes place, Souhad refuses to speak her father's language and unconsciously negates every part of herself that may be associated with his North African culture. She starts to despise and hate her father. Instead of mourning her loss, she seals herself off in a deeply buried violence related to the never-explained death of her brother. Cutting off her roots, she flirts with death symbolically and touches on the suffering inherent to human language, as Pascal Quignard states in his analysis of the experience of memory:

> [L'expérience] où l'oubli de l'humanité qui est en nous agresse. Où le caractère fortuit de nos pensées, où la matière involontaire de notre mémoire et son étoffe exclusivement linguistique se touchent avec le doigt. C'est l'expérience où nos limites et notre mort se confondent pour la première fois. C'est la détresse propre au langage humain. (Quignard, 1993: 57)

[The experience] where the oblivion of humanity within us assaults us. Where the fortuitous character of our thoughts, where the accidental nature of our memory and its exclusive linguistic fabric can be touched. This is the experience where our limits and our death mingle for the first time. This is the suffering inherent to human language.

Souhad's suffering memory is an experience that can be read through the critical lens of Khatibi's concept of a '*mémoire tatouée*' (tattooed memory). Khatibi defines it as a memory that contains 'les signes et les événements qui frappent un corps et le marquent définitivement' (Khatibi, 1976: 11) (the signs and events which strike a body and mark it permanently). In Khatibi's autobiographical novel, the child's memory bears the mark of the original trauma or *tattoo*, which can be familial, social, cultural, economic, and political. In a veiled witness account, the narrator realizes that the scream of his childhood – which may be interpreted as the direct consequence of his 'tattooed memory' will keep coming back and haunt him, if the mystery surrounding his identity is not solved: 'Bien que le cri de cette enfance épargne mon salut, l'énigme à dénouer – quitte à demeurer sur la plage déserte – renvoie encore à cette identité nouée' (Khatibi, 2008: 108) (The screams of my childhood may spare my salvation, but the unsolved riddle – even at the cost of being condemned to remain on the deserted beach– refers back to this knotted identity). In Zaoui's novel, Souhad's memory is marked by trauma, and the psychological scars are the expression of her incomplete identity. Haunted by a 'returning memory' herself, Souhad, like the narrator in Khatibi's text, is unable to untie the Gordian knot of her identity (Dosse, 1998: 10). She has carried out her father's will and espoused French ways, yet, she still wonders why her father forced her and her brothers to be the exact opposites of who he was:

> Pourquoi toi, avec ton histoire normale, ton immigration banale, le bled, Alger, le bateau, Marseille, Dijon, Saint Denis direct, sans accident, sans diplôme ni argent, sans rien qu'une femme tatouée et quatre enfants basanés, pourquoi toi, tu as voulu, comme ça, si fort, que nous soyons différents? Je ne comprends pas. Mais je sais que tout vient de là. Tout … La réussite de tes enfants et la mort, l'agrégation, le grec et le latin … les parapluies, les sacs à mains, tout, je te dis … Jusqu'à ces vieux arabes qui se jettent sous mes yeux maintenant. (Zaoui, 2010: 21–2)

> (Why did you, with your simple story, your plain immigration story, your hometown, Algiers, the boat, Marseille, Dijon, and your uneventful, non-stop travel to Saint Denis, with no degree and no money, with nothing else but a tattooed wife and four brown children, why did you want so badly, that we'd be different from you? I don't get it. And yet I know that's where it all comes from. I know … Your children' success, and death, my *agrégation* diploma, Greek, Latin … umbrellas, handbags, everything, I tell you … Even these old Arab men who are thrown in front of my eyes today.)

For Souhad's father, Ali Etthari, as for his daughter and the three migrant workers, the past is still a haunting presence. Ali voluntarily isolated himself from his wife and children in France to make sure that none of them would become who he was. He was ready to sacrifice his life so they could become well-integrated French citizens, which, according to Souhad, cost her brother his life. *Chibani* parents certainly want their offspring to succeed in France; yet, they do not all react like Ali. On the contrary, many pass on some form of their cultural heritage. In this sense, Ali promotes and even enforces assimilation in its original definition, one tainted with colonial connotations. He appears to be a father who wants his children to be more French than the French themselves, to fit in at all costs, even if he has to impose his idea on his family. This behavior is far from successful, as Ali's assimilation takes on the definition put forth by Alec Hargreaves: 'Assimilation tends to imply not only acculturation but also the complete abandonment of minority cultural norms' (2007: 37). According to the identity framework developed by sociologist Adil Jazouli, Ali's behavior falls under the category of 'identity affirmation,' where French cultural norms are embraced to the point of complete exclusion of the cultural heritage and ethnic forms of differentiation (Jazouli, 1982: 25–32).

Thus, Souhad's father chose to stay away from the working neighborhoods crowded with North African immigrants and preferred to live in *zones pavillonaires* (residential areas not far from the ghettos), where he and his family were despised by some of their neighbors. The narrator reminds the reader of her father's work as a mason and compares the brick walls he built to the symbolic fortress he erected around his memory: 'Tout autour de toi, tu montes des murs pendant des années, des dizaines, ni tu vois les Français ni tu vois ta femme, tu élèves même pas tes enfants. Et quand tu rentres au bled, tu es tellement pâle qu'on te regarde comme si tu sortais de prison' (Zaoui, 2010: 51) (For years, you've been building walls around yourself, by the dozen, you don't see the French, you don't see your wife, you don't even raise your children. And when you go back home to Algeria, you're so pale that people look at you as if you just got out of jail). Completely isolated from his home territory, Souhad's father's identity is walled in.

Three types of memories seem to be drawn on the canvas of the novel: those of the 'old Arabs,' who do not speak with each other and have a truncated memory; Ali's, the absent father who never communicated with his children, and whose memory is walled in; and in the center of the symbolic triptych, the self-censored memory of Souhad, who refuses to speak to her father in her parents' native tongue.

As the novel unfolds, the reader, alongside Souhad, has to solve the riddle of the protagonist's suffering, as it derives from her father and her younger brother. The mystery associated with her brother's death looms in the text, undisclosed and secret. As she walks into the park to go to her father's home, Souhad passes her brother's murderer, Mr. Le Vent,[12] whom she believed to be dead. Painful, scattered, and unexpected memories assail and nauseate her. She questions herself and her father in an uninterrupted interior monologue composed of short, sometimes incomplete, sentences. At this point, Souhad begins a desperate search for her father. She silently converses with him in a sort of epiphany: 'Depuis trois jours je vois des vieux arabes partout, papa, et passe mes après-midi assise sur les bancs publics. Je suis à cent mètres de chez toi. Donc lui aussi ... C'est pour ça que tu es parti? C'est à cause de Monsieur Le Vent?' (Zaoui, 2010: 13) (For three days now I've been seeing old Arabs everywhere, dad, and I spend my afternoons on the public benches. I am 50 feet away from your home. And so he is too. Is this why you left? Is it because of Mister Le Vent?).

Eventually, the Gordian knot that prevented Souhad's identity from developing will be cut, as she violently reacts to a racist situation. Her floating memory, suspended in grey areas, surfaces as her concealed psychological violence is externalized, and transforms into physical mayhem. At the supermarket next to her father's house, Souhad knocks over the shopping cart of a customer who called the three old men *bicots* (dirty Arabs). Indeed, the apple juice carton that she kicks bursts open, a metaphor for her dead brother's shattered skull. The customer's screams sound like her mother's yells when she found out about her son's death:

'C'est un magasin pour les bicots[13] ou quoi, faut le dire si on a plus le droit de venir ici.' Souhad met toute sa force pour renverser le caddie. L'autre crie toujours mais des cris rauques de désespoir, qui lui arrachent la gorge. Ces cris ce sont ceux de sa mère, les mêmes cris. Son fils est mort. Les mêmes cris insupportables. Il est mort sans raison. Elle crie sans raison. C'est seulement un caddie, pas un fils, sans raison. Elle donne un coup de pied dans un pack de jus de pomme qui éclate comme un crâne. Il est mort le crâne. Vas-y, crie! (Zaoui, 2010: 77)

('Is this a shop for dirty Arabs, here or what? Just say if we can't come here any longer.' Souhad knocks the cart over with all her strength. The lady is still wailing, long, guttural screams that tear at her throat. These screams are her mother's screams, the same piercing cries. Her son is dead. The same unbearable howling. He is dead for no reason. She screams for no reason. It's just a shopping cart, not a son, for no reason. She kicks a carton of apple juice that bursts open like a skull. The skull is dead. Go on, scream!)

This climactic point in the narration allows Souhad to come to terms with the language of her childhood – of her father – in order to communicate with the old Algerian men. It is her first moment of recovery. Her new voice will articulate what was previously hidden behind silence and oblivion. As Souhad speaks her father's tongue again, words become the key to their joint quest for individual memory. Thanks to these words, the diegetic past and the main protagonists' histories will be reconstructed also through the power of observation.

Reconstructing history: toward an appeased memory

The road trip that lies at the heart of the novel is planned by the protagonists and will help reconstruct history, which in turn will allow for the construction of an appeased collective memory. By telling the story of her brother's death, Souhad calls the forbidden past back to life for the first time, and this prepares her to reconstruct her personal history. After the violent scene at the supermarket, Souhad is arrested and taken to the local police station. When her new friends come to pick her up, she wants to thank them by inviting them to her father's house. For the first time, she will tell her story in her father's language, so they can all understand her: 'Le temps ne compte plus avec les vieux ... Elle sait désormais qu'elle devra raconter, mais elle a le temps. Toute la nuit. Plus s'il le faut. Depuis qu'elle est enfermée avec ces vieux, le temps ne compte plus pareil' (Zaoui, 2010: 90–1) (In the company of old men, time no longer matters. She knows now that she will have to tell her story, but she has time. The entire night. More, if need be. Ever since she entered these old men's world, time has no longer unfolded in the same way).

Each of the protagonists will articulate his past and reconstruct his individual story, in his own time. Malek, for instance, is distressed by Souhad's tale. For the first time in his life, his voice can be heard when he finds and confronts the killer. After spitting chewed tobacco onto his face, he tells him: 'Assassin! Il dit cela sans crier. Assassin. Trois fois. Assassin de Jaouad Etthari! ... Le visage de Le Vent se décompose. Il respire comme un bœuf. Un peu de chique rentre dans sa narine, il l'aspire et tousse ... Le Vent est figé, son cœur bat si fort que son ventre tremble' (Zaoui, 2010: 96–7) (Murderer! He says this without shouting. Murderer. Three times. Murderer of Jaouad Etthari ... Le Vent's face loses all composure. He breathes like an ox. A piece of chewing tobacco finds its way into his nose, he inhales it and coughs ... Le Vent is transfixed, his heart beats so hard that his belly trembles). The walls imprisoning Souhad's memories fall apart, as Malek is able to repair her past and deliver justice by his deeds and even more by his words. The return of memory shows that the past can be revisited. As such, the future may become the place of possibilities and new beginnings. Souhad will be able to rewrite her own history as they start their long road trip across France.

Before accepting the challenge of going back to Algeria, the old men impose their conditions and request that they stop in a series of French places where they will engage with their past. Each stop stands in for one of the towns they spent time in when they first arrived in France, before they reached Saint Denis. To come to a decision, they deliberate for a long time:

> Saint Denis bout du monde, elle pense ... Elle ne dit plus rien. La contradiction dans leur tête. Ils pensent le contraire de ce qu'ils pensent. Elle sent dans sa poitrine l'écrasement de toute leur vie (Zaoui, 2010: 126) ...

On reste? Non. On part? Non. Merde! Vous me faites chier. Le paradoxe ... Elle pense: le paradoxe est une structure discursive, pas une structure mentale.

– On est en démocratie, on n'a qu'à voter. Qui veut rester? Personne. Qui veut rentrer? Personne. Qui veut quoi?
Qui veut entre les deux? ... Les trois vieux lèvent la main . . .

– On peut partir sans rentrer. S'approcher juste et voir venir (Zaoui, 2010: 128)

– On s'en va d'ici mais on va pas là-bas, on va vers là-bas, c'est tout. On décide plus tard. (Zaoui, 2010: 129)

(Saint Denis, the end of the road, she thinks ... She keeps quiet. Contradiction inhabits their heads. They think the opposite of what they think. She feels the weight of their entire life in her chest ... Should we stay? No. Should we go? No. Shit, you make me crazy! Paradox ... She thinks: paradox is a discursive structure, not a mental structure. We're in a democracy, let's vote. Who wants to go back? No one. Who wants to stay? No one. Who wants what? Who wants something in-between? ... The three old men raise their hands ... We can leave now without going back. Come close to it, and let things happen ... We leave this place here but we don't go there, we go toward there, that's it. We'll decide afterwards.)

Their itinerary traced on the map of France includes numerous detours before reaching Algeria, the land of their ancestors. Zaoui's novel stands apart for the way it transforms the trope of the return to the native country currently found in migrant literature. The characters do not reach their destination, Algeria, as expected. Rather, they decide to stay in between here (France) and there (Algeria), 'ni là, ni là-bas' (Zaoui, 2010: 110) (neither here nor there) as they retrace their initial voyage, taking the detours that bring them back to their past. This calculated meandering may be seen as a metaphor of memory itself, the collective memory that is being written by the sum of their individual memories. The old men are ready to dig up the past and connect it to the present. The main characters are now entering what Pierre Nora calls the 'eternal present': 'La mémoire est un phénomène toujours actuel, un lien vécu au présent éternel' (Nora, 1984: xix) (Memory is a phenomenon that is ever present, a living link to the eternal present). Indeed, the different stages of their journey and the intensity of their encounters matter more than the final destination. In an unpublished poetic song, Hafid Gafaïti highlights this idea. 'Ô je n'ai que toi, ici et maintenant, ô je n'ai que toi, aurons-nous assez de temps?' (Oh I only have you, here and now, oh I only have you, will we have enough time?). Revisiting the loci of previous hardships, they accept their encounter with the past, aware of temporal constraints, and from there, they will do justice to the past and repair its wrongdoings, in order to be able to mourn. For the three old men, remembering requires resilience, but for Souhad, remembering brings peace, a form of mnemonic appeasement.

In order to penetrate the old men's universe, Souhad goes through many transformations. In just a few days she changes, as she frees herself from the pain of her past thanks to the men. She mentally hated her father and blamed him for never telling her his story, her family's story. She hated him for his lack of understanding and the effects of the mandatory oblivion he imposed on his family after her little brother's death. Spending time with the old men on the roads of France leads her to question her complex relationship with her father and to come to a new form of understanding. With the old men she speaks Arabic, the language of her father, in order to fully enter their universe and be a part of it. In this way, she grows closer to her father. Souhad knows that she cannot understand everything they say and focuses on learning how to observe their behaviors. She learns the importance of the gaze and of gestures: 'C'est en les regardant qu'elle apprendra' (Zaoui, 2010: 90) (She will learn by watching them). This gaze becomes essential to learning and discovery. As Marguerite Duras has said: 'De bien regarder, je crois que ça s'apprend' (1960: 41) (Close observation, I believe, must be learned). In so doing, the main protagonist slowly adopts the old men's way of thinking and reactivates her own memory to build her family history in light of theirs. The memories she and her father have in common come back to life by listening to the old men's stories and by visiting the places they have known, which are pregnant with their personal histories. As Maurice Halbwachs explains, memory is dependent upon the social environment:

> Le plus grand nombre de nos souvenirs nous reviennent lorsque nos parents, nos amis, ou d'autres hommes nous les rappellent ... Le plus souvent si je me souviens c'est que les autres m'incitent à me souvenir, que leur mémoire vient au secours de la mienne, que la mienne s'appuie sur la leur ... Ils me sont rappelés du dehors, et que les groupes dont je fais partie m'offrent à chaque instant les moyens de les reconstruire, à condition que je me tourne vers eux et que j'adopte au moins temporairement leurs façons de penser. (1994: vi)

> (The greatest number of memories come back to us when our parents, our friends or other persons recall them to us ... Most of the time, when I remember, it is others who spur me on; their memory comes to the aid of mine, and mine relies on theirs ... They are recalled to me externally, and the groups of which I am a part at any time give me the means to reconstruct them, upon condition, to be sure that I turn towards them and adopt, at least for the moment, their way of thinking.) (1992: 38)

The memorial quest initiated by the road trip gives Souhad the capacity to fill in the blanks of her family history. The young woman in search of a father started off with a paternal absence and journeyed with three father figures, who opened the gates of memory for her. The stories of the three *chibanis*, who bear a striking resemblance with her own father, allow Souhad to reconstruct her family history through their memories. Now, she can answer the questions that her father had left unanswered: 'Elle comprend tout doucement le silence de son père, la résignation, l'acharnement, le travail, les parpaings, tout. Doucement. L'acceptation de la solitude. Le refus des Arabes. Le refus des Français … La maison vide comme un hôpital, pour se soigner lui-même. Pour se carreler le cerveau' (Zaoui, 2010: 105) (She slowly understands her father's silence, his resignation, fierceness, his work, the bricks, everything. Slowly. His acceptance of solitude. His rejection of Arabs. His rejection of the French … The house, as empty as a hospital, to cure himself. To tile his own brain). She eventually forgives her father and thanks him in her mind. Hatred turns into love. Her lack of understanding turns into a new burning desire to know why her father left for Algeria, now that she can tell him that she understands him, that she understands everything.

She is able to reread her own story, her family's history, and also the collective story of her father's immigration. In this way, she becomes the repository of migratory history. Souhad gets ready to narrate and relate every single fact and memory, as she prepares to talk to her father again, once they meet in Algeria: 'Je vais essayer de tout bien retenir, j'ai la tête comme un gros cahier, tu disais toujours ça' (Zaoui, 2010: 157) (I am going to remember everything, my head is like a big notebook, as you always said). Souhad, the classics professor, belongs to a culture of writing. Like most of the *chibanis* population, her father is illiterate and relies on the oral tradition for transmitting stories. The big notebook, a metaphor for the mnemonic ability of people evolving in the oral culture, shows that her father has already found a way to meet the literary written culture of his daughter, by telling her how he used his brain as a notebook to memorize and record events in their lives. Yet, before the trip, Souhad never reached out to her father's oral culture: she was cut off from it. The symbolic moment when she calls to mind her father's 'big notebook' represents the second and last moment of recovery for her, where the daughter's culture (writing) reaches out to her father's culture (orality). From now on, she is going 'to remember everything well,' and use her brain to record her life events as she reaches out to her father and to his culture.

Yet, the more she understands, the more she memorizes, the closer she gets to her father, and the more she seems to lose him:

> Depuis 30 ans je veux t'oublier et maintenant je pense à toi tous les jours. Et tous les jours je te perds un peu plus. Hier Mustapha. Aujourd'hui Hachimi. Demain Malek. Dans quel état je vais te retrouver?

C'est quoi ce jeu? Pour retrouver ton père, sème des petits Arabes sur ton chemin ... Plus qu'un. Je serai là bientôt. J'ai le sentiment que je ne reverrai plus Hachimi ... tu gagnes si tu en retrouves un vivant. (Zaoui, 2010: 217)

(For thirty years, I've wanted to forget you, and now I think of you every day. Every day I lose you a little more. Yesterday, Mustapha. Today, Hachimi. Tomorrow, Malek. What state will I find you in when we meet? What is the purpose of this game? In order to find your father, sow a few little Arabs on your way ... Just one more. I will soon be there. I have a feeling that I will not see Hachimi again ... You win if you find one alive at the end).

She foresees the loss of her father, as she loses her friends, one by one, after they come to terms with the past during the road trip. Mustapha decides to interrupt his trip back to Algeria in the city of Saint-Nazaire, where he finds solace living with the children and grandchildren of his deceased Maghrebi worker friend. He has found a new family. Hachimi falls into a coma and will probably never wake up again, but he repaired his past: he visited the old woman who willingly carried out a violent abortion on his French wife, leaving her infertile solely because she was carrying the child of an Arab. Malek, who was once grossly abused by his French boss, gets his revenge by stealing the motorcycle of his employer's son to head alone for the sheep farm he was dreaming of in the French mountains. Finally, the main protagonist reaches Marseille, ready to board the ferry to Algiers, but she will not be able to share her road trip story with her father, as she finds out that he has died in Algeria. She realizes that she is now the repository of their individual stories; she is responsible for passing the torch of her journey back in time and for conveying the oral memory of immigration. Indeed, as the novel concludes, Souhad, who has become all the old men's symbolic daughter, ponders over a maternal thought and becomes, as the biblical figure, the mother of all men: '*Je* suis leur mère à tous' (Zaoui, 2010: 217) (I am the mother of all of them).

Conclusion

The novel redraws the memory map of immigration in France to reveal the theme of coming back (memory) in order to become (identity). 'Becoming' takes on the meaning of being present in the world and taking responsibility for one's humanity. 'Coming back' takes the form of resilience, where Souhad and the old Arab men give each other the chance to exorcize the past and build an appeased memory, as they reinvest the memory of French territories, past and present. Their memorial quest brings the reader to the heart of the history of immigration in France.

Hence, their achievements and inner evolution during the journey are at the core of the novel, while the final destination is de-emphasized, since they will never reach Algeria.[14] Did the characters realize during their trip across France down memory lane that it is not the place where we live that matters, but how we stand for our values and beliefs, and how we live our lives in exile? Did they come to develop a sense of belonging to France that had been lost? The novel is open-ended, and offers multiple interpretations. Souhad lost all of her friends along the way. She is alone in the port of Marseille, as she is about to board the ferry when the novel ends. The reader may think that she will reach Algeria for her father's burial and be reunited with her mother, whom she has not seen in twenty-two years. The end of the novel beckons the reader's questions. A necessary incompleteness. Transforming the myth of the return to the native land, the *chibanis*' cathartic coming-to-terms with their past as immigrants in France reveals a new direction in migrant literature as a genre.

Samuel Zaoui's novel portrays first generation immigrants in a new light. Their children can now tell the story of the forgotten, invisible, and voiceless fathers. The reader is not only able to perceive the *chibanis*' faces and their inner beauty but also to hear their voices and share in their memories. The written text becomes a history book, in which oral testimonies shed new light on the 'mono-vocal master narrative' of history (Enjelvin, 2014: 85, quoted by Machelidon, Chapter 9 in this volume, p. 164). In this masterpiece, Samuel Zaoui thus makes a significant contribution to the way the *chibanis* will be remembered and pays a moving tribute to the retired workers (Ireland, 2011: 89). It is now up to the following generations to observe and spend time with their elders: to narrate the history of their fathers and grandfathers, which is also their story, in order to turn oblivion into memory, to hear their silence, record life, and make history out of it. We could say to conclude that 'il n'y a pas de mémoire sans histoire personnelle ou collective, sans locuteur capable d'énoncer cette mémoire – même choisie, même fragmentée – et pas de mémoire sans transmission, c'est-à-dire sans la présence d'un receveur, qui écoute et transmettra peut-être à son tour" (Lefranc-Morel, 2012: 6) (There is no memory without personal or collective history, without a teller able to narrate the memory – be it chosen or fragmented – and no memory without transmission, i.e. without the presence of a receiver, who listens and may transmit in turn).

Moving away from the traditional, largely negative, narratives of loss, the novel partakes of new narratives of staking claims and repairing, or what Susan Ireland calls 'a kind of narrative recovery,' as 'Souhad becomes the repository of the men's stories and helps them find a form of empowerment' (2011: 88). To go even further, a new narrative of reconciliation triggers the shift in the *episteme* of migrant literature. The novel can thus be read as the story of a forgotten generation, which is repairing collective amnesia as it regains memory, in order to reconcile itself with the past, in a trans-generational model, where the forgotten generation (the fathers) and their children (Souhad's generation) are able to jointly mend the amnesia.

The characters' oral narratives establish a bridge between the past and the 'here and now,' setting in motion *la mémoire en marche*, or 'memory in motion,' as Pierre Nora explains. According to him: 'Un objet devient lieu de mémoire quand il échappe à l'oubli … et quand une communauté le réinvestit de son affect et de ses émotions' (Nora, 1986: 7) (an object becomes a place of memory when it manages to escape oblivion … and when a community reinvests it with its affect and its emotions). This allows for the *reconnaissance de la mémoire* (Nora) (recognition of memory), turning contemporary French literature itself into a *lieu de mémoire*. The book, as an object, becomes *un lieu de mémoire*, a 'place of memory,' which may well be, as Ricoeur beautifully says, a never-ending process:

Sous l'histoire, la mémoire et l'oubli.
Sous la mémoire et l'oubli, la vie.
Mais écrire la vie est une autre histoire.
Inachèvement.
          (Ricoeur, 2000: 657)

(Beneath history, memory and oblivion.
Beneath memory and oblivion, life.
But writing life is another (hi)story.
Incompleteness.)[15]

Notes

1 For an overview of *beur* literature, see for instance Alec Hargreaves (1990: 47–58) and Michel Laronde (1988: 684–92). On the shifting paradigm between *beur* literature and *banlieue* literature, see Mireille Le Breton (2013: 12–26).
2 On the different waves of labor immigration, see Gérard Noiriel (2005: 38–48).
3 Numerous authors since the 1950s have written fiction about the life of single immigrant workers in France, such as Driss Chraïbi, *Les Boucs* (1955) and Tahar Ben Jelloun, *La Réclusion solitaire* (1976), to name but two. Yet, until today, there have been very few fictional works devoted primarily to the character of the *chibanis*.
4 Most *chibanis* moved to France from Algeria alone – either because they were single or had to leave their wives and children behind. They contributed to rebuilding post-World War II France and revitalized the French automobile and metallurgy industries, among others. Once called "young Algerian workers," these men are now seniors. Today, 40,000 of them still live in a *foyer Sonacotra*, in the 7.5 m^2 room that was attributed to them when they were young. The 350,000 *chibanis* aged over 65 today do not have access to healthcare, housing benefits, or elderly social solidarity benefits (François, 2013). Their wives, called the *chibanias*, are mostly absent from literary or cinematographic representations. Souhad's mother in *Saint Denis bout du*

monde, for instance, returned to Algeria after her son's death, abandoning the family. Some feature-length films tell their stories and portray their difficult living conditions, such as, for instance Abdellatif Kechiche's *La Graine et le mulet* (2007) or Rachid Bouchareb's *Indigènes* (2006). The documentary by Rachid Oujdi, *Perdus entre deux rives, les Chibanis oubliés* (2014) is a tribute to this generation.

5 Traditional migrant literature portraying the *chibanis* include, among others, Tahar Ben Jelloun's *Les Raisins de la galère* (1996) and *La plus haute des Solitudes* (1997), Fawsia Zouari's *Ce Pays dont je meurs* (1999), and Leïla Sebbar's *Mon cher Fils* (2008).

6 Unless otherwise indicated, all translations are mine.

7 On the migratory process as an essentially economic phenomenon, see Alec Hargreaves (2007: 75).

8 This image is persistent in Yamina Benguigui's feature-length film *Inch Allah Dimanche* (2001), which highlights the transitory nature of the *chibanis*' stay in France. It is one of the first feature-length films presenting the point of view of a *chibania*.

9 The *Seine-Saint-Denis* department, where the city of Saint Denis is located on the Paris beltline, bears the departmental number '93' for a colonial district in Algeria (Lang, 2012: 55). According to Claude Rocca, the city of Saint Denis, presents itself as 'un livre d'histoire à ciel ouvert' (an open-air history book). It used to be a medieval city, then a necropolis for French monarchs, before becoming an important site for the French industrial revolution. The city then belonged to the *ceinture rouge* of Paris – the 'red belt' referring to the communist political orientation of numerous industrial cities near Paris. It became a very important blue-collar district and the destination of numerous waves of immigrant labor (Rocca, 2015: 1). In her documentary *9/3 Mémoire d'un Territoire: L'histoire du 93 de 1860 à nos jours* (2010), Yamina Benguigui gives a historical account of the sometimes disastrous migrant and housing policies that accompanied the different waves of immigration, and reveals the negative working and living conditions of North African men.

10 In his studies of medieval history, Jacques Le Goff acknowledges the importance of speech in the writing of history and questions how the oral can be apprehended in the past, in order to write history: 'We can make out the great dialogue between the written and the oral. That most important absentee from the history of historians, speech, can be heard, at least in the form of echo, rumor, or murmur' (1982: xiv).

11 Sonacotra stands for *so*ciété *na*tionale de *co*nstruction pour les *tra*vailleurs (emphasis added). It was a governmental agency responsible for providing housing to immigrant workers of all ages. Created during the Algerian War of Independence, it was initially designed to host Algerian workers and was then called Sonacotr*al* – the last two letters "al" standing for the first two letters of the word *Al*gerian (emphasis added). Since 2007, Sonacotra has been renamed Adoma. A *foyer Sonacotra* is a hostel or residence housing usually single immigrant workers, each of whom rents a very small room. See Marc Bernardot (1999).

12 The name of the murderer, Mr. Le Vent, is spelled differently in the novel, as Souhad becomes increasingly able to revisit the murder of her little brother and slowly starts to untie her own identity knot. *Le Vent* in two words means "the wind." At the beginning of the novel, it represents one of the three elements that are omnipresent in the text and escape Souhad's control. As she develops the strength to unveil her family's secret, Souhad calls the killer by his real name: *Leven*.
13 *Bicot, bougnoule, crouille, crouillat, melon*, etc. are derogative, racist nouns to name Arab men. Some of these terms are borrowed from French colonial jargon from North Africa or West Africa (*bicot* derives from the Arabic term *arbico* which means 'Arab.' *Bougnoule*, meaning 'black,' is borrowed from the Wolof language of Senegal).
14 The one character who ironically manages to go back to Algeria is the absent father figure, Ali Etthari, who also set the plot in motion. At the end of the novel, his unexpected death can be read as a '*testament*' or legacy to his daughter and the younger generations. On this idea of legacy, see Chapter 11 in this volume.
15 I would like to thank my colleagues Dr. Lisa Cerami, Dr. Nevan Fisher, Dr. Bill Hopkins, and Mrs. Erica Ragan for giving me precious leads when I started working on this project. I also would like to thank my colleague, Dr. Cara Welch, for her constructive criticism in reviewing the draft of this chapter and for her steadfast support. Heartfelt thanks go to Laurent Estienne and Thomas Greiner for their critical scrutiny and to Joyce, Véronique, Philippe, Jean, and Yvette, and Meriem for their patience, support, and love.

References

Abidat, A., Begag, A., and Barême, C. (2003). *Chibanis, chibanias, Portraits d'une génération sans histoire?*, Marseille: Images plurielles.
Benguigui, Y. (1997). *Mémoires d'immigrés, l'héritage maghrébin*, Paris: Albin Michel.
Ben Jelloun, T. (1976). *La Réclusion solitaire*, Paris: Denoël.
Ben Jelloun, T. (1996). *Les Raisins de la galère*, Paris: Fayard.
Ben Jelloun, T. (1997). *La plus haute des Solitudes*, Paris: Seuil.
Bernardot, M. (1999). 'Chronique d'une institution: la "sonacotra" (1956–1976),' *Sociétés contemporaines*, 39–58.
Chraïbi, D. (1955). *Les Boucs*, Paris: Denoël.
Coleman, D. (1998). *Masculine Migrations: Reading the Postcolonial Male in 'New Canadian' Narratives*, Toronto: University of Toronto Press.
Collin, D. (2001). 'Histoire ou mémoire?,' *Philosophie et politique*. Web. July 15, 2015.
Djemaï, N. (2011). *Invisibles. La tragédie des Chibanis*, Paris: Actes Sud-Papiers.
Djemaï, N. (2015). 'Invisibles. Création 2011.' Web. July 15, 2015.
Dosse, F. (1998). 'Entre Histoire et Mémoire: Une histoire sociale de la mémoire,' *Raison présente*, 5–24.

Duras, M. (1960). *Hiroshima mon Amour*, Paris: Gallimard.
François, J. B. (2013). 'Les Immigrés âgés, souvent confrontés à la précarité,' *La Croix*, January 25. Web. July 15, 2015.
Gafaïti, H. *Ici et Maintenant*. [n.d.] MS. Collection of Hafid Gafaïti, Lubbock. Song.
Halbwachs, M. (1992). *On Collective Memory*, trans. Lewis A. Coser, Chicago: University of Chicago Press.
Halbwachs, M. (1994). *Les Cadres sociaux de la mémoire*, Paris: Albin Michel. [first published 1925]
Hargreaves, A. G. (1990). 'Language and Identity in Beur Culture,' *French Cultural Studies*, 1, 47–58.
Hargreaves, A. (2007). *Multi-Ethnic France: Immigration, Politics, Culture and Society*, 2nd edn, New York: Routledge.
Ireland, S. (2011). 'Masculinity and Migration: Representations of First-Generation Maghrebi Immigrants Living in France,' in E. Biegler Vandervoot (ed.), *Masculinities in Twentieth- and Twenty-First Century French and Francophone Literature*, Cambridge: Cambridge Scholars, 76–92.
Jazouli, A. (1982). *La Nouvelle Génération issue de l'immigration maghrébine: Essai d'analyse sociologique*, Paris: L'Harmattan.
Khatibi, A. (1976). 'Entretien,' *Pro-Culture*, 12, 9–13.
Khatibi, A. (2008). 'La Mémoire tatouée,' in *Œuvres complètes*, vol. 1, *Romans et récits*, SNELA Paris: Editions de la Différence.
Lang, G. (2012). 'Le Code officiel géographique,' *INSEE, Courrier des statistiques*, 108, 53–62.
Laronde, M. (1988). 'La "Mouvance beure": Emergence médiatique,' *French Review*, 61, 684–92.
Le Breton, M. (2013). 'De la Littérature beur à la littérature de banlieue: Un changement de paradigme,' *Présence francophone*, 80, 12–26.
Lefranc-Morel, S. (2012). 'Nathalie Burnay (dir.), *Transmission, mémoire et reconnaissance*,' *Lectures*. Les comptes rendus. April 5. Web. July 15, 2015.
Le Goff, J. (1982). *Time, Work, and Culture in the Middle Ages*, trans. A. Godhammer, Chicago: University of Chicago Press.
Le Goff, J. (1992). *History and Memory*, trans. S. Rendall and E. Claman, New York: Columbia University Press.
Noiriel, G. (2005). 'Histoire de l'immigration en France: État des lieux, perspectives d'avenir,' *Hommes & migrations*, 1255, 38–48.
Nora, P. (1984). 'Entre Mémoire et Histoire,' in P. Nora (ed.), *La République*. vol. 1 of *Les Lieux de mémoire*, Paris: Gallimard.
Nora, P. (1986). 'La Nation,' in P. Nora (ed.), *La Nation*, vol. 2 of *Les Lieux de mémoire*, Paris: Gallimard.
Quignard, P. (1993). *Le Nom sur le bout de la langue*, Paris: Folio.
Ricoeur, P. (2000). *La Mémoire, l'histoire, l'oubli*, Paris: Seuil.
Rocca, C. (June 5, 2015). Cours à la Basilique de Saint-Denis, Chambre de commerce et d'industrie de Paris and Lauder Institute-Wharton School of Business, 1–2.

Sajed, A. (2013). *Postcolonial Encounters in International Relations: The Politics of Transgression in the Maghreb*, New York: Routledge.

Sayad, A. (1980). ' Le foyer des sans-familles,' *Actes de la recherche en Sciences Sociales*, 32–3 (April/June), 89–103.

Sebbar, L. (2005). 'Notes de lecture,' [review of *Chibanis, Chibanias, portraits d'une génération sans histoire?* by A. Abidat, C. Barême, and A. Begag] *Confluences Méditerranée* 2(53), 139. Cairn. Info. Web. July 15, 2015.

Sebbar, L. (2008). *Mon cher Fils*, Tunis: Elyzad.

Zaoui, S. (2010). *Saint Denis bout du monde*, Paris: Nouvelles Editions de l'Aube Poche.

Zouari, F. (1999). *Ce Pays dont je meurs*, Paris: Ramsay.

Filmography

Benguigui, Y. (2001). *Inch Allah Dimanche*. Film Movement.

Benguigui, Y. (2004). *Mémoires d'immigrés, l'héritage maghrébin*. Mk2.

Benguigui, Y. (2010). *9/3 Mémoire d'un Territoire: L'histoire du 93 de 1860 à nos jours*. Canal+.

Bouchareb, R. (2006). *Indigènes*. Mars Distribution.

Kechiche, A. (2007). *La Graine et le mulet*. Pathé Distribution.

Oujdi, R. (2014), *Perdus entre deux rives, les Chibanis oubliés*. Comic Strip Production.

13

Harragas in Mediterranean *illiterature* and cinema

Hakim Abderrezak

Refugees and migrants: all in the same boat

A three-year-old lies face down on the shore of the Ali Hoca Burnu beach in Bodrum, Turkey. This photograph, showing the lifeless body of young Syrian Aylan Kurdi appeared in European and Turkish newspapers, circulated on social networks, and moved a huge number of media users. Commentators have speculated that this image effected a noticeable shift in public opinion about Mediterranean Sea crossings from the Middle East and Africa. Initially, the journeys involved migrants leaving Tunisia and Libya for western European shores, but the media's attention turned dramatically with the sudden movement of Syrian migrants across the Mediterranean.[1] This geographic shift in media focus was accompanied by a shift in tone, which was so drastic that it revolutionized the official position of conservative European governments. Accustomed to lumping together "legal" and "illegal" migrations, Prime Minister David Cameron's government had to tone down its anti-migratory discourse in order to gain British voters' approval. In Germany, Chancellor Angela Merkel's unexpected call for a welcoming of war refugees put her on the list of 2015 Nobel Peace Prize nominees.

When Nilüfer Demir, the Turkish photographer who brought Aylan Kurdi to the world's attention, was questioned about her motive for photographing the toddler, she stated that she did what she had to do. Her statement suggests that it is journalistic photographers' mission to inform the world about tragedies with the hope that their work will make a difference. Do other media that participate in the shaping of our understanding of current events and thus constitute information sources on world affairs and *faits divers* have the same objectives? In this respect, what are the goals and roles of novelists and filmmakers who have covered similar phenomena in their fictional works?

In this chapter, I will look at literary and cinematic representations of unauthorized maritime journeys. While the situation discussed above involves refugees from the eastern Mediterranean, my analysis below looks at migrants from the western part of the basin who happen to still constitute the main bulk of individuals crossing the sea. Apart from the important difference in legal status between migrants and refugees – often obfuscated in the media and politics – these two migratory trends have much in common. Both groups undertake a perilous crossing in a clandestine fashion. Both hail from the global South and hope to make it to Europe. Furthermore, they are often labeled as Arabs or Muslims, but not all of them are. Hence, in spite of inherent national, cultural, linguistic, ethnic, and religious distinctions, refugees and migrants often suffer from a biased and simplistic treatment by the mass media as well as stigmatization and vilification through populist political propaganda.

Based directly or not on real events, *illiterature* consists of literary works that tackle the phenomenon of clandestine migration. It comprises mostly novels, but also short stories, testimonies, etc. published in various languages and countries, notably from around the Mediterranean, but not limited to this region.[2] It represents an interesting avenue for understanding related complexities and incongruities. Some of the characteristics of what I call *illiterature* are revealed in the unpacking of this coinage. First, this is an *ill-literature* in many respects. Indeed, numerous works feature characters who are ill before, during, or after the journey. Moreover, this literature teases out the diseases of globalization, the deleterious effects of which are seen in the countries of emigration. An example of this is Tahar Ben Jelloun's novel *Partir*, where the physical and mental health of local individuals declines in spite of seeming 'opportunities,' which benefit Western hegemonic economic and sexual transactions. In this regard, illness is a metaphorical and somatic expression of transcontinental abuse. Furthermore, the relatively new terrain of *illiterature* (*île-literature*; literally, island-literature) points to Fortress Europe perceived as a distant island using the Mediterranean as a protective moat to keep its less prosperous neighbors at bay. In addition, except for a few notable exceptions, *il-literature* (he-literature) has thus far been a stronghold of male writers. Finally, the obvious phonetic proximity with illiteracy reminds us that, while *beur* literature was mostly written by the offspring of Maghrebis who undertook a state-sponsored voyage to make a living in France, the bulk of *illiterate-ture* aims to educate the average reader on widespread misconceptions about burning that he or she will likely have inherited from generalizing mass media accounts and chauvinistic disinformation. I would like to argue that there are different forms of illiteracy since brainwashing by mainstream or ideologically biased media results in a modern type of illiteracy. In turn, works of *illiterature* contribute to another kind of literacy. Although a number of people and characters who set out to sea are college graduates, white-collar professionals, and members of their countries' elite, many *harragas* are illiterate. Their inability to communicate their experiences to us necessitates the intervention of writers.³ In any case, when recounting the stories of the poor and the well-to-do, the educated and the illiterate, the novelists give a voice to those who have been deprived of the possibility of putting down their stories in writing.

Just as in western Mediterranean cinema, *illiterature* strives to document the undocumented. The referential aspect of this literature is undeniable. Its genesis proves that the subgenre has emerged in order to provide a different testimony from the prevailing mass media narrative. Indeed, writers, including Youssouf Amine Elalamy, Salim Jay, and Laila Lalami, have indicated that their works would not have been possible had they not come across a horrifying headline or news report, which is sometimes included in their novels. Finding the journalism incomplete, faulty, or biased, they felt compelled to provide another side to the story. Therefore, I will deal with the notion of *illiterature*, which highlights a division of the world along ideological lines criticized by filmmakers and authors alike. This coinage should help assess the field of francophone Maghrebi studies, which, especially thanks to *illiterature*, have taken a new turn over the past few years, notably by featuring a diversification of geographic settings, integrating other places of origin like Libya, Egypt, and Syria, and other destinations like Spain and Italy. Additionally, this field has been gradually examining Mediterranean-focused themes instead of exclusively treating matters concerning the Maghreb–France dyad. This paradigm shift can be seen in the recent literary and cinematic productions I will be discussing here. I will look at how literature and film have addressed the issues at the core of clandestine migration, a topic Mediterranean writers and filmmakers born and living in Morocco, Algeria, Tunisia, France, and Italy have tackled increasingly since the late 1990s.⁴ Here, I will focus on Tahar Ben Jelloun's *Partir* (2006), published in English under the title *Leaving Tangier* (2009), and Mohamed Teriah's *Les "harragas" ou Les barques de la mort* (2002), which translates as '"Harragas," or, the Boats of Death'. My examination of *illiterature* will help frame my exploration of the films *Harragas* (2009) and *Io, l'altro* (2007).⁵

It is necessary to define a few terms that have circulated widely in general discussions, scholarly discourse, and media coverage of clandestine migrations from the global South. First, *patera* is a Spanish term designating a dinghy used by clandestine migrants heading north from Morocco, but the word historically and literally refers to a fishing boat loaded with ducks (*patos*). As Inés d'Ors (2002) demonstrates, *pátera*, often discussed in combination with *patera*, is associated with the notion of sacrifice, which is very present in Maghrebis' conception of clandestine sea crossings, as I will show when I discuss two other terms, those of sainthood and martyrdom, which are correlated with regard to clandestinity. Second, *harragas* (sg. harrag) designates those who migrate clandestinely, burn their documents to prevent repatriation should they be caught, and burn the road or, in the context of this chapter – which is concerned primarily with the Mediterranean crossing

– the sea.[6] Clandestine migration is identified by related Arabic words, such as *hrig* and *harga*, both designating 'fire' and 'burning.'

Burning passages: *illiterature's seametery*

In this light, *illiterature* is a *littérature engagée* (engaged literature). It includes personal reports of violent deaths relayed by direct witnesses as well as intimate accounts by empathetic storytellers. Interestingly, *illiterature* and the cinema focusing on clandestinity use similar devices. Tropes and code words are commonly employed to convey the writers' and directors' views on contemporary trans-Mediterranean migration and the criminalization of those involved in crossing the sea from the global South. These include the archetype of the sickly character and the practice of nicknaming, which I will examine throughout the chapter. In both artistic genres, the characters' names are chosen to resonate with the sea.[7] For example, in both the novella *Clandestins* (Elalamy, 2001) ('Sea Drinkers') and the film *Harragas*, one of the protagonists is named Omar, a common Arabic name, which happens to contain the word 'mar/mer' (sea). The inference is that the characters and the sea share a morbid intimacy. *Illiteraturists* aim to press the idea of the sea-turned-cemetery, or what I term the *seametery*. Often hailed as a crossroad where many types of exchanges have taken place in history, the Mediterranean must also be beheld as a space that has now morphed into a cemetery. This has been the viewpoint of a rising number of writers and film-makers originating mainly from the global South but also from others part of the world such as the Middle East and Europe. Such is the case of Chus Gutiérrez's film *Retorno a Hansala* (Spain, 2008), Lodewijk Crijns' film *Hitte/Harara* (the Netherlands, 2008), Emanuele Crialese's film *Terraferma* (Italy, 2011), and Hakan Günday's novel *Encore* (Turkey, 2015).

As we will see in this section, the seametery is a mass grave and in spite of its being located between Europe and Africa, it is depicted as a highly sophisticated apparatus designed to screen, select, and stop unwanted migrants from the global South. Describing it as 'un système de surveillance électronique, avec infrarouge, armes automatiques, ultrason, ultra tout' (2006: 41) ('an electronic surveillance system along its beaches, with infrared and ultrasound equipment, ultra everything, along with automatic weapons' (2009: 34)), Ben Jelloun refers in a sarcastic fashion to the state-of-the-art sieve called SIVE (*sistema integrado de vigilancia exterior*), a surveillance system in place in Spain, to point at Europe's responsibility for the transformation of a *mer* (sea) into what one could designate a *mur de la mort de Musulmans* (wall of death for Muslims). To this effect, he writes, 'Azel a décidé que la mer qu'il voit face à lui a un centre et ce centre est un cercle vert, un cimetière où le courant s'empare des cadavres pour les mener au fond, les déposer sur un banc d'algues' (2006: 13) ('Azel has decided that this sea has a center and that this center is a green circle, a cemetery where the current catches hold of corpses, taking them to the bottom to lay them out on a bank of seaweed' (2009: 5)). The author's choice of color is not random. Green happens to be the color of Islam. The association Ben Jelloun makes between green and the seametery insinuates that drowned Muslim migrants are martyrs, saints in their own right. Indeed, in the Maghreb the tombs of saints are covered with a green fabric, representing their privileged attachment to Islam. Visitors will utter prayers while touching the green drapery to request the Muslim saint's intercession before Allah. Besides portraying the drowned as martyrs, the writer implies that even the dead Muslim migrants are not free to move around in their final home, for they are ascribed a place in the seametery recognizable by its green circle. Albeit potentially problematic, the parallel drawn between clandestine migration and martyrdom has historical and contemporary roots. 'Seek knowledge all the way to China!' is a *Hadith* (saying attributed to the Prophet) presented in the form of a command. In order to become accomplished Muslims, *harragas* deem it their mission to cross modern borders. Should they perish in the attempt, they will die as saints-martyrs. Thus, it is not surprising to see the term 'kamikaze' used in relation to *harragas* aboard rickety *pateras*, since *pateras* (dinghies) is a term closely related to *páteras* (which connotes sacrifice). Ben Jelloun's passage makes the association between martyrdom and sainthood clear and thus reminds his readers that although *hrig* is straightforwardly branded as a crime in mainstream media and politics, it finds a religious and cultural impetus on the other side of the Strait. Protagonists do not always face a tragic death. In fact, sometimes – because they were not able to board the boat – they are spared a fatal end. Whether it strikes or not, death is intimately coupled with the phenomenon of sea crossings.

Tahar Ben Jelloun's *Partir* tells the story of Azz El Arab (Azel), an unemployed graduate, and his sister Kenza, who works part-time for the Red Cross. Azel meets Miguel Romero López, a gay Spanish art collector who falls in love with the young Moroccan man. Miguel takes his companion to Spain and agrees to a marriage of convenience with Azel's sister. Azel becomes gradually miserable because, as a straight man, he questions his sexuality for sleeping with his benefactor. To prove to himself that he has not become impotent, he arranges to meet clandestinely with a Moroccan woman who ends up being murdered. Shortly afterwards, Azel faces the same tragic fate. In *Partir*, special attention is given to the smuggler. His name is 'Al Afia,' which happens to be a nickname meaning 'fire' in Arabic. This is an obvious reference to his function, which consists in helping migrant hopefuls to 'burn' the Strait of Gibraltar. Additionally, his sobriquet draws a parallel with his clients' consuming yearning to leave the country, which the narrator calls an 'obsession' and a 'folly.' The relationship between Al Afia and his clients is one of love and hate. Locals praise the trafficker whom they see as a philanthropist. Yet Azel abhors this man for charging his cousin Noureddine twice for a sea journey that will ultimately cause his death.

The smuggler, or *passeur*, is a commonly decried figure, and not only among Westerners. Salim Jay sums up the despicable function of this individual: 'Nous sommes des joueurs à la roulette russe qui auraient besoin de se faire interdire, au casino du détroit, de pactiser avec ce diable, le passeur' (2001: 23) (We are gamblers, playing Russian roulette, who ought to be barred from the casino of the Strait and prohibited from making a pact with this devil).[8] Echoing Jay's demonization of the *passeur*, Ben Jelloun asserts that corruption enables dishonest people to undermine an entire society, thus forcing honest individuals to search for better opportunities abroad on perilous journeys. The author upholds that the Moroccan kingdom fails to retain its most promising constituents, including Azz El Arab, whose name signifies in Arabic 'La fierté, la gloire des Arabes' (2006: 49) ('The pride, the glory of the Arabs' (2009: 43)). Instead of confronting drug traffickers, the police arrest Azel. When they discover he is in a homosexual relationship, they rape him, thus committing an unpunished crime. Ben Jelloun's contention is that the big fish is not caught, whereas the small fry is constantly harassed for the wrong reasons.

Partir seeks to demonstrate that *hchouma* and *hogra* (shame and institutionalized shaming/harassment) are two major driving forces in the Maghreb that lure desperate individuals into potentially deadly choices. Clandestine migration is one of these. Al Afia's popularity springs from the fact that he markets himself as a genuine philanthropist. His calculated acts of kindness are smart investments that bring him much profit in return. His business is so fruitful that he is in a position to turn clients away. Islamists are another group identified by Ben Jelloun as taking advantage of widespread misery and lack of hope. Because the state is unable to provide welfare, Islamist networks supply what is lacking (money, medical attention, judicial assistance, etc.). Their aid is an effective recruiting strategy. Through Azel's death, Ben Jelloun points to the dangerous nature of complex surrogate social networks that thrive on the disenfranchised and impoverished individuals who have lost faith in traditional institutions. The novel attempts to hold criminals accountable for their acts by calling alleged traffickers by the names of shunned animals: Dib (Wolf), Hmara (Mule), and Hallouf (Pig).[9] Besides referring to a reviled animal in Muslim-based cultures, Hallouf also characterizes individuals who stand out for their sly nature, as does Dib. Hmara, a mistreated animal in the region, points to the other extreme, namely, gullibility: 'Ton patron, c'est Al Afia, Hallouf ou Dib? Pour qui tu fourgues la drogue qui part la nuit vers l'Europe?' (2006: 67) ('Your boss is Al Afia, Hallouf, or Dib? Who's the guy you get the drugs for, the stuff that goes out at night to Europe?' (2009: 50)). There is no evidence that these nicknamed individuals are linked to human trafficking, for they are suspected of drug trafficking. Yet the implication is unavoidable and thus shows that "trafficking" has become a catch-all term and that in a corrupt environment, charges can be interchangeable or added at ease.

In Mohamed Teriah's *Les "Harragas" ou les barques de la Mort*, the mule is the animal used to smuggle merchandise across the border.[10] The two contrabandists are Jamal and Mahjoub, the hunchback, whose animal name is 'the Camel.' The smuggler (Ahmed)'s acolytes are given sea creature names: 'le Squale' (the Shark), 'l'Alligator' (the Alligator), 'la Pieuvre' (the Octopus), 'l'Orque' (the Orca), 'le Crabe' (the Crab), and 'Bernard l'ermite' (the Hermit Crab). In addition to the nickname's function of granting anonymity, the implication is that the group of people in the burning industry are involved in a fishy business. Teriah's choice to paint a realm of animalized humans implies that prospective migrants entrust their lives to networks of influential businessmen who straddle two worlds in their dual position as denizens of the sea and purveyors of fresh meat. Does the boss not call *harragas* 'nos espadons' (our swordfish)? Upon accidentally coming across weapons, the narrator suspects the smuggler to be involved in arms trafficking. Arms sales and human trafficking are handled as similar transactions undertaken in dehumanizing ways. Indeed, the *harragas* are referred to as 'La Cargaison' (The Boatload). Such congruence induces a criminalization of the smuggler in the narrator's eyes and, as I shall develop in the next section, reflects a pervasive overlap of various types of criminality associated with clandestinity.

Although bearing names of animals traditionally associated with violence and constituting a threat to humans, the Shark, the Octopus, the Alligator, etc. can appear as likeable characters. Some Moroccans who benefit from the smugglers' contributions to the micro-economy see them, as well as middlemen and their bosses, in a positive light. In the novel, they evoke the Shark in laudatory terms. 'Le père Mouloud,' once a miner, now owns a restaurant where Jamal likes to eat. It is 'le père Mouloud' that tells Jamal about burning. He views smugglers as 'les braves types qui font passer la frontière à bord de leur petite embarcation, et qui vous sauvent tant de familles de la misère' (46) (the good guys who help you cross the border onboard their small boat and who save so many families from misery). The Shark too presents himself as a savior: 'Payez-moi et je vous sauverai' (86) (Pay me and I'll save you). Jamal draws a similar sympathetic profile of this figure: 'Il était sévère mais efficace' (53) (he was stern but efficient). The trafficker is characterized as someone determined to provide the best customer service: 'j'ai un contrat à remplir' (53) (I have a contract to fulfill). Ironically, his professionalism and perfectionism are not directly imputed to the masses of money he makes but to a purportedly humanitarian call to assist those in need:

> Il ne laissait rien au hasard. Normal, non? Il y allait de sa carrière de passeur. Son procédé était simple: éviter les incorruptibles ... Il avait dans la tête la carte du pays, avec ses moindres recoins; ainsi que le tableau de service des agents de police, des gendarmes, et même des médecins et des pharmacies de garde au cas où l'un de ses clients se trouvait mal. C'est vrai qu'il exigeait de grosses sommes pour vous faire passer la frontière, mais il ne manquait jamais à ses engagements. (53)

(He didn't neglect a single thing. That's normal, right? His smuggling career was at stake. He had a simple trick: avoid the untouchables ... He had memorized the map of the country, in all its minute details; as well as the names of the police agents, gendarmes, and even doctors and pharmacies on call in case one of his clients were to feel ill. Sure, he required hefty sums of money to take you across the border, but he never failed to fulfill his obligations).

In light of this embellishing portrait, is the 'Shark' a misnomer? The novel is dominated by ambiguity and existential questions. Jamal, who studied theater, is obsessed with Hamlet's question 'To be or not to be,' which he applies to his financial predicament and its impact on his mother for whom he feels responsible. 'Le père Mouloud' explains to Jamal that thanks to his son's remittances from Spain he is able to run a 'superbe restaurant' (45). When he maintains that 'toujours est-il que tu pourrais en faire autant et aider ta mère' (45) (in any case you could do the same and help your mother out), the young man is seduced by the idea despite the risks of boarding 'les barques de la mort' (dinghies of death), which the old man downplays right away: 'des ragots que tout ça!' (46) (nothing but gossip!). Having witnessed his business partner murder a stranger, Jamal is convinced that he will be charged with the crime. Consequently, the young man brushes off the dangers of burning as well, since 'tôt ou tard, il partirait, ne fût-ce que pour éviter la prison' (48) (sooner or later, he would leave, if only to avoid jail time). His reasoning builds on the idea that a dangerous departure becomes necessary when inaction promises, at the very best, the same living conditions. Teriah's book title implies a connection between '*harragas*' and the 'dinghies of death' through the peculiar use of 'or' between these two markers. It is as if the *pateristas* were conflated with the modes of travel they use. The question is whether the narrative performs a thingification (to use a term borrowed from Aimé Césaire) of *pateristas* or a humanization of the dinghies, or both. It is clear that one of the main ideas contained in the title of Teriah's novel is that migrant hopefuls travel in coffins; in other words, that the Mediterranean crossing is a tragic passage through an earthly Hades. The equation "Mediterranean and Burning equals Death" is posited not as a mere hypothesis but rather as a plain fact.

Whether or not they make it to the other side or the other shore, it is common for characters in *illiterature* to suffer from sickness. In *Les "harragas" ou Les barques de la mort*, Jamal aboard the *patera* is seasick, an expected discomfort as he finds the dinghy to be 'un peu vieillote, mais elle s'accrochait tout de même' (148) (a bit antiquated, but it still held its own). The level of discomfort is minimized to the point where the narrator indicates: 'Jamal n'avait pas à se plaindre. Au contraire, il trouva même exagéré de titrer dans les journaux "*Les barques de la mort*"' (148) (Jamal had no reason to complain. On the contrary, he even found headlines reading 'The dinghies of death' to be an exaggeration).[11] The quote conveys the idea that Jamal's indisposition is merely due to preconceived ideas gleaned from the press. It should be noted that when seasickness seems to be a factor, it covers up a deeply rooted cause. The characters may be having a fever, symbolic of their burning desire to leave, but whatever the symptom, it betrays an angst-ridden somatization associated with danger. Akka's physical ailment is particularly troublesome for the narrator. Ever since the reader's first encounter with him, the young Berber is identified with two alienating elements: his inability to speak Arabic and his poor health. His linguistic deficiency makes it hard for him to verbalize his incapacitating condition, while his disabling digestive issues lead to a nauseating scene. The degrading process he must endure, which includes having to outwit officers chasing him with a trained dog, makes the harrag sick to his stomach, so to speak.[12] In the van transporting them closer to their point of departure, the prospective migrants must endure the foul smell of excrement, and the vomiting adds another layer of abjection to their objectification.

Screening (for) *Harragas*: a hegemonic or demonic discourse?

Cinematic works, like their literary counterparts, provide crucial information on the subtleties of maritime clandestine migration in general. Additionally, they are significant representative and representational mirrors of a Mediterranean reality that concerns legislators, activists, and advocates of burning. Even the most well-intentioned reports and policies struggle to initiate change, which literature and cinema attempt to achieve as well. Last but not least, these areas of cultural expression often present themselves as competitive voices, bringing the views of the global South into a Western-dominated epistemology.

The films *Harragas* and *Io, l'altro* were directed by Merzak Allouache and Mohsen Melliti respectively. My choice of these two productions is motivated by my intention to examine clandestinity from wide-ranging angles, including diverse spoken languages in the region (Arabic, French, and Italian). Here, I will focus on ethnicity, gender, class, media, and terrorism. One may legitimately wonder why a film in Italian should find a place in a volume focusing on Maghrebi-French works. I am including *Io, l'altro* to show how it illustrates – as does *Harragas* – a recent evolution in Maghrebi migratory patterns and their representations through artistic forms of expression. Indeed, I argue that contemporary migratory trends have become progressively *ex-centric*, in that they do not exclusively feature journeys along the common Maghreb–France axis.[13] Clandestine migrants from Tunisia have recently settled in a diverse range of countries that includes non-francophone ones like Spain, Italy, Germany, and the Netherlands and have thus remapped Maghrebi migratory patterns exemplified by Melliti's film. This chapter strives to inform our understanding of a major migration trend and its referencing in Mediterranean cinema.

Harragas (2009) recounts the sea journey undertaken by strangers and a trio of friends – two men and a woman – Nasser (Seddik Benyagoub), Imène (Lamia Boussekine), and Rachid (Nabil Asli), from Mostaghanem, Algeria, to Europe. They leave after Imène's brother committed suicide following his third failed attempt at emigration. *Harragas* exemplifies the concept of ex-centric journeys in that the passengers are not traveling to France but Spain. In this filmic narrative, a sickly character stands out. The first time he appears on-screen, he is being assisted walking down a dune. The second time, the wide-angle shot focuses on his coughing, which leads Hassan (who is supposed to smuggle the migrants) to ask, 'What's wrong with that one? Is he sick?'[14] Wrapped in blankets, the man is shown as frail and passive. In one instance, he is brought bread and soup by a fellow *harrag*. Later, he sits with a few *harragas* facing the sea. The others are giggling at Mounir, Hassan's dumb assistant.[15] The camera frames the scene from behind, showing the sick man's back shaking together with his companions, but we soon realize that what actually causes his body to shake is his cough. His presence in this film is two-fold: first, it highlights the assumption that contemporary global South prospective migrants are seen as foreign bodies likely to contaminate Western nations; second, they are shown to be the victims of a partial (in the sense of "incomplete" and "unfair") globalization which institutes a strict divide between the North and a global South forbidding the free movement of those who are sick of their confinement. Another harrag blames Hassan for the man's sickness because they have been lodged in a damp cabin, an act which mimics Europe's desire for *harragas* to be quarantined and kept separate.

Hassan (Okacha Touita) is another iconic figure in *Harragas*. While he welcomes his clients' money, he views them as a yoke and their complaints as a joke. Rachid, who is also the first-person narrator in the voiceover, remarks that Hassan used to be a fisherman living overseas. The implications of the smuggler's conversion from seller of small fish to dealer of big fish (read: humans) are clear. The narrator adds that Hassan now smuggles people to Spain and that his career change has been lucrative. This information confirms the opinion of those who see burning as a brain drain – instead of using his experience abroad to benefit his *bled*, the smuggler instead bleeds his homeland.[16] While his valued patronage in the local cabaret earns him the title 'merchant king,' the narrator emphasizes the old man's wickedness by referring to him in debasing terms, including 'son of a bitch' and 'Hassan mal de mer' (Hassan-seasickness).[17] The narrator even notes that if Hassan's own mother wanted to emigrate clandestinely, he would charge her for the voyage. The spectators understand why the *passeur* should be named 'seasickness,' for his handling of sea-related matters as a mere business, without any care for the *harragas*' lives, makes the travelers sick. In addition, because 'Hassan' means 'the one who does good,' it becomes obvious why the narrator feels the urge to rebaptize him and correct the oxymoronic misnomer.

Albeit not a conventional one, the *bote* (dinghy in local Arabic) is a character in its own right. A major portion of the narrative takes place on the *bote*, where the passengers act out societal tensions. It is a microcosm of Algeria in terms of the represented categories of class, gender, and ethnicity. The passengers comprise nine men and one woman. One of the Algerian characters criticizes the three main protagonists for belonging to the bourgeoisie.[18] He comments on class differences revealed by sartorial appearance and embodied in language politics (the use of French instead of Arabic, which causes the exasperated southern Algerian to feel excluded). Three other characters are lumped together. They are Hassan-seasickness the smuggler, Mustapha the former police officer, and Hakim the 'bearded man' who stands for the Front Islamique du Salut (FIS) held responsible for the Algerian civil war. Hakim is shown chatting on the Internet with a sheikh who remains invisible and inaudible to the extradiegetic viewer in a short scene that casts ambiguity on Hakim's motives for burning. The trio symbolizes the contemporary forces that have driven Algerians out of the country. The irony lies in that all of them will perish away from Europe while absconding. First, Mustapha is an intruder in that he did not pay his fare, he was not among the ten selected individuals to embark, and he invited himself by force just before the journey. He shoots Hassan who is thus unable to fulfill his smuggling job. From then on, Mustapha, a bully, makes all decisions related to the crossing operations until he and Hakim drown while fighting in the water. Claiming to have fought against the FIS, the enigmatic Mustapha takes the life of the Islamist years after the end of the civil war. This betrays entrenched feelings of resentment within the Algerian social matrix. The vessel will continue its course over the seametery that the two men have now joined and which acts as an extension of the Algerian cemetery, hosting as a final resting place those who were thrown into the national mass grave of the 1990s.

Once purged of the bad guys, the *bote* shelters the remaining *harragas*, portrayed as victims. The topos of the vessel as testing ground, modeled on the medieval Ship of Fools, is thwarted by immutable hierarchies and is used ironically in that its passengers are not able to stick together. Allouache's dystopian floating polis is a triptych: the trio of villains, three bourgeois, and the final three, darker-skinned individuals who cannot swim and whose phenotype further marks their vulnerability and marginalized status. The villains die, the bourgeois protagonists quickly vacate the scene, and the final three are left to fend for themselves. Allouache's contention is that the most innocent and least powerful are the ones most disadvantaged in the context of clandestine migration.

Positions aboard the *bote* are costly and coveted, for the dinghy can only hold ten passengers. Holding the group at gunpoint, Mustapha determines who will remain aboard. Hoping to ensure a spot for himself, one of the hostages – an older man – tells Mustapha that the sick man should stay behind. The sick man denies the claim about his infirmity. Mustapha tells the older man to mind his own business and rhetorically asks him if he has heard of *immigration choisie*. 'Selective immigration,' as opposed to *immigration subie* (endured immigration) or *immigration jetable* (disposable immigration), is a policy instated by then-president Nicolas Sarkozy to grant visas to select migrants based on France's economic and professional needs. Mustapha remarks, 'eh bien, aujourd'hui, c'est moi qui choisis' (well, today, I'm the one who chooses). He deems the older man unfit for a Europe with stricter selection criteria and therefore a non-candidate for the journey. The ex-policeman is adamant about how things should be done and what they should be called. As the passengers notice an approaching coastguard ship, they duck. Mustapha, still holding his gun, warns, 'S'ils approchent, je les brûle' (If they come close, I'm gonna burn them), thus reversing the roles in the hunting game, shifting power relations and turning the authority figures into fugitives. The significance of this reversal is to establish a comparison between the *passeur* and international institutional bodies: neither of them is capable of addressing (sufficiently or adequately?) the causes of trans-Mediterranean migration.

The insertion of Mustapha and his life history into *Harragas* enables Allouache to connect his plot to the aftermath of the recent national narrative, namely, the Algerian civil war known as 'the Black Decade,' or 'the Dark Years,' and thus to tease out the connections often drawn between colonial and civil wars, clandestine migration, and terrorism. Whereas the relationship between war and terrorism is an age-old one, the linking of clandestine migration to terrorism is a more recent practice. Recently, European nation-states have used the conflation of terrorism and migration to justify their harshening of migratory laws and to enforce compliance from their Southern neighbors. As Virginie Lydie contends, 'Le 11 septembre 2001 a marqué un nouveau tournant sécuritaire dans le discours politique, créant l'amalgame entre clandestinité et risque terroriste, amplifiant le durcissement des dispositifs de lutte contre l'immigration irrégulière' (2010: 25) (9/11 signaled a new security shift in political discourse, lumping together clandestinity and terrorist risk, increasing the harshening of measures to fight illegal immigration). As such, authorities in Europe have cited the 9/11 tragedy to support an ever-growing suspicion that undocumented migrants from the global South consist of a category of individuals endowed with evil intentions.[19]

The film *Harragas* shows that the lack of a guarantee of a better future at home combined with the impossibility to make it abroad drives many desperate North Africans to suicide,[20] as is the case for Imène's brother, or to terrorism, as Imène threatens Rachid: 'If you leave without me, I'll kill you. I'll find you and kill you. Or I'll join the zealots and turn into a kamikaze.' Imène's point is that when society does not offer much hope, the prospect of washing ashore does not appear any more morbid than that of taking one's life. The film does not end on an optimistic note, as it leads to a dead-end and is a return to square one. Indeed, as soon as they set foot on a Spanish beach, the three protagonists are caught by two Guardia Civil officers. Imène is sent back, while Rachid and Mounir are detained in a detention center with 3,000 other inmates from countries like Senegal, Mali, and Morocco.[21] As for the southern Algerians, their marginalized status is mirrored by their relegation to the fringes of the narrative – in fact, their fate remains unknown to us: they could have been regularized or deported. Allouache implies that Islamophobia, wars (on terrorism), and racial profiling all influence immigration practices and policies.

In *Io, l'altro*, director Melliti examines amalgams in a more straightforward fashion. As we see in this film, hostile exclusionary discourses are directed at the Muslim 'Other,' construed as an enemy. *Io, l'altro* (I, the Other) came out in 2007. Most of the plot unfolds aboard a fishing boat owned by two fishermen, an Italian and a Tunisian. Giuseppe (Raoul Bova) and Yousef (Giovanni Martorana) have been best friends for a decade. Yousef is a former *harrag*. One of the major contributions of this film lies in the director's emphasis on a Maghrebi character in the Italian context, which constitutes an eccentric approach to Maghrebi film history in that it offers a different view of contemporary North African emigration. Furthermore, *Io, l'altro* takes place predominantly off the coast of Sicily, which is an ex-centric site in that the sea was at the margin of the traditional Maghreb–France nexus, where most of the North African narratives were anchored during the last decades of the twentieth century. Melliti focuses on the issues of terrorism and clandestinity, which make their way into the plot insidiously at first and then more forcefully. Both are treated as sources of anxiety. Due to the scarcity of fish and thus with plenty of time on their hands, the two partners play cards, chat, and listen to the radio which broadcasts commercial programs and news, including that of a wanted terrorist involved in the 2004 Madrid bombings. Most of the script is in the form of a dialogue. The radio program provides a forum for Italians to express their opinions on national security, migration policies, and *extracommunitari*.[22] The points of view are of a reproving nature, prompting the moderator to invite listeners to express a more positive message. Giuseppe learns that the terrorist who has mobilized the media, Youssef Ben Ali, bears the same name as his best friend.[23] The Tunisian admits that he has been once to Spain. Yet, though Yousef has proven to Giuseppe that he is a well-integrated *harrag* who 'has benefited from the 1990 amnesty granted by the Martelli law and has got a regular residence permit,' the tensions soon reach a crescendo (Pastorino, 2010: 325).[24]

The film dialogue is in none of the languages common in Maghrebi cinematography, namely Arabic, Berber, and French. Instead, it is in Italian.[25] Just as in *Harragas*, the migrant characters do not aim to migrate to France, but are heading to Italy instead, or already live there. Mainly for historical and linguistic reasons, migrants have traditionally shown a preference for the land of their former colonizer. Following this logic, the Somali woman in *Io, l'altro* was likely on her way to Italy when Giuseppe and Yousef fished her out of the sea, since Somalia used to be an Italian colony. Yousef's presence in Sicily, however, appears atypical because Tunisia is a former French colony. At first sight, the film seems to deviate from an instituted norm. Yet, in the context of clandestine migration, it inscribes itself in a new norm, so to speak. As Europe is tightening its external borders, unauthorized maritime crossings are one of the very few remaining passageways. Therefore, migrant hopefuls have had to factor in geographic proximity in their migratory habits. As Allouache's *harragas* are heading for Spain, Melliti's characters choose Italy as their primary destination. Due to the hazardous nature of burning, shortcuts to a peninsula, an island, or an enclave have become a modus operandi. This did not use to be the case in the context of State-sanctioned immigration where other criteria such as binational agreements, language, and the presence of settled relatives determined the destination country.[26]

Therefore, it is no wonder that the Italian island of Lampedusa has been highlighted in international news for the arrival of thousands of Tunisians, notably during the Arab Spring. As a report from Migreurop indicates, since 2009 Italian *carabinieri* have sent 'back' to Libyan coasts boatloads of migrants hailing from various African countries, thus causing thousands of drownings. Yousef hypothesizes that the dead Somali woman lying on the deck may have been thrown overboard by smugglers when they tried to outmaneuver coastguards by making their boats lighter. Nonetheless, given practices unknown to the public until their recent media treatment, it is equally possible that she was a victim of Italian repatriation procedures. Symbolic of a colonial past, she is now drifting back like a haunting presence while an Italian neocolonial hegemony of sorts spreads about with European support. Like the other works studied here, *Io, l'altro* posits that international/Western authorities may be just as guilty as the *passeur*. Advocates of stringent migration policies will argue that clandestine migration to the northern continent constitutes a threat to Western values, identities, and way of life and that Europe ought to protect itself by strengthening its external borders. Others contend that it is because Europe has become a fortress that clandestine migration is on the rise. Scholars have claimed that borders are counterproductive and have theorized a world without borders.[27] Finally, opponents of a gradually fortified world have regarded the closing of borders as homicidal. Various sources and agencies, like Migreurop, have used the expression 'war on terror' to denounce the implementation by the North of 'murderous borders' and other deterrents to the practice of burning.

Generally speaking, the idea of terrorism evokes images of destruction and fire. In this film, the topic of terrorism is omnipresent – on the marine VHF radio, in conversations of people on the mainland, and between Giuseppe and Yousef on their boat – yet we never see images of it. We only hear about it. In the film, terror is a fantasy entertained by the characters themselves, which is Melliti's way of mocking preconceived ideas. The two friends imagine a scenario in which Yousef would turn himself in, sell his story to the media, and make money on his new fame. Yousef comments on how easily the media can manipulate their audience, but more importantly, how easily they can be manipulated as well, thus showing how false stories may be feeding our knowledge of current events. Through the presence of the radio, the topic of terrorism serves as the backdrop against which another rhetoric, that of the migrants as a potential threat, is explored, showing how terrorism and clandestine migration are commonly conflated, especially in Western migration politics. To this dyad, another "crime" is traditionally added – another traffic – usually involving drugs. Virginie Lydie confirms this view: 'Les discours sécuritaires qui mélangent, pêle-mêle, clandestins, terroristes et trafiquants en tous genres, se chargent de nous les rendre carrément hostiles. Et comme s'il fallait en rajouter, la stigmatisation de l'Islam est là pour convaincre un peu plus ceux qui ne le seraient pas' (2010: 22) (The security discourses that indiscriminately mix clandestine migrants, terrorists, and traffickers of all kinds strive to depict them to us as totally hostile. And, as if it was not enough, the stigmatization of Islam is added to convince those who needed more persuasion). Thus, it is not rare for some media to serve political agendas that feed nationalist fervors. The media and politics share responsibility in fear mongering based on opaque beliefs. As Glissant and Chamoiseau suggest, 'Ces refus apeurés de l'autre, ces tentatives de neutraliser son existence, même de la nier, peuvent prendre la forme. . . [du] brouillard d'une croyance transmise par beaucoup de medias qui, délaissant à leur tour l'esprit de liberté, ne souscrivent qu'à leur propre expansion, à l'ombre des pouvoirs et des forces dominantes' (2009: 8) (The fearful rejection of the other, the attempts to neutralize his/her existence, or even negate it, can take the form … [of a] shady belief transmitted by many media, which, by renouncing in their turn the spirit of freedom, only serve their own expansion, in the shadow of hegemonic powers and forces). *Io, l'altro* scrutinizes the negative effects that the media and dominant discourse have on migrants. 'La radio non è il Corano! È diventata il Corano la radio?' (Radio is not the Quran! Has radio become the Quran?), Yousef shouts, surprised to see Giuseppe's feelings so easily swayed by media speculations. In spite of the two men's long-term friendship, rumors soon become gospel truth for Giuseppe, turning him against his friend.

Io, l'altro interrogates the fine line between belief and mediated truth by proposing that there are always two sides to a story. This message is cleverly borne both literally and metaphorically in the scene where Giuseppe finds in Yousef's coat pocket a newspaper page devoted to AlZarkawi.[28] Meanwhile, the camera, the omniscient conveyor of multiple perspectives, records the scene from a worm's-eye view. This allows the extradiegetic viewers to read the other side of the newspaper's page, which is about Ali Zidan.[29] Presented with the flipside of the coin, the spectator is better equipped to make a judgment, whereas Giuseppe, being satisfied with only one point of view, remains couched in his fear. At first, Yousef does not rebuff Giuseppe's accusations, partly because he has a hard time believing his friend could give credit to rumors, and then, when proved wrong, he tries to gauge how far Giuseppe is willing to jeopardize their friendship. The building tension invites the spectators to test their own judgment of where the truth lies and to articulate their views alongside those who were encouraged to share their opinions on the national radio.

Burning is associated with terrorism because it is often presented as an invasion that takes the other by surprise and is perceived as having a bomb-like effect upon existing circumstances. The Somali woman and Yousef are portrayed as intruders and due to fear, their 'existence' is, to use Glissant and Chamoiseau's aforementioned quote, neutralized, or even negated when they are made to vacate the boat physically or metaphorically.[30] From the picture that Yousef and Giuseppe find on her body, we discover that the Somali woman is a mother. Constructed on the model of the Greek tragedy, *Io, l'altro* features another mother figure, 'Medea.' The name of this mythological murderess is written in Arabic and Roman letters in blood-red paint beside the wheelhouse, signaling the devouring nature of the sea, which kills her children and brings them to the ground (Medea-terranean). The Mediterranean thus becomes the stage for the duality-turned-antagonism between the two men. Yousef and Giuseppe share the name Joseph across languages (Arabic and Italian). Despite the two characters' underlying commonality, the film title contains a comma, which embodies the separation between the one and the other. We watch media and misinformation gradually drive the two friends apart, until, in the end, Giuseppe stabs Yousef to death. The Medea-terranean sea/mother (*mer/mère*) has devoured one of her two sons, but which one actually? In one of the final scenes, Giuseppe hears on the radio that the terrorist used to be a CIA agent – and thus cannot be his friend whom he has just killed. The closing scene exposes the shattered murderer weeping and begging Yousef to come back to life. Giuseppe is left alone with his gnawing guilt. The camera-witness-accomplice extricates itself from the scene, swiftly backing away from a drifting ship lost in the middle of an immense sea-cell.

Closing in on no closure

Alongside coverage of Maghrebi migrants washing ashore Spanish beaches and well before images of refugees made it to our screens, novels and films called our attention by providing alternatives to the dominant script of the mass media. Literary and filmic representations of clandestine migration show that from the seametery the dead continue to haunt us until we acknowledge their stories. Western Mediterranean writers and filmmakers have taken on this task in such works as *Partir*, *'Les harragas' ou Les barques de la mort*, *Harragas*, and *Io, l'altro*. Artistic creations from the eastern part of the basin are to be expected. Will they aim to rectify a biased media vision of the sea crossings following the Syrian war waged by Bashar Al-Assad's regime and the exactions of ISIS? While most of the works examined in this chapter tackle the phenomenon of burning from the Maghreb, *Io, l'altro* turns the camera around. Looking southward from the vantage point of an Italian region frequently represented in the media as a migration destination, it traces the path of an allegorical boat in which neither old nor new migrant is welcome to stay or to make it to the mainland, the gateway to Europe – or rather, the gate-no-way to Fortress-Murderess Europe. The film's vessel is not a *patera* or a *bote* transporting clandestine migrants alive, but rather a trawler whose net brings to the surface the body of a dead migrant returned to the sea-cemetery or sea-prison. In *Partir*, the sea is a spider. Just like SIVE, it weaves its web around its Moroccan prey. Throughout this novel, characters perish in their attempts to emigrate by sea; meanwhile, Azel makes it to the gilded Eldorado by airplane. This decision to contrast modes of travel taken by his Moroccan characters, all of whom irremediably end up leading miserable lives overseas, enables Ben Jelloun to indicate that migration efforts from the global South have become excessively more straining and the outcomes no more profitable. In *Les "harragas" ou Les barques de la mort*, the migrants-objects manipulated by the Shark and his business partners are postmodern disposable goods locked up in a van, then stuck in a *patera*, and finally sunk in an insatiable sea. In *Harragas* too, some of the passengers' final home is the anthropophagic seametery. But while Allouache's plot documents the actual maritime crossing, Teriah's narrative scrutinizes the perils leading to the awaited journey and then concisely discloses the fatal outcome in an anticlimactic fashion to stress the preposterously insurmountable forces facing the frail hopes of *harragas*. In all these works, the Mediterranean is represented in a negative light. A sieve-like sea, the Mediterranean has become a lethal web of nets as European anti-immigration policies strive to catch *harragas*, holding their dreams captive and turning this seametery into the world's deadliest body of water.

Notes

1 In this chapter, I will mainly use the word 'migrants' as an umbrella term to refer to those who cross the sea. There are other categories, such as 'asylum seekers' and 'refugees,' which necessitate a discussion of legal terms for which there is not enough space here. I will use the last term solely in the context of the Syrian refugee crisis since these individuals have fled armed conflicts and have been recognized as needing protection under international law and the 1951 refugee convention.

2 A growing number of these fictions have been published by (North) African and European writers of Maghrebi ancestry. Such is the case of Youssouf Amine Lalami's *Les Clandestins* (2001), Rachid El Hamri's *Le Néant bleu* (2005), Ahmed Bouchikhi's *Le Cimetière des illusions* (2006), Salim Jay's *Tu ne traverseras pas le détroit* (2001), Nasser-Eddine Bekkai Lahbil's *Le détroit ou le voyage des vaincus* (1995), Laila Lalami's *Hope and Other Dangerous Pursuits* (2005), and Hamid Skif's *La Géographie du danger* (2006). However, this subgenre has also been tackled by authors with other origins. Laurent Gaudé's *Eldorado* (France, 2006) and Antonio Lozano's *Patera* (Spain, 2002) are examples of accounts from beyond the Maghreb.

3 Examples include Fawzi Mellah's *Clandestins en Méditerranée* in which the author, who also happens to be a lawyer, scholar, and reporter, allegedly accompanied *harragas* to provide a personal report on the experience of burning.
4 Instead of identifying the writers and filmmakers under scrutiny by their respective nationalities, I prefer to qualify them as "Mediterranean" because some of them claim transnational identities across the Mediterranean and because the sea is a locus at the center of all the studied works. There are various clandestine migratory patterns but I will use clandestine "migration" in its singular form throughout the chapter to refer to the concept of leaving one's country with the intention of entering another in an unauthorized fashion.
5 For a comprehensive examination of *illiterature*, see Abderrezak (2016).
6 'Harraga' can be spelled without an 's' but, given that a female migrant is a 'harraga,' in order to avoid confusion, I have used the plural form, as seen here.
7 Nicknames are not alien to Maghrebi literature and cinema, but the works about clandestinity have tapped into halieutics and the seascape. In Mahi Binebine's novel, *Cannibales* (*Welcome to Paradise*), the character's name Morad evokes the notion of death ('mort') and yet – or precisely for this reason – the sea is in him, since three letters of his name make up the word 'mar' – phonetically close to *mort*. The inference is that death and the sea are intertwined.
8 All translations are mine unless otherwise indicated.
9 In the context of clandestine migration to the Unites States, the smuggler is known as the 'coyote.' In Ben Jelloun's novel, the characteristics selected to describe the members of the trafficking network are far more negative.
10 For a study of this novel, see Yvette Bénayoun-Szmidt's, 'Un aller sans retour: Les "Harragas" ou les barques de la Mort de Mohamed Teriah.'
11 This sentence is evidence that the author, like a good number of his peers, used his novel as a reply to newspaper accounts of burning. As for Jamal's name (Sabiri), which means 'the patient one' in Arabic, it connotes the character's quietude and the long wait imposed on *harragas*, which generally contrasts with smugglers' impatience to charge their clients, get rid of them, and then look for more as soon as possible.
12 In Mahi Binebine's *Welcome to Paradise*, a character experiences similar debilitating health problems, which prevent him from boarding the dinghy. As for the only female character, she manages not to be caught by the police by biting the trained dog from under the *patera* where she is hiding with her baby.
13 See Abderrezak (2016) for a thorough study of the concept of ex-centric migrations.
14 I am providing English translations only for the Arabic quotes in the film.
15 Mounir is mute, but it is important to note that Mustapha sees him as 'dumb' in the other sense as well – as shown when he calls him *bahloul* (idiot).

16 In Arabic, *bled* is an umbrella term that refers to the notion of location and can signify village, region, area, and country. In French, it means village or a place in the middle of nowhere.
17 Note that the nicknames 'merchant king' and 'Hassan-seasickness' reflects a linguistic hybridity in the original dialogues, mixing Arab and French. 'Merchant' is in Arabic while 'king' is in French (roi); Hassan is an Arabic name while 'seasickness' is a translation of the French expression 'mal de mer,' pronounced like an Arab word, rolling the 'r' of 'mer.'
18 As this was confirmed to me by the filmmaker himself, because of their accent and the fact that they 'traveled 700 kilometers,' these three characters are fellow citizens from the desert and not sub-Saharan migrants.
19 Media reports have revealed that among refugees crossing over to Europe from the Middle East through the Greek island of Leros were terrorists responsible of the attacks in Paris on November 13, 2015. This type of information has reinforced prejudices against refugees, migrants, and European citizens of alleged Muslim faith. Additionally, it has boosted the electoral scores of European far-right candidates in such countries as Austria, where the leader of FPÖ Norbert Hofer ranked the highest in the first round and almost won the presidential election in May 2016.
20 Mohamed Bouazizi, the 26-year-old who set in motion the Arab Spring, which prompted the clandestine sea crossing of thousands of Tunisian migrants and Syrian refugees among others, set himself on fire in front of the Préfecture of Sidi Bouzid on December 17, 2010. For more about this event and the correlation between physical and symbolical burnings, see Abderrezak (2016).
21 The subtitles wrongly indicate '300.'
22 As Alessandro Dal Lago remarks, though technically this term applies to individuals from North America, Japan, and Switzerland, 'Everywhere that the terms "foreigner" or "*extracommunitari*" appear – in legal decrees, in the press, in "scientific" debates – those terms actually apply to those migrants in search of a job, a refuge, a new existence' (2009: 55).
23 Yousef jokes, arguing that he will become as famous as the soccer player and trainer Zinedine Zidane, but it is clear that Melliti's choice of name is not random; it enables him to draw a parallel between another famous public person, the president of Tunisia, who bears the same last name and is thus equated to a potential terrorist.
24 This organic law on migration, also known as Law 39/90, granted legal status and work permits to unauthorized foreigners who had entered Italy prior to December 31, 1989. Under strong pressure from the European Union, the law was accompanied by the intensification of anti-migration measures.
25 The two protagonists speak to each other in a Sicilian dialect and the radio broadcasts in Italian.
26 The shortest distance between Algeria and Marseille is 700 kilometers.
27 See Pécoud and de Guchteneire (2009).
28 Though the image aims at making the link between AlZarkawi – spelled this way in the newspaper – and Abu Musab Al-Zarqawi, a terrorist from Jordan

known for a series of acts of violence during the Iraq War, including suicide bombings and beheadings, the article alongside the picture is in Latin. The writing is intentionally disconnected from the image. Instead of having the function of illustrating and hence confirming beliefs, the juxtaposition adds to the complex nature of parallels that run through the film and alerts us to the importance of always questioning appearances.

29 In a savvy manner, Melliti lays the foundation for another moment of confusion and misunderstanding, since the headline indicates that Zidan dreams of a soccer team, but the major league in question (C1) is in Acireale, in the region of Catana, and 'Zidan' is Ali and not the world-renowned Zinedine Zidane.

30 It should be remarked that one of the two *extracommunitari* is nameless and the other bears the same name as his killer. Identity, usually granted by (unique) naming, is not an option in this film since, regardless of his status, the other remains out of place as reflected by the double meaning of the French and Italian terms *étranger* and *straniero*, namely, 'foreigner' and 'stranger.'

References

Abderrezak, H. (2016). *Ex-Centric Migrations: Europe and the Maghreb in Mediterranean Cinema, Literature, and Music*, Bloomington, IN: Indiana University Press.

Bénayoun-Szmidt, Y. (2008). 'Un aller sans retour: Les "Harragas ou Les barques de la Mort de Mohamed Teriah,"' in N. Redouane (ed.), *Clandestins dans le texte maghrébin de langue française*, Paris: Editions L'Harmattan, 107–30.

Ben Jelloun, T. (2006). *Partir*, Paris: Editions Gallimard.

Ben Jelloun, T. (2009). *Leaving Tangier*, trans. L. Coverdale, New York: Penguin.

Binebine, M. (1999). *Cannibales*. Paris: Editions Fayard.

Binebine, M. (2004). *Welcome to Paradise*, trans. L. Norman, London: Granta.

Dal Lago, A. (2009). *Non-Persons: The Exclusion of Migrants in a Global Society*, trans. Marie Orton, Vimodrone: IPOC.

D'Ors, I. (2002). 'Léxico de la emigración,' in I. Andres-Suárez, M. Kunz, and I. d'Ors (eds), *La inmigración en la literatura española contemporánea*, Madrid: Verbum, 21–108.

Elalamy, Y. A. (2001). *Les clandestins*, Vauvert: Au Diable Vauvert.

Elalamy, Y. A. (2008). *Sea Drinkers*, trans. J. Liechty, Lanham, MD: Lexington Books.

Glissant, E. and Chamoiseau, P. (2009). *Quand les murs tombent: L'identité nationale hors-la-loi*, Paris: Galaade Editions.

Jay, S. (2001). *Tu ne traverseras pas le détroit*, Paris: Editions Mille et une Nuits.

Lalami, L. (2005). *Hope and Other Dangerous Pursuits*, Chapel Hill, NC: Algonquin Books.

Lydie, V. (2010). *Traversée interdite! Les harragas face à l'Europe forteresse*. Le Pré Saint-Gervais: Editions le passager clandestin.

Mellah, F. (2000). *Clandestin en Méditerranée*. Paris: Le Cherche-Midi.
Migreurop, *Les Frontières assassines de l'Europe: Rapport Migreurop 2009 sur la violation des droits humains aux frontières*. Web. August 15, 2015.
Pastorino, G. (2010). 'Death by Water? Constructing the "Other" in Mohsen Melliti's *Io, l'altro*,' in G. R. Bullaro (ed.), *From Terrone to Extracommunitario: New Manifestations of Racism in Italian Cinema*, Leicester: Troubador Publishing, 308–40.
Pécoud, A. and de Guchteneire, P. (eds) (2009). *Migrations sans frontières: Essais sur la libre circulation des personnes*. Paris: Unesco.
Teriah, M. (2002). *'Les Harragas' ou les barques de la Mort*, Casablanca: Afrique Orient.

Filmography

Allouache, M. (2009). *Harragas*. Librisfilms, Baya Films, Centre National de la Cinématographie, France 2 Cinéma production, Canal +, Cinécinéma, France 2.
Melliti, M. (2007). *Io, l'altro*. Trees Pictures, Pulp Video, Passworld.

Index

Notes: 'n' after a page reference indicates the number of a note on that page

Literary works can be found under authors' names

For films and literary works that are the subject of entire chapters, please refer to the Contents

accented cinema 197–8
Ali-Ben Ali, Z. 160
Allouache, M.
   Harragas 241–4
Arabicides 120
Arzoune, M. 43
Azzeddine, S.
   Mecque-Phuket, La 36–40

banlieue 99, 119–20
Barclay, F. 5–6, 10
Beaud S. and Masclet O. 9
Begag, A. 4
Benguigui, Y. 212–13
   Aïcha 9, 99–100, 107–8, 111–12
Ben Jelloun, T.
   Partir 236–7
Ben Yadir, N.
   Marche, La 9, 121–3, 126–7, 128–30, 131
Bergson, H. 108
Besnaci-Lancou, F. 188–9, 192–3n.12
beur 2–3, 17, 22, 27, 31–2
beur cinema 63
Boulin, J-E.
   Supplément au roman national 23
Bourdieu, P. 110
Boutouba, J. 31–2
Bouzid, N.
   Quand Beretta est morte 41–3

Charef, M.
   Cartouches gauloises 186–8
Cheb Sun, M.

D'ailleurs et d'ici: L'affirmation d'une France plurielle 26
Chevillot, F. 3, 42
Chibane, M.
   Douce France 181–2, 191–2
chibanias 227–8n.4
Chroniques d'une société annoncée 17
Collin, D. 217
colonial fracture 153, 172n.1
communauté intersticielle 188
contact zone 129

Deleuze, G. 80, 93n.10
Deleuze G. and Guattari, F. 80, 82, 93n.11, 93n.12
Détrez, C. 42
Djaïdani, R. 8, 77–8, 88, 91, 92–3n.4
   Rengaine 8
Durmelat, S. 182
Durmelat, S. and Swamy, V. 22

Egaliberté 117
Emery, M. 35
Enjelvin, G. 158, 164
Ervine, J. 101
Esclangon-Morin, V. 171
Esposito, C. 74

Fabbiano, G. 154, 156–7, 180
Faucon, P.
   Trahison, La 185–6
Fernane, A.
   Celui qui écrit une lettre au président 23

Foerster, M. 84, 90
Fortunes 9, 100–1, 103–5, 105–7, 109–10
Foucault, M. 127
Freedman, J. and Tarr, C. 36, 40

Galdeano, T.
　Pieds-noirs, Harkis, nos cœurs orphelins 155–6, 157–8, 164–8
Guène, F.
　Du rêve pour les oufs 53–7
　gens du Balto, Les 33–6, 57–8
　Kiffe kiffe demain 24, 51–3
　Un homme, ça ne pleure pas 58–61
Guénif-Souilamas, N. 44

Hajjat, A. 120
Halbwachs, M. 223
Hall, S. 5
Hargreaves, A. G. 2, 18, 33, 37, 39, 40, 41, 44, 94n.18, 99, 103, 105, 119, 149n.5, 209n.12, 219
Hargreaves, A. G. and Gans-Guinoune, A-M. 2, 31
harkeology 160
harki 173n.3, 173n.6
harragas 234–5
Harzoune, M. 59
Higbee, W. 3, 7, 13, 32, 63–4, 69, 72–3, 98, 178, 181, 186, 188, 208n.8, 209n.15
Hirsch, M. 10, 143–6, 156, 158, 167, 175n.16
homophobia 84
Howell, J. 11

illiterature 13, 233–4
Imache, T. 3, 42
Ireland, S. 154, 160, 212, 226

Kaganski, S. 78–9
Kealhofer-Kemp, L. 4
Kechiche, A. 6, 8, 65, 71
　Faute à Voltaire, La 65–7
　Graine et le mulet, La 69, 73
　L'Esquive 67, 68, 70–2

Kerchouche, D.
　Mon père, ce harki 154–5, 156–7, 160–3, 168–70
Khiari, S. 18

Lacoste-Dujardin, C. 7, 38, 59, 79, 80–1
Laronde, M. 42–3, 46n.14, 209n.16
Le Breton, M. 40, 58
Leherpeur, X. 97, 103

Maalouf, A. 43
Maghrebi-French 92n.1
Manceron, G. 173n.3
Mandelbaum, J. 65
Mandin, D.
　Banlieue Voltaire 24–5
Mehrez, S. 32
Mehta, B-J. 33, 53
Melliti, M.
　Io, l'altro 244–7
mémoire tatouée 218
Mills-Affif, E. 102–3
mission civilisatrice 169
Moumen, A. 173n.6

Naamane-Guessous, S. 51
Nettelbeck, C. 67, 70, 72
Nora, P. 227

patera 234
pied noir 173n.3
Pierret, R. 188
political *dissensus* 124–5
post-*beur* 2–3
postmemory 10, 143–5
Pratt, M. L. 129

Raack, R. C. 121
Rancière, J. 116–17, 124, 131
Redouane, N. 2, 22, 44n.1, 50
Reeck, L. 26
Ricoeur, P. 203, 227
road movie genre 127, 197
Rosello, M. 45n.12, 86–7

Sayad, A. 18
Sciolino, E. 50

seametery 235
Siri, F.-E.
   L'Ennemi intime 183–5
Smouts, M-C. 18–19
Stora, B. 11, 153, 159, 168, 179, 180–1, 183, 185, 187, 192n.12
Swamy, V. 4, 71

Tarr, C. 9, 15n.3, 63, 72, 77, 79–80, 92, 99

Tasma, A.
   Harkis 188–91
Taubira, C. 1, 5, 14
television 4
Teriah, M.
   "Harragas" ou les barques de la Mort, Les 237–40, 249n.10
Thomas, D. 50

urban culture 7
urban literature 19–22, 27

EU authorised representative for GPSR:
Easy Access System Europe, Mustamäe tee 50,
10621 Tallinn, Estonia
gpsr.requests@easproject.com

www.ingramcontent.com/pod-product-compliance
Lightning Source LLC
Chambersburg PA
CBHW070236240426
43673CB00044B/1816